The Role of the

CHIEF HUMAN

RESOURCES

OFFICER

The Role of the CHIEF HUMAN RESOURCES OFFICER

Perspectives, Challenges, Realities and Experiences

Edited by
Dave van Eeden

KNO RES
PUBLISHING

2014

First published in 2014

ISBN: 978-1-86922-490-5
eISBN: 978-1-86922-506-3 PDF ebook

Published by Knowres Publishing (Pty) Ltd
P O Box 3954
Randburg
2125
Republic of South Africa

Tel: (011) 706-6009
Fax: (011) 706 1127
E-mail: orders@knowres.co.za
Website: www.kr.co.za

Printed and bound: Shumani Printers (Pty) Ltd, Parow Industria, Cape Town
Typesetting, layout and design: Stephani Krugel, steph.krugel@gmail.com
Cover design: Dina Nel, dina@knowres.co.za
Editing and proofreading: Elsa Crous, getitedited@mweb.co.za
Project management: Cia Joubert, cia@knowres.co.za
Index created with: TExtract, www.Texyz.com

TABLE OF CONTENTS

FOREWORD

In a recent article in the *Harvard Business Review*, Ram Charan suggests that now is an apt time for the Human Resource (HR) department to be split up. Charan argues that the transactional part of the function (including payroll) should report to the Chief Financial Officer (CFO), while the transformational part that focuses on people capabilities (leadership and organisation) should report to the Chief Human Resource Officer (CHRO). His viewpoint stems from a credibility gap between HR's promise and its actual delivery. This was confirmed by the last HR survey conducted by Knowledge Resources, where CHROs ranked low in terms of their ability to work as part of the executive team, as well as their understanding of how the business makes money.

In addition, the challenges facing the HR fraternity and the CHRO in particular have never been greater. To name but a few: economic stagnation, high unemployment levels, volatile labour relations, low labour productivity levels, transformation requirements and change at break-neck speed. Leaders have to be developed who can elevate the organisation to new heights through innovation and transformation. Also, managers are needed who can deliver on the vision and promise of the organisation; and can provide and maintain a consistent pipeline of high-quality talent.

Above all, the CHRO should guide the organisation to be sensitive to the contextual realities of poverty, unemployment and present levels of societal distrust. Organisations should be instrumental in creating a better society in which generations to come will thrive, grow and reach their full potential. This book provides the CHRO and HR leaders across the African continent and in other emerging markets with the inspiration, direction and guidelines to effect much-needed change, specifically within HR functions.

The contributors to this book have done an outstanding job in providing different perspectives, challenges and realities for CHROs to consider, so that they are better able to deliver on their critical transformational role.

Pearl Maphoshe, HR Director, Massmart
September 2014

ACKNOWLEDGEMENTS

When Wilhelm Crous casually approached me in August 2012 and asked whether I would be interested in editing a book on the role of the Chief Human Resource Officer in emerging markets, little did I know what I was in for, as we embarked on this journey. Since then the book has metamorphosed somewhat to what it is now, but more on that later.

I would like to acknowledge and thank most profusely the 22 authors who gave so willingly of their time, and most of all their expertise. Writing a book chapter requires dedication; it is lonely, hard work and the contributors to this book have been excellent. It must also be acknowledged that they are all highly competent, busy practitioners in their own right, which makes their efforts even more appreciated. What is also a source of great pride to me is that this is a human resource book written by South Africans – I believe we are among the best HR practitioners globally and, given our rich and troubled past, have a story to tell. Evidence of this is in each chapter of this book!

Thank you, Steve, for the excellent template you provided through your book on talent management – it helped me a great deal with structure and practicality.[1]

To Cia Joubert and her editorial team behind the scenes: your calm, organised efficiency deserves a special thank-you. Your ability to create order and produce a professional manuscript is truly amazing.

Wilhelm Crous, your understated yet focused encouragement and consistent enthusiasm are hugely appreciated. Thank you for this – the book would not have happened without your counsel and vision, interspersed with comments on the woes of the Stormers and Western Province rugby! Backing you is the Knowledge Resources team whom I would also like to sincerely acknowledge for their consistent, professional support.

Finally, I would like to thank Luciano and Tjaart, and indirectly Andries and Andre, for giving me the break I really needed.

Dave van Eeden
Cape Town
September 2014

---

1   Bluen, S. (Ed.) (2013). *Talent management in emerging markets*. Johannesburg: Knowres Publishing.

ABOUT THE EDITOR

Dave van Eeden has 30 years of corporate human resource management experience in several economic sectors. Prior to becoming an independent consultant, he was Executive Director of Human Resources at the University of Cape Town for eight years. Dave's areas of expertise are human resources strategy and practitioner development, leadership and team development, and organisational transformation and change. In addition to his expertise in higher education, Dave has worked in the sugar manufacturing, chemical, retail and food manufacturing, and consumer goods industries. He is currently in a full time role as Executive: People and organisation for Rialto Foods. He has qualifications in Psychology, Business Administration and Knowledge Management, and has participated in various international executive development programmes. As a Master Human Resources Professional, Dave is registered with the South African Board for People Practices.

ABOUT THE CONTRIBUTORS

Penny Abbott is one of the founding partners and directors of Clutterbuck Associates South Africa, a leading consultancy in support of organisations' coaching and mentoring programmes. Penny uses her experience in management and leadership development, gained during her long and successful career in human resource management, as the basis for her consultancy work in the field of coaching and mentoring. She has an MPhil in Human Resource Development from the University of Johannesburg and is engaged in doctoral research at the same institution. She is actively involved in Coaches and Mentors of South Africa, serving on the Research & Definitions Committee, and leads the Mentoring Special Interest Group. She is a Master Human Resources Practitioner and a mentor with the South African Board for People Practice.

Steve Bluen, who previously held key positions at South African Breweries (SAB) and directorships at several businesses in Africa and Asia, has extensive experience in Human Resources and Industrial Psychology. He is the current head of the Wits Business School, which forms part of the University of the Witwatersrand's Faculty of Commerce, Law and Management. His aim is to position the Wits Business School as both nationally responsive and globally competitive, and as a national and continental asset located at the heart of the African economy. Steve holds a Doctorate in Psychology from Wits, and is the former Head of the Psychology Department at the university. In 2002, he was appointed Human Resources Director of SABMiller's South African operation and, from 2005, he headed Human Resources in the brewer's beer and soft drinks divisions. In 2007-08 he served as SAB's acting Corporate Affairs Director. Prof Bluen also ran a consultancy where he worked closely with top South African companies.

Mark Bussin holds a Doctorate in Commerce and is the Chairperson of 21st Century Pay Solutions Group, a specialist reward consultancy employing nearly 50 deep technical specialists. He has remuneration experience across all industry sectors and is viewed as a thought leader in the remuneration arena. He has appeared on television and radio, and in the press for his expert views on remuneration. He serves on and advises numerous boards and remuneration committees, and has consulted in several countries. An Associate Professor at the University of Johannesburg, he has been a guest lecturer at various academic institutions and supervises Master's and doctoral theses. He is a Commissioner in the Presidency as a member of the Independent Commission for the Remuneration of Public Office Bearers. Mark is the current President of the South African Reward Association (SARA) and is a Global Reward Practitioner (GRP) tutor. He is the author of *The remuneration handbook for Africa* (2011).

Johann Coetzee, a former Professor in Industrial Psychology and Management, is a psychologist and management consultant. He holds doctorates in Industrial Psychology from the University of the Free State, and in Innovation and Technology from the Da Vinci Institute. His areas of specialisation are varied, and include public administration, sociology, criminology, forensic medicine, ethics and philosophy. Following a stint as a lecturer at the University of Durban-Westville, in 1972 he served Edgars as group human resources consultant. Since 1977 he has worked as a human development consultant and consulting psychologist, and lectured at North-West University and the University of the Free State. In addition, he has experience as an aviation psychologist. Johan is registered as a psychologist with the Health Professions Council, and serves as a Fellow of the Da Vinci Institute, the Institute of Management Consultants and the Institute of People Management.

Wilhelm Crous, who holds an MBA from the University of Stellenbosch, is the Managing Director and founder of Knowledge Resources, established in 1991. Wilhelm previously served as Executive Director of the Institute of Personnel Management (IPM) (1981–1991) and is also a past Chairman of the South African Board for People Practices (SABPP). His past experience includes working as a part-time and guest lecturer at various business schools and universities, including the University of Johannesburg. Wilhelm is a member of many international associations such as ASTD, AMA and the Academy of Management. In 2012 he received a Lifetime Achievement Award from the SABPP for his outstanding contribution to the Human Resources Management profession.

Tony Davidson is a medical doctor with postgraduate qualifications in sports medicine, occupational health and health technology assessment. He also holds an MBA from the University of Cape Town (UCT). After leaving his traditional medical practice in 1992, he began focusing on workplace issues. With 20 years of experience, he offers organisations integrated, cost-effective and results-orientated health systems designed to enhance employer–employee relationships, and to manage health-related risk and productivity issues. Current and past clients include universities and Johannesburg Stock Exchange-listed corporations in the packaging, financial services, retail and petroleum industries. With his associates, he offers programmes ranging from incapacity and absenteeism management; substance abuse, HIV/AIDS and wellness interventions; and medical advisory services. For more information, see www.orghealth.co.za

Dave Duarte is an educator and entrepreneur whose passion is growing digital leadership in Africa. He is the Chief Executive Officer at Treeshake, a company that offers courses and workshops in social media and digital marketing for managers and leaders. Dave also serves as a trustee for MXit Reach, as Principal of the Ogilvy Digital Marketing Academy, and as young global leader of the World Economic Forum.

Nolitha Fakude is Executive Director at Sasol Limited, member of the Risk and SHE Committee and Chairman of Sasol Mining. As Executive Vice-President of Sustainability and Business Transformation she has global responsibility for human resources, safety, health and environment, public and regulatory affairs (PRA) as well as shared services. The first woman President of the Black Management Forum (2003–2006) and its Managing Director prior to that, she now serves as Chairman of the Elders and is a respected authority on transformation and empowerment in South Africa. Nolitha led the initiative to set up and implement the Sasol Inzalo Fund, a broad-based black economic empowerment platform which enabled previously disadvantaged South Africans to hold ten per cent of Sasol's shares. With more than 22 years of corporate experience earned in the retail, mining, oil, gas and financial services industries, she held a number of senior positions developing expertise in areas such as strategy and governance, human resources development and corporate affairs. In 2014, she was awarded the prestigious South African 'Most Influential Woman in Business and Government' award in the mining and petrochemical sector. In 2004, she was recognised as one of South Africa's ten most influential businesswomen by the Financial Mail, and in 2003 she received the Impala Platinum Young Entrepreneur Award. Nolitha is Chairman of Sasol Mining Holdings (Pty) Ltd and non-executive director of Sasol Oil (Pty) Ltd; Chairman of Datacentrix Holdings Limited and Council Member and Second Deputy Chairman of the Human Resources Development Council of South Africa, in addition to being a member of the University of Cape Town (UCT) Business School's Advisory Board. Before joining Sasol she was a member of the group executive committee at Nedbank Group Ltd. She is a former director of Harmony Gold Mining Company Ltd, BMF Investment Ltd and Woolworths Holdings Ltd. Nolitha holds an Honours in Psychology from the University of Fort Hare and completed a Senior Executive Programme at Harvard Business School in 1999.

Linda Fine is the Human Resources Executive for Dimension Data Middle East and Africa. In this role she is responsible for three trading operations across almost 20 countries (encompassing South Africa, Africa and the Middle East), with over 6 000 employees. She has held this role since 2005, but started her career with Dimension Data as Global Marketing Manager in 2001. Linda holds a Business Science degree from the University of Cape Town (Honours in Marketing and Economics) and also has a postgraduate diploma in Project Management from Unisa's School of Business Leadership. Linda has previous experience lecturing at the University of Cape Town, and in the instructional design of courseware for marketing qualifications. She has a distinct passion for learning and development – especially leadership and management development and business effectiveness. Her application of marketing and business principles to the Human Resources discipline ensures that employees are always top of mind, and she believes that service delivery, in the form of employee engagement and experience, to this audience is paramount.

Amanda Glaeser has been Executive Human Resources Director at the University of the Western Cape (UWC) since 2003. She previously held senior human resources posts at Woolworths, with her last role encompassing national staff training and development. She has a Master's degree in Industrial Psychology (Cum Laude) from the UWC, having previously studied at the universities of Johannesburg and Pretoria. Her main focus is on good, generalist HR practitioners' work which conforms to the 'Value Add' model (Ulrich), as well as leadership development work and capability building at the university, achieved through transformative organisational development processes. Amanda believes the challenges facing the UWC environment are a microcosm of the current environment in South Africa, with its emerging world challenges.

Frank Horwitz, BA(SocSci), HDPM, MPM PhD, serves as Director and member of the Advisory Board at Cranfield School of Management, Cranfield University. He served as Director of the Graduate School of Business (GSB) at the University of Cape Town (UCT) from January 2004, having been a senior member of faculty for some 23 years. During this time, GSB achieved full EQUIS (EFMD) accreditation (five years), the school's MBA programme attained a *Financial Times* top 100 ranking for five consecutive years, and its executive programmes were listed in the *Economist*'s top 12. Frank specialises in human resources management, organisation change and industrial relations. He has been a visiting professor at the Rotterdam School of Management (RSM) Erasmus University in the Netherlands; Nanyang Business School in Singapore; the University of Calgary, Canada; and research associate of the Industrial Relations Centre, Griffith University, Australia. He has some ten years' executive experience with AECI and ICI in England. He has published over 90 refereed articles, books and book chapters, locally and internationally, and serves on the editorial boards of numerous leading international and local journals. In 2007 and 2008 he received the Emerald Literati Network Outstanding Reviewer Award for his work on the editorial boards of the *Journal of European Industrial Training* and *Corporate Governance – The International Journal of Business and Society*. His research interests include human capital strategies, workplace flexibility and high-performance work practices, leading and managing knowledge workers, organisational redesign, performance incentives, mergers and acquisitions, cross-cultural and international Human Resource Management, employment discrimination and diversity. He is a board member of a number of companies, has acted as a consultant in organisational change and human capital strategies for several companies and governments. He was educated at Grey College and the University of the Witwatersrand.

Barney Jordaan was Professor of Law at Stellenbosch University until 1997. He obtained a BA (Law) LLB and a doctorate in law from Stellenbosch University and is currently Professor of Management Practice at Vlerick Business School, Belgium, Extraordinary Professor at the University of Stellenbosch Business School, and teaching fellow at the Graduate School of Business of the University of Cape Town. He has been involved in the theory and practice of employment law and employment relations for many years, and is a senior arbitrator and mediator in dispute resolution, practising as mediator since 1989 and as arbitrator since 1990; part-time senior commissioner at the Commission for Conciliation Mediation and Arbitration and several bargaining councils between 1996-1999; ADR Grp (UK) certified, 2008; International Mediation Institute certified, 2010; trainer of mediators; programme director: Postgraduate Diploma in Dispute Settlement (USB); and consultant to the World Bank Group's Office of Mediation Services.

Tjaart N Kruger is Chief Executive Officer of the Premier Group. From 2007–2011 he served as Chief Executive Officer of African Oxygen LTD, a gas company listed on the Johannesburg Stock Exchange. Prior to that he served as an executive of Tiger Brands Ltd, where he was responsible for the Adcock-Ingram Pharmaceutical Division and the Grain Division. Tjaart is a Chartered Accountant and a Commerce graduate from the University of Johannesburg, and in 1995 he participated in the Harvard Business School's programme for business development (MDP).

Johan Ludike is the Talent Management Development and Succession Director at Emirates Telecommunications Co (Etisalat), the Dubai-based Telco, overseeing operations in Africa, the Middle East and Asia. An international Human Resources practitioner for the past 25 years, he has mainly worked in global financial services and telecoms, and recently served as Head of Talent Management for Yum Restaurants International. In South Africa he was Head of Leadership, Management and Organisation Development at Wesbank, prior to heading up Barclays and then First National Bank's Centre for Management Studies (corporate academy). Shortly after completing a Master's in Human Resource Management and Occupational Psychology he pursued an international career in London, spending several years with the Royal Bank of Scotland Group, involved mainly in executive leadership and organisation development for RBS Insurance. For the past three years Johan has been back in South Africa working for MTN Group, spearheading leadership talent management efforts in 21 countries across Africa and the Middle East for 25 000-odd employees.

Lele Mehlomakulu has a BSc Honours from the Medical University of Southern Africa (Medunsa), and a Master's in Business Leadership from Unisa, where she submitted a thesis on the topic 'Psychological characteristics of black female entrepreneurs'. She has held various middle-level and senior Human Resources Development and Organisation Development positions in the finance and retail sectors, the last being as Head of Human Resources at Allan Gray Pty (Ltd), a leading asset management company in South Africa. She is a Director at Accelerate Cape Town, a business-led initiative aimed at bringing together stakeholders in the Cape Town region, with a view to developing and implementing a long-term vision for sustainable, inclusive economic growth. She has held various other leadership roles in industry bodies in the city of Cape Town. Lele, a renowned speaker and a certified Daring Way™ Facilitator Candidate, is the founder and Managing Director of mPower People Solutions (mPS), which focuses on the development and transition management of graduates, young professionals and women in corporate environments. mPS also offers human resources services to small and medium-sized companies.

As Chief Executive Officer of Operational Improvement Management (OIM)*, **Tjaart Minnaar** serves as advisor to several South African blue-chip companies. With international consulting experience in areas such as organisational change and development, employee engagement, executive coaching, strategic planning, business structuring, industrial relations and conflict resolution, his main interest is the design of large-scale organisational performance improvement processes. He has led numerous projects in the food, financial services, engineering, construction and mining industries, and has consulted for parastatals and local government. Before joining OIM, Tjaart spent ten years with Foodcorp and Barlow Rand, holding senior human resources positions in subsidiaries such as Table Top, ICS Group, Renown and Dairy Maid. In the late 80s he achieved ground-breaking successes in industrial relations, establishing one of the country's first effective employee-engagement partnerships in a highly unionised internal and politically volatile external environment. In 1992 Tjaart joined OIM as a consultant, where he spearheaded the design and roll-out of the company's integrated approach to building high-performance organisations. This included the conceptualisation of OIM's performance improvement cycle and the INVOCOM® offering. In 2006 Tjaart took over the company reins and has grown the business tenfold within eight years. OIM has since branched out into specialist units, addressing the full spectrum of people management, organisational performance and operational optimisation. Tjaart holds a BComm Honours (Industrial Relations) from the University of South Africa. (* Prosperity partnership is a registered trademark of OIM Group (Pty) Ltd.)

Seshni Samuel, who holds an MBA from the Rotterdam School of Management, is the Area Talent Leader for Ernst & Young (EY) in Europe, the Middle East, India and Africa (EMEIA) and is a member of the executive. In 2005 she joined EY South Africa as a senior manager and was instrumental in setting up the company's SAP implementation assurance business in Africa, before becoming a partner in 2007. Seshni also sits on EY's Global Emerging Markets committee. Prior to joining EY Seshni worked for Unilever, IBM and PwC. Seshni is focused on ensuring that EY retains its leading reputation as an employer of choice and that employees feel engaged, excited and proud to be a part of the organisation. Having grown up in apartheid South Africa, creating an environment where diversity is respected and appreciated, and in which inclusiveness is achieved at all levels, is a real priority for her.

Linda van der Colff is a business strategist, leadership strategy and leadership development expert, executive coach and business mentor. Her consulting practice focuses on business model development, organisational change and re-engineering initiatives, as well as the development of learning and development strategies with a specific focus on creating a global learning architecture. Her clients include corporates from the healthcare, mining, banking and manufacturing sectors. Linda has held a number of executive corporate positions over the past decade, in particular as Global Head of Leadership and Learning at Standard Bank, as Director of Education at Netcare, and as Managing Director of Milpark Business School. Of the more than 75 articles, book chapters and international journal papers she has published, a significant number deal with the issues of leadership strategy, diversity, innovation and entrepreneurship. Further to delivering conference papers at international and national conferences, and being invited as guest speaker on a range of business-related training and development topics, she has featured on several television and radio broadcasts, speaking on a wide range of education-related matters. She graduated with a Bachelor degree in Economics, and her postgraduate qualifications include an Honours in Sociology, a postgraduate qualification in Labour Law and a Master's in Business Administration.

Clifford van der Venter is currently enjoying a career break and is touring in Africa. With a wealth of business and Human Resources experience, in his most recent role he was employed by Anglo American as Executive Head of Human Resources for Kumba Iron Ore. He previously held the position of Human Resources Director at Unilever SA and Caltex respectively, and was appointed Human Resources Director of British American Tobacco South Africa in October 2009. He completed a Bachelor of Commerce in 1988 at the University of South Africa and a Master's of Business Administration (MBA) in 1994 at the University of Cape Town. Clifford has a passion for people – in particular, he derives satisfaction from watching people develop and helping them grow. He believes that the role of Human Resources must contribute to the overall success of the business.

Theo Veldsman has been Professor and Head of the Department of Industrial Psychology and People Management, University of Johannesburg, since 2008. He holds a doctorate in Industrial and Organisational Psychology, and is a registered psychologist (Industrial and Research Psychology), as well as a registered personnel practitioner. Theo has more than 30 years' extensive research and development, as well as consulting experience in the fields of strategy formulation and implementation, strategic organisational change, organisational (re)design, team building, leadership/ management development, strategic people/talent management, learning, and development. Apart from consulting for many leading South African and global companies in the roles of advisor, expert and coach/mentor, he has authored of over 180 reports and articles, published the book *Into the people effectiveness arena –*

navigating between chaos and order (2002), and has contributed five book chapters on organisational culture, organisational change interventions, strategic talent management (two chapters), and people competence modelling respectively.

Peter Warrener attended school in Botswana and later in the United Kingdom. He holds a B Social Science degree from the University of Natal (Pietermaritzburg), and has a diploma in Financial Management. Throughout his career he has held various Human Resources roles in corporates across the mining, employee benefits and healthcare industries. Peter also completed a four-year stint in consulting. His career has been underpinned by the dual concepts of the purpose of human resources as being that of a contributing support function and attempting to lead through the principles of servant leadership. Peter is currently the Group Human Resources Director of Netcare Ltd, which employs 30 000 staff members in South Africa and Britain.

Shirley Zinn is a former Human Resources Director of Standard Bank South Africa and Deputy Global Head of Human Resources for the Standard Bank Group. Her previous positions include Group Executive Human Resources at Nedbank, General Manager for Human Resources at the South African Revenue Service, Executive: Employment Equity at Computer Configurations Holdings, Regional Human Resources Director for Middle East and Africa for Reckitt Benckiser, Training Manager at Southern Life and Director in the Department of Public Service and Administration's South African Management Development Institute. She is Extraordinary Professor at the University of Pretoria's Department of Human Resource Management. She serves on the board of Monash South Africa, and is past Chairperson of the Institute of Bankers of South Africa, past President of the Institute for People Management, and sits on the Council of the Banking SETA. She served on the Human Resources Committee of the Board at the South African Institute of Chartered Accountants, is a patron of the South African Association for Learning and Educational Differences, is past Honorary Patron of the Corporate Governance Framework, and a patron of the Friends Daycare Centre for children with disabilities. Shirley, who holds an M.Ed from the University of the Western Cape and a D.Ed from Harvard, was awarded the Top Woman in Business and Government and Top Executive in Corporate South Africa by Topco Media in 2008. She was recognised by the *Black Business Quarterly* and received the award for Top Woman in Business and Government and most Visionary Woman in 2008. In 2007 she received an award in Mumbai for Global Human Resources Leadership.

INTRODUCTION

In 2010, the Society for Human Resource Management (SHRM) published the findings of a survey on the top competencies needed by senior Human Resource (HR) leaders.[1] The survey found that the top two competencies needed were *effective communication* and *strategic thinking*. These two competencies were followed by the competencies of *HR knowledge, business knowledge* and *persuasiveness/ influencing others*. The next most important competencies were *integrity, ethical behaviour, credibility* and *leading change*.

In September 2010, the Boston Consulting Group, in conjunction with the World Federation of People Management Associations, published an excellent report entitled *Creating people advantage 2010 – how companies can adapt their HR practices for volatile times.*[2] In this report, four HR topics stood out as the most critical: *managing talent; improving leadership development; employee engagement* and *strategic workforce planning*. Also notable in the report is that high-performing companies emphasise certain HR practices which low-performing companies tend to play down, inter alia: performance management and rewards; and a focus on fewer, carefully chosen HR projects. Perhaps the most significant part of the report is the emphasis it places on the need for companies to reboot their HR function and boost resources devoted to it. This is stated with two caveats, namely 'that HR professionals should be viewed as functional experts and partners to business units, similar to corporate finance. HR professionals themselves acknowledge that they have big capability gaps in business analytics, business planning, and client relationship management'; and second, that

> while both HR professionals and business managers recognize the need for training and other developmental initiatives, the differences in their perceptions must be addressed. Business managers view HR professionals' expertise as less important than their skills in business planning and conflict resolution. And, while both groups agree that business managers' handling of poor performers is their most important people – management skill, business managers see a far smaller gap in their own performance than HR professionals do.

In the *Harvard Business Review* blog of July 2014, Ram Charan wrote an article entitled 'It's time to split HR',[3] in which he predicted, quite correctly, that there would be plenty of opposition to splitting the HR function into HR-A (for Administration) and HR-LO (for Leadership and Organisation). His concluding comment was that 'the problem is real. One way or another, it [the HR function] will have to gain the business acumen needed to help organisations perform at their best.'

A storm of comment and articles followed: 'What it will take to fix HR';[4.] 'Do not split HR – at least not Ram Charan's way';[5] 'Why managers and HR don't get along';[6] and 'It's time to retool HR, not split it'.[7]

This debate is not a new one – what is interesting is that it is assuming greater urgency as the strategic role and contribution of the function become increasingly crisp.

This book addresses many of the issues raised in these two excellent and succinct reports, while indirectly contributing to the debate on splitting the HR function. The original title of this publication was mooted to be 'The role of the Chief Human Resources Officer in emerging markets'. A framework was prepared, and as the respective chapters were produced, addressing the various aspects of the outline, it became clear that the issues to be addressed by the CHRO are no different in emerging markets from any other markets – only the emphasis is different, hence the current title of 'The role of the Chief Human Resources Officer: Perspectives, Challenges, Realities and Experiences'.

The book consists of five parts.

- **Part I** provides a context in which the CHRO plays his/her role:
  - **Chapter 1** identifies global trends and challenges which the CHRO needs to focus on, especially in an emerging market environment;
  - **Chapter 2** counter-balances this with an analysis and overview of the changing world of work and its implications for HR;
  - **Chapter 3** addresses the critical contribution of social capital and its importance in the role of the HR practitioner;
  - **Chapter 4** again counter-balances this with a practical reality check on what a Chief Executive Officer (CEO) expects from his/her CHRO.

- **Part II** focuses on the issue of leadership, with the emphasis falling on emerging markets:
  - **Chapter 5** comprehensively addresses leadership challenges with a focus on Africa, although many of the issues addressed are arguably global – especially in respect of creating a 'language' of leadership;
  - **Chapter 6** raises several HR issues and challenges arising from the changing world of work, focuses especially on emerging markets, and then suggests possible responses to these scenarios;
  - **Chapter 7** is a challenging and thought-provoking piece on the role of the HR practitioner – past, present and future;

- **Part III** is a practical section which addresses a number of the functional challenges facing the CHRO:

  - **Chapter 8** broaches the critical question of talent attraction and retention;

  - **Chapter 9** presents a thoughtful discussion of leadership and development paradigms for the future, in an uncertain world;

  - **Chapter 10**, which offers a comprehensive and cutting-edge review of reward and recognition practices, deals with the complex options and choices in this important area.

  - **Chapter 11** addresses an issue which has arisen frequently in the book, in the context of the changing world of work, namely the role and use of social media for communication and employee engagement. The chapter concludes with a useful case study;

  - **Chapter 12** addresses the issue of collective relationships and challenges in emerging markets and highlights how socio-economic and employment relationships are inextricably linked;

  - **Chapter 13** addresses the oft-neglected issue of health and wellness in the workplace.

- **Part IV** is the 'so-what?' section of the book. It addresses the CHRO directly, via models, processes and case studies, in order to provide practical direction to the important issue of execution. There are eight chapters in this section, emphasising the importance of strategic execution as well as theory.

  - **Chapter 14** emphasises the importance of the HR practitioner knowing her/himself and having a personal vision;

  - **Chapter 15** provides guidelines on how to approach a new position or role during the first 100 days, with some useful dos and don'ts.

  - **Chapter 16** describes the importance of aligning organisational core purpose and culture and the impact this has on employees;

  - **Chapter 17** challengingly describes the various aspects of leading the HR function of an organisation, particularly in a changing world order.

  - **Chapter 18** refreshingly adopts a marketing approach to positioning and aligning the HR function in a new world of work, and in so doing poses several critical questions about the future role of HR;

  - **Chapter 19** uses an architectural metaphor to describe, in detail, the design and crafting of an HR function, including the various options and choices involved in this process;

- Chapters **20** and **21** describe, in a very practical and tangible way, several critical success factors to be considered in designing and executing HR strategy, based on actual case studies in two large South African blue-chip organisations.

- **Part V** concludes the book with two chapters:

    - **Chapter 22** describes a useful and comprehensive model for organisation improvement, encompassing, inter alia, the key people dimensions of organisation transformation and change;

    - **Chapter 23** summarises the various diverse aspects of the content by way of a checklist for action.

My sincere wish is that the content of this book will be both useful and valuable to people practitioners, academics, students and line managers.

Dave van Eeden
Cape Town
September 2014

Endnotes

1. What senior HR leaders need to know: Perspectives from the United States, Canada, India, the Middle East and North Africa (SHRM, 2010).
2. Creating people advantage 2010: BCG and WFPMA, September 2010.
3. Charan, R. (July–August 2014). It's time to split HR. Boston: Harvard Business School.
4. Benko, C. & Volini, E. (2014). What it will take to fix HR. Boston: Harvard Business School.
5. Ulrich, D. (2014). Do not split HR – at least not Ram Charan's way. Boston: Harvard Business School.
6. Ashkenas, R. (2014). Why managers and HR don't get along. Boston: Harvard Business School.
7. Boudreau, J. (2014). It's time to retool HR, not split it. Boston: Harvard Business School.

PART I: Context

CHAPTER 1: Global Trends and People Challenges in Emerging Markets

Clifford van der Venter

Introduction

The pace of change has accelerated dramatically in recent decades, producing large-scale changes in business and society. For corporates, one consequence of these shifts is the realisation that ultimately the best-laid strategies and plans are delivered through people, and that companies can create competitive advantage through their people strategies and outperform their competitors.

While we have witnessed a significant increase in the number and complexity of human resource (HR) challenges, so too have opportunities for companies to excel through their people strategies.

In this chapter, we will

- describe the common features of emerging markets in relation to corporates;

- take a closer look at South Africa as an emerging market;

- identify some of the common HR trends and implications which are prevalent in emerging markets; and

- consider actions which the HR function can take, in response to these situations.

Emerging markets – who/what are they?

Emerging markets are nations with social or business activities in the process of rapid growth and industrialisation. Typically, the so-called BRICS (Brazil, Russia, India, China and South Africa) countries are used as a proxy for emerging markets. Although each of these countries is unique, they do have a lot in common: large populations, underdeveloped economies, and the willingness to embrace global markets and explore opportunities for rapid future growth. Furthermore, almost without exception, these economies are characterised by large social and economic disparities, poor and often dysfunctional education systems, and volatile economic and political environments – all of which have a direct impact on employment markets.

Given the benign growth prospects in developed economies relative to developing economies (2013–2017 growth is forecast to be 4.0 per cent versus 8.3

per cent [Thornton, 2013]), it comes as no surprise that there is a growing shift of economic power towards emerging economies. While there are obvious challenges facing businesses operating in these markets (new regulatory environments, different education and skills levels as well as cultural/linguistic barriers), indeed, many opportunities exist. According to Roland Berger Strategy Consultants (2012), 80 per cent of the world's employees work in emerging markets. This statistic highlights the importance of identifying and understanding global trends and the people challenges prevalent in emerging markets.

The role of corporates

The relationship between corporates and society is important, to the extent that, historically, corporates have often been important drivers of societal change.

A common feature of corporates and governments in emerging markets is the extent to which their fortunes are interlinked. Consequently, the ability to jointly address both social and economic factors within those emerging markets can potentially provide win-win outcomes for all stakeholders.

In South Africa, for example, corporates contribute ±19 per cent to the country's income from taxes (National Treasury, 2013), however despite this income benefit, due to policy implementation issues within local political structures, significant socio-economic challenges still prevail.

There is also great opportunity in the principle of shared value, which involves 'creating economic value in a way that also creates value for society by addressing its needs and challenges. Shared value is not social responsibility, philanthropy, or even sustainability, but a new way to achieve economic success' (Porter & Kramer, 2011). Businesses operating in emerging markets must reconnect company success with social progress. Business leaders and managers should now be required to develop new skills and knowledge, such as a far deeper appreciation of societal needs, a greater understanding of the true drivers of company productivity, and the ability to collaborate across profit/non-profit boundaries.

Macro considerations in emerging markets

Before considering specific HR trends in emerging markets, it is necessary to examine those broader macro-environmental factors which could impact businesses operating in these countries. The World Economic Forum, in its 2012/13 *Global competitiveness report* (2013, p. 4), defines competitiveness as 'the set of institutions, policies, and factors that determine the level of productivity of a country'. It identifies 12 pillars of competitiveness, some of which have a direct bearing on business (and the role of HR).

These aspects are highlighted below.

Institutions

The institutional environment is determined by the legal and administrative framework within which individuals, corporates and governments operate in order to generate wealth. Many emerging economies are characterised by excessive bureaucracy and red tape, overregulation, corruption (especially in dealing with public contracts), as well as a lack of appropriate services to the private sector. These factors often impose significant economic costs on businesses and retard development.

Infrastructure

It is a given that the effective functioning of an economy is heavily dependent on the availability of an extensive and efficient infrastructure, as it connects businesses with consumers. Effective modes of transport, a reliable electricity supply, as well as efficient telecommunications are key enablers of economic activity, yet are often lacking in emerging markets. Again, these factors add significantly to cost structures, as this burden is shifted onto corporates which then need to provide alternative resources.

Healthcare and education

In general, the health of a workforce has a direct bearing on productivity and the competitiveness of a country, as poor health may lead to increased labour costs through absenteeism and low levels of efficiency.

Similarly, having a good basic education improves the efficiency of employees, as they are typically able to advance to more challenging production processes and techniques which, in turn, enables the company to produce more sophisticated products. In the context of a rapidly globalising world, the development of well-educated talent pools that are able to respond to the many complex challenges in a changing environment remains an essential ingredient of competitiveness. While good progress has been made in many emerging markets towards addressing deficits in the quantity and quality of higher education, a great deal of work remains to be done. According to the 2008–2009 *Global competitiveness report*, South African executives expressed concerns about the quality of the education system which, in their view, does not meet the needs of a competitive economy, with mathematics and science lagging behind global standards. Executives also noted that limited access to the Internet in schools makes it increasingly difficult to attain benchmarked standards (World Economic Forum, 2008).

Stakeholders within the economy must contribute to the quest to find viable solutions to eradicate (or at least mitigate) development issues through local initiatives (Corrigan, 2009).

The economic environment

The relevance of emerging markets has been closely linked to the impact of the financial and economic crises on traditional, developed economies. Emerging markets are now projected to play a key role in restoring ailing global markets as a result of their superior growth prospects (John, 2012). However, growth alone will not resolve the problems facing emerging markets, if these markets do not change at the same time (Bertelsmann Stiftung, 2012). Developing economies – and more specifically BRICS states – face considerable obstacles to their individual development paths. The threat of political and social instability arising from extreme social inequality and rampant corruption will have a great influence on individual economic environments (Hartman, Hofmeyer & Schmidt, 2011).

The political landscape

There is a strong connection between a country's political landscape and the economic environment within which corporates operate.

Kenya, for example, is well serviced with a body of laws, programmes, commissions and agencies that could potentially make it the best-governed democracy in Africa (Corrigan, 2009). However, a frequently encountered problem, and arguably the greatest challenge to Kenya's democracy, is the poor implementation of policies and programmes.

The situation is similar in South Africa. While commendable policies exist, the cross-cutting problem in Africa, as well as India and Brazil, is that progress in these countries is often frustrated by poor implementation. While the state has been good at identifying the most serious bottlenecks to development and has formulated sophisticated policies in response, its ability to implement such policies in several critical areas has been limited. Much of this relates to issues of skill and capacity, but nepotism, patronage and corruption have also played significant roles in bleeding the state of scarce resources.

In South Africa specifically, much has been said about the country's miraculous transition to a new democratic dispensation post-1994 and, indeed, many successes have been achieved in restoring economic fundamentals and freeing up capital for the establishment of a comprehensive social welfare system. However, various structural flaws exist and these have been well articulated in a country report published by the Bertelsmann Stiftung (2012), titled 'A deeply unequal society and a welfare state in the making'. While recognising the strides made in addressing poverty through an expanded welfare system and access to critical infrastructure, the South African government has failed to forge a more inclusive, labour-intensive economy, which has resulted in greater social inequality. The country has now surpassed Brazil as the most unequal society amongst the BRICS nations. Furthermore, an economy in which the ratio of welfare recipients to taxpayers is 3:1 (and increasing) is not sustainable, and a new structural model is desperately needed. This growing inequality is further exacerbated by high unemployment levels of around 25 per cent (35 per cent, if discouraged workers are included) of the economically active population, of whom almost 70 per cent are younger than 34. Current demands for wage increases far exceeding inflation and productivity gains will place additional strain on the prospects of reducing unemployment, as private capital investment remains significantly lower than in many other emerging markets.

South Africa's education system is seriously flawed. The system fails to produce learners with the skills needed to facilitate a stronger growth trajectory, and this represents one of the most significant obstacles to employment growth. The South African government's failure to transform the education system has resulted in an over-supply of lowly and unskilled workers, and a scarcity of skilled workers. While approximately 20 per cent of the annual budget is spent on education (representing the largest single allocation), the impact thereof has not been felt in the labour market, and appears unlikely to be felt in the next generation.

While at least two comprehensive strategic plans to address the structural flaws in education and employment (the New Growth Plan and the National Development Plan produced by the Department of Economic Development and the National Planning Commission, respectively) clearly demonstrate a good understanding of the issues and propose seemingly plausible actions to fix them, government's track record on implementation remains questionable and is fraught with issues of skill and capacity, nepotism and corruption.

Despite these significant challenges, South Africa is still the second-highest-ranked African economy, having recently been overtaken by Nigeria, which has significantly improved its position over the past few years.

Global HR trends

In its report entitled *Creating people advantage*, the Boston Consulting Group (BCG) (2013) analysed trends in terms of ten HR topics, with a view to establishing the relative strategic priority of each topic. While the findings of this study primarily dealt with companies based in Europe, the topics are assumed to be relevant across geographies, with specific nuances expected with regard to emerging markets. The following is a brief comment on each topic, in the context of emerging markets.

Talent management and leadership

In recent years, talent management and leadership have consistently been identified as the number one priorities for executives. Identifying and developing employees for more senior positions and ensuring a healthy leadership pipeline remain critical to the success of any organisation.

Given the economic growth prospects in emerging markets, businesses the world over are actively competing for both customers and talent in these markets. However, nationals from key growth markets are often grossly underrepresented in the leadership structures of Western multinationals. Thus, the race for talent is global, and a key challenge facing organisations in emerging markets is having the right people, in the right jobs, in the right locations.

The gap between talent demand and supply is pervasive in the developing world. Multinationals often have trouble recruiting managers and other skilled workers, because the quality of talent is difficult to ascertain. This has led to an increasing trend of corporates returning to the talent fundamentals and focusing on growing their own talent through training, development programmes and experiences, managing career paths and job opportunities, as well as retention programmes.

A 2008 *Harvard Business Review* article, 'Winning the race for talent in emerging markets', identifies four factors to consider in attracting and retaining talent in emerging markets:

- *Employer brand:* Companies that have a reputation for excellence, as well as leading global businesses and those associated with inspirational leadership, are well placed to attract talent since these opportunities may lead to personal advancement;

- *Opportunity:* Talented individuals in emerging markets are especially drawn to those companies that offer opportunities in the form of challenging work, stretch assignments, ongoing training and development, and competitive rewards. Moreover, there is an expectation that opportunity includes an accelerated career track to senior positions;

- *Purpose:* Emerging market job candidates place a premium on companies that have a game-changing business model which will allow them to be part of redefining their nation and the world economy. Furthermore, these candidates express the value of global citizenship and are attracted to companies involved in helping the less fortunate (as many have experienced poverty firsthand);

- *Culture:* A company's culture matters to job candidates in emerging markets in distinct ways. The authenticity of its brand promise, meritocracy, teamness, as well as a truly talent-centric culture, are key attractions within any company.

The BCG article (2013) identifies a number of ways in which the HR function can respond to these challenges:

- *Treat talent as an organisational asset,* rather than being narrowly focused on business units or locations, and use fair and transparent decision processes to fill leadership pipelines;

- Given that approximately 60–80 per cent of a typical company's leaders are promoted from within, it is imperative that a good talent plan takes a *long-term view* (at least five years) and anticipates talent needs by business unit, expertise and location. Investing in the development of talent to meet these needs (through thoughtful career plans, critical work experiences and formal training programmes) will ensure the readiness of these candidates;

- Clearly *define the leadership competencies* required for the future and ensure that these are reinforced in all people processes (e.g., selection, promotion and reward).

As expected, talent management cuts across several key HR processes, and the need for an integrated strategy based on sound analytics and insights goes without saying. In an article entitled 'Talent edge 2020', Deloitte (2010) identifies several focus areas adopted by so-called world-class talent leaders:

- *A strategic approach to talent:* Their talent plan is aligned to their business priorities, and has clear metrics and key performance indicators (KPIs). Furthermore, there is a clear focus on addressing generational issues as well as gender and global diversity;

- *Stronger global outlook:* By recognising the effects of globalisation, they rank global and new market expansion as top priorities and focus on managing a globally diverse workforce;

- *Making future investments:* They focus on future skills requirements (and critical skills in particular), and invest in training programmes to ensure their readiness to meet new skills demands;

- *Engaging current employees:* Such talent leaders proactively manage their employee value proposition (EVP), and maintain excellent communications with their staff;

- *Preparing for the next decade:* They take a long-term view in attracting top talent and invest in the development of their future leaders through succession planning and accelerated leadership development programmes.

Education and skills

'Human capital' is routinely listed as a precondition for economic growth and development, and in this regard a well-functioning education system is of paramount importance. The unreliability of the education system is a common trend amongst emerging markets. In Brazil, the education system has lagged behind in producing job-ready young people, and many workers do not have the skills to fill the jobs being generated. The education system is in disarray, with teacher truancy a significant problem (CIPD, 2010). Russia has also seen a decline in the quality of education despite an increase in the number of universities (Foong & Lim, 2011). Much like Brazil, the education system is playing catch-up, with demands for new skill-sets arising from new or fast-growing sectors. There is a mismatch between the skills learned at school and what employers need from graduates, which is also a challenge in India (Foong & Lim, 2011). The situation in South Africa is no different, with the country facing a major challenge in respect of low-quality education. The declining quality of education, which is also noted in Kenya and Ghana, is linked to inadequate pupil–teacher ratios, the quality of instruction, teacher truancy and poor infrastructure (Corrigan, 2009).

There is an opportunity for corporates to collaborate with educational institutions to facilitate the process of aligning the education curriculum with industry needs: currently, the emphasis is on theoretical learning, rather than practical skills training. Corporates also have an obligation to put pressure on government to improve education and alleviate other socio-economic inequalities, especially given the interdependence of corporates on the availability of human capital and the impact this human capital has on economic growth.

Given the flaws in most education systems in emerging markets, the need for employers to take responsibility for the training and development of their employees is amplified. The current trend is to establish corporate universities or internal learning facilities and programmes dedicated to the skills development of employees. Such initiatives build capacity for sustainable growth within their own organisations, in their markets, and ultimately in the economy more broadly.

HR analytics

Given the increasingly important role of HR as a partner in driving the strategic agenda of the business, analytics are becoming critical in making more effective decisions related to workforce planning, reward, employee development, and culture and engagement management. Quality insights enable the organisation to predict, monitor and improve people management processes.

This trend has been aided by a new breed of data-savvy HR leaders who appreciate the need to develop HR foresight, and are comfortable with using new technologies. Furthermore, the cost of technology is decreasing, and new solutions are proving to be easily scalable, creating greater and easier access for companies.

In its report on human capital trends, Deloitte (2012) identifies certain practical implications resulting from the trend to focus on HR analytics:

- Get started (use your existing data and a real business challenge) and plan a multi-phase journey to develop towards a world-class analytics system;

- Focus on building a sustainable analytics capability and culture.

Deloitte (2012) further identifies a number of entry points in developing towards an analytics mindset which focuses on building capability while addressing point solutions:

- *Workforce planning and optimisation* – understanding current and future talent demand and supply across the business and geographies;

- *Recruitment* – identifying which strategies are most effective in attracting talent;

- *Retention* – which categories or individual employees pose retention risks;

- *Organisation design* – what kinds of organisational structures can aid growth;

- *Leadership development* – understanding the quality of the succession plan;

- *Workforce safety* – anticipating workplace accidents by understanding current data/risks;

- *Workforce transitions* – developing insights aimed at assisting in workforce deployment decisions;

- *Health and productivity* – effectively correlating benefits and investments in wellness and productivity.

While HR analytics is still in its infancy, relatively speaking, the growing diversity and complexity of workforce challenges demand that organisations develop new solutions, specifically in the context of economic environments experiencing huge volatility, as evidenced in emerging markets.

Engagement, behaviour and culture management

The degree to which an organisation can establish company-specific norms and behaviours for employees, while engaging them through a common purpose, is key to organisational success. Companies that proactively define and shape their desired culture and take active steps to embed it (by focusing on those processes that impact culture as well as communications), are more likely to realise a benefit to the bottom line as a result of its culture. Some practical steps to achieve this include the following:

- Measure how much value your culture is creating, by using tools to gauge the impact of culture initiatives and by performing regular engagement and culture assessments aimed at identifying positive or negative trends;

- Use a clearly defined management cascade process to improve engagement and steer the company culture. This should involve using the right mix of communication channels to ensure the active involvement of all employees. It has also been demonstrated that the active involvement of middle managers in the co-design of culture change initiatives is often more successful than merely using these managers to communicate the change process;

- Managing performance and establishing a reward system linking compensation to critical behaviours are key enablers for driving a desired culture and behaviours. Successful companies set very clear expectations, focusing on both the 'what' (results) and the 'how' (behaviours) of performance; they provide regular, constructive feedback and reward employees accordingly.

HR communications and social media

The rapid increase in digitalisation, coupled with the entry of Generation Y into the job market, has made it imperative that companies embrace and leverage their HR communications and social media platforms to create and share information and knowledge.

Social media in particular have created an unprecedented level of transparency through which companies are assessed by both employees and job candidates, mostly without any controls or oversight on the part of the company. This requires companies to develop a clearly defined and integrated strategy aimed at leveraging multimedia, and that they customise it to the preferences and habits of the target audience(s).

Companies need to constantly monitor their social media presence and use these insights to improve their image and reputation. Increasingly, employees are assigned to social media activities, acting both as surveyors and activators to proactively shape a company's image.

Specifically with regard to recruitment, the use of social media can play a critical role in attracting talent via the following means:

- *Employer branding* – use all available channels to create an attractive EVP that resonates with prospective employees and talent pools, and use multiple platforms (company websites, online job forums and social networks, etc.) to reach out to target groups through campaigns;

- *Recruiting strategy* – use career networks to identify candidate groups and apply filters to ensure specific relevance;

- *Candidate recruiting* – make use of streamlined online application and screening processes;

- **Onboarding** – use both internal (intranet) and external social networks to assist new recruits in settling into the company.

The HR target operating model

Although we have witnessed a significant improvement in HR processes, as well as the organisation, governance and repositioning of the HR role as a strategic business partner over the past few years, a lag remains between having the right organisational structure and the available capabilities amongst HR people. It is critical that the HR function effectively link its activities to the strategic goals of the organisation. To achieve this, HR must have a sound understanding of the business context and must be accepted as a partner on all people-related issues. Obviously, a prerequisite for this acceptance is that the basic HR processes need to function smoothly and efficiently.

HR can address these deficits by breaking down silos and building expertise in critical areas across various disciplines (such as talent, development, organisational effectiveness and reward), as problems are often multi-dimensional. Furthermore, strong collaboration is required to provide the business with clear points of contact, while creating integrated solutions. Specifically in the context of multinational organisations, the HR function needs to establish the right balance between global and local responsibilities, in order to respond effectively to local requirements and needs. This entails having a set of global standards that are implemented through localised roles and responsibilities, with some flexibility to customise to local conditions.

Training and development

This involves all activities aimed at equipping employees with the skills necessary to do their jobs and improve their performance. It includes formal classroom training, job experiences, extramural studies, as well as on-the-job coaching and mentoring. Companies that invest in the development of their employees are more likely to improve their capabilities, particularly in a world where the rapid pace of change demands continuous learning and the development of new solutions.

In emerging markets in particular, it has been highlighted that employees place a premium on those companies that invest in their development and display a commitment towards addressing human development issues within the particular country. This can, in turn, improve employee engagement and serve to attract prospective job candidates.

Increasingly, training and development are not simply activities that are outsourced to a third-party provider. Successful companies allocate their resources to those activities that will drive their strategic agenda, and they furthermore use company leaders to actively promote, teach and sponsor such programmes.

It is becoming increasingly evident that meeting future business challenges will require new skills and different qualities as well as fresh approaches to finding, developing and engaging the next generation of leaders. For example, increased globalisation has highlighted the need for leaders to be more culturally aware and to guide business into new markets. Hence, organisations are increasingly including diversity initiatives in their leadership development agendas, as the leadership teams of the future should appreciate and reflect the evolving diversity of the global workforce.

Furthermore, given the dynamics of the business environment, leaders who can manage assimilation and change are more in demand than ever before. Similarly, the new generation of leaders will have different expectations, values and work preferences.

From an HR perspective, traditional leadership competency frameworks used in selection and assessment are unlikely to produce the kinds of qualities expected of future leaders. Companies that grow their own leaders will need to rely on a range of work experiences such as job assignments, projects and scenario-based learning, supplemented by support networks (coaches and mentors) to develop new skills and knowledge.

Finally, measuring the return on investment of development initiatives is increasingly underpinned by an understanding of how value is created, as opposed to measuring the outcomes of single programmes.

Diversity and generation management

Diversity management is defined as 'a managerial process that is planned, systematic and comprehensive for the purpose of developing an organisational environment in which every employee, each with his or her similarities and differences, has the opportunity to contribute to the strategic and competitive advantage of the organisation, and where no person is excluded on the basis of factors unrelated to productivity' (Uys, 2003, pp. 30–48).

According to the Deloitte report on human capital trends (2011), corporates have historically viewed diversity management as 'the right thing to do', whereas there is growing acceptance that 'in today's dynamic business environment – where knowing your customer is so critical to growth – diversity is also the smart thing to do' (Deloitte, 2011, p. 12).

The business case for diversity is clear and compelling: 'having people from different backgrounds engaged in thoughtful debate leads to groundbreaking solutions. Innovation in today's environment depends on bringing all kinds of minds to the table' (Deloitte, 2011, p. 12). A diverse workforce can help companies capture new and expanding markets through their unique consumer insights.

Managing employee diversity with regard to demographics (gender, race, age, etc.) as well as social, cultural and religious differences has received much attention in recent years and will continue to do so as greater awareness is raised.

Globalisation, stronger economic growth in emerging markets and the development of new business opportunities in these markets have significantly changed the distribution of jobs in the world, as well as in the global workforce. From gender to generations, ethnicity to culture, to changing family structures; today's workforce is more diverse in every sense of the word. Workers' needs, expectations and definitions of success now vary widely, rendering obsolete a one-size-fits-all approach to talent management. The implication for HR as a whole therefore is to establish a culture that allows individuals to bring their uniqueness and difference to the table, instil a culture of trust and respect for difference within the organisation and foster an environment in which everyone feels they can reach their full potential.

According to the BCG (2013) there are several key drivers in diversity and generation management:

- *Diversity is not an end in itself* – ultimately, the objective is to bring diverse perspectives into the business, to improve performance;

- *Make diversity a top priority for leaders* – top management must take primary responsibility for driving diversity and must act as role models;

- *Diversity does not mean preferential treatment for certain groups* – use fair and transparent processes to hire and promote the best employees;

- *Diversity is not a public relations gimmick* – back up diversity communications with concrete actions;

- *Diversity is both local and global* – balance the use of international staff with addressing local diversity realities and objectives.

In order to fully leverage the benefits of diverse perspectives, organisations need to ensure that there is a free flow of communication. The synergies arising out of blending different viewpoints may lead to richer solutions than merely focusing on a single point of view. However, a prerequisite for achieving this is a culture that encourages everyone to express their views freely.

Diversity initiatives which are aimed at integrating groups rather than creating many diverse, separate groups, are likely to be more successful.

Finally, merely focusing on recruitment in managing diversity is not sufficient, as too often companies end up losing their diverse talent. Thus, establishing mechanisms and plans to retain diverse talent groups remains critical.

Recruiting, branding and onboarding

The competition for talent – especially in emerging markets where the gap between the demand for and supply of skilled labour is significant – has resulted in companies with superior recruiting processes (including employer branding, recruiting strategies, onboarding and retention) enjoying a definite competitive advantage.

An employer brand represents the corporate identity or personality of an organisation. It is a communicative tool that reflects certain organisational qualities and images to prospective and current employees, communities, and other stakeholders associated with the company.

According to Roland Berger (2012), another growing trend is the increasing importance of a company's brand in attracting and retaining the best talent. As organisations continue to compete in the global marketplace and enter into new markets, they must design and promote distinctive employer branding strategies that will differentiate them from their competitors. A distinctive brand should position the organisation as an employer of choice that is responsible, desirable and attractive to highly talented individuals.

While organisations must have a coherent and consistent brand across all cultures and regions, managing an employer brand in the global marketplace must allow for some local customisation, in order to attract the best local talent in each market. Successful companies appreciate that customised approaches need to be adopted to reach various talent pools, differentiating on the basis of job levels, skills categories, target groups and recruitment channels. Furthermore, they proactively invest in developing an EVP both internally and externally, with core attributes differentiated for the various target groups. Most importantly, they understand that their employees are their best brand ambassadors and ensure that their brand promise is aligned with and kept alive through their actions.

Finally, the successful onboarding of new hires will enable companies to avoid early (regrettable) attrition. This requires a comprehensive programme which not only addresses administrative and professional onboarding requirements, but also the cultural and leadership integration of the new employee.

Labour costs, flexibility and restructuring

The significant economic volatility that has characterised the business environment in recent years has challenged the ability of companies to scale up or down by adapting their cost structures, the size of their workforce and their capability sets.

In emerging markets this problem is often compounded by rigid labour legislation which is designed to keep people in jobs, thus limiting the company's ability to hire and fire workers.

From an HR perspective, it is imperative that there be a clear understanding of ongoing business challenges and resource implications, and of using workforce planning and forecasting tools to anticipate future workforce supply and demand across functions. Successful companies are quite transparent about the workforce implications of their strategic plans and share these with employees and representative groups, thereby also affording employees an opportunity to plan their careers proactively.

Where possible, companies could facilitate some flexibility within their workforce plans by utilising third parties to undertake non-core activities, while keeping critical strategic capabilities and knowledge in-house. Needless to say, HR people need a thorough understanding of legislative requirements in order to avoid costly and time-consuming legal wrangling that will further inhibit their ability to respond to these challenges.

Conclusion

In this chapter we focused on what emerging markets are, and highlighted certain common features of these markets with a view to identifying potential implications for businesses in general and the HR function in particular. While emerging markets generally display better growth prospects than their developed market counterparts, they also share some structural flaws, mainly in the areas of poverty, poor infrastructure, skills and education, and huge volatility in their economies. Amongst others, we highlighted the interdependence between corporate and country success, especially in emerging markets, where significant developmental issues still exist.

Furthermore, we examined HR trends globally and considered these in the context of emerging markets. It is evident that rapid change, increased globalisation, turbulent economic conditions and the high growth prospects of emerging markets have created conditions that require corporates to tap into their available resources, and human resources stand out as one factor that can ensure competitive advantage and superior results.

References

Bertelsmann Stiftung, BTI. (2012). *South Africa country report*. Gütersloh: Bertelsmann Stiftung.

Boston Consulting Group (BCG). (2013). *Creating people advantage*. Retrieved August 26, 2014 from https://www.bcgperspectives.com/content/articles/human_resources_organization_design_creating_people_advantage_2013/

Chartered Institute of Personnel and Development (CIPD). (2010). *Talent development in the BRIC countries*. London: CIPD.

Corrigan, T. (2009). *Socio-economic problems facing Africa: Insights from six APRM country review reports*. Cape Town: South African Institute of International Affairs (SAIIA).

Deloitte. (2010). *Talent edge 2020: Blueprints for the new normal*. Retrieved August 26, 2014 from http://www.deloitte.com/assets/dcom-unitedstates/local%20assets/documents/imos/talent/us_talentedge2020_121710.pdf

Deloitte. (2011). *Human capital trends 2011: Revolution/evolution*. Retrieved August 26, 2014 from http://www.deloitte.com/assets/Dcom-UnitedStates/Local%20Assets/Documents/us_consulting_HCTrends2011_051211.pdf

Foong, A. & Lim, T., compilers. (2011). *HR risks in emerging markets: A panel discussion focusing on BRIC countries*. Aon Consulting. Retrieved August 26, 2014 from http://www.aon.com/thought-leadership/asia-connect/2011-may/hr-risks-in-emerging-markets.jsp

John, L. (2012). Engaging BRICS – Challenges and opportunities for civil society. A study supported by Oxfam India, New Delhi.

Porter, M.E. & Kramer, M.R. (2011). *Creating shared value*. Retrieved August 26, 2014 from http://adamantconsult.com/wp-content/uploads/2014/05/11-porter-creating-shared-value-ss-highlights.pdf

Ready, D.A., Hill, L.A. & Conger, J.A. (2008). Winning the race for talent in emerging markets. *Harvard Business Review, 86*(11), 62–70.

Roland Berger Strategy Consultants. (2012). *Human resources – How the emerging markets are changing the global HR agenda*. Retrieved August 26, 2014 from http://www.rolandberger.   com/media/pdf/Roland_Berger_8_billion_HR_goes_global_Emerging_markets_change_the_HR_agenda_20121109.pdf

Uys, I. (2003). Diversity management: Reasons and challenges. *Politeia, 22*(3), 30–48.

World Economic Forum. (2008). *Global competitiveness report*. Retrieved August 26, 2014 from http://www.weforum.org/reports/global-competitiveness-report-2008-2009

World Economic Forum. (2012). *Global competitiveness report*. Retrieved August 26, 2014 from http://reports.weforum.org/global-competitiveness-report-2012-2013/#=

CHAPTER 2: The Changing World of Work – Emerging Markets

Frank Horwitz

Introduction

'A brave new world of work' which reflects increased digitalisation and work individualisation; a new risk regime of work, with 'spacialisation' of work to multi-locations and virtual, flexible working by connected individuals and groups, is the new scenario of work (Beck, 2000). Global digitalisation and networking, according to Beck (2000, pp. 74–75), 'are aimed at an economy with a capacity to operate in real time across the planet'. This is part of a new literacy which will result in the social exclusion of those who do not master the language of technology, those without 'technological literacy'. The Internet and social media represent what Christopher (2013) argues is a third industrial revolution, which follows the first industrial revolution from cottage to factory industries, and the second to the mass production of Fordist assembly-line manufacturing with command and control managerial cultures.

This third industrial revolution is evident in Africa, too, where cell phone communication in countries such as Nigeria and Kenya has circumvented the traditional provision of landline telephone systems. Mass mobile communication has developed enhanced access to communication at much lower cost to both individuals and the state, which no longer has the same imperative to provide landline infrastructure. A Kenyan company, M-Pesa, has developed an innovative money transfer system which relies on cell phone use. In both mature and emerging market retailing, Internet versus store purchasing has had a significant impact on the labour market. Recently, in the United Kingdom (UK), the decades-old music store HMV went into provisional administration, as did the giant video store firm Blockbuster, with hundreds of job losses as more consumers purchase music online or download music onto their cell phones and other devices. The 'old world' of compact disks (CDs) and digital video disks (DVDs) is transitioning to a new world of digital distribution. Large computer outlets in the UK, such as Comet, have closed hundreds of stores as these types of purchases are increasingly made online or through individual service-oriented firms.

Digital communication, rapid manufacturing processes, customised solutions and the 'servitisation' of products are increasingly individualised, as customer needs become more pre-eminent over traditional standardised products (Christopher, 2013, pp. 4–5). Similarly, standard versus tailored individual service, underpinned by real-time data analytics and multiple supply chain pipelines, occurs. In the context of emerging markets, these countries now have more than 1 000 firms with annual sales exceeding US$1 billion (the *Economist*, January 19, 2013, p. 68); more of these emerging market multinational companies (EMMNCs) with their own distinctive organisational cultures and brands – such as the Indian giant, Tata Corporation; the Chinese computer multinational, Lenovo; Naspers, the South African media company with successful strategic partnerships with Chinese and Russian Internet firms; the Chinese e-commerce MNC Alibaba, which has been buying e-commerce sites in America – all reflect new organisational and human resource cultures diffusing from their home countries to increasingly operate in other markets. These include both mature and emerging markets such as those in Africa, in which China has now become the largest foreign direct investor. This said, while more than two decades ago, the shift of traditional manufacturing jobs from high labour cost to low labour cost countries such as China and India was a common narrative (Van Liemt, 1992), labour costs in several large emerging markets have increased significantly, as their economies have liberalised under recent high levels of gross domestic product (GDP) growth (e.g., over seven per cent in China and India).

With the rising purchasing power and labour costs, and growing middle-class populations in these markets, however, Western firms have sought to relocate certain forms of production elsewhere, seeking further reductions in labour cost and lower labour standards – examples include Bangladesh and Vietnam. However, a notable development is that the hitherto taken-for-granted trends of off-shoring and international outsourcing are being reviewed by many mature market MNCs, and are arguably on the wane (the *Economist*, January 19, 2013, pp. 1–12). General Electric's traditional approach in pioneering off-shoring has now been reversed and has been referred to by Jack Welch's successor, Jeff Immelt, as 'yesterday's model' (the *Economist*, January 29, 2013, p. 11), with the manufacturing of several products previously outsourced to China, including fridges and washing machines, now 'insourced' or 're-shored' back to America.

With the threat of lower wages in mature markets which are in the midst of a prolonged recession, concerns about job losses and downward pressure on middle-class wages have, to some extent, reduced support for the globalisation of traditional manufacturing processes. EMMNCs such as Lenovo, from China, with its IBM manufacturing operations, plan to shift certain operational functions to North Carolina in America. Wages for Chinese manufacturing workers are rising up to 20 per cent per annum. Pay for senior managers in several emerging markets (e.g., China, Brazil and Turkey) matches or exceeds executive pay in America and Europe (the *Economist* Special report on outsourcing and offshoring, January 19, 2013, p. 7). A key feature of emerging markets is the increased purchasing power of its workers, given sustained high levels of GDP growth. This means that labour market supply chains have become more flexible and fluid, almost amoeba-like, as work processes shift from mature markets to emerging markets and back again (with 'in-shoring' or diffusing employment and HR practices) in a much more organic way.

Although global labour arbitrage that saw companies relocating operations abroad is declining, the growth strategies of emerging market firms have seen many become major players and investors in foreign markets, for instance Tata Corporation in the UK and Africa, as well as Chinese investment, especially in the commodities sector in African countries such as Angola, Botswana and Tanzania. The diffusion of their employment and HR practices is not uncontroversial, as minimum employment standards and worker rights are variable in these firms. Emerging markets will need to compete not only in terms of labour costs, but also in respect of increasing the work motivation of employees, their skills development and training, flexible work practices, and realistic labour market regulation.

With the new digital age revolution the globalisation project has not ended, it has simply changed. It is no longer only about globalising supply chains, labour and the skills mobility of expatriate workers, or capital and technology. Today, with the profound third industrial revolution of social media, it is about the simplicity, speed and ease of globalising communication, knowledge and information. With this shift, decision making has become much faster. Witness, for example, the impact of social media communications as a mass mobilisation tool for the Arab Spring revolutions, and in the higher education sphere, the increasing provision of mass online open courses (MOOCs) by eminent universities such as MIT and Stanford.

These changes suggest either an evolution or a profound revolution in the nature of work. Either way, the continuity or nexus between the past and future, presents important questions for the management of organisational and work transitions.

Does history still matter?

Organisational history forms underlying values and reflects something positive that people often wish to preserve. It shapes the culture of an organisation. A firm's 'history can be instrumental in transforming cultures that are no longer useful' (Seaman & Smith, 2012, p. 3). In the fast-changing world of work, the collective memory of organisational history is often forgotten.

Why is this important? The institutional memory of key organisational values and culture not only binds people together, but is 'a rich explanatory tool with which executives can make a case for change and motivate people to overcome challenges' (Seaman & Smith, 2012, pp. 1–3).

Over the past two decades, mergers and acquisitions have often proved unsuccessful because 'soft' key elements of due diligence have been neglected, such as the compatibility of the two organisations' values, culture and work processes (Horwitz, Anderssen & Bezuidenhout et al., 2002). Seaman and Smith (2012, p. 3) relate the following story:

In 2010 Kraft Foods acquired the British confectioner Cadbury. There was considerable resistance to this acquisition from the management and employees of Cadbury, one of Britain's oldest and most well-known firms, and itself a strong brand. Many of its 45 000 employees feared a loss of their values and an end to the fine quality products it made. A clash of cultures occurred and it was predicted that the post-merger integration process would fail. Fortunately the senior executives soon realised this concern and turned to the archives of both organisations. They launched an intranet site called 'Coming Together' that identified and acknowledged the common values in both firms' institutional history and memory. The company archivists indeed discovered that there were several common values including those of the founders of both organisations, James L. Kraft and John Cadbury. This narrative and the common values identified were communicated by the CEO and senior executives using social media, training sessions and other communication channels. This discovered sense of common history helped smooth the integration.

The corporate cultural and HR intent is to retain local talent which understands the importance of, and can access, local markets due to historically developed networks and connections (Chattopadhyay, Batra & Ozsomer et al., 2012, pp. 123–124.) EMMNCs such as Tata Corporation tend to retain the senior executives of the firms they acquire (in contrast to many Western firms, which replace them with executives from the acquiring company). The philosophy here is to be considered a local, rather than an Indian company. Tata Corporation did the same in acquiring Daewoo Commercial Vehicles in Korea. Post-acquisition integration of the acquired firm is gradual and incremental, yet systematic and phased, for example in the Mahindra Group. Investing in local talent is considered vital in these emerging market MNCs, in order to fully benefit from local networks established over time, to leverage existing skills and intellectual capital along with corporate memory, and hence to ensure high retention levels (Chattopadhyay et al. 2012, p. 253). The issues of talent management and the changing nature of work are discussed in greater detail later on in this chapter.

The rapidly changing world of work too often seeks glib, quick-fix solutions to people and organisational culture issues. Understanding organisational history and memory can help unite and inspire people in turbulent markets and in times of uncertainty and complexity – features which characterise emerging markets.

Does place still matter? What does the changing world of work mean for HR management?

Two fast-moving trends have changed the way companies manage talent (Drucker, 2002). First, is the significant number of people who work for organisations, but who are no longer traditional employees of those organisations. Second, is the move – especially in mature market economies – to outsource what might have been considered 'core' people management functions, such as employee relations (Drucker, 2002, pp. 1–2). Outsourcing certain maintenance HR work may indeed be a sound concept, if this permits a more strategic HR orientation internally and the provision of flexibility and organisational agility to adapt quickly to rapidly changing markets.

There has been a significant growth in temporary, interim and part-time labour markets in emerging markets, including in the BRICS countries (Brazil, Russia, India, China and South Africa). A key concern is who will take responsibility for developing the skills and competencies which firms need, if HR development is outsourced. This may, at one level, be part of a formal contract or partnership with independent human resource development (HRD) organisations such as business schools, consultancy firms, sector training authorities (such as in South Africa) and labour suppliers and agencies – where feasible. Alternatively, the broader societal responsibility for skills development is becoming increasingly individualised, as was noted earlier in this chapter. Obviating the red tape of labour regulation is clearly also a motive, and this has indeed been found to be a factor in the rise in part-time or temporal flexibility in BRICS countries (Horwitz, 2013). Peter Drucker (2002, p. 7) argued over a decade ago that 'the traditional work force serves the organizational system. In a knowledge intensive work system, the system might come to serve the worker'.

That said, at least two dual labour markets are at work especially in emerging markets. Traditional command and control mass production factories (such as footwear, clothing and textiles) will continue to be major employers, as is the case in China. However, they, too, will experience similar pressures to those felt in mature economies, as wage costs rise and government regulation impacts on their employment and HR practices. The second economy is the brave new world of work, as described in this chapter, driven by rapidly changing technology, and easy and instant communications in real time through mass social media. This development requires highly skilled technologically literate knowledge and professional workers. Those without these skills will be left behind, and earnings inequalities, which are evident in emerging markets such as Brazil and South Africa, will grow.

National variations continue to occur in employment laws and regulations, even though some regions (such as the Eurozone) have regulated for consistency of labour standards and protections across national boundaries. One example relates to hours of work and part-time work, as outlined by the European Working Time Directive. Some attempts have even been made to regulate flexible work with the construct of 'flexicurity' in Europe; the idea being that flexibility and employment security can be reconciled at both policy and enterprise levels. But the domestic and regional (e.g. European Union) institutional and social policy context still matters. Government labour market policies still affect the conditions and nature of work, as well as the regulation of workplace relations, including flexible work such as part-time and temporary work. The world is not completely flat, as Thomas Friedman (2005) might have us believe.

Quelch and Jocz (2012, p. 1–3) argue from the title of their book, *All business is local*, that 'place matters more than ever in a global, virtual world'. They note that businesses, irrespective of size, must be local as well as global in order to succeed (Quelch & Jocz, 2012, p. 3). Although their focus is largely on marketing, their reference to different fundamentals of place (including psychological place, physical or geographical space, virtual and global place) is most pertinent for product, service and labour market mobility and adaptability. They note that competing trends include both the convergence of culture and values, and tensions between the foregoing and place, where the local is still as significant as the global (Quelch & Jocz, 2012, pp. 7–8). Quelch and Jocz (2012, p. 8) cite the HSBC slogan of 'the world's local bank' and McDonald's, which has to have authentic, locally customised menus to appeal to local customers, even though the brand itself is global. McDonald's, for instance, plans to introduce vegetarian-only outlets in India. Colgate-Palmolive adapts toothpastes to local flavour preferences, while Google is considered a 'placeless firm', with all its products being offered worldwide via 'the cloud'. But despite the fact that its products have no physical form, Google has experienced political and legal difficulties in China and Germany.

Both employees and consumers still have connections to place, which explains why the concept of 'new localism' is evident in case examples such as Pepsi, which puts a great deal of effort into building relationships with local communities (Kotkin, 2009). Examples of organisation culture as a feature of the nature of work in EMMNCs include the strong emphasis which the Indian MNC, Wipro, places on fostering a culture of innovation by encouraging employees to report on any innovations they have helped their clients achieve. HTC, the China Taiwan MNC, does something similar (Chattopadhyay et al., 2012, pp. 87–88). Investing in local employees is a key facet of the strategies of highly successful EMMNCs such as SABMiller, Mahindra and Tata Corporation. Just as geography matters for products and services, so it matters for the labour market and the nature of work, given regulatory regimes of employment laws in countries around the world. These, coupled with social, cultural and language diversity, impact on consumer choices, remuneration and spending patterns, social interactions and interrelationships between regions. Yet social networks such as LinkedIn, Facebook and others also add 'geographically agnostic virtual communities weakening the importance of social ties based on face-to-face proximity' (Quelch & Jocz, 2012, pp. 19–20). By respecting local values and tastes and rooting themselves in a community, employers with global brands broaden their appeal and build trust with consumers and employees (Quelch & Jocz, 2012, pp. 20–22).

Referring to 'dynamic' rather than emerging markets, White (2012) argues that Anglo American and SABMiller have largely retained their corporate culture in markets as diverse and as far afield as Chile, the Czech Republic, Peru and El Salvador. They have done this by being open to learning from and adapting to the needs of their customers, suppliers and other stakeholders (such as regulators) in the global markets in which they operate. Corporate culture and its readiness or openness to change underlie the way in which managerial practice and work are defined in successful EMMNCs. The question of agility and readiness for change is discussed later in this chapter.

Finder's keepers – managing talent

Van Agtmael (2007, pp. 227–247) refers to a revolution in 'cheap brainpower' in discussing the knowledge worker emergent market example of Infosys, India's leading software exporter with a market value of over US$18billion in 2005, and over 49 000 employees. Infosys recruits less than one percent of the more than one million job applicants annually, in what is clearly a very selective recruitment and hiring process. It has consistently been rated the best employer to work for in various surveys in India. Ranbaxy Laboratories Limited, with experienced international managers in its leadership team, and focusing on both developed and emerging markets, has become the biggest manufacturer of antibiotics in India, with plants in seven countries and exports to 70 others. Countries such as India and China Taiwan have invested heavily in HR development to address the brain drain – or, indeed, to reverse it, as appears to be occurring in India in the technology field. While China has been dubbed the world's manufacturing hub, some call India the back office of the world. 'Brainpower hub might be a better name,' according to Van Agtmael (2007, p. 233).

Coats (2009) argues that the 'big story' is the growing importance of employment in high-value knowledge-intensive services. He notes that the changing occupational structure is a consequence of the rise and fall of certain industries, with fewer manual workers in traditional manufacturing sectors and more white-collar knowledge workers in others. Coats notes that this changing occupational structure occurs across the developed world. Arguably, it also occurs in rapid-growth emerging markets. Associated with these developments is the notion of flexible work practices, such as increased part-time and temporary work, and (as discussed earlier) the profound impact of digital technology on the nature of work. Structural changes have always been part of the changing nature of work, but the impact of the third industrial revolution (Christopher, 2013) is the most recent, given the globalisation of information communication in particular, and shifting patterns of production and supply chains.

India graduates over 100 000 highly qualified engineers a year, many with software skills. A substantial number of these graduates work in Bangalore. The establishment of country-wide institutes of technology has gone some way in increasing the supply of skilled and professional labour market entrants in India and Taiwan. Large-scale science parks, with closely-linked training institutes, have been developed in countries such as Brazil, China, India, Singapore, Taiwan and Malaysia. These nations seek not only to make education and skills development a national competitive advantage, but also endeavour to reverse the brain drain by creating new, white-collar jobs in emergent markets.

Talent management research in Africa and East Asia shows that professional workers at high skill levels in knowledge-intensive industries rate the following as critical to their work motivation, effective utilisation and retention (Horwitz & Mellahi, 2009; Horwitz, Chan & Quazi et al., 2006; Sutherland, 2006; Sutherland & Jordaan, 2004):

- Autonomy and the opportunity to plan and control their own work;

- Challenging, 'stretching' and stimulating work;

- Collegial relations with peers and superiors;

- Career development and personal growth opportunities;

- Competitive, flexible remuneration;

- An 'engaging' culture with direct, informal communications, work–life balance and 'decent work', which nurtures and mentors leadership talent.

One study of some 20 global companies, which identified factors that differentiate successful firms in emerging markets, which are able to attract and retain talent, found four key attributes that go beyond salary and bonuses: 1) company brand reputation; 2) internal opportunities in the firm; 3) a purpose beyond profit (companies such as Novartis, Standard Charter Bank in China and Tata Corporation); and 4) a continuous growth culture (Ready, Hill & Conger, 2008). These factors are consistent with other findings relating to changing values to work in knowledge-intensive firms in emerging markets (Horwitz & Mellahi, 2009; Horwitz et al., 2006). These studies underline a degree of convergence in work expectations especially amongst professional and managerial employees in emerging and mature labour markets, given the more traditional instrumental attitudes to work which were considered to be prevalent until very recently.

This shift towards 'existential needs' (Maslow, 1943) or 'intrinsic motivation needs' (Herzberg, 1968, pp. 87–96) is an important feature of the changing world of work in emerging markets, although these factors have long been associated with work motivation in mature labour markets. Getting to this point begins with understanding and addressing the unique needs and scarce skills which knowledge and professional workers have, which include 1) competitive, market-based flexibility in work practices – pay, benefits and employment practices (e.g., flexible contracts); 2) intrinsic work factors such as autonomy and job satisfaction, planning and control over work, recognition and reward; 3) an opportunity to do challenging work that is exciting, stimulating and at the leading edge in an industry or sector; and 4) growth and skills development. According to an Economist Intelligence Unit (EIU) survey (2007), raising pay to above market rates was only the fourth most effective HR strategy amongst Asian firms. The top three all revolved around personal growth: increased training was first, using a mentoring system was second and personal development road maps/plans third. In South Africa, it was in the area of opportunities for growth that many firms appeared to be failing. The Deloitte National Remuneration study (2007) showed that in regard to staff turnover, most South African workers quit their jobs because of a lack of career advancement and the ineffective utilisation of their knowledge and skills.

A fifth factor is that of social networks, peer group relations and organisational context. These include an open and engaging culture, with peer interaction that creates opportunities for collegial learning, value diversity as essential for innovation, high-quality relations with the organisation's leadership, and fair employment practices. Workplace contextual factors, such as unfair discrimination (explicit or often subtle, but still with the net result of underutilisation), lack of job satisfaction and resultant under-performance all play a role.

Research by Deloitte (2007), entitled 'Connecting people to what matters most', describes three keys to creating a high-performance work environment and culture in the changing world of work context:

- *Connecting people to people*. People rely heavily on the knowledge and insight of others, which means personal relationships are more important than ever. This is not only about attracting and developing local talent, it also concerns engaging constructively and playing a developmental role in local communities and enhancing ethnic/local representation in the governance structures of the EMMNC in the country/countries in which it operates. MTN, the South African-based telecommunications company, is an example of these practices in respect of its operations in Nigeria (White, 2012, p. 18). In this sense, the nature of work is not defined exclusively in a narrow 'job-sense', but in a broader social way;

- *Connecting people to purpose*. This implies actively building and sustaining a sense of personal and organisational mission; connecting people to the core purpose or mission of the organisation through resources, for example, via knowledge management, cutting-edge technology and flexible working time; and doing this in ways that enhance performance, adaptability and work–life balance. The so-called Generation Y (i.e., younger professional and knowledge workers) greatly values work–life balance;

- *Connecting people with the right resources through others*. Related to this is the first key factor (see above) which considers the cultural constructs of Confucian 'guanxi' social networks and African 'ubuntu', the sense in the latter being that personal identity is developed within a social and community context. The single biggest foreign investor in Africa over the past decade is China. Although it can be argued that its main interest is Africa's commodity resources, and that its own employment practices are sometimes problematic, Chinese firms in several countries have made tangible investments in developing local infrastructure and resources, such as roads and medical facilities.

The changing world of work in the past decade has seen a so-called 'war for talent' which is not unique to mature market economies or to BRICS countries. It is also evident in other large, emerging markets such as Indonesia. An increasing level of labour mobility in labour markets with high economic growth (e.g., China, India, South-East Asia, Dubai and other Middle East emergent markets) reflects a massive demand for knowledge worker talent at premium wage prices (Horwitz & Mellahi, 2009). Although China and India appear to have deepened their shallow talent pool, South Africa has been less successful. This has resulted in a rising 'churn', as more executives, professionals and skilled technical people job-hop, creating an artificial demand in the labour market.

Nevertheless, two-tier labour markets will continue to exist in emerging markets characterised by high earnings differentials, such as Brazil, China, Nigeria and South Africa, which have the four highest Gini coefficients in the global economy (the *Economist*, January 26, 2013, p. 53). But sustained high economic growth in emerging markets, increased domestic consumption, and prospective or concomitant social development and service delivery are dependent on the ability to develop the requisite skills in domestic markets, to motivate people and to retain scarce skills.

Organisational responses to the changing world of work

New forms of organisation often typify the new world of work, as organisation seek to move from command and control managerial cultures and mechanistic hierarchical structures with narrow job definitions, which are characteristic of a stable environment, to more flexible, organic organisational structures, which respond speedily and with agility to a rapidly changing environment. This new environment is characterised by change – ongoing, often relentless change, high in complexity and uncertainty. Organisations need a different set of competencies at all levels to navigate these changes. The impact of technology, product obsolescence and increased competition from emerging market firms are probably the most significant factors in how work and the requisite skills needed for effective performance, have changed.

Two key attributes are vital to modern organisations, namely organisational agility and flexible work practices.

Organisational agility and readiness for change

How to achieve organisational agility through human resource management (HRM) practices in turbulent times is receiving increased attention (Nijssen & Paauwe, 2012). This involves the 'dynamic capabilities' of organisations; continuous organisational adaptation; and a readiness to reconfigure and transform strategy, structure, workplace skills and processes, capacity and workforce scalability. These reflect the capacity of an organisation to keep its human resources aligned with its business needs (Nijssen & Paauwe, 2012, pp. 3317–3318).

Also required is a capacity to consistently create, adapt, distribute and apply knowledge (Nijssen & Paauwe, 2012, p. 3319). Organisational agility is the opposite of organisational rigidity. However, the potential risk of such organisational agility is a loss of knowledge as people configurations change constantly, which affects, for example, headcounts, skills mix and patterns of deployment.

The degree of strategic alignment of the workforce with its strategic goals or its organisational fit is never totally guaranteed, nor is it indeed desirable. An element of tension between alignment and autonomy/fluidity is needed for change and innovation to occur. In organisation design or redesign, a term such as 'agility' is a function of the 'Five Ds':

- *Downsizing* (doing more, with fewer people) by increasing shared services, rather than duplicating service functions;

- *Delayering*, which involves flatter and networked amoeba-like structures, with virtual working occurring individually or in virtual teams, seamlessly or in a seemingly boundaryless manner. Virtual teams working across countries and cultures is a significant development; one which presents a unique set of managerial challenges given the freedom, autonomy and fluidity intrinsic to this work type, in contrast to the certainty and rigidity of Fordist command-and-control micro-management;

- *Decentralising* authority, decision locus and responsibility, but within coordinated, shared information and decision-making parameters;

- *Disaggregation*, which involves outsourcing or subcontracting non-core functions, also redefining what is core and non-core work;

- *Deployment* – the 're-words' – organisational redesign, reinvention, (the now older notion of) re-engineering, and the redeployment and retraining of people in redundant jobs or their retrenchment, if internal redeployment into suitable positions is not possible.

New forms of flexible work practices

Included among these attributes are the following:

- Functional flexibility, including multiskilling, job rotation;

- Numerical flexibility – a variation of staffing types and levels;

- Temporal flexibility, such as part-time and temporary work; and

- Pay flexibility, for example, performance-related variable pay. (Blyton & Lucio, 1995)

Of course the prevalence of these practices and organisational types is a moot point. However, these practices may be packaged in part, and in different ways. The Brazilian manufacturer, Semco, is a good example of a firm which has consciously sought such agility by using various forms of flexibility, including functional, numerical and pay flexibility. Traditional 'Fordist' organisational types are characterised by predictability and stability, or by relatively slow, incremental change, in part because of an inflexible mass production industry type which provides relative employment security. However, even in these sectors flexible practices and agile structures have become more necessary (as in the auto industry, for example), as these organisations fight to remain competitive and to survive.

Conclusion

Often, over the past two decades, one response on the part of large, multinational firms to the dynamic, changing world of work, has been to seek cheap labour markets in low-wage emerging markets with abundant labour supply. But, as discussed earlier, there is some evidence now of a move to 're-shoring' or in-sourcing again, as the price of labour rises in major emerging markets such as China. Yet, organisational change and responses to the new world of work should not be oversimplified. Firms often respond in quite individual ways, in seeking to make distinctive strategic choices which aim to give them the edge over their competitors. And it is rare that all of the above forms of organisational agility and work flexibility will be implemented together, in a bundle, or in combination.

High-performance cultures, using some or more of these practices, do indeed have a downside. Excessive downsizing with high levels of skills loss can result in a firm becoming 'too lean to be mean', losing its institutional memory and its sense of binding ideology, derived from its organisational history. Work intensification, with fewer people having to do more, does not usually result in employee wellbeing or job satisfaction. Large-scale downsizing often results in a loss of trust and growing insecurity which are inimical to teamwork, sound employee relations, and the cooperation needed for effective problem solving. This raises serious questions about job quality in a changing labour market (Coats, 2009, pp. 118–119).

The way in which work is organised in this, the 21st-century third-phase industrial revolution, is clearly different from traditional, single physical location, mass production operations. One could well ask whether, with the rising trend of individual work; home-based working; outsourced work; technology and virtual working in any place, at any time and indeed even in cyber space, are we not returning to the first-phase industrial revolution of the small, more atomised cottage industry as a supplier business? It is an intriguing question.

References

Beck, U. (2000). *The brave new world of work*. Frankfurt and New York: Polity Press, 72–81.

Blyton, P. & Lucio, M. (1995). Industrial relations and the management of flexibility. *International Journal of Human Resource Management, 6*(2), 271–291.

Chattopadhyay, A., Batra, R. & Ozsomer, A. (2012). *The new emerging market multinationals*. New York: McGraw-Hill, 87–88, 123–125, 252–254.

Christopher, M. (2013). *The 3ʳᵈ industrial revolution and what it might mean for retailing*. Address to School of Management, Cranfield University, January 17, 1–8.

Coats, D. (2009). Changing labour markets and the future of work. In J. Storey, P.M. Wright & D. Ulrich (Eds.), *The Routledge companion to strategic human resource management*. New York: Routledge, 106–122.

Deloitte National Remuneration Guide, South Africa. 2007. Deloitte, Touché and Tohmatsu Survey – 'Connecting people to what matters most', 1–15.

Drucker, P.F. (2002). They're not employees, they're people. *Harvard Business Review*, February, 2–7.

Economist Intelligence Unit (EIU). (2007). *Global Corporate Network Survey*, August 16.

Friedman, T. (2005). *The world is flat*. New York: Allen Lane.

Herzberg, F. (1968). One more time: How do you motivate employees? *Harvard Business Review*, February, 87–96.

Horwitz, F.M., Anderssen, K., Bezuidenhout, A., Cohen, S., Kirsten, F., Moseunyane, K., Smith, N., Thole, K. & Van Heerden, A. (2002). Due diligence neglected: Managing human resources and organisation culture in mergers and acquisitions. *South African Journal of Business Management, 33*(1), 1–10.

Horwitz, F.M., Chan, T.H., Quazi, H.A., Nonkwelo, C., Roditi, D. & Van Eck, P. (2006). Human resource strategies for managing knowledge workers: An Afro-Asian comparison. *International Journal of Human Resource Management, 17*(5), 775–811.

Horwitz, F.M. & Mellahi, K. (2009). Human resource management in emerging markets. In D.G. Collings & G. Wood (Eds.), *Human resource management: A critical approach*. London: Routledge, 264–277.

Horwitz, F.M. (2013, forthcoming). Employment relations in the BRICS countries. In A. Wilkinson, G. Wood & R. Deeg (Eds.), *The Oxford handbook of comparative employment relations systems*. Oxford and New York: Oxford University Press, 1–18.

Kotkin, J. (2009). There is no place like home – Fewer Americans are relocating. *Newsweek*, October 19, 42.

Maslow, A.H. (1943). A theory of human motivation. *Psychological Review, 50*, 370–396.

Nijssen, M. & Paauwe, J. (2012). HRM in turbulent times: How to achieve organisational agility? *International Journal of Human Resource Management, 23*(16), 3315–3335.

Quelch, J.A. & Jocz, K.E. (2012). *All business is local. Why place matters more than ever in a virtual world*. London: Penguin Books, 1–3, 4–5, 7–8, 17–22.

Ready, D., Hill, L. & Conger, J. (2008). Winning the race for talent in emerging markets. *Growing talent in growth countries: EFMD Global Focus, 1*, 20–23.

Seaman, J.T. & Smith, G.D. (2012, December). *Your company's history as a leadership tool.* Harvard Business Review Insight Centre website. Retrieved January 13, 2014 from http://hbr.org/2012/12/your-companys-history-as-a-leadership-tool/ar/1

Sutherland, M. (2006, April). *How do senior people attract and keep staff? The role of HR in South Africa.* Retrieved May 2, 2006 from http://MBA.co.za

Sutherland, M. & Jordaan, W. (2004). Factors affecting the retention of knowledge workers. *South African Journal of Human Resource Management, 2*(2), 55–64.

The *Economist*. 2013a, January 19. The best thing since sliced bread, 68.

The *Economist*. 2013b, January 19. Offshoring – welcome home, 11–12; and Special report on outsourcing and offshoring, 3–7.

The *Economist*. 2013c, January 26. Inequality – Out of the bottle, 53.

Van Agtmael, A. (2007). *The emerging markets century.* London: Simon & Schuster, 227–250.

Van Liemt, G. (1992). *Industry on the move.* Geneva: ILO Publication, v–vi.

White, L. (2012). South Africa, the home of global champions. In M. Makura (Ed.), *Going global.* Johannesburg: MMEmedia and GIBS, 17–19.

CHAPTER 3: The Role of Social Capital

Penny Abbott

Introduction

Social capital provides the glue which facilitates co-operation, exchange
and innovation.

> – Organisation for Economic Co-operation ·
> and Development (OECD), 2001

What is social capital and why is it important for organisations in general and the
CHRO in particular? The term 'social capital' is unfamiliar to many people, although
the concept is probably just as important to organisations (and therefore to HR
practitioners) as 'human capital'.

The two terms are, in fact, often linked. 'The full range of our human capital –
from the state of our health to the level of our learning – affects, and is affected by,
our relations to wider society' (OECD, 2007, p. 96). 'Human and social capital don't
exist in isolation from each other. The two are linked in complex ways and, to some
extent, feed into each other. In other words, social capital promotes the development
of human capital' (OECD, 2007, p. 105).

Human capital refers to the assets of a nation or any organisation which reside in
the knowledge, skills and experience of that nation's citizens, or in an organisation's
employees. The OECD (2007, p. 3) defines human capital as 'the knowledge, skills,
competencies and attributes that allow people to contribute to their personal and
social well-being, as well as that of their countries'. For the HR profession, one could
add that a contribution is also made to the employing organisation.

Social capital refers to assets which reside in inter-connectedness, expressed
through relationships, whether these are:

*   within small, local communities, between the members of that community or
    between that community and its neighbours;

*   between citizens and the state;

*   between employees and their employer(s), and amongst employees;

*   between organisations and their external stakeholders.

The wider the networks of relationships and the more constructive the relationships,
the more social capital exists.

The OECD (2007, p. 102) notes that although there are many definitions of social capital, these can basically be simplified as 'the links, shared values and understandings in society that enable individuals and groups to trust each other and so work together'. This manifests or is expressed through

- bonds – links based on a common identity;

- bridges – links stretching beyond the bonds to other groups;

- linkages – linkages across social groups further up or down the social ladder.

Bonds can perform positive or negative functions – they can, for example, help a child obtain an education with the assistance of the community; but bonds can also isolate a community, for instance, an immigrant group may keep to itself and fail to build bridges with the local people.

High levels of social capital can work either positively or negatively. A close-knit gang of criminals has a high level of social capital – but so does a well-functioning business.

Relating social capital directly to Human Resource (HR) work, Krebs (2008) states:

> Human Resources used to focus only on within-employee factors. The new competitive landscape requires focusing on between-employee factors, the connections that combine to create new processes, products and services. Social capital encompasses communities of practice, knowledge exchanges, information flows, interest groups, social networks and other emergent connections between employees, suppliers, regulators, partners and customers. [...] Organizations with better connections in the network of industry alliances and joint ventures report higher patent outputs, a higher probability of innovation and higher earnings and chances of survival in rapidly innovating industries. Social capital, within the firm and across the firm's border to other firms, seems to be a prerequisite for organizational learning, adaptability and agility.

It is clear that, from an HR point of view, social capital is a concept that needs to be looked at in three ways:

- As a factor that contributes directly to the success of the organisation, through employees networking and sharing knowledge;

- As a factor that can impact positively or negatively on the organisation, through the relationships that the organisation builds with external stakeholders;

- As an important indicator of societal stability and future sustainability, which therefore impacts on the organisation's ability to operate in that society.

Within the organisation a number of attributes characterise those individuals who are better at building their own social capital, i.e., building and using networks. People with better social capital

- find better jobs more quickly;

- are more likely to be promoted early;

- close deals faster;

- receive larger bonuses;

- enhance the performance of their teams;

- help their teams reach their goals more rapidly;

- perform better as project managers;

- help their teams generate more creative solutions;

- increase output from their research and development (R&D) teams;

- coordinate projects more effectively;

- learn more about the firm's environment and marketplace;

- receive higher performance evaluations. (Krebs, 2008, p. 38)

Social capital as a form of capital

Why are these relationships considered to be a form of capital? Some theorists argue that such relationships do not constitute true capital, because there is no element of giving up value today in order to derive greater value tomorrow.

The OECD considers that education generates capital which produces a long-term return in the form of employment and income. This is the basis of human capital. The basis of social capital is made up of those structures in society that enable the development of relationships and shared values which generate a long-term return, in that they make it easier for people to work together, and therefore to achieve economic success (OECD, 2007).

Capital can also be viewed as a stored form of value (assets), and thus '[n]etworks and the associated norms of reciprocity have value' (Putnam, n.d.). Positive, constructive relationships lead to greater trust and therefore to greater social cohesion, which leads to greater peace and less waste of energy in handling conflict. Greater trust between a state and its citizens leads to the improved spending of state funds on nation-building activities such as education, rather than channelling those funds to safety and security activities such as policing. Higher levels of trust are also linked to higher levels of economic growth and government performance. Greater trust within an organisation leads to improved employee relations, fewer instances of industrial action, higher productivity (because employees are more willing to use their knowledge and skills to benefit the employer), lower employee turnover, increased innovation and quicker change in response to changing demands on the organisation.

The concept of social capital is therefore of interest not only at a national and a macro-economic level, but also at the level of a single community or organisation. It is also of interest at an individual level, because researchers have found that 'the quality of our social relationships is one of the most important factors shaping well-being outcomes throughout the life course ... our social connections are the single most important determinant of people's level of life satisfaction' (Scrivens, 2013). This being so, the concept of individual social capital is clearly linked to the study of happiness – research which is growing in popularity and has gained greater acceptance. The concept of gross national happiness (GNH), which originated in Bhutan, has, for instance, been recognised and adopted by several countries in Europe.

The concept of social capital is also of interest to economists, because they hypothesise that higher levels of social capital are associated with higher levels of political and social stability, which reduce investment risk within markets.

Furthermore, there is a direct link between the extent and the quality of social contacts (networks), and the ability to find employment. Poverty works in multiple ways to disadvantage an individual in respect of achieving economic success – be it through lack of education, poor health or a lack of social contacts. The same applies to the poor as a sector of society – they become marginalised and unable to participate in a modern, knowledge-based economy.

The close links between social capital and socio-economic development in a country become increasingly evident as the understanding grows that socio-economic development encompasses much more than economic development. The OECD's project to measure social capital focuses on four specific areas:

- Social connections (the people you know and how you know them);

- Individual resources (the support, information and opportunities provided by your social connections);

- Civic engagement (your contribution to community life, such as volunteering or other forms of social involvement);

- Public resources (the shared values, attitudes and trust which facilitate collective action).

The World Bank (2012), which has also conducted research in this area, developed questionnaires at the household, community and non-governmental organisation (NGO) levels.

At a formal organisational level (public or private sector), the measurement of social capital concentrates largely on measuring networks of information sharing, both inside and outside the organisation (Krebs, 2008). From this point of view, social capital links into knowledge management. However, based on the focus areas listed above, it would seem that measuring social capital in relation to an organisation could widen its focus to include similar areas – this would take social capital closer to employee engagement and social investment.

Authors in the field of sociology, with which social capital is mainly associated, stress that the concept is multi-dimensional and highly complex. For the purpose of this chapter, the focus will be on how social capital impacts on the success of the organisation, and therefore why it is important to the CHRO.

Emerging markets and social capital

White (2013), in his analysis of the defining features of emerging markets, prefers to use the term 'dynamic markets', because he sees such a wide diversity of economies in the so-called emerging markets that it is hard to classify them into a single group. However, all the markets in this group are characterised by 'significant political, social and cultural change ... and general ambiguity and complexities are often prevalent' (White, 2013, p. 14). In addition, White (2013, p. 17) analyses markets within this group on dimensions that include, apart from economic growth, 'key environmental attributes like political stability, governance and innovation'.

If emerging (or dynamic) markets are defined by change, and governance is important, then the concept of social capital becomes extremely important as an enabler of change and a precursor to good governance. Conversely, rapid and ambiguous change with poor governance would result in low levels of trust and therefore decreasing levels of inter-connectedness.

Rapid change can lead to problems with stability within a country. Social capital is closely linked to social stability. It would appear, from a paper by one of the pioneers of the concept of social capital, Robert Putnam (n.d.), that social capital even in one of the world's largest and politically most stable countries, the United States of America (USA), was on the decline, from about 1960 to 2000. The OECD notes that 'even developed countries are worried about how they can maintain cohesion in societies that are home to ever-more disconnected communities' (2007, p. 15). According to Moller, author of *The Creative Society of the 21st Century*, 'a growing dichotomy between the elite and the rest of the population puts a question mark on the social cohesion inside many societies – a cohesion that has been and still is the foundation for stability' (Moller in OECD, 2007, p. 15).

In an analysis of the differences between states within the USA, Putnam (n.d., p. 10) shows that the lowest levels of social capital manifest in those states where slavery was prevalent: 'It is not an accident that the low social capital is very clearly associated with the depth of slavery in the nineteenth century, and that is because slavery as a system and the post-slavery reconstruction period were institutionally designed to destroy social capital'. There are analogies here to the likely situation as regards social capital in other societies which, in the past, saw the imposition of slavery or similar types of systems. Clearly, many emerging economies fall into this group.

Putnam (n.d., p. 12) also discusses the relationship between social capital and the welfare of young people – his measure of welfare 'includes teen pregnancy, infant mortality and a variety of other measures of how well kids do' – and 'again there is a very strong relationship showing that, in general, the welfare of children is higher where social capital is higher'. Also, 'the strongest predictor of the murder rate is a low level of social capital. It is stronger than poverty; it is stronger than other plausible measures' (n.d., p. 12). This relationship holds true for all measures of lawlessness, including tax evasion. Again, this observation has relevance for emerging economies.

Can a ranking order of countries in terms of social capital reveal anything useful? Lattin and Young (n.d.) compiled a rank order of countries on a social capital achievement score, using an index of various measures which include economic freedom, purchasing power, economic growth, the human development index (DHI), governance and corruption indicators. The ratings for countries identified as 'dynamic markets' (White 2013) are shown below, with positions given from highest to lowest.

Table 3.1: Rank order of countries based on a social capital achievement score

Position	Country	Rating
1	The Netherlands	0.9698
23	Chile	0.8143
54	South Africa	0.5977
64	Brazil	0.5009
78	India	0.4531
80	Turkey	0.4313
84	China	0.4016
90	Russia	0.3865
114	Indonesia	0.2855
117	Vietnam	0.2784
142	Nigeria	0.1553
155	Democratic Republic of Congo	0.0406

Source: Lattin and Young (n.d.)

As with all such rankings, the selection and weighting of measurement components has to be carefully scrutinised before drawing any conclusions. A ranking, as the authors point out, represents a specific point in time, and it would appear that a more useful approach is to look at trends over time, as Putnam has done in the USA, because then changes in social capital can be compared with changes in other variables which are considered important, and correlations (if not causations) can be identified.

From the point of view of a CHRO, measuring social capital at a societal level is of interest as it gives some indication of levels of trust and 'citizenship' in the society from which employees are drawn. Estimating the level of social capital could be devised by looking at the degree of homogeneity within a society, the degree of income inequality, and the quality of the public healthcare and education systems.

Building social capital in emerging markets

Within organisations

For building social capital inside the organisation, in the form of connected employees who can leverage those connections, Krebs (2008) offers this guidance:

- Identify what connections exist

    - internally (formal and informal information flows)

    - between the organisation and stakeholders to ensure two-way flow of information;

- Develop connections within groups and between groups through awareness-raising and training;

- Retain – target less-connected groups to help them build connections, as this increases commitment to the organisation and therefore improves employee retention;

- Enhance – look at the pattern of relationships (vertical, horizontal and diagonal) and consider which patterns need to change to achieve greater organisational success.

Between the organisation and its stakeholders

For any organisation, its relationships with its various stakeholders is a critical asset. Poor relationships can literally destroy a company.

Investor relations is often a high-level function in a company, because it is so critical. Customer relationships take high priority, as do supply chain relationships.

But often community relations are not taken equally seriously, despite the fact that poor relationships can significantly impact on a company.

The difficulty with stakeholder relationships is that it takes a long time to build positive, trusting relationships, but those relationships can be destroyed very quickly, as many companies have discovered. Reputational damage is expensive and can be long term – oil companies which see their share price drop and customers boycotting their products after major oil spills are a prime example; consumers boycotting the products of sportswear manufacturers, due to revelations of sweat-shop conditions in the factories of their Asian suppliers, is another case in point.

Stakeholder relations in the public sector are extremely important. One example here is the imposition of visa requirements for South African visitors to the United Kingdom (UK), due to the poor reputation of their identity documents (failure to comply with security requirements).

Within society generally

If social capital is concerned with trust and governance, then it follows that building social capital has to do with improving levels of trust between individuals, groups and institutions; and also with ensuring good governance in public institutions. While this may seem to be the role of governments and the public sector, it is increasingly accepted that private sector organisations cannot divorce their economic success from that of the society in which they operate. In more developed economies, the private sector is better able to leave the building of social capital at a community and national level to the government and the public sector. However, it is generally a feature of dynamic/emerging economies that the capacity of government/the public sector is insufficient to do all that is needed to grow the economy, while at the same time ensuring the equitable distribution of the fruits of that growth, such that social capital is increased. Thus, the role of business in an emerging economy is expanded to that of an active community builder.

In South Africa, this finds concrete expression in the work of the Institute of Directors and the King reports on corporate governance. The King III Report (2009) puts the responsibility for an organisation's ethics squarely in the hands of the board of directors, and pertinently outlines the importance of investing in the community.

The impact of low levels of trust in, and poor governance of, public institutions within a particular society extends to various aspects of people management within an organisation. Organisations draw their employees from the society in which they function – at least to some extent, depending on the use of migrant or expatriate labour. If those employees have low levels of trust and are used to having low levels of inter-connectedness, it will be difficult to implement modern HR practices such as self-governing work teams, the sharing of knowledge, and encouraging individual responsibility for work and career development. Similarly, poor governance within state institutions usually results in corruption, which is also associated with higher levels of misconduct, including fraud in the private sector workplace. Abbott (2012), reporting on research among HR practitioners in South Africa, demonstrates the impact which poor social conditions have on the workplace, where up to 60 per cent of the work of HR practitioners may be focused on mitigating the effects of employees' social challenges or problems. Such problems usually manifest as poor productivity or absenteeism/presenteeism due to factors such as financial difficulties, drug abuse, family or transport problems, poor health and a lack of essential skills due to poor education. Individuals' inability to deal with their problems can be attributed to low levels of social capital.

Parallels may be drawn between the issues of trust in social capital, and trust in employment/industrial relations (E/IR). Good practice in E/IR involves training supervisors to take the initiative to show respect for their subordinates and to consciously work to build a relationship of trust with them. Values-based initiatives, such as the Care and Growth models, have had success in increasing trust levels in the workplace (Schuitema, 2013): 'It is possible to take a moribund business beset with industrial conflict and employee distrust and to turn it into a successful organisation that can count on the loyalty and commitment of its people. And it is possible for people to rise above the alienation and victimhood that besets modern man to achieve authentic personal mastery.'

CHRO's role and actions needed to build solid social capital

The leadership role of the CHRO may be considered in three important areas of work:

- Contributing to the business strategy of the organisation;

- Leading the organisation in developing the people strategy to deliver on the business strategy;

- Translating strategy into the HR business plan.

Business strategy and social capital

In his/her work with the leadership team in strategy development, the CHRO is uniquely placed to bring to the table interpretations of the socio-economic environment and probable trends in changes to that environment. The changing environment can impact on products, markets and logistics, as well as on the pipeline of human capital required. This highlights the need for excellent knowledge of trends in several areas, including

- economic growth and the distribution of that growth amongst groups in society;

- demographics, especially concerning age distributions and urbanisation;

- globalisation;

- public policy, especially in areas such as labour law, education, health and international migration;

- unionisation.

In this strategic thinking role, the CHRO also needs to consider how social capital in each national, local and labour-supplying market impacts on the organisation, and how this might change in the short, medium and long term.

For example, an organisation selling products to the developed world, producing its products in the so-called 'dynamic markets' and sourcing its supplies from countries with a low level of development, needs to consider all the above factors in three very different situations. A well-informed interpretation of this environment is essential for making sound judgements on risk and, therefore, good strategic choices. One or more of these situations may be characterised by considerable income inequality, potential instability, and poor levels of education and health in the population. This could lead to different strategic choices being made when doing business in a situation with reasonable and rising social capital.

As another example, a financial or retail company wishing to expand its business in an environment with poor social capital will need to factor in risk mitigation strategies that take into account likely corruption, internal fraud, and low levels of employee skills in sophisticated technologies.

Another strategic choice for an organisation is its degree of involvement at the national, local and community levels, in terms of policy making and policy implementation.

In other words, what is the social investment approach of the organisation? This will depend, to a large extent, on the nature of the organisation – it is imperative for capital-intensive businesses in the mining and extractive sectors to be heavily involved with social investment, whereas for a fashion design house this might not be an important issue. The decision largely depends on an assessment of the impact the environment has on the organisation – if it will have a critical impact on the organisation, it is strategically important to strive to influence that environment. Assessing the impact on the organisation must include the extent to which present and potential employees will bring negative effects from the environment to work with them, in so far as it works to the detriment of the organisation. If such effects are significant, then the organisation will benefit from investing in improving that environment.

In social capital terms, if the organisation needs a social licence to operate, then it must devote time and other resources to building constructive relationships with groups in the external context. This can be tricky, as the social dynamics involved can be highly complex and dynamic. The CHRO needs to monitor these social dynamics and must advise the executive team on how to navigate such complexities.

People strategy and social capital

The CHRO must lead the executive team in making essential choices involved in crafting a people strategy to deliver on the business strategy. In human capital terms, that may mean choosing between 'building, buying and borrowing' skills, and designing 'high or low tech' production/transaction processes. In social capital terms, it can involve making a choice between designing production/transaction processes that emphasise employee empowerment and high command/control processes. A people strategy can be built on high or low levels of trust; it can explicitly build social capital or work with the existing (perhaps poor) social capital.

Any people strategy that is crafted by an organisation will have a powerful impact on the employer value proposition (EVP). A strategy that builds relationships and connectedness is likely to result in higher employee commitment and retention, since such factors have been proven to contribute directly to the sense of wellbeing of individuals.

A well-known example of a people strategy that builds high levels of social capital is a Brazilian tool manufacturing company, described in *Maverick* (Semler, 1999). Through work teams being granted an unusual level of self-governance, the company, Semco, has achieved both economic success and high levels of employee engagement over many years.

This people strategy is something that has to be crafted by the executive team, because it is implemented by line managers, and supported by HR processes and programmes.

HR business plan

In developing the HR business plan, the CHRO should consider how each HR programme and process contributes to building social capital, both inside and outside the organisation. All programmes and processes need to fit together coherently to deliver on the people strategy.

The concepts of building connectedness and enabling relationships in order to deliver innovation, increase productivity and improve skills levels, impact heavily on the learning and development function, the performance and reward management function, and the organisation development functions in particular, although other functions (e.g., employee wellness) are also affected.

The design of learning and development interventions can be transformed if considered through a social capital lens – current trends towards e-learning and mobile learning need to be integrated with methods which encourage knowledge transfer, peer learning and team learning.

The HR business plan also needs to consider investment priorities which allow for the building of social capital outside the organisation. This can include the corporate social investment (CSI) programme, talent pipeline programmes and employee services programmes (e.g., housing, sport and recreation, and wellness). HR organisation structures need to make provision for positions which can monitor and influence the environment, by building and supporting communities.

The CHRO as a role model

The CHRO is inevitably regarded as a symbol of the people strategy of an organisation, and as such serves as a role model. As the leader of the HR function s/he should ensure that the function works in such a way that it builds social capital for HR employees.

Furthermore, the CHRO must be visibly involved outside the organisation.

The critical personal attributes that the CHRO models, must help build trust and relationships, foster connectedness and encourage the sharing of knowledge.

Potential barriers the CHRO may face

As outlined earlier, social capital is an important but not well-known concept. It is likely, therefore, that attempts by the CHRO to introduce the concept to the organisation, may face some difficulties or even barriers – some of these may lie in the organisation, and others in the CHRO him/herself.

Role expectations

Expectations of the role of the CHRO differ across organisations. Factors influencing such expectations may include

- the maturity of the organisation in its life cycle (start-up, expanding, mature, declining);

- the world view of the chief executive officer (CEO) and board – whether they see the role of the organisation as extending beyond purely business into its role as a corporate citizen;

- the level of thinking of the CEO in terms of cognitive complexity – in developmental terms, whether the CEO him/herself can deal with many mutually contradictory realities, or whether s/he is rather conventional and sees complex problems as having one, simple solution;

- the industry sector/type of organisation – as explained earlier, capital-intensive companies differ from small design houses;

- the maturity of the HR profession in the country. In many emerging market countries, HR as a profession is relatively young and therefore concentrates more on the core functions and processes of transactional HR. This differentiation was identified in the work of Dave Ulrich and his co-researchers from the HR competencies survey of 2008, elaborated on in a later publication (Ulrich, Brockbank, Younger & Ulrich, 2013);

- the history of the HR function in the organisation. If the role has traditionally been limited to transactional rather than strategic leadership functions, it will be difficult to change this outside of a general leadership change.

The role expectations pertaining to HR practitioners have been greatly influenced by the writings of Ulrich and his fellow researchers, who introduced the idea of HR as a business partner (Ulrich & Brockbank, 2010). In many cases, although not intended by those authors, the 'business partner' idea has been interpreted as meaning that HR practitioners should work only on those business issues identified by line managers, thereby subordinating the HR contribution to the purely commercial agenda of the organisation. However, the concept – as intended by Ulrich and Brockbank (2010, p. 2) – implies that HR practitioners should be 'partners to the business as they work to create value for employees, customers, shareholders, communities and management'.

Thus, the role of the CHRO in introducing the concept of social capital as a source of value to the organisation is completely in line with this thinking.

Personal competencies and approach

In order to play the progressive role of introducing the concept of social capital to the organisation, the CHRO needs to be well equipped.

Competencies

Ulrich et al. (2008) propose following a bi-axial model of HR competencies (see Figure 3.1). In this diagram, certain competencies are highlighted as being relevant to the promotion of social capital.

Building on this and other work done on competencies by the Corporate Leadership Council and the Chartered Institute of People Development, amongst others, in 2013 the South African Board for People Practices launched a South African HR Competency Model (see Figure 3.2).

Although the model was developed specifically for the South African context, it may well be applicable to other emerging markets. Elements which are emphasised here, more than in other models, include duty to society; citizenship for the future; and HR governance, risk and compliance.

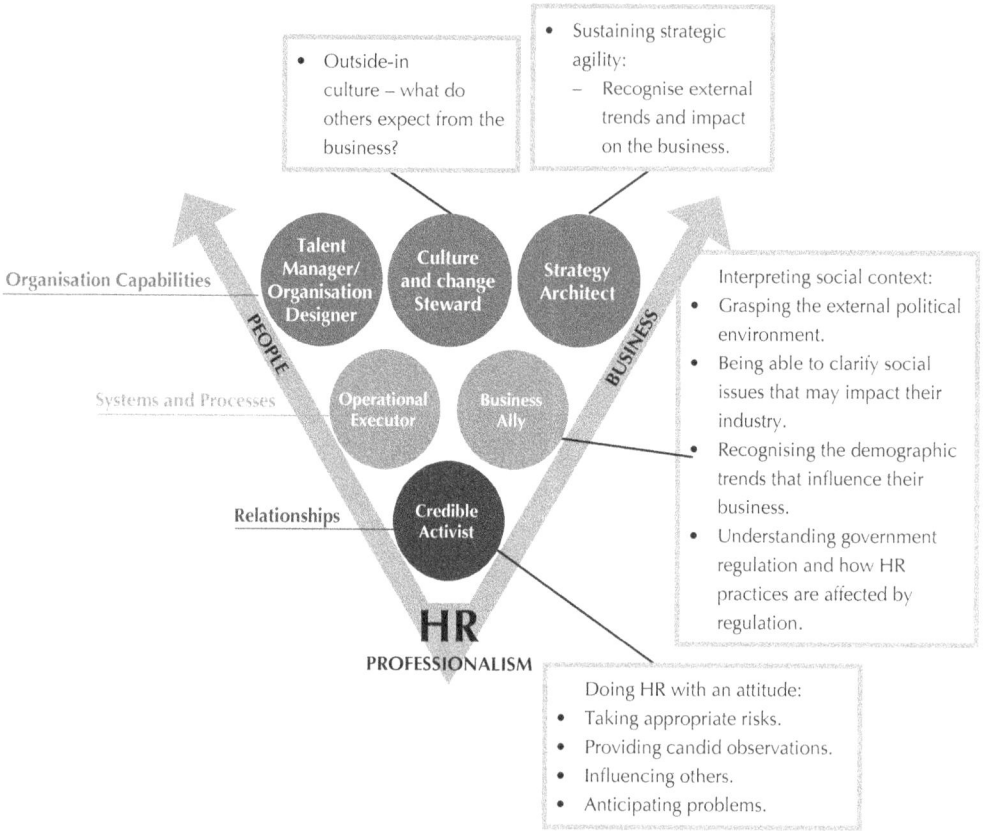

Figure 3.1: A bi-axial model of HR competencies
Source: Adapted from Ulrich et al. (2008)

Relevant extracts from this model show that CHROs need certain knowledge and skills in order to be able to develop appropriate social capital externally to the organisation.

Approach

Even when well equipped to do so, some HR practitioners seem reluctant to take on the role of progressive advocates who put forward new ideas. According to Abbott (2012), the following factors may influence the willingness of an individual to take on this role:

- *Career choice.* Why did the individual choose HR as a career, or, indeed, did the individual actively choose HR at all? If the choice was a conscious one, was it with the aim of entering a profession with a duty to society as a whole, or was it simply to do a job using their knowledge of the social sciences?

- *Locus of control and personal value system.* If the individual has a strong internal locus of control and his/her value system includes the promotion of personal dignity and development for all, then advocacy will come more naturally;

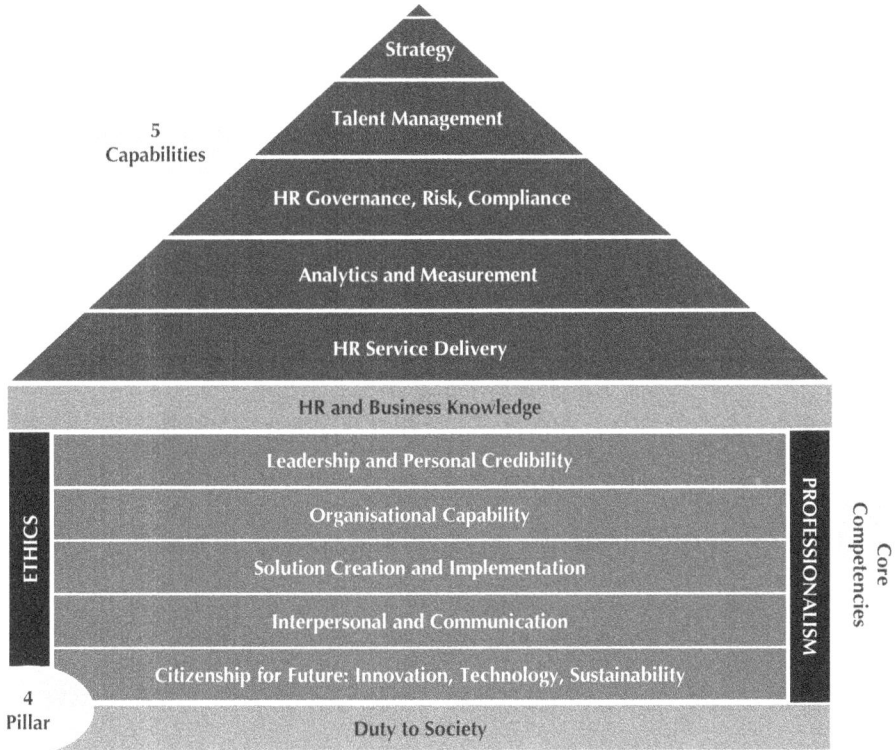

Strategy

Talent Management

HR Governance, Risk, Compliance

Analytics and Measurement

HR Service Delivery

HR and Business Knowledge

Leadership and Personal Credibility

Organisational Capability

Solution Creation and Implementation

Interpersonal and Communication

Citizenship for Future: Innovation, Technology, Sustainability

Duty to Society

5 Capabilities

ETHICS

PROFESSIONALISM

Core Competencies

4 Pillar

Figure 3.2: South African HR Competency Model
Source: SA Board for People Practices

- *Ability to deal with complexity.* Social capital issues, as explained in this chapter, are complex and involve many dynamics. Thus, an evolved ability to deal with high levels of complexity is required;

- *Career experience.* If the individual has worked exclusively in very transactional HR departments with traditional practices, it would be hard to draw on experience and intuition in dealing with the complex issues of social capital.

It is therefore clear that a combination of knowledge, experience and attitude is essential for coping adequately with building social capital both inside and outside the organisation.

Table 3.2: HR competencies relevant to developing social capital outside the organisation

Element of the model	Definition	Illustrative competencies
Duty to society	Delivering high-quality HR work that has an impact on society. Being custodians for good people practices in organisations, ensuring that people are treated fairly and with respect and dignity, and driving transformation, skills development and sustainability.	Understands the macro-economic and socio-political landscape and how this impacts on organisation and employees. Devises mitigation strategies.
		Participates at industry, sectoral and national level in institutions which seek to find solutions to macro-economic and socio-political problems.
		Puts in place systems to monitor the social circumstances of employees and surrounding communities, and leads the organisation to contribute to finding solutions to problems.
Citizenship for the future	The ability to drive innovation, optimise technology and contribute to the sustainability of organisations.	Advocates for people issues in balance with social and environmental issues internal and external to the organisation.
		Advocates for the organisation to become involved in building social capital nationally and internationally.
		Proactively identifies ways to contribute to social policy at all government levels and contributes to a positive relationship between government and the organisation.
HR governance, risk management and compliance	The ability to take a proactive approach to HR governance, risk and compliance, understanding this to be a strategic capability in growing the business and its people as legitimate role-players in their industry.	Monitors external environment for HR risks and advises line management on mitigation strategies.
		Advises management on the implications of labour legislation for organisation strategy and objectives.

Conclusion

The abundance (or otherwise) of social capital that an organisation has can have a significant impact on its success. Clearly, it is one aspect of capital that requires the attention of a CHRO.

S/he needs to understand the concept, how it might manifest in and around the organisation, and how to build more of it. This requires particular competencies and also a certain attitude and approach.

Greater awareness is needed of the social capital aspect of the role of the CHRO. The hope is that this chapter has facilitated such awareness-building. Professional bodies representing HR practitioners in emerging market countries need to play a role in building competence in this area.

References

Abbott, P. (2012). *Human resource management in the South African socio-economic context.* Unpublished PhD dissertation, University of Johannesburg, Johannesburg, South Africa.

Krebs, V. (2008). Social capital, the key to success for the 21st century organisation. *IHRIM Journal* XII (5). Retrieved May 5, 2013 from http://orgnet.com/IHJour_XII_No5_p38_42.pdf

Lattin, R. & Young, S. (n.d.). *Country ranking: Social capital achievement.* Retrieved May 5, 2013 from www.cauxroundtable.org/view_file.cfm?fileid=43

OECD Insight. (2007). *Measuring human capital.* Paris: OECD Publishing.

OECD. (2001). *The new economy: Beyond the hype.* Paris: OECD Publishing.

Putnam, R. (n.d.). *Social capital: Measurement and consequences.* Retrieved May 5, 2013 from http://www.oecd.org/edu/country-studies/1825848.pdf

Schuitema, E. (2013). *The Care and Growth Leadership Model and employee commitment.* Retrieved May 26, 2013 from http://www.schuitema.co.za/article_12.asp

Scrivens, K. (2012). *Valuing relationships.* OECD blog. Retrieved May 5, 2013 from http://www.oecdbetterlifeindex.org/2013-03/valuing-relationships/

Semler, R. (1999). *Maverick – The success story behind the world's most unusual workplace.* London: Random House.

Ulrich, D. & Brockbank, W. (2010). The Business Partner Model: Past and future perspectives. *Human Capital Review*, November.

Ulrich, D., Brockbank, W., Younger, J. & Ulrich, M. (2013). *Global HR competencies – Mastering competitive value from the outside in.* New York: McGraw Hill.

White, L. (2013). The new world of dynamic markets. In S. Bluen (Ed.), *Talent management in emerging markets.* Rosebank: Knowledge Resources, 14–28.

World Bank. (2012). *Social capital: Measurement tools.* Retrieved May 5, 2013 from http://web.worldbank.org/WBSITE/EXTERNAL/TOPICS/EXTSOCIALDEVELOPMENT/EXTTSOCIALCAPITAL/

CHAPTER 4: What Chief Executive Officers Want and Need from their Chief Human Resources Officer

Tjaart Kruger

Tjaart Kruger,
Chief Executive Officer,
Premier Foods,
in conversation with
the editor.

Ed: What do you believe the key role of the Chief Human Resources Officer (CHRO) is?

TK: I believe that 80 per cent of the Chief Executive Officer's (CEO) job is to do with people. Research has shown that the IRR (internal rate of return) on people is of the order of 35 per cent. People capital is by far the most important capital on the balance sheet. I do not believe the CHRO must manage the payroll – that should sit in Finance. The key role of the CHRO is to help me formulate the people agenda of the business, and develop and grow the right culture.

To take this further: when organisations fail to deliver on their promises, the most frequent explanation is that the strategy was wrong, but this is often not the case. Strategies most often fail because they are not executed well. No company can deliver results unless all leaders practise the discipline of execution – execution has to be part of the culture!

This means that the right people must focus on the right things at the right time.

The CHRO is key in understanding – to use an information technology analogy – that the organisation's hardware, its strategy and structure, will not work without the necessary software, i.e., peoples' beliefs and behaviours.

My simple view is that the strategic process defines 'the why and the what' of the business's direction; the operations process provides the path, or the how; and the people process defines 'who' is going to get it there. The CHRO's role is critical in the latter process.

Larry Bossidy, former Chairman of Honeywell, said that 'the people process is more important than either the strategy or operations processes, because, to put it starkly and simply, if you do not get the people process right you will never fulfil the potential of your business'.

Ed: What are the particular issues that the CHRO needs to deal with in an emerging market?

TK: The people issues in an emerging market are no different from those in a developed market – the challenges are merely greater. We are faced with low education levels, inadequate skills and competencies, and a need for systems and procedures to fill these gaps. In addition, in South Africa there are the imperatives of a transforming society, such as employment equity (EE) and broad-based black economic empowerment (BBBEE).

We need the right people with the right development. The more we develop people, the more they will be poached – which is fine, as long as we have a good talent pipeline in place. It is not only about the individual, but also about the collective, the team.

Another major challenge is the issue of ethical behaviour and practices in emerging markets – I would rather have someone with a sound value system than a competitive set of skills and competencies. Obviously I look for both!

At a practical level it is even more important in emerging markets to be clear about the roles and responsibilities needed to execute strategy, to have a well-designed operational blueprint or value chain structure, and to ensure structured collaboration between the people and the teams who execute the plan.

So, to repeat: the right organisational capability and skills and the right people focusing on the right things is needed!

Ed: What contributions would you like more of, from your CHRO?

TK: I see the key contributions of a CHRO as the following: 1) S/he needs to be a key executive team member, 2) who will give me, as the CEO, honest feedback, and 3) will show exemplary leadership.

My CHRO needs to help me ensure that my team is aligned and working well. The role is not a soft one – the soft stuff is actually the hard stuff!

I need the best teams and teamwork available – the role of my CHRO is to put in place processes which will assist in building the best possible teams.

S/he must attract the right people, use the right methodology to choose the right people, and then ensure that the right people are retained. This includes practices like recognition, reward, creating the right climate and culture and, where necessary, the right operating procedures, without encouraging bureaucracy.

People need to be part of the DNA of the organisation. There is a lovely South African example of an under-13 rugby captain, named Stanley. Whenever the team was in trouble in a game the call was *'Gee die bal vir Stanley'* (give the ball to Stanley) – the team knew they could rely on him, and this is what I need from my CHRO.

Ed: What do you believe a CHRO should focus less on?

TK: Human Resource (HR) people are great at building bureaucracy! HR professionals should do themselves a favour and spend less time on forms, job grading, organograms and intricate job specifications, and spend much more time in the business, working on the culture.

   HR must move from being reactive to proactive, and from being sweepers, nurses and firemen to being business partners. HR must focus on building an employee value proposition (EVP) which is aligned with the organisation's strategy; on being a business leader; and on being the drivers and custodians of critical business systems.

Ed: What do you believe the key performance areas of a CHRO should be?

TK: Obviously, one of the key performance areas must be that the requisite, fundamental people systems are in place and working efficiently. This means that the CHRO, and by implication the HR function, must have a clear grasp of what creates value for both the organisation and the employee; a clear understanding of and the ability to implement these organisational systems to create such value; and the ability to measure and improve these systems. Let me add that this foundation must be established before value can be added.

   For me, the true value-adding key performance areas should focus on the development of organisational culture and everything it entails; leadership and competency development and aligning the organisation as a whole around the strategic goals of the business.

   There needs to be an understanding of three critical levers: 1) the need for crucial accountability conversations which focus on evaluating individuals accurately and in-depth, as well as on managing positive (and negative) consequences; 2) the development and maintenance of a talent pipeline focused on leadership development, succession and critical skills; and 3) the provision of a fit-for-purpose, non-bureaucratic HR support system.

   I would like to expand a little on my view of the role of the HR function, since this is the kind of function I would expect the CHRO to establish.

   In practitioners' roles as business partners, I see HR as being involved in all HR parts of the organisation, participating in discussions on, for example, using our capabilities to make more profit; how to improve our margins; what growth strategies we should adopt; how we can grow our brand equity; how we can improve our customer proposition; what our ideal business model is; how we can drive change within the organisation; and so on.

Ed: What are the key competencies and personal attributes you look for in a CHRO?

TK: I am very clear on what I look for in a CHRO. There are five competencies or attributes I require, and I will list them (in no particular order).

First, business acumen is important, as is an understanding of the related demands of business performance on leadership and management. Reasonable knowledge of profit margins and business functions is critical.

Second, I look for an individual who is a good leader, who leads by example and is honest and ethical – these aspects are non-negotiable. I have found, in choosing the right person, that there is too much reliance on the content of a CV, and too little emphasis on the essence of the person. In-depth personal reference checks are very important.

The third area is the ability of that individual to give me good advice on people as well as the organisation. This obviously implies knowledge of human and organisational psychology, but what is vital, I think, is the combination of abstract knowledge and its practical application which enables someone to do an in-depth analysis and give sound advice.

The fourth area, which is somewhat less tangible, is passion! A CHRO must be passionate about working with people on both hard and soft issues, understanding people's behaviour and being able to constructively resolve conflict, which inevitably arises in any organisation. In addition, a CHRO must be passionate about business, and should understand and deal effectively with the pressures of the business.

The last attribute, which is a combination of all of the above, and which I would classify as very special, is the ability and the desire of a CHRO to be happy to see others achieving success, to be a leader 'in the shadows', as it were. I hope that makes sense!

I would add that for a CHRO to be successful, the HR business partners within the organisation must have business acumen, they need to understand how profit is made, they must think critically, have a passion for people, business and results, drive performance and have the ability to link strategy and execution.

Ed: If you were to give a few words of advice to a CHRO in an emerging market, what would you say?

TK: Follow a holistic systems approach. Strive to be competent, credible and confident, yet humble. Be ethical and honest! In the words of Gandhi, you must 'be the change you wish to see in the world'.

PART II: Leadership and the Role of HR

CHAPTER 5: Leadership Challenges in Africa: Creating the Language of Leadership

Linda van der Colff

Introduction

Africa continues to enjoy robust economic expansion, and, according to the *Economist*, is home to six out of the top ten growing economies in the world. New opportunities within industries such as telecoms, banking, retail, private healthcare, insurance, infrastructure and hospitality are being driven by the demand for raw material, infrastructure development, the evolution of financial systems, and the rise of the African consumer class. Africa is often seen as the last 'one billion person market' yet to be 'trapped'.

In the latest findings of the Corporate Executive Board Leadership survey, the challenges facing global leaders include the fact that they work with 17 per cent more people whom they do not directly manage, they are 32 per cent less likely to have accurate market information, they have a 74 per cent broader span of responsibilities and work with 160 per cent more stakeholders. In addition to facing such a dramatic increase in role complexity, the global village is now also a borderless workplace where technology has removed many of the borders between people, to connect employees, customers, partners and suppliers, with the result that traditional corporate hierarchies are fast disappearing. People are working in cross-cultural, diverse teams within flatter organisational structures, which impacts on the type and level of relationship skills needed to be successful within a connected workplace.

This chapter will highlight the key leadership skills needed in Africa to overcome these challenges and to assist successful leaders in managing through innovative thinking, across geographic and cultural borders, thanks to a keen understanding of local markets and customs.

Leadership challenges in emerging markets

In essence, developing a key understanding of the leadership challenges companies face within Africa will help to clarify the role companies can play in establishing more sustainable business practices within the African context and on the continent.

The challenges facing African leaders can be clustered around four main themes.

Leading within increasing uncertainty and complexity

One of the most important factors to take into consideration when doing business in Africa, is the complexity inherent in the interconnectedness of economic and social systems. In developing an appreciation for this complexity, leaders face the challenge that no amount of linear planning and formulaic risk management will decrease the high degree of uncertainty or define the 'right' answer.

Building sustainable strategies within this environment takes into account the ability to balance dilemmas, to focus on creating a broad-based approach to risk assessment and to respond to continuing change. It includes the ability to engage with a wide range of stakeholders who often represent a diversity of sometimes conflicting interests. Faruk and Hoffman (2012) describe this as a move away from an optimisation mindset towards a resilience mindset.

In some ways, it can be said that we now find ourselves in the era of the thoughtful provocateur.

'Stepping outside the system'

In many interviews with leaders managing regional African portfolios, it became clear that one of the most critical challenges they face is that of managing context. Leaders need to see themselves as active participants in shaping the social, political and policy environments within the country and the context they work in. In many ways, they must actively participate in the broader debate around the future of their industry and, in some cases, engage in debating future growth strategies for the country as a whole. In essence, it is about being a leader as well as a citizen. In one interview, a leader referred to it as being both a 'pathfinder and team player'.

Moving from valuing difference towards strategic inclusivity

Another challenge facing leaders within the African marketplace is the shift from managing diversity in the traditional sense, to valuing difference and creating strategic inclusivity. Strategic inclusivity has as its premise the notion that organisations have an openness to different views, i.e., that they focus on 'cognitive diversity'. Ironically, most organisations' diversity agendas, which are already well established, have become quite narrow in their scope as a simple taxonomy that tends to focus on gender, race and ethnicity.

A move towards strategic inclusivity would include a conscious strategy of trying to be more representative of the society within which the organisation operates. For this strategy to succeed, however, leaders within the organisation must possess a level of cultural agility that goes far beyond a simple understanding of different cultural norms.

The exponential war for talent

Building the right level of talent in emerging markets is critical to ensuring any organisation's sustainable success and achieving growth targets. However, the war for talent has, in the last decade, turned into an exponential war for talent, with companies unable to deliver the quantity and quality of talented technical experts and leaders required to successfully implement the organisation's strategy. Later in this chapter, the basis for defining a successful talent management strategy and appropriate practices within Africa is discussed. In essence, winners of the war for talent on the continent will have to adapt their talent management practices appropriately, as an overreliance on global processes to close the leadership gap simply does not work, and is not the most appropriate strategy to follow.

The remainder of this chapter focuses on how to successfully address the challenges that prevent companies from realising the full potential of doing business in Africa.

Leadership strategy

Any organisation that aims to overcome a highly challenging environment (as discussed in the preceding section) must formulate a clearly defined leadership strategy. The function of such a strategy is to develop not only a clear view of the current situation, but also an informed view of the future. The main function of implementing a leadership strategy is to put a clear set of recommendations in place to close the gap between the current situation and the desired future. Once an organisation has outlined its leadership strategy, a leadership development strategy can be formulated to produce the desired future state. Added to this is the ability of the organisation to clearly articulate the implications for its talent management processes. In essence, the conversation around a well-constructed leadership strategy is two-fold: 1) it centres around the behavioural expectations the business has of its leaders, and 2) expectations in respect of what leaders need to deliver (i.e., the results expectations, as directly related to the organisation's strategy).

Quantity and quality

The leadership strategy should firstly define the quantity (bench strength) and secondly the quality of leaders that will be needed over the next five to ten years, to implement the organisation's business strategy. In other words, such a strategy should clearly articulate *when*, *where* and *at what level* these leaders need to be. This must be done through clear demand planning. In terms of leadership qualities, according to the CCL White Paper (2009), the focus should be threefold, namely on demographics (age, gender, education, experience, race, etc.); on internal promotions versus external hires; and on targeted diversity such as job level and location.

A lack of sufficient and accurate data related to the labour market outside of South Africa makes demand planning so much more difficult. Also, the lack of cross-border data makes talent mobility complex and often incidental, rather than planned using future demand as a basis.

Capabilities, competencies, skills and behaviours

An organisation should focus on creating the *leadership capabilities, competencies, skills* and *behaviours* needed to implement the business strategy and create the desired organisational culture. In the section on defining and implementing a leadership competency framework, it is argued that such a framework allows organisations to focus on the leadership requirements flowing from the unique contexts and diverse challenges which leaders in Africa face. A leadership competency framework also creates a bridge between the characteristics leaders need in order to execute the organisation's strategy, and it creates a framework for skills and capabilities to be built through the leadership development strategy.

Collective leadership capability

What is important for an organisation are the *collective leadership capabilities* of leaders, i.e., the way in which leaders act together to implement the organisation's business strategy. This concept is aligned to Gestalt, i.e., the capabilities of the leadership team as a whole are more powerful than the sum of the parts of individuals' leadership abilities. Collective leadership capabilities also contribute to the leadership brand and the leadership culture defined within any organisation.

According to the CCL White Paper (2009), capabilities include

- providing direction, demonstrating alignment and generating commitment as a collective leadership team;
- solving problems or making improvements that require collaboration across internal and external boundaries;
- engaging employees in decision making and gaining their active support in implementing cross-functional actions;
- developing talent on behalf of the enterprise, rather than for individual business units;
- being responsive to customers in ways that demand cross-unit coordination.

Leadership practices

Leadership practices such as employee engagement, developing other leaders, learning to learn, and creating opportunities for others to lead, will fundamentally impact on creating the desired leadership culture. Further to these core requirements, there are a number of additional practices that leaders working in Africa should develop and focus on. Aiken (2010) defines such practices as they apply to change leadership, which, in essence, could be extended in its application to any leaders doing business in Africa:

- *Future sense-making combined with strategic thinking ability.* Leaders need to keep abreast of their operating environments, by looking out for emerging trends in products, services, customers and markets, so as to innovate workplace practices aimed at building sustainable businesses;

- *Become a co-creator of the organisation's learning culture.* Given the exponential war for talent and capability across organisations and industries within Africa, leaders need to take personal responsibility and accountability for enabling the organisation's learning culture. This responsibility is further explored in the section on crafting a leadership development strategy, as well as the fact that growing global capability is seen as one of the differentiating leadership competencies which successful leaders need to possess;

- *Develop 'one-to-many' dialogue skills, action learning and process consulting.* The ability to use learning to solve real business problems, to generate ideas for improving workplace practices, and to ask critical questions that challenge status quo assumptions about problems, is imperative in the context of the high level of complexity and uncertainty involved in doing business in Africa;

- *Access 'broadband' capability from across the leadership membership.* Given the complex context within which leaders in Africa need to do business, it is imperative that they continue to draw on knowledge, experience, ideas and insights from across the organisation's leadership. This practice forms the basis for the leadership competency known as purposeful collaboration;

- *Develop 'transcultural' capability.* This practice is pivotal in creating an inclusive culture. Leaders not only need to understand their own personal values, they also need to value diversity, and be able to connect and relate to people from all parts of the business and the wider community. This practice influences the 'cultural agility' of leaders and their ability to see themselves as part of a wider economic and social community;

- *Develop one-on-one relationship skills through coaching and mentoring.* Both these processes assist in facilitating learning, adapting to change, and providing fresh insights into solving business problems in new and innovative ways. These skills underpin the people leadership competencies of inspiring performance, fostering teamwork and growing capability (more on this later);

- *Create a 'no surprise' culture through high-quality performance conversations.* One of the most impactful leadership practices is where everyday performance conversations feel normal, and where feedback is constructive, well framed and welcomed. It will inherently lead to more sustainable organisational improvement and talent growth, and will generally help to reduce the anxiety emanating from insecurities around performance expectations. It will not only assist organisations in achieving outstanding people development, but will underpin significant business results.

Leadership brand

Developing a common leadership brand is one of the most important elements underpinning any leadership strategy. Leaders should therefore be the kind of people who embody the promises a company makes to its customers. A leadership brand is an identity which is shared among an organisation's leaders, and which differentiates what they can do differently from their rivals' leaders. A company with a great leadership brand inspires the faith that employees and managers will consistently make good on the firm's promises.

According to Dave Ulrich (2007), defining a cohesive leadership brand extends thinking about leadership in two ways: 1) the focus is less on the individual leader and more on the leadership capability within the organisation; and 2) effective leadership is defined less by what happens inside an organisation and more by how leaders turn external customer and investor expectations into employee abilities and organisational capabilities.

The leadership brand sets a company apart from the competition by developing a cadre of exceptional leaders with distinct talents geared towards fulfilling customer and investor expectations. What differentiates branded leaders is their ability to reflect, in their leadership style, both the attributes and results customers want to see in the organisation. According to Ulrich (2007), the importance of a customer brand extends to employee relations as well; should the company promise its customers timely and responsive behaviour, it should also do so with employee relations. As an example, a company's best customer should be treated as if they were also the best employee and vice versa.

Leadership culture

Culture is the soul of the organisation; it is based on the organisation's meaning and values. It provides meaning, direction and mobilisation. Unless the culture fits the strategic approach, the organisation will struggle to achieve and maintain superior performance. Leaders must set about encouraging a positive climate in which the company culture reflects the beliefs, values, norms and spirit of the organisation. It is imperative that leaders develop an inclusive culture that is representative of all employees' values.

Leadership culture can be defined as the key attributes of the organisational culture created by leaders through the way in which they lead. Key attributes include the degree of interdependence among leaders, the key values that are reinforced through their collective behaviour and actions, as well as the leadership attributes which the majority of them display (CCL White Paper, 2009).

Leadership culture starts with the personal culture of the organisation's leadership, i.e., anyone who significantly influences people within the organisation. Personal culture consists of everyday observed behaviour which is driven by the personal values that motivate leaders to act, and which define and express what they truly value.

The stronger the alignment between leaders in this respect, the more clearly defined and more strongly enacted the leadership culture of the organisation will be. According to Aitken (2010, p. 4), 80 per cent of a workplace culture is shaped by demonstrable leadership culture.

A strong leadership culture enables clarity of communication and connects people through well-aligned and well-expressed artefacts that help to embed 'what it feels like to work around here and what is seen as top priorities', in other words – their workplace culture.

Leadership development strategy

Once the organisation has set out its leadership strategy, the leadership development strategy needs to focus on specifying the actions that should be taken to acquire, retain and develop both the leaders and the leadership skills required by the business strategy.

Although each organisation may build its leadership development strategy in a highly customised and contextual way, any successful strategy must be focused on the following outcomes:

- *Leadership effectiveness*. Our leadership team has the capabilities needed to manage the business successfully;

- *Leadership confidence*. Our employees have faith in our leaders and believe that they demonstrate our core values;

- *Leadership brand*. We are recognised internally and externally as a top organisation for developing leaders;

- *Succession pipeline*. Our organisation has a strong bench of candidates for key leadership positions.

All the actions within the strategy should be focused on attaining these underlying outcomes. At its root, leadership development is about creating world-class leaders.

Building world-class leaders through exchange, education, exposure and experiences

Although there are numerous methodologies for building the leadership pipeline, the focus should be on providing world-class *experiences* using a wide variety of methods; providing world-class *content* through access to leading thinking and tools; and aligning with the individual's development needs in creating a *personal learning journey*. Any learning journey should, in the final instance, align with the business strategy and link learning to business performance as its key objective.

Without entering into a debate around the 70:20:10 principle of learning (70% of new learning comes from doing; 20% comes from observing or being coached and 10% training or reading) and development, perhaps a more constructive conversation would centre around the three elements that must be present in any strategy aimed at building leadership capability. Using the principles of 1) exposure and experiences, 2) exchange and 3) education, every organisation should focus on integrating an appropriate mix of these elements into their leadership development strategy. What the actual contribution is of each element, will be determined in the context of the organisation's strategy and learning objectives. Another factor in determining an appropriate 'mix' is the level of the leader being developed, i.e., whereas first-level leaders may be spending the greatest portion of their time on education, as they progress through the ranks, their development will become more heavily focused on exchange and exposure. The main learning elements per category are the following:

- Education includes classroom and virtual classroom sessions, e-learning and m-learning, webcasts and podcasts, video learning, case studies, simulations and role plays and all elements of self-study;

- Exchange includes leader-led dialogue and guest speaker programmes, programme-based coaching, 'dilemma dialogues', panel discussions, virtual collaboration, executive coaching and mentoring, round table discussions, 'leaders teaching leaders' and peer learning;

- Exposure and experiences include action learning projects (ALPs), job rotations, stretch projects, job shadowing, secondments, immersion experiences, talent development forums, developing international 'crucible experiences' (experiences outside of a leader's area of expertise; in a new market/new business), international assignments, career sponsors and short-term attachments.

To be effective and successful, these learning elements must be underpinned by thorough learning integration. The role of the learning integrator is to bring all the parts of the learning experience together into a meaningful whole which makes sense to participants. The learning integrator should be part of creating the learning architecture and design process from the beginning, so as to ensure that during the programme key themes are reinforced, the golden threads that were designed into the programme are highlighted, and that emerging themes are discussed. The main role of the integrator is to help frame and 'language' the content and context of the leadership journey.

Signature solutions for leadership development in Africa

Underpinning the need to use the most appropriate learning methodologies in developing world-class leaders in Africa, is the requirement to compress 15 years of development and experiences into five years; the need to develop trust and accountability at warp speed (see Richman and Wiggenhorn, 2006); and the need to keep talent supply optimal during both good and bad economic cycles. Organisations that succeed in these markets need not be afraid to partner with major customers, suppliers, joint venture partners and government agencies in sourcing and developing talent.

Given these challenges, it is clear that leadership and talent development strategies cannot rely on traditional, outdated education models. What follows is a discussion of the main elements of successful signature solutions that should underpin any leadership development strategy within Africa.

Leaders teaching leaders

The core of every successful leadership development strategy rests on the premise that it is 'leader owned' and 'learning facilitated', i.e., leaders themselves play a pivotal role in executing a successful leadership development and talent management strategy, and the learning team acts as technical experts in the design, development and execution of the programme. In this way, it builds a forum for leaders able to demonstrate corporate values, share the business strategy and clearly set expectations of what the company requires of effective leadership. This, in essence, articulates corporate citizenship to leaders at all levels of the organisation.

According to the latest Bersin report (2012), leaders play four key roles in executing a 'leaders teaching leaders' philosophy:

- *Strategist*. In this role, leaders impart knowledge of the organisation's business strategy and business imperatives to course delegates;

- *Change agent*. As a change agent, a leader is able to encourage others to move the organisation forwards, and demonstrates breakthrough effort via practical experience and company-specific examples;

- *Relationship builder*. Leaders within the organisation are best placed to show others how to leverage partnerships, build the right networks and understand the underlying power dynamics within the organisation;

- *Talent developer.* A large part of developing the next generation of leaders is based on top leaders' active participation in developmental initiatives, as they can have a profound impact on other participants by drawing on their own experiences, and being able to 'decode' and unlock unwritten complexities within the organisation.

Action learning projects

Action learning is an educational process whereby people work and learn together, by tackling real issues and reflecting on their actions. Learners acquire knowledge through actual actions and practice, rather than through traditional instruction. In ALPs, participants solve real business problems while focusing on what they are learning, and how their learning can benefit each group member as well as the organisation as a whole. In this way, we 'teach' leaders how to reflect on change, and how to respond to change more effectively. It is imperative that these projects make use of project sponsors who champion the project and the team within the organisation, as well as project coaches who guide team members throughout their projects to ensure that individual and organisational learning takes place. As a methodology, ALPs can only be deemed successful if projects are implementable within a reasonable time frame, are focused on solving business-critical problems, have a high-profile and impactful business sponsor, and have the outcome of raising the visibility of the project team members.

'Dilemma dialogues' and leader-led conversations

One of the essential leadership challenges within Africa is leading in the face of increasing uncertainty and complexity, as most of the difficulties leaders face are not around problems with a right or wrong answer, but around dilemmas where various courses of action are available, each with their own set of advantages and disadvantages. In essence, dilemma dialogues within learning initiatives are conversations aimed at discussing the polarities of the most critical challenges the organisation faces, and creating a framework for leaders to discuss the 'trade-offs' between several potential plans of action. These dialogues therefore create a space for 'real talk', they examine the organisation's strategic shifts and what dilemmas need to be managed in order to make these shifts, while 'teaching' the leader how to trigger necessary conversations within the workplace, to ensure that the strategic direction is implemented in a conscious way. Notable here is the work of Nancy Kline, who argues that the quality of everything we do depends on the quality of our thinking.

Once participants understand the insights gained through identifying strategic polarities within the business, they are able to truly participate in leader-led conversations. These dialogues are set up as structured discussions aimed at collective learning through sharing insights, knowledge and experiences – this is where real, collective learning happens.

Being a successful leader in Africa means being able to think with rigor, imagination and courage.

Programme-based coaching

For real organisational transformation to take place through leadership development journeys, the first imperative is for all programmes to have a high level of programme-based coaching, where required behaviour changes and mindset shifts can be discussed. Real behaviour change will only take place where key leadership behaviours are modeled by leaders and delegates alike, with programme-based coaches helping delegates to reflect on the actual changes required. Second, mindset shifts will only occur if delegates fully comprehend the rewards and incentives for behaviour change, when they understand what type of value reframing must be done, and have a clear sense of the trade-offs between what they stand to gain and what they may have to give up. Third, true organisational transformation will only happen if businesses are able to provide a space for the behaviour and mindset changes to 'land' back in the business. This clarifies why all leadership development must be business driven and owned, and emphasises why the role of strategic learning partners is to support the journey and craft the technical learning architecture necessary for creating world-class leaders.

Programme-based coaches may play a variety of roles within the learning experience, depending on the learning architecture and the overall learning objectives. These roles mainly fit into the following three categories:

- Technical coaching happens where a coach may be used during a programme to build participants' technical skills. This includes calling on experts (internal or external to the organisation) to help delegates develop their technical skills and commercial acumen, by sharing insights, posing questions and through using real-life challenges related to the topic;

- Personal mastery coaching focuses on providing delegates with feedback on assessments they have completed and coaching them around actions that need to be taken, in order to align with the organisation's overall leadership strategy. It can provide one of the 'landing mechanisms' for behaviour changes and mindset shifts. This type of coaching normally deals with the full range of personal mastery topics, such as self-awareness, interpersonal skills, social awareness, political acumen, etc.;

- ALP coaching is pivotal to the successful conceptualisation and implementation of any action learning project. ALP coaches guide team members throughout the duration of their projects and play an active role in facilitating both individual and team learning. Ideally, one of the roles of these coaches is to engage with business sponsors within the business and to act as intermediaries between the teams and their business sponsors – this, to ensure that the relationship is driven in an active and business-focused way. These coaches also assist business sponsors in understanding their role in and the potential value they bring to ALPs. In many ways the coach can bring significant credibility to the process, in terms of the role they can play for the team and the business sponsor. The role of the coach is therefore to help team members reflect on what they are learning and how they are solving problems. For instance, the coach can help team members reflect on how they listen, and can assist them by reframing the problem and giving feedback on how they plan and work together.

Creating and developing 'crucible experiences' through immersions, shadowing, secondments and short-term assignments

There are a variety of ways to build 'crucible experiences', depending on whether they focus on developing bench leadership, or talent. Such experiences are designed to supply leaders with an experience in a new market, a new business or even outside of his/her area of expertise. The easiest way to build these experiences for both target audiences, is through immersions which are designed to place the delegate in either an unfamiliar context, or a context where problems need to be solved in new and innovative ways. Immersions are aimed at integrating individual, team and organisational learning in such a way as to develop fresh perspectives and solutions. Delegates can, for instance, be taken to an unfamiliar location with the aim of deciphering the market and market conditions. Further to using familiar economic data to understand the market, the immersion process can make use of socio-economic and political data to explain the context, key cultural patterns that impact business within the geography, and the level of cultural adaptivity leaders will need, in order to make them successful in the market.

Development methodologies such as shadowing, secondments and short-term attachments are mainly used in talent development, and focus on the following:

- Building the leader's networks by engaging with stakeholders across all levels and business units. The latest research shows that successful global leaders spend more time with clients, government/community officials and their global peers than with other global leaders, making it imperative for these leaders to build the best networking skills possible;

- Developing leaders' commercial acumen through gaining practical exposure to new products, processes, systems, strategies and controls;

- Developing leaders' cultural agility through building strategic relationships that expose them to different customer mindsets and by establishing effective partnerships (internal and external to the organisation), i.e., developing the skills needed to become a good citizen;

- Using stretch roles to build essential influencing skills through creating cross-functional and cross-geography experiences.

Although this does not touch on all the methodologies used, the focus has been on those which are most likely to drive a successful leadership development strategy within Africa. Should the leadership development initiative specifically be focused on developing talent, the roles of the career sponsor and talent development forums should be included as essential methodologies for driving a successful talent development strategy.

Leadership competency framework and modelling

Setting and implementing a well-constructed leadership competency framework is far from a silver bullet, but it does give organisations the ability to focus on the leadership requirements flowing from the unique contexts and diverse challenges faced by leaders in Africa.

Why is a leadership competency framework important for leaders in Africa?

- It determines accountability by defining a clear standard for effective leadership to which leaders can hold themselves and each other accountable;
- It defines the behaviours and approaches that enable leaders to deliver on the organisation's strategy and desired culture, and further plays a role in enabling the employee value proposition;
- It assists in defining the leadership brand and language that can be used to attract, engage and develop leaders in a way that differentiates an organisation from its competitors;
- It provides a framework that fosters leader–employee relationships which are characterised by transparency, honesty, trust and openness;
- Creating effective leaders leads directly to improvements in employee engagement, which results in a more consistently positive client experience and focus;
- The framework can be used as a tool to learn, leverage and replicate what the best leaders do, thereby creating energised and effective leaders.

Key characteristics of a successful framework

- Competencies define what separates the best leaders from the rest;

- Competencies are based on what leaders actually think, say and do that differentiate outstanding from average performance, as well as the new behaviour required to achieve strategic business priorities;

- A successful framework highlights the small number of competencies that drive exceptional performance;

- Competencies do not establish baseline performance levels; rather, they are used to raise the bar on employee performance and provide employees with roadmaps for increasing their capabilities incrementally;

- Competencies include a focus on an organisation's culture and values;

- Competencies reflect the organisation's strategy, i.e, they are aligned to short- and long-term missions and goals, and enable the delivery of the strategy;

- Competencies focus on how results are achieved rather than merely the end result. In this way they bridge the gap between performance management and employee development, and form an integral component of personal development plans;

- Competency data can be used for employee development, compensation, promotion, training and new hire selection decisions.

Four core principles for creating and operationalising a leadership competency framework

- It is imperative that there be a clear line of sight between the framework and the organisation's key strategic business priorities. For example, if the company is implementing a matrix organisation as a business model, the competency of fostering cross-unit cooperation becomes pivotal for all leaders;

- The framework must be unique to the organisation, i.e., it should stipulate the small number of leadership behaviours that are pivotal in driving success in the organisation's culture, as opposed to the many competencies found in competitor frameworks that will neither differentiate nor drive the company's culture and success;

- The framework must be clearly differentiated, i.e., it should answer the question: What is it about the way we do leadership round here that marks us out from the competition and builds a clear leadership brand?

- Finally, it is about usability. Very often frameworks are highly conceptual and do not clearly indicate what the behaviours are and how leaders should develop them. The only way in which a framework will be deemed credible, by employees and leaders alike, is if it has practical usability and simplicity.

An example of a great framework is one that indicates both positive and negative behaviours (i.e., also the behaviour of someone who has not mastered a required competency). For instance, the behaviour of someone who is able to lead courageously includes the ability to challenge a fellow leader or employee whose decisions and behaviours are not in line with the organisation's best interests. An individual who does not possess this competency is likely to keep quiet despite disagreeing, and will consequently fail to execute agreed actions. In this way, competencies are directly linked to clear behavioural standards in the performance management process, as they offer a very practical way in which to discuss behaviour.

Defining the model: Building blocks

When organisations work on defining and implementing a competency framework, a number of standard elements can be used. At the level of the 'quarters' (see below), organisations should clearly customise the leadership behaviours needed to be successful, given their strategy, long-term vision and capability requirements.

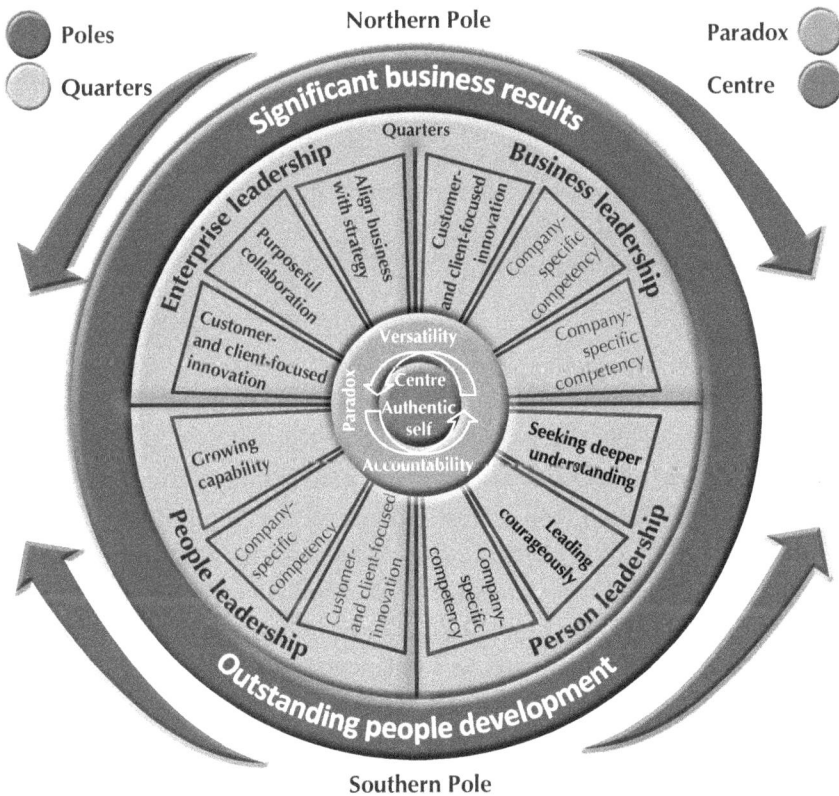

Figure 5.1: The four quarters of a competency framework

The centre

At the centre of the model is the concept of the authentic self, the point of departure for all leadership behaviour. In principle, this centre is not about 'individualism', but rather about 'interconnectedness'. Leaders need to understand themselves and their responsibility in creating a culture and a language of leadership. Introspection and self-reflection are some of the main components in reaching a point where interconnectedness is possible. In essence, it encompasses communal enterprise, leadership legitimacy and value sharing, i.e., principles of *ubuntu*. Traditionally, African leadership legitimacy is built on participation, responsibility and the spiritual authority underpinning the leadership centre of the authentic self.

The paradox

The second dimension of the framework talks to versatility (flexibility) and accountability. A growing component of responsible leadership in the 21st century is balancing paradox with dilemmas. This dimension demonstrates the tension that occurs when using one's discretion responsibly. For example, leaders are expected to be versatile (creative) in respect of innovation and decision making, and to accept full accountability for their actions. Within the context of doing business in Africa, managing paradox is one of the main elements used to define successful future leadership. Successful leaders in Africa are those who work in an integrative, rather than a polarising, way. This dimension must be fully understood as it will assist leaders in overcoming the challenge of moving from diversity towards strategic inclusivity.

Quarters

The third dimension identifies appropriate leadership behaviours in clusters, namely enterprise, business, people and personal leadership. Each of these dimensions should be customised per company, given its unique strategy and future vision. However, it is imperative that organisations invest in creating 'well-rounded' leaders, rather than leaders who do well in certain clusters, but fail in others – especially in industries that traditionally attract large numbers of technical experts, such as banking, engineering and healthcare. Other than individual contributors who may not have a high level of people management responsibilities, key to success are leaders who excel in all four clusters, in a balanced way.

The personal leadership cluster focuses on the dimensions of leadership in developing a high level of personal mastery – especially those capabilities that impact on how leaders make decisions and lead others. The people leadership cluster is focused on elements related to interpersonal capabilities and on leaders' people management expertise. These two quarters drive outstanding people development.

The business leadership cluster focuses on the capabilities needed to manage a business unit or the organisation as a whole, in an integrative way, by being results-oriented, driving execution, and initiating and driving change. A leader's ability to navigate the complexity of doing business in Africa will make him/her successful and sustainable, both from an individual and organisational perspective. The final cluster, enterprise leadership, focuses on the leader's ability to think and act in a systemic and integrative way, i.e., whether s/he is able to balance the many polarities and dilemmas being faced. Here the leader shows the capabilities needed to be an active participant in creating and managing the overall organisational context and, in certain instances, even the policy environments within the country where s/he is working. If successful, the leader will be able to overcome the leadership challenge of 'stepping outside the system'. The business and enterprise leadership clusters drive significant business results.

For a discussion of the differentiating competencies in each cluster, i.e., the competencies that will give leaders and organisations an advantage over their competitors and the ability to drive a leadership brand that is both inspirational and aspirational, see below.

The poles

The next dimension is the most important in differentiating success from failure, as it pertains to leaders in the African context. The great polarity within African leadership remains the ability to successfully balance significant business results with outstanding people development. In this competency model, the north deals with tasks (significant business results) while the south deals with the human element (outstanding people development). The business- and people-related clusters are positioned in the northern and southern hemispheres respectively. In essence, 21st-century leadership is clearly defined by the principle of 'and' rather than 'or'. Those who are capable and excel in their ability to balance the polarities of both dimensions will define the future cadre of leaders within Africa.

Defining the differentiators within each cluster

As stated above, it is at the level of the different clusters that organisations should customise according to their requirements and overall long-term vision. However, that does not mean certain leadership behaviours can be seen as standard differentiators and can therefore be included as building blocks in all competency frameworks. Before mentioning the actual behaviours, it is imperative to understand the rationale of why such differentiating competencies exist in the context of doing business in Africa.

This context is underpinned by what can be referred to as 'the new networked environment'. First, an increasingly geographically dispersed workforce means that leaders must have the ability to work across multiple regions and time zones. Second, organisations are adopting more matrixed organisational structures, which impact on changes in terms of the number of individuals involved in decisions – according to the Corporate Executive Board (2012), this has increased by more than 50 per cent since 2009. Third, there has been an increase in cross-silo coordination, i.e., the percentage of leaders who regularly coordinate with different teams, functions, job levels and locations. Leaders have had to improve their ability to navigate complex work processes and numerous work relationships. Lastly, there is an increasing business need for data and information – something of a dichotomy within an environment where these are sometimes seen as scarce resources. However, this factor impacts on leaders' ability to develop and use their analytical competencies to process data, as much as on their intuition when it comes to making effective and efficient decisions.

Personal leadership cluster differentiators: Leading courageously and seeking deeper understanding

Leading courageously is the ability to believe in yourself, your judgement, skills and experience, and using this self-confidence to challenge others, for the benefit of the organisation.

In the first instance, leaders need the self-confidence to take ownership of and drive organisational initiatives which will help them deal with criticism and disagreements in a professional, objective manner. In the new networked world, leaders must have the ability to challenge popular values, decisions and opinions, and to accept that this comes with personal risks and consequences. In the final instance, this competency will enable leaders to speak up when others are not behaving in line with organisational values, and will help them to persist in the face of opposition or fear.

A leader who *seeks deeper understanding* is actively curious, seeking a broader and more objective understanding of not only the internal environment, but also the wider social context within which the organisation functions. This skill will reveal the necessary information on which the leader can base commercial decisions and actions. As part of this competency, the leader must actively seek to understand not only different cultures, but also diverse viewpoints. By building an extensive and in-depth awareness of macro-environmental trends, s/he is able to take a global view of critical decisions to be made, even in an environment fraught with market complexities and an absence of key data.

These two competencies form the basis of a differentiated personal leadership cluster, and give organisations the ability to customise additional organisation-specific competencies based on the vision and strategy of the organisation.

Business leadership cluster differentiator: Customer- and client-facing innovation

Traditionally, this functions as the most 'generic' cluster of competencies, focusing on 'operation-specific' requirements such as results delivery and operational excellence. In being able to build sustainable business solutions in African markets, the differentiating competency within this cluster is *customer- and client-facing innovation*. This competency is defined as the ability to focus attention and effort on understanding customers (or customer segments), and proactively addressing different customer and client needs by focusing on how to action organisational changes/innovations when addressing customer needs.

As a starting point, the leader needs a deep understanding of the local customer segment, including cultural customs, approaches and norms. Second, this competency revolves around the leader's ability to focus or reframe his/her team's attention on specific customer needs, with the intention of building closer relationships as well as organisational credibility.

Again, environmental scanning is of the essence as it enables the leader to identify customer needs and to design new products and business-appropriate solutions, with speed and adaptable execution.

People leadership cluster differentiator: Growing world-class capability

Given the talent crunch across markets and industries, a leader's ability to *grow world-class capability* in a resource-constrained environment remains one of the key challenges and opportunities of doing business in Africa. This competency revolves around the ability to identify, develop and retain capability for the benefit of the broader business, based on a genuine intent in fostering the long-term learning and development of others.

It all starts with a leader's ability to provide on-the-job guidance, by making specific recommendations to help others achieve set performance standards. Second, leaders grow capability by providing balanced development feedback. Not only is it about the ability to provide ongoing feedback with the purpose of reinforcing employees' positive attributes and discussing areas of development, but of equal importance is the leader's ability to tolerate well-intentioned mistakes and treat these as potential learning opportunities. Third, it is about the leader's ability to grow capability by delegating full areas of accountability and decision making, to allow others to grow and learn from managing new responsibilities. Here, the role of the leader is to provide developmental guidance or coaching along with the developmental assignment. Lastly, this competency describes the ablity of leaders to grow capability by managing careers, i.e., redeploying and promoting individuals for developmental purposes. For this to be successful, the leader needs to be explicit and clear as to what the skills and competencies are that the individual is expected to learn in the new role.

Other leadership competencies that organisations may include are *fostering teamwork* and *inspiring performance*. These competencies, which are reflected in the personal leadership and people leadership clusters, must be directly aligned to the dominant behaviours the organisation would like all employees to manifest. It also indicates which behaviours are valued within the organisation.

Enterprise leadership cluster differentiators: Purposeful collaboration

Purposeful collaboration is the competency with the strongest link to the capabilities needed for the new networked environment. In essence, a leader needs to understand and leverage dependencies across the organisation, and must comprehend the impact his/her own actions have on the rest of the organisation, in striving to create an organisational climate of effective decision-making and quality outcome delivery. To understand this competency, it may be useful to look at the antithesis of purposeful collaboration, which is being overly inclusive. Such indecisiveness will lead to leaders involving everyone in endless discussions and consultations, without actually making any decisions. Being over-inclusive means that leaders collaborate for collegiality, rather than for the decisive delivery of outcomes. At its most dysfunctional, leaders may agree 'in the room', but then work 'behind the scenes' to veto decisions or may allow others to veto decisions. These types of managers mainly attend meetings 'to be seen', rather than to contribute substantively to decision-making.

At the base level, leaders must be able to include the smallest effective number of people in the decision-making process. Leaders should also build cross-functional teams to arrive at the best solution for the business as a whole, when coming up with new plans or even in the day-to-day focused execution of the organisation's strategy. The next level of this competency is the leader's ability to ensure cross-functional alignment by using a clear, disciplined process to fearlessly work from purpose and principles to decisions. The ability of the leader to lead across structures, manage across borders (such as geographies, product and functional lines, potentially including third parties) and to influence without authority make up the main characteristics of this level of the competency.

Purposeful collaboration forms the basis of a differentiated enterprise leadership cluster and, as a competency, cannot be emphasised enough for its role in the new networked environment.

The next competency within this cluster that defines competitive advantage is *aligning business to strategy*. This competency is defined as the leader's ability to understand the line of sight between strategy and organisational implementation. It translates organisational strategy into specific decisions and actions to ensure strategy implementation, and aligns resources in an effective manner to ensure that business execution is directly aligned to the organisation's strategic direction. Although it is a standard feature of most competency frameworks, it is also the one at which organisations often fare badly. The success of this competency depends on the leader's ability to execute on four actions, with each building on the next level in terms of complexity and ambiguity.

First, leaders must put the right people in the right place to achieve strategy execution. This includes clarifying the structures and accountabilities of each person, along with their relevance for the business strategy. Second, leaders must align resources and structures to strategy, which includes adjusting resources, roles, processes, systems and accountabilities to ensure strategy implementation. Third, leaders have to align business to local market conditions, which includes adjusting strategy implementation to the specifics of local conditions or needs. This will ensure a disciplined balance between the need for centralised and local processes. Often, organisations are unable to negotiate the right balance between global versus local, which directly impacts on successful strategy execution. Lastly, leaders have to create the right strategic insight for action which recognises interdependencies and underlying patterns between different systems and opportunities, in order to develop an optimal strategic response. It is the ability to take a long-term, macro view of strategy, and to not only make the most appropriate strategic choices, but also to prioritise actions so as to implement longer-term strategy. Often leaders who are accountable for aligning business to strategy only focus on the first two actions, which leads to a disconnect between long-term strategy and short-term strategic actions.

How, then, would this competency be applied within the context of 'stepping outside the system'? It is the responsibility of leaders within Africa to determine and communicate a compelling future for the business that is reflective of its social responsibilities, creates value for many, and recognises the varying aspirations and expectations of stakeholders. It would also encompass the co-creation of strategy with people across the company, and would be informed by those within the wider social environment in which the company operates.

It is about recognising the value of a broad based, flexible and multi-stranded approach. In essence, it is about developing socially responsible products and services, with a view to making a positive impact across the value chain (Faruk and Hoffman, 2010).

Key factors to successfully implementing a leadership competency framework

Irrespective of the quality and appropriateness of the actual model, it will only be successfully implemented if the following factors are present:

- Visible top management and CEO ownership and sponsorship through their collective leadership capability and through them enacting competencies in tangible leadership practices;

- Visible business buy-in and ownership, especially the role leaders play as 'leaders teaching leaders' in leadership development programmes;

- The competency framework must tie in with the organisation's and leaders' overall aspirations. It does not help if the 'clever' model does not reflect what is valued within the organisation's values and leadership practices;

- It has to be integrated into all the organisation's value propositions, i.e., talent development proposition, employee value proposition, and management and leadership development proposition;

- The organisation has to use the language of competencies in all its internal and external communication.

Addressing leadership challenges – key recommendations

Guiding principles of leadership development

In 2007, Robert M. Fuller and Jared L. Bleak, in *The leadership advantage*, defined five guiding principles which are applicable to the challenges facing the development of future leaders within the African context.

Start at the top

Starting at the top is not only about sponsorship and endorsement – best practice states that top leaders must be used as teachers, coaches and mentors. In fast-growing emerging markets especially, where practical experience is often the key differentiator between success and failure, it is imperative to develop well-structured coaching and mentoring programmes for young and experienced leaders alike.

More than that, it is not only about structured programmes, but also about creating a culture of mentorship, where leaders see it as one of their most important people practices and leadership imperatives. In fact, this should be seen as an entry point into their balanced scorecard. In a well-defined leadership development architecture, 'leader-led conversations and dialogues' form an integral part of the learning process.

However, is time being set aside to improve leaders' teaching and coaching skills, or are we assuming an inherent capability? Where many coaching and mentoring processes fail is when leaders are not given the actual skills and toolsets to become great mentors – they merely practise the methodologies they were taught as they 'came through the ranks'. Often these styles included a heavy-handed 'tell' approach, rather than a facilitative and experiental 'practice' approach.

One of the most effective ways of learning is by 'failing in a safe space'. More often than not, such a space is best achieved through organisations creating a positive culture of mentorship. One of the core applications of a leadership competency framework is to guide leaders in understanding the capabilities being built for the future, and to ensure that they focus their mentoring efforts in these areas.

Build an integrated leadership strategy

Leadership development programmes are but one element of leadership strategy. Other elements include competency models, assessments, talent management and succession planning, rewards and recognition, job rotation, special projects, coaching and mentoring. Leadership development architecture must bring together these elements into a consummate whole. Underpinning this is the fact that the architecture must be integrated with and linked to strategy and the needs of the business, in order to increase the impact of the investment in leadership development. In many of our interviews with regional leaders in Africa, it became clear that a number of these processes tend to exist in isolation, making it impossible for regional business units to show the links between processes or to show real return on investment.

Link leadership development directly to the business and deliver results

Leadership development should begin and end with the company's business strategy and objectives in mind. Organisations must clearly emphasise business objectives when crafting leadership development plans, to ensure that delegates clearly understand the purpose and focus of the learning experiences, as well as leaders' expectations of the learning process. Bearing this in mind, it is clear that a 'one-size-fits-all' approach will not be successful for organisations doing business where the growth expectations; the social, political and policy environments; as well as the business environment may differ radically from country to country. It is imperative for the organisation to decide which are the 'common themes' globally and which capabilities should be built per country/region. In many of our interviews it became clear that there are significant differences within the talent market in various countries (i.e., talent supply and demand), which of course impacts on the focus of leadership development programmes.

Drive consistency in the execution of leadership programmes and practices

Given the above, this does not mean that enterprise-wide standards, practices and metrics for leadership should not be defined and implemented, just that there should be flexibility in terms of execution when addressing specific business needs.

The better the level of customisation (in respect of developmental solutions for business units being directly linked to their core objectives), the higher the level of management support and engagement in such activities. Programmes and processes should be cascaded down the organisation in order to improve impact, drive cultural change and broaden employees' understanding of the organisation's strategic goals and objectives, and therefore the ability of the business unit's specific leaders to execute strategy.

Hold leaders and the organisation accountable
for developmental and business results

Organisations will have to become as disciplined in holding people accountable for developmental goals as they are in creating scorecards focused on making people accountable for achieving business results, especially in an increasingly competitive environment where any investment is carefully considered and monitored for returns. Leaders manage leaders, develop leaders, hire and promote leaders, therefore they should be fully accountable for the people scorecard which is linked to leadership and talent development ROI measures.

Best practice companies anchor their leadership development efforts with lean competency models tied to performance and reward systems. According to Fuller and Bleak (2007), best practice organisations use competencies as a baseline for identifying and then developing high potentials and leaders, as part of their succession planning. In this way, competencies are established as behavioural standards for both leaders and managers.

Building a cadre of future leadership talent

According to James Eyring (2011), several insights can be used as the basis for defining a successful talent management strategy as well as appropriate practices within emerging markets.

Build appropriate practices aligned to market demand

It is key to the success of the strategy that organisations operating in Africa change their mindset and start building appropriate planning processes and tools which are aligned to local market conditions. Leaders within these markets may, for instance, face a number of challenges that are significantly more complex than those in developed markets, such as poorly defined and changing legal and regulatory environments, complex government relations, core infrastructure and supply chain issues, and highly matrixed environments.

Further to these identified challenges, growth itself can outpace leadership capacity and capability, which places added pressure on the talent strategy.

To accommodate these challenges, a talent management model should be built, taking the following into account:

- *Market complexities.* One of the most common mistakes organisations make, is to adopt a 'one-size-fits-all' approach. This continent is made up of a significant number of countries, each with its own context, complexities and differences. Organisations would therefore be ill advised to see Africa as a single, homogeneous marketplace. In the same way, 'matching' talented individuals to the market complexities faced by each country is imperative.

During interviews with regional leaders it became clear that the assumption that success in one market directly leads to success in another, is too simplistic. However, there is a sense that leaders who possess the competencies of flexibility, cultural agility and the ability to work integratively, seem to transfer more seamlessly into different localities.

- *Growth rate demands on leaders.* Localising the talent strategy in relation to the country and the company's growth rate targets may demand very different leaders per region and/or locality. As an example, in high growth rate markets, leaders may have to deal with geographically dispersed markets that are characterised by large populations spread across a vast geographical area; there may be cultural barriers, lifestyle and language differences; as well as challenges brought on by an immature business environment (e.g., inadequate distribution infrastructure, poor payment cycles, and a lack of local knowledge and customs).

The leader's ability to environmentally scan both the internal and external environment, and at the same time contextualise the organisation's growth strategy in relation to the country's growth rate, may make the difference between success and failure. In large-scale mature markets, these characteristics may only come into play at much higher levels in the organisation, but may be required of a larger number of leaders within emerging markets.

- *Leveraging local talent networked relationships.* One of the most interesting insights gained from working outside the borders of South Africa, is that employees are highly networked individuals who have a keen sense of their peers' career aspirations and are aware of those peers' current roles in other companies. Identifying talent may have a very different definition and require a different methodology if talented individuals are acutely aware of their 'peers and competition' for certain roles. We are so used to formal talent mapping processes in South Africa, that we may be missing a trick if we are unable to leverage these already-formed relationships.

- *Hiring ahead of the curve by hiring for the size of the job three years from now, not for the size of the job today.* In hiring practices, a great deal of time is spent on clearly identifying and structuring job descriptions. Although there is logic and practical relevance for doing this, the more appropriate way is to define broad-based role profiles which include a 'future focus', rather than merely a current list of skills and responsibilities. Given market growth expectations and the overall shortage of experienced talent in some emerging markets, it may be a much more strategic proposition to build a talent mobility conversation at the start of the talent planning cycle, rather than three years down the line.

An issue which a number of expatriates identified during the interviews, is that their skill sets are frequently 'dragged and dropped' into geographies deemed 'most in need', and that they are often unaware of where their next role will be. Although this is mainly done unintentionally, they feel the company does not invest enough time and effort in having medium- and long-term career conversations with them. This makes them nervous and more disposed to being headhunted by competitors who offer them long-term opportunities. Another issue that must be better managed is the fact that conversations about career opportunities, once employees are back at HQ, are limited. Also, they feel that their colleagues who do not take up the challenge of working in more unsure environments, have more stable and clearer career paths. In one interview a manager described as follows the situation when he returned to HQ after spending four years outside South Africa: there was no 'debriefing' around what he had learnt and what knowledge he had built. He stated that it was quite a culture shock coming back, as his own thinking and experience had grown so much. Yet, his colleagues 'seemed the same, not having built better skills sets'.

Focus on high-impact practices

One of the single biggest factors in defining a successful talent strategy, is to ensure that the focus is not on implementing all the practices through a shotgun approach, but to define those with the highest impact in a particular marketplace. A 'lift and drop' approach often ends up having very little, if any, benefit, and continues the complex relationship of head office not appearing to understand their marketplace.

In research on talent practices in emerging markets, the following stand out as having high-impact returns:

- A clear focus on developing leaders from the early stages of market entry;
- Building close relationships with local universities, where possible, improves the effectiveness of recruitment, internships and leadership development;
- A stable, local leadership team, kept in play for a minimum of two years, impacts positively on outcomes and fosters a culture of mentorship;
- Hiring ahead of the curve on seniority for key roles;
- Hiring into the talent pool, but not for a specific position.

Avoid the 'global standard trap'

A number of global firms, as standard practice, limit the portion of high-potential candidates to about ten per cent of the population, which allows them to focus their development resources. Although this common practice may be appropriate in low- to medium-growth markets, it does not accommodate fast-growing developing marketplaces where, if applied, it loses pace with growth in demand for skilled and talented leaders. In such markets, a more accurate measure would be to look at a three- to five-year future demand cycle, inclusive of both attrition and growth rate needs. In many interviews with leaders in African countries, it became clear that this was one of the criticisms leveraged at a central model, where HQ defines such standards without understanding the supply and demand cycles and trends per country. A further challenge exists where regional leaders identify very different supply and demand curves per country, and find it difficult to timeously create opportunities for talented individuals, i.e., a lack of talent mobility may result in them losing these individuals.

Adapt and customise your design to accommodate local needs

In no way should this be construed as advice against leveraging global and regional practices. The focus should, however, always remain on having the flexibility to adapt and add to these practices at a local level. A one-sized global programme may not have enough relevance and value to identify the leadership and talent growth needed to match local market growth needs. In designing leadership and talent learning architecture, a successful leadership development strategy will be differentiated from an unsuccessful one, based on decisions about what must be common, and what must be customised. A key challenge of implementing leadership and talent development programmes is that there is seldom sufficient feedback and communication between different geographies, in learning what works and what does not. In a number of cases, interviewees complained that they were not asked for feedback on whether programmes actually achieved the set objectives. Also, more often than not, they were not involved in scoping and designing the learning intervention.

Segment markets by growth rate

Further to implementing a focused, locally relevant, customised and adaptive strategy, organisations should clearly articulate the appropriateness of their strategy based on the market growth rate, and should not try for local implementation without taking into account the growth rate – an important variable which impacts on the type and number of talent practices to be used in an effective talent management strategy. In countries with high growth rates, a level of flexibility in the actual practices that are relevant to the market should also be taken into account when implementing talent management practices.

Practise evidence-based implementation

Rather than focusing on what is seen as best practice in other organisations, or looking at new global 'fads', it is imperative that companies build discipline in terms of implementing what works by using metrics to track progress and talent output, evaluate programme output, and track success stories, irrespective of what is seen outside the organisation as the latest trend. This type of discipline needs to be exercised as soon as the first phase strategy is defined, not when the strategy has been implemented and is seen as 'mature' and ready for ROI. An evidence-based approach must therefore be the starting point of the strategy.

In summary, building an appropriate leadership strategy is critical to achieving business growth in challenging high-growth environments. Any talent strategy must be designed in such a way that it suits the market as well as the organisation's growth targets.

Rein in programme enthusiasm

Very often companies subscribe to a 'more is better' philosophy, where programmes are created at all levels of the organisation and in multiple countries to assist in growing talent. According to research conducted by Eyring (2011), this philosophy has the opposite result than what was intended. Companies showed no incremental value for executing additional practices.

What did make a significant impact, however, was the level of management commitment. Companies with the highest level of management commitment executed 22 per cent of practices at the highest level, versus nine per cent for those companies with lower levels of management commitment. A single-minded focus may certainly deliver better results. In a number of interviews with learning and talent professionals, they mentioned that so many initiatives were 'landed' in a country that they had no way of actually providing the right level of ROI for these initiatives, and that it may be a much better and more consolidated strategy to ensure the right level of investment per geography, with a clear focus on ROI, practice relevance and appropriateness.

Conclusion

For organisations to be successful in Africa and fully leverage the multiplicity of available opportunities, they need to focus their energy on balancing risks and opportunities in such a way that the dominant mindset within the organisation is that of optimisation, not resilience alone.

In developing an integrated leadership strategy, organisations must not only ensure that the right quality and quantity of leaders are developed, but must focus most of their attention on defining the leadership culture, the leadership brand and the collective leadership capabilities needed to drive and implement strategy. Underpinning this would be clearly defined and implemented world-class leadership practices, which effectively drive the behaviours needed in order to be successful in a networked environment characterised by poorly defined regulatory environments, complex government relations and core infrastructure challenges.

In implementing the leadership strategy, the specific actions required to deliver the desired future will be defined in the leadership development strategy, underpinned by a fully integrated learning architecture that defines the roadmap for delivering highly agile, innovative leaders. The architecture must define the level and type of crucible experiences to be built and implemented, aligned to the core capabilities needed within the organisation's cadre of leaders. Important here is the fact that in building these signature solutions, action learning methodologies (e.g., immersions, programme-based coaching, leaders teaching leaders, dilemma dialogues and ALPs) form the basis of a highly effective leadership development journey.

In defining a highly customised leadership competency framework that is well differentiated, unique to the organisation, clear and usable, and articulates a clear line of sight to the organisation's business priorities, organisations will be able to build leaders who lead courageously, are able to collaborate in a purposeful manner, and focus on growing world-class capability within their teams and in the organisation at large. With a high level of top management sponsorship and ownership, such a framework defines clear standards for leadership to which leaders can hold themselves and others accountable, while also playing an enabling role in defining the desired leadership culture and brand.

To address the leadership challenges experienced by organisations doing business in Africa, it is imperative that companies balance the dilemmas facing them. First, they must be able to balance adoption versus adaption, i.e., when should global practices be implemented in a standardised way, and when should practices be adapted at local level? Second, quality versus quantity should be defined on a number of fronts, including in talent management practices and leadership development programmes. Organisations need to make trade-offs between the type and number of programmes and practices to be implemented, given the context of market demand and growth rates. In the final instance, remember that in developing a consistent language of leadership within an organisation, there is no alternative to leader-owned and leader-facilitated development journeys. It is the only way in which we will truly be able to develop leaders as both pathfinders and team players.

References

Aiken, P. (2010). *The 10 leadership practices for highly capable change leadership.* United Kingdom: The Centre for Applied Leadership Research.

Centre for Creative Leadership (2009). *Developing a leadership strategy: A critical ingredient to organisational success.* White Paper Series.

CLC Learning and Development (2012). *Building high-performance capability for the new work environment.* Virginia: Corporate Executive Board (CEB).

Corporate Executive Board (CEB) (2012). *Strengthening the global leadership pipeline: Build management capabilities to keep pace with growth strategies.* Virginia: CEB.

Eyring, J. (2011). *Building leadership talent in emerging markets: Eight insights to act on today.* New Jersey: Organisation Solutions Pty Ltd.

Faruk, A. & Hoffman, A. (2010). *Sustainability and leadership competencies for business leaders.* New York: BSR, Executiva.

Fulmer, R. and Bleak, J. (2008). *The leadership advantage: How the best companies are developing their talent to pave the way for future success.* New York: Amacom.

Goldsmith, M. (2007). *Developing your leadership brand, an interview with Dave Ulrich.* Businessweek.com. Retrieved September 2, 2014 from http://www.businessweek.com/stories/2007-10-02/developing-your-leadership-brandbusinessweek-business-news-stock-market-and-financial-advice

O'Leonard, K. & Loew, L. (2012). *Leadership development factbook: Benchmarks and trends in U.S. leadership development.* Oakland: Bersin and Associates.

Richman, H. & Wiggenhorn, A. (2006). Developing leadership talent in emerging markets. *Leadership in Action, 25*(5), 1–7.

Van der Colff, L. (2003). Leadership lessons from the African tree. *Management Decision Journal, 41*(3), 257–261.

Van der Colff, L. (2007). Understanding culture-based diversity through the development of a skills-based model of leadership. In K. April and M. Shockley (Eds.), *Diversity in Africa: The coming of age of a continent.* New York: Palgrave MacMillan, 35–50.

CHAPTER 6: The Role of the HR Function in Emerging Market Organisations

Johan Ludike

Introduction

> HR is the corporate function with the greatest potential, the key driver
> in theory of business performance and also the function which most
> consistently under delivers.
>
> – Dave Ulrich

It should at this stage, after progressing through the respective chapters of this book, dawn on most readers and practitioners that we are living in times of unprecedented change. Many insights, recipes and quick-fixes from the past, as they relate to the competitive advantage of nations (see Porter, 1990) are eroding and/or have evaporated, and no longer offer a means to sustainable competitive differentiation.

Charan (2013) describes the world as tilted on its axis, elaborating that the economic center has shifted from the northern hemisphere to fast-developing countries such as China, India, Indonesia, Brazil and a selection of states in the Middle East and Africa, where the majority of wealth and jobs are migrating.

That said, many authors in preceding chapters have alluded to the envisaged prosperity and human potential of the emerging market countries – as Sharma (2012) terms them, 'breakout nations'. It would, however, be prudent to heed Sharma's caution that only one-third of these nations have been able to grow at an annual rate of five per cent or more. Johansen (2007) argues that such growth may be the result of tumultuous volatility, uncertainty complexity and ambiguity in terms of an accentuated range of drivers such as globalisation, shifting demographics, multicultural intelligence and/or agility, as well as new technologies – all of which impact labour economics.

Having defined and described dynamic, pioneering and/or emerging markets, for the purposes of this chapter it is useful to offer a general perspective on globalisation and human resource management (HRM). Also important is to reiterate the complexities of a fast-evolving workforce and of the workplace as an increasingly permeable context, before briefly attempting to align the characteristics, challenges and capabilities of a 21st-century HR function. Further, this chapter will endeavour to integrate a repositioning of what the business of an HR function should be. To do so, it will be necessary to explore the changes required of the HR function, and to conceptualise its delivery models as well as its leadership, so as to establish a rapid, agile, relevant and lean HR function which provides a sustainable degree of value innovation that is unique to emerging markets.

Human resource management amidst an evolving, globalising landscape

Thanks to the perceived increasing importance of HRM as a driver of as much as 85 per cent of intangible value in organisations (see Lev, 2001; Warner, 2004), the role of globalisation is attracting a compendium of research-based insights from scholars in both developed and developing/emerging markets.

Until very recently, exponential growth in international trade was linked to globalisation related to the unification of markets, consumer preferences due to increasingly mobile investor capital, as well as the rapid and ubiquitous reach of technology. Ohmae (1990) postulates that in most organisations' internal and external actions, processes are becoming increasingly multinational and borderless, which implies that economies are becoming globally integrated. As a result, global management techniques, including those of HR, have increasingly been converging around the notion of 'best practice' (see Sera, 1992). If practitioners accept this perspective in isolation, it implies that HRM, once exposed to forces of globalisation, merely succumb to the dominant worldwide practices of 'leading-edge' companies (this being something of a value-laden term, supposedly designed to enhance competitiveness).

Contrarians such as Rugman (2000) and publications such as the *Economist* (2000) argue that multinationals are extremely local in their practices and that, surprisingly, on average two-thirds of employees are nationals of their home country, who in turn produce two-thirds of their output in their home countries.

Thanks to global trade, international and national boundaries are becoming increasingly permeable, which accelerates the convergence of practices and their universal transfer. However, dramatic changes in the workforce of 2020 will most likely require organisations and their HRM functions to be locally responsive.

Chattopadhya and Batra (2012) compellingly argue that very credible strong competitors to global brands are emerging in local markets, and that this is happening at a far greater pace and much sooner than anticipated. These so-called multinational emerging countries are developing both the confidence and the ambition to become global giants themselves. Govindarajan and Ramamurt (2010) give credence to the notion of reverse innovation, where innovation from emerging markets literally trickles up to rich, developed countries – a phenomenon they consider to be without historical parallel.

Bartlett and Ghoshal (2002) believe a new form of organisation – the so-called transnational company – needs to strive not only to achieve global efficiency and competitiveness, but also to be nationally responsive and to develop, generate and disseminate knowledge.

In many contexts, imposing best practice and universalist processes and philosophies may lack the necessary degree of legitimacy. Brewster (1999) advances the notion of best fit (given the specific context) as opposed to best practice at all costs in order to advance the interests of all stakeholders.

It is against the above contextual paradigm that this chapter will briefly explore the avalanche of anticipated changes in both the workforce and the workplace, in terms of how these might in future drive the transformation of the HR function in emerging markets.

The 21st-century revolutionary workforce and workplace

An accelerated pace of change, which can only be described as revolutionary, is sweeping and impacting emerging market workforces and workplaces. Pfeifer and Sutton's (2000) early pronouncements on the so-called 'knowing–doing gap' have never been more relevant, nor has the HR function ever been more disempowered through a lack of discernible strategic business impact and credibility.

It is no coincidence that Nagpal (2013) identifies the need to 'reinvent employment', given the profound impact of globalisation, disruptive technologies, shifts in demographics (both in terms of age and gender), and transient worker expectations – all of which are expected to impact on anticipated workplace realities and employee experiences by 2020.

Many of the trends and challenges present in these markets (be they changing demographics or evolving employee labour participation rates) are evolving concurrently; they are complex and are gaining momentum at a dramatic pace not only in developed but also in developing markets.

A good example would be the manner in which telecoms companies now provide voice, Internet and video services as easily accessible bundles which grant employees swift access to the Internet on their phones, at relatively low cost.

Notable challenges are dramatic shifts in employee expectations as they relate to flexible work arrangements that support their individual circumstances, heightened stakeholder demands for greater gender equality, increased female representation, and greater employee diversity within organisations and on the boards of companies.

In respect of customising work experiences for employees, Cantrell and Smith (2010) state that the next generation of workers will increasingly choose to work remotely, electing to use their own technology when and where they want, and opting to manage technological advances on their own. This could present significant challenges, as employees will expect employers to segment and differentiate them according to not only their individual lifestyles, but also their preferred modes of learning and their respective life stages.

With constant change expected to be a consistent theme amongst future workforces, many experts believe it is crucial that HR keep up not only with rapid technological advances, but also with how different generations value and integrate technology into their lives: the millennial generation, in particular, believe it is their right to work hard and play hard, while maintaining a lifestyle which is increasingly connected to social media.

Social media are viewed as a potential game changer in emerging markets (Charan, 2013). Already, social media are being used extensively as tools for branding, recruiting and engaging. Often, social media platforms are the first place job seekers look for employment opportunities. Similarly, HR can use this to their benefit by leveraging social media platforms such as LinkedIn, Pinterest, Twitter and Facebook, blogs, wikis, etc. to refresh, unearth and engage with a sizeable talent community for new hires, as well as a new breed of consultative contingent workers who transcend both the developed and the emerging worlds of work. HR can also exploit this trend transnationally by extending its communication strategy to the next level, and providing employees with the opportunity to share feedback and ideas, in real time, on internal blogs and forums. This creates a heightened sense of belonging, community and collaboration.

Being physically based in an office does not ensure employee productivity. Similarly, working away from the office does not necessarily equate to a lack of productivity. HR practitioners have to accept that social media are integral to the lives of not only the new generation workforce but also of existing employees – it is futile to resist the phenomenon, therefore working proactively to embrace it may help to leverage a more mobile workforce.

According to Meister and Willyerd (2010), employers will face huge challenges in recruiting, developing and motivating employees of all ages and backgrounds, amid breakneck organisational changes. In fact, five generations of employees will soon be working together – from aging Traditionalists and Baby Boomers to 'Generation 2020s', i.e., those born post-1997. By 2020, more offices will be mobile, serving employees and team members stationed around the globe. The best employees will demand innovative, imaginative contracts. Employers who are unable or unwilling to supply such new-paradigm agreements will come up short – and their attempts to recruit top talent will suffer.

Meister et al. (2010) and Gratton (2011) concur that a wide array of elements will impact the workforce and will dramatically affect workplaces by 2020. These include:

- *Shifting workforce demographics.* Compared to the 2010 scenario pertaining to workforces in many developed countries, employee pools will, by 2020, include more people older than 55, and more women. Age, gender and ethnicity will pose challenges to employers as five generations are forced to collaborate and cooperate in the workplace, specifically: Traditionalists (born pre-1946), Baby

Boomers (1946–1964), Generation X (1965–1976), Millennials (1977–1997) and Generation 2020s. This may be the result of a drop in fertility rates impacting particularly the European and Asian workforces, which are not only aging but also shrinking in numbers. Given different working styles and ways of thinking, HR will need to find ways to manage conflict and support collaboration among the different generations, by tapping into their respective strengths and expertise levels.

- *The knowledge economy.* As work evolves to become increasingly technical in nature, organisations will require workers with more conceptual, tacit skills, such as problem-solving abilities, sound judgement, the ability to listen, the capacity to analyse data, to foster relationships, and collaborate and communicate with co-workers. Work is becoming increasingly characterised by 'datafication' meaning huge amounts of information are being automated, extracted, and sourced in an applied attempt to generate solutions. The new generation of workers places greater importance on achieving work–life balance and the need to work smart. HR should, therefore, focus on creating the right environment, providing suitable tools and resources, breaking down hierarchical barriers, allowing greater transparency in decision-making and inculcating an inclusive culture.

- *Globalisation.* A significant number of *Financial Times* Global 500 companies are now based in Brazil, Russia, India and China (BRIC countries). Experts forecast that by 2020, BRIC nations will be among the world's economic leaders. As the world 'flattens' according to Friedman (2005), workforces will become 'virtual', with fewer employees working on-site and operations emanating from smaller, centralised headquarters. It will increasingly be vitally important to appreciate differences between employees and to create a system that values such diversity.

- *The digital workplace.* This is the realm of digital information, i.e., where data are 'created, captured or replicated in digital form', and it is growing both constantly and rapidly. Companies will need employees who can manage vast amounts of content, while simultaneously keeping it private and secure. Wired since birth, the new networked employees expect companies to furnish them with the same networking, collaborative and brainstorming tools they have used all their lives. Work–life balance will continue to be very important – Generations X, Y and Z are already refusing to work as hard and as long hours as their Baby Boomer parents.

- *The ubiquity of mobile technology.* In many countries, mobile phones now outnumber people. Going beyond communication, they also function as learning devices. The field already offers in excess of 10 000 education-related applications for the iPhone. A significant trend is that many leading institutions now increasingly deploy and use mobile phones and tablets for sales and compliance training, for disseminating product knowledge and offering online performance support. The real challenge is probably hidden in how employees embrace such technology and leverage it as hype. Connectivity and an 'always on' presence are blurring the boundary between home and office.

- *The participation society.* Increasingly, both consumers and employees will be compelled to proactively participate and improve products, services and business. Employees now unite via online social networks to improve business operations, forming collaborative groups such as Tripadvisor, Glassdoor and Monsterthinking, not to mention Learnist, which goes beyond mere social learning to literally crowdsource and leverage the world's knowledge.

- *Corporate social responsibility* (CSR). Already a pivotal trend in big companies, CSR will be even more crucial by 2020. Significant numbers of graduates are striving to work for companies with CSR ideals that mirror their own. One exceptional example is IBM's Corporate Service Corps, which deploys interns on CSR projects in emerging countries where the company expects to experience growth during the coming decade. To draw the best talent, traits such as diversity and flexibility, as well as CSR, are becoming more important to job-seekers. Likewise, company culture and branding will in future be key differentiators.

The world is becoming increasingly unpredictable, and organisations that are able to adapt to changing business conditions will outperform their competition. On a fundamental level, HR will need to reshape itself in order to create new organisations designed around nimble and responsive HR, which has been reinvented to meet the needs of a contemporary, 21ˢᵗ-century agile organisation.

Reinventing and transforming the HR function and operating model

Given the disruptive changes to the landscape of work, as popularised by the acronym VUCA (volatility, uncertainty, complexity and ambiguity), it is not surprising that esteemed scholars such as Ulrich and Allen et al. (2009) and Lawler and Boudreau (2009) are challenging HR practitioners to renew, reinvent and transform their HR functions – inclusive of their operating and delivery models, capabilities, competencies, etc. – in order to be fit for the future.

Wright and Boudreau et al. (2011), on reflecting on the business partner, centre of excellence and shared services model which was almost universally adopted by global multinationals during the 1990s, highlight the following structural flaws and other impediments:

- *Resources are inflexible and efforts fragmented* – this is because the original intention was to spend a higher proportion of HR resources on delivering HR strategy, and less on HR administration. However, given timing differences between the deployment of HR business partners (HRBPs) and so-called shared services coming online, for instance, many HRBPs still had to pander to the needs of line management, while centres of excellence became mini-specialist functions beavering away in silos. Often, policies and processes were poorly defined and inferior data quality from legacy systems did not contribute to the flawless execution of services, or to the generation of cutting-edge business-enabling or -enhancing solutions.

- *Deterioration in HR planning, with limited-impact solutions.* These plans increasingly represented little more than a random consolidation of activities and programmes. In the main, they originated in either business units or geographies with very little (if any) strategic alignment or sense of prudent governance. This was further exacerbated by the internal voice of the customer and/or HRBP surveys which, if anything, proved that the latter were enslaved by the transactional demands of line managers who were involved in activities such as leave approvals, grievances, and compliance issues – many of which did not add any value or have any business impact.

- *Poor, sub-optimal resource deployment and/or little alignment with business strategy.* Resources were allocated on the basis of revenue and/or number of employees, with little consideration of business strategy and/or context, e.g., innovation, emerging market growth, new start-up, etc. In addition, line managers did not readily adopt the much-touted 'self service delivery' approach, preferring a 'high touch' by expensive HRBPs and/or CEO specialists, who were all driven to serve their internal customer irrespective of cost, and without consideration of either relevance or fit of solution(s). Implementing and/or deploying a global technology platform that provides common HR standards, frameworks and tools could be very relevant; however, at times there might simultaneously be a need to up-skill, re-skill and empower local teams to innovate and to customise or localise corporate programmes. HR success will not be simply and narrowly defined in terms of cost-cutting, but in terms of the ability to drive strategic business performance and growth.

- *Frustrated and uncoordinated efforts.* These predominantly stemmed from unclear roles and responsibilities, as well as poor governance of HRBPs and centres of excellence efforts. In addition, in the past a plethora of challenges arose around HR service centres, which tended to display an inability to leverage various rather diverse HR technology platforms and were inept at dealing with outsourced vendors in a misguided effort to drive down costs. In the main, these shared service centres remained oblivious to the overall business imperative for either strategic integration or differentiation, given their isolated focus on performing transactional activities at the lowest possible cost (be it via a hotchpotch array of fragmented technologies or through poorly aligned outsourcing efforts to reckless vendors). Huge insights derived from this, including the realisation that shared services, in order to be both effective and efficient, require much more than the simplistic centralisation of services and/or the adoption of the latest fad-driven technologies.

- *Poorly conceived HR strategies which are badly executed.* This contributed to an incestuous internal drive and a focus on cost and service delivery, at the expense of enabling the organisation to meet its current or future competitive business needs (operational excellence, fast growth in pioneering markets, or the ambitious pursuit of offshore merger and acquisition opportunities). The continued challenge for HR is to design the right balance between the new and the traditional, the proposed and the feasible, so that it can still bring innovation to its practice while not only supporting but also enabling the diverse needs of the business.

- *Diminished HR capability with insufficient geographic focus.* This led to many expensive initiatives not being adopted locally, in various host countries where specialist knowledge and local expertise were honoured. Many central or global centres of excellence (COE) or 'exported' Chief Human Recource Officers (CHROs) and HRBPs were unable to adapt to the multicultural, geopolitical and social nuances required to make solutions stick. Many HR generalists and/or past administrative personnel were unable to transition to a more strategic business focus. In addition, they were slow to either adopt or leverage technology – either centrally, or in a quest to serve their ever-expanding geographical footprint via partnerships or specific geographical alliances.

It would be reasonable to conclude (although shockingly so) that due to these impediments as well as the disruptive forces referred to, many HR functions and their operating and delivery models are literally being rendered obsolete. Many an HR function has become irrelevant, as it relates to the strategic sustainability of the organisation.

Hence the burning questions are: What should be done under these circumstances? How does one go about ensuring that organisations' HR functions and their operating delivery models are future-proofed? How should HR functions be designed and resourced to ensure that they contribute to – if not enable – sustainable performance and growth?

A new generation of HR agility solutions

According to Josh Bersin (2011) of Deloitte, the purpose of the HR function is not merely to implement controls and standards and drive execution, but rather to strive to facilitate and improve organisational agility. This not only significantly and strategically repositions, but also drastically changes, HR's mission and focus. Incorporating an element of agility into the HR function allows it to be nimbler and enables an organisational culture that is more responsive to the needs of all its stakeholders – be they shareholders, customers and/or the larger community in which the organisation operates.

An agile organisation is able to change direction quickly and easily, and HR needs to be responsive to the ever-changing needs of such an institution, as speed and sustainability are vital for generating high value-added solutions and executing them expeditiously. Social media are incredibly powerful and effective, but a hidden risk lies in using social media such as Twitter and Glassdoor – if word gets out that a company does not walk the talk, its authenticity is questioned, and this leaves HR and its leadership very vulnerable.

In addition to 21st-century organisations having to innovate faster and in new, often unrecognisable and disruptive ways, they also need to execute their strategies at speed – or at least faster than their competitors – and they must therefore be highly capable of change and learning.

This requires the HR function to harness its ability to anticipate, sense and respond to volatility in the markets in which the organisation operates, and to proactively add value in such a way that it creates a competitive people advantage. Cultivating and fostering agility implies driving future-focused HR programmes and solutions which result in adaptability, innovation, collaboration, and speed. It represents a further stage of evolution, beyond merely being a provider of a service or a process owner to internal customers, be it through performance evaluation, talent development and/or reward schemes.

Many practitioners such as Fitz-enz (2010), Boudreau (2007) and Ulrich (2012) advocate that in order for HR functions to renew, they need to adapt from the outside in. Increasingly, they need to be guided by metrics and measurements, while flawlessly executing agile and lean solutions which enable a business to achieve its strategic objectives, rather than inhibiting it. HR functions should be insight-driven and must be positioned such that they inform the organisation's future course of action and/or opportunities.

It is thus obvious that HR functions need to become more strategic. This demands a set of skills and capabilities which will enable businesses to achieve competitive advantage and differentiation via configuring delivery models which seamlessly execute at speed. The new generation of workers will look for employers which offer attractive packages beyond big salaries and benefits. Companies that win this war will be those which clearly differentiate their brand and create meaningful HR programmes that are irresistible to the talent pool they attract.

As a result there is a pressing need for HR functions to be far less fragmented and isolated or hived off into HR services and specialist, insular advice centers. There is a growing need for a more refined HR strategy, yet there is less capability to deliver it. There is a demand for support to transform organisations, yet HR has struggled with change management, technology deployment and/or the progressive organisational design methodologies required to proactively transform itself. Every quarter the HR services market bustles with new entrants, mergers and acquisitions. New skills are required for analytics, influencing behaviour change, vendor management, and for HR to become workforce technology 'evangelists'.

It is anticipated that HR functions will be far less enslaved by and judged in terms of external benchmarks, and more on their ability to make a measureable, tangible impact on business results.

This demands a significant shift in focus in terms of practitioners' strategic thinking, with renewed emphasis being placed on the quality (depth and breadth of inputs) of the decisions being made, rather than the quality and cost-effectiveness of the services HR provides.

As a suggested starting point, HR governance will drastically have to be revisited, in order to clearly and explicitly define the policies, processes, as well as the roles and responsibilities of all sections involved. Any changes will have to be executed at speed, within accepted risk management margins – be they local, regional or global. Encapsulated within this new generation of agile business-centered delivery and operations models is the need for all solutions to show a clear return on investment, and to deliver proof of business impact. Businesses will require HR to account for the results it delivers, and such results will need to be validated with solid facts and figures.

Once again, HR will be deemed integral to business as a value creator and enabler, given the application of its unique expertise to the specific business context. It will move away from being seen merely as a series of disjointed initiatives. Both the structures and roles within HR would need to be resourced and deployed in such a manner that they display flexibility. Structures and roles would need to be scalable to meet changing business needs within multiple contexts, be it a start-up, pre- or post-merger integration, or downsizing and disinvestment, locally or internationally. The organisation's use of technology, outsourcing, co-sourcing, offshoring, etc. of solutions will influence the geographic scale and scope of HR services. HR practitioners employed in legacy centres of expertise or excellence will, for instance, be required to resolve (if not proactively anticipate) business issues, and to be organised into resource pools which deliver bespoke solutions per business or per workforce segment. In order to accelerate and enrich HR transformation efforts, a concerted effort will need to be made to leverage global technology platforms in support of the global HR organisation. Easy-to-use self-service capabilities should be available to managers and employees. Relevant alliances that encourage country initiatives which align with global processes must be nurtured. Once these global processes, roles and expectations are locally embedded, teams could be expanded to include communities of expertise. That will allow local HR leaders to create, customise and deliver local programmes at speed. They can then leverage the corporate infrastructure and standards to further enhance and/or optimise strategies and HR programmes in each business and geography, to drive impact at the host country level. The solutions generated in such a way are likely to be driven by local insight, therefore they will be genuinely relevant, timely and (most of all) strategically impactful. Jobs will have to be redesigned to create meaningful and challenging work that optimises the skill sets of the future workforce. To this end, HR must consistently re-examine itself and ensure that jobs remain challenging, rewarding and meaningful.

For HR, the emphasis should be on empowering team members to work where, how and when they choose, so as to maximise productivity and deliver the greatest value to the business. This will help to build a strong, diverse workforce, as well as a strong employer brand and work culture that employees will both recognise and appreciate.

Becker and Huselid et al. (2009) envisage the HR function providing strategic differentiation to develop top talent and to focus the relationship between workforce measures and the drivers of firm financial performance. They propose that complete accountability for administrative and transactional work be transferred to a third party, i.e., another part of the business or to an entirely new function. In their view, centres of expertise should be focused on traditional programme design and collaboration across silos, so as to design and deliver integrated, performance-centred outcomes. The implications of this include building expert teams which are much smaller and designed around human capital and business outcomes. HR resources would be assigned responsibility for a specific part of the operating model, and would be governed/managed vertically against specific functional objectives. Similarly, as previously mentioned, the majority of HR resources would be deployed from a flexible pool, and supposedly leveraged horizontally against various business solution-centered initiatives. In this manner, HR strategy would be perceived as being both more responsive and relevant, and connected to the business in a proactive manner.

In articulating an 'outside in' perspective as it relates to renewing the HR function, doyens Ulrich and Younger et al. (2012) argue that in order to execute an agile business-centred mandate, HR leaders need to embody the following competencies:

- *'Strategic positioner.'* This is someone who understands the business and develops stakeholder relationships, both inside and out. Such practitioners gather knowledge and feedback from many sources and understand the context in which the business operates, including the pivotal players. They are adept at recognising the organisation's differentiators and competitive challenges. As strategic positioners, HR practitioners produce actionable advice that aids in better, faster decision-making, leads to enabling and executing strategy, helps to avoid unacceptable risk and allows management to seize promising opportunities.

- *'Credible activist'*. Such leaders follow through on their commitments, thereby earning a reputation for reliability and results. These individuals become authorities in their fields of expertise and proactively contribute evidence-based recommendations to help solve problems affecting the organisation. To gain the trust and respect of both inside and outside stakeholders, they bring their knowledge, experience and insight to bear on pressing issues. To both galvanise and sustain stakeholder relationships in a credible manner it is considered more than prudent for practitioners to develop and espouse a distinctive, teachable point of view which transcends HR jargon and integrates business acumen and skills. Integral to this competency is the notion of not merely adding value, but creating it and ensuring that their contribution makes a tangible business impact. Practitioners therefore have to continually strive to develop their profession, while fostering a heighted self-insight which enables them to function as trusted advisors and creators of future business value-driven solutions.

- *'Capability builder.'* Increasingly, practitioners are tasked with being guardians of the organisation's stature within the greater community, and are being held accountable as ambassadors of the organisation's values and beliefs. This is in addition to ensuring that the organisational culture is both agile and future-proof. A concerted effort is needed to acquire, develop, communicate, encourage, measure and improve the relevant capabilities which ensure that the organisation remains distinctive and can be differentiated from competitors in the marketplace. In this way it aligns all critical aspects of HR leadership (including culture, values and branding) which are integral to this vital competency.

- *'Change champion.'* In HR's 21st-century quest to remain relevant and impactful, it faces relentless pressure to facilitate change within the organisation. Practitioners continuously need to be on the bleeding edge (also known as the pioneering edge) of developments, both internally and externally, to ensure not just a sense of transformational renewal, but also to contribute proactively and in so doing to embed those changes which will make the organisation future fit. Run-of-the-mill best practice and benchmarking efforts will no longer suffice. Change needs to be directed at creating a greater degree of differentiation in the marketplace, and contributing significantly to overall competitiveness. A compelling case for change would need to be made, supported by evidence and facts. The inevitable generational resistance and inertia will need to be overcome via networks of change advocates within the organisation. It will be beneficial for practitioners to develop and/or select change methods that fit the organisation's culture, create teams of the right people, give them sufficient resources and gain long-term commitments from powerful sponsors, so that the change effort is sustained and the commercial benefits of transformational change are realised.

- *'HR innovator and integrator.'* Following on from the aforementioned competencies, it will further be necessary for practitioners to commit to dismantling HR silos, so that value innovation which originates from insightful, enabling solutions can be realised. It is possible to align HR's efforts with the business by interpreting corporate strategy and assigning high priority by additionally considering and integrating HR's perspective. This will require practitioners to become specialists or experts in the fields of talent, leadership and cultural diversity, as these impact the firm's main strategic objectives. Strategically integrating HR practices around those priorities will ensure that an insight-driven approach drives value creation efforts. Innovation will become a key differentiator and HR's job will not merely be to promote innovation, but to leverage it.

- *'Technology proponent.'* It is frequently asserted that, generally speaking, HR professionals rank poorly in terms of their technological knowledge, and are lagging in their propensity to explore and adopt a wide array of social networking tools, technologies and platforms. In addition, they are uncomfortable with what has become known as 'big data' and/or evidence-based insights. Practitioners will be required to expand their knowledge of IT beyond standard HR recruiting, learning and performance-management tools. Deepened expertise in social networking and social learning platforms will be required, as will be the driving force behind the building of networks that connect employees, leaders, customers and other stakeholders. In addition, there might be some value in revitalising old knowledge-management initiatives, by utilising the power of technology and networks to give data meaning and impact. Strategically, what is necessary is for practitioners to assemble and combine information into actionable insight, and to collaborate with stakeholders who need it and can derive value from it. Technology can be constructively deployed to connect those inside and outside the firm, and to further expand the broader community (the so-called ecosystem). Valuable knowledge could be harnessed to help the organisation make better, faster decisions which are in the interest of all concerned, and to do so in a sustainable manner.

Meister and Willyerd (2010), looking ahead at the time, argued that by 2020, HR teams would grow and/or evolve to include new specialists such as the following:

- 'Capability planners' – they ensure that the company develops much-needed skills;

- 'Chief technologists' who serve as HR's IT experts;

- 'Community gardeners' who help to create and nurture online communities;

- 'Futurists' who work with companies to anticipate their future needs;

- 'People capability planners' who map out employees' career path and/or route for development;

- 'Place planners' who ensure that site-specific features work well at presentations and at 'virtual and collaboration sites', professional career paths and/or routes of development;

- 'Social connectors' who provide expertise in using social networks and social media;

- 'Talent scouts' who spot emerging talent and approach experienced professionals for hiring;

- 'Talent development agents' who help to plan and create accelerated as well as enriched learning experiences, if not widened opportunities for employees.

Conclusion

The purpose of this chapter was to reflect on the impact of globalisation and its potential to effect change in the workplace and the workforce, and to investigate the HR function's ability to rise to this wide array of challenges and contradictions, by interrogating its capability as an agile, future-fit division. What is obvious from this deliberation, as it relates to the vast changes in the nature of work, the workplace and the workforce, is that globalisation drastically impacts both the HR practitioner's profession and function. This is significant in terms of how HR is designed to operate, deliver and create value, in the interest of an increasingly broader or extended ecosystem. Practitioners will be compelled to respond to such changes (perhaps not proactively), but CHROs in particular, as credible and effective board members, will need to demonstrate and apply deep levels of strategic business foresight and agility. Their contribution, results and performance will be considered not merely in terms of enabling the business, but also in terms of how they help the organisation generate value and achieve innovation-based growth which is sustainable and in the best interests of all stakeholders in the 21st century.

References

Bartlett, C.A. & Ghoshal, S. (1989). *Managing across boundaries: The transnational solution.* Boston, MA: Harvard Business School.

Becker, B.E., Huselid, M.A. & Beatty, R.W. (2009). *The differentiated workforce: Transforming talent into strategic impact.* Boston, MA: Harvard Business School.

Bersin, J. (2011). *The Agile Model comes to management, learning and human resources.* Retrieved July 18, 2014 from http://www.bersin.com/blog/post/The-Agile-Model-comes-to-Management2c-Learning2c-and-Human-Resources.aspx

Brewster, C. (1999). Strategic human resource management: The value of different paradigms. *Management International Review, 39*(9), 45–64.

Brewster, C. (2000, January 29). The world's view of multinationals. *The Economist, 354*(8155), 21–22.

Cantrel, S. & Smith, D. (2013). *Workforce of one: Revolutionizing talent management through customization.* Boston, MA: Harvard Business Press.

Charan, R. (2013). *Global tilt: Leading your business through the economic power shift.* New York: Crown Publishing.

Chattopadhyay, A. & Batra, R. (2012). *The new emerging market multinationals: Four strategies for disrupting markets and building brands.* New York: McGraw Hill.

Friedman, T.L (2005). *The world is flat: A brief history of the twenty-first century.* New York: Farrar, Strauss & Giroux.

Govindarajan, V. & Ramamurti, R. (2011). Reverse innovation, emerging markets and global strategy. *Global Strategy Journal, 1*(3-4), 191–205.

Gratton, L. (2011). *The shift: The future of work is already here.* London: Harper Collins.

Johansen, B. (2007). *Get there early: Sensing the future to compete in the present.* San Francisco: Berrett-Koehler.

Lawler, E.E. & Boudreau, J.W. (2009). *Achieving excellence in human resource management: An assessment of human resource functions.* Palo Alto: Stanford University Press.

Lev, B. (2001). *Intangible assets: Values, measures and risks.* Oxford: Oxford Psychology Press.

Meister, J.C & Willyerd, K. (2010). *The 2020 workplace: How innovative companies attract, develop and keep tomorrow's employees today.* New York: Harper Collins.

Nagpal, G. (2013). *Talent economics: The fine line between winning and losing the global war for talent.* London: Kogan Page.

Ohmae, K. (1999). *The borderless world: Power and strategy in the interlinked economy.* New York: Harper Collins Business.

Pfeffer, J. & Sutton, R. (2000). *The knowing–doing gap: How smart companies turn knowledge into action.* Boston, MA: Harvard Business School.

Porter, M.E. (1990). *The competitive advantage of nations.* London: MacMillan.

Rugman, A.M. (2000). *The end of globalisation: Why global strategy is a myth and how to profit from realities of regional markets.* London: Random House.

Sera, K. (1992). Corporate globalisation: A new trend. *Academy of Management of Executive, 6,* 89–96.

Sharma, R. (2012). *Breakout nations: In pursuit of the next economic miracles.* London: Penguin.

Ulrich, D., Allen, J., Brockbank, W. & Nyman, M. (2009). *HR transformation: Building human resources from the outside in.* New York: McGraw Hill.

Ulrich, D., Younger, J., Brockbank, W. & Ulrich, M (2012). *HR from the outside in: Six competencies for the future of human resources.* New York: McGraw Hill.

Wright, P.M., Boudreau, J.W., Pace, D.A., Sartain, E., McKinnon P. & Antoine, R.L. (2011). *The Chief HR Officer: Defining the new role of human resource leaders.* San Francisco: Jossey-Bass.

CHAPTER 7: Once Upon a Time ... Human Resources were Otherwise (Reflections of a South African HR Executive)

Johann Coetzee

Introduction

Once upon a time people went to work differently and worked differently. A career was cherished and a job protected. The employer was respected not merely as a provider of income, but as someone sanctioned to employ people and deploy talent.

Once upon a time most people had no job, no revenue and even no hope. Deprivation was the norm and this sensation made every opportunity to engage in economically active endeavour, a very special gift. The relationship between employer and employee was not a psychological contract, but a moral charter. Job security was regulated by devotion to duty, relentless commitment to the job at hand and the universal willingness to do more than was asked for. I miss those days. I also miss my peers who miss that work ethic of yesteryear. I call on them to announce themselves so that we can arrange a reunion for those occupational fundamentalists. Yet, as I write this reflexive commentary, I am filled with ambivalence and guilt. Yes, we resurrected an economy after two world wars and a depression within a constitutional ideology which dehumanised all people of colour and sublimated whites. I was part of the privileged few!

While contemporary human rights, labour legislation, revised job contracts, position charters, collective bargaining and recognition agreements may argue differently, there once was a different and better way of getting things done.

I am talking about 50 years ago. We refer to them as the 'good old days', while modern-day employees would probably ridicule those times, by comparison, as slave trade, exploitative and universally unfair. We may even be accused of 'enduring' this because we didn't know any better. The point is, we didn't have to know better – it was actually good enough.

What I am referring to, are the following:

- Work was not a right, but a privilege. We worked harder than called for, because it was the only criterion we knew.

- Job content was not negotiated. It was delegated and you accepted the terms as decreed by the *boss*. There was no uncertainty about the exact nature of expectations. You went to work, devoted yourself absolutely to the corporate call and returned home, grateful that you had a job.

- Being employed in itself was a unique status symbol. You made no demands and you conformed to the requirements of the job at hand. Nothing was left open to interpretation or speculation. Everyone knew exactly what to do and work life was essentially uncomplicated.

- We worked six days a week and had 12 working days' leave per annum, which were taken when it suited the employer.

- We frowned upon anybody who suggested collective bargaining, unionisation, petitions and pressure groups. Grievances and gripes were discussed, and dialogue and consensus-seeking served as mediation and arbitration. It was generally acknowledged by all parties that there was always a better option than conflict or strike action. In fact, we looked down upon those who allowed disenchantment (at enterprise level) to convert into any form of aggression or remonstration.

- Interventions or notions such as team building, 'bosberaad', emotional intelligence, values clarification, ethics, situational leadership and corporate re-engineering did not exist. The reason: none of these were necessary. We just got on with it!

- It is fascinating how much additional education, training and development sophisticated and technologically advanced managers, leaders and executives require in order to cope with their jobs – jobs which we simply performed, one generation ago. Our instinct, intuition, gut and guts guided our decision making – mostly in the right direction.

- Families were still intact; common courtesy was inculcated at home; and values, norms, principles and standards were driven by interpersonal respect and dignity.

- The workplace was never regarded as a rehabilitation centre or a vestibule for educating people in the rudiments of courtesy and candour. This you received at home! Nobody needed emotional intelligence training, coping, coaching or empathy guidance. You were brought up properly.

- The normative context in which we engaged with our jobs demanded that we work according to our beliefs, so we believed in the way we worked.

- We were uncompromising on many issues. Religion and faith were not ridiculed because of the corporate call. Certain things were just not done, and those who did do wrong became universally marginalised.

- Customer service and customer care did not exist, either as subjects or as processes. Your word was your bond and making a commitment was an absolute undertaking. If you said so, you did so! Yes, we did (incorrectly) refer to the customer as king and treated customers accordingly. But, we never lied. The truth was an absolute, and that truth set us free, but also apart.

• The first time I was subjected to a corporate code of conduct and values intervention, I was both amazed and insulted. I was aghast to learn that intelligent people would isolate themselves for a weekend and return inspired by their consensus on honesty, integrity, truth, trust, support, openness and uncompromising commitment. These moral attributes were a natural and intrinsic part of every executive, not the consequence of some seminar which educated people on its relevance, and so ignited a new level of moral commitment. What a joke!

• An incentive was something you paid for by using your own energy. Why must people incentivise in order to optimise? Why do people hold back until such time as additional money releases optimal energy, appropriate morality or subsequent productivity? Those were the days when people worked hard and produced their best, regardless. Moreover, a bonus (13th cheque) is typically money paid out in December, but spent in September. It is not viewed as a gift of acknowledgement for extraordinary effort, but rather as an expected, integral part of normal pay.

• Why should any worker be enticed to work? There was a time when people automatically extended themselves beyond the call of duty, purely because of personal pride and consistent professional commitment.

• Again, it is the mentality of entitlement, a subconscious mindset of exploitation and a fundamental antagonism between employees and employer which predominate. People so inclined actually suffer from an inherent dereliction of duty, because the fruit of such labour is fraught with negativity.

• I am looking for those few remaining people who still enjoy making a plan, alleviating consumer anguish and saving money for the employer because it is the right thing to do, and creating good fellowship amongst colleagues instead of frivolous team 'stuff'. Where are those people? Have they been corrupted by 'the modern way' and have they succumbed to the notion that honesty is career limiting? I am looking for those few unique people who can anticipate, who possess a fundamental logistical inclination, who are sensitive to infrastructure and are circumspect enough to see things coming which will interfere with good process and progress. They are individuals who enter any space and immediately detect those things that are wrong. They actually lie awake early in the morning, thinking through the day, visualising potential situations and the obvious misconduct of those employed to execute instructions. They consistently think on behalf of others and are regularly unpopular because they express their views on what is wrong, and deploy interventive energy where bad things have to be fixed.

- The sad thing is that too many of these incredibly astute people have left the corporate fold in frustration, and have either prematurely retired (opted out) or are now self-employed so that they can exercise control over what is otherwise tolerated as mediocrity.

- But, as I complete this historical chronicle and investigation, I recognise my own residual racism and utterances based on false privilege.

Yes, while so much of devotion to duty, commitment, unstinting engagement and vocational pride was evident then, it was all founded on an ideology which was inherently immoral and terminal. White people succeeded in separating colour, race and gender, and designated group areas for living, recreation and social interaction. Whites constituted the superior grouping, and the rest of society was deemed not only inferior, but even insignificant. Every white was a *BAAS* (boss) by virtue of colour, and the rest were labourers and slaves. Yes, the majority were subservient to a self-appointed minority.

This ideology and colourisation as norm for stratification could not last. It merely served to ignite a groundswell of collective disenchantment and concomitant compounding anger. Even though liberation, democracy and equity have ensued, it would be naive to believe that the legacy of exploitation has disappeared. In fact, despite the invitational benefits of liberation, the oppressed still witness and remember the extent of deprivation and the compounding gap it created.

Today, these people are still at work seeking out a livelihood, pursuing a quality of life and striving toward education, training and development. Roles and status have changed, though, and reversals have been effected. Billionaires of colour are known, empowerment has been legislated and opportunities for equality affirmed. Normal sociology has assumed its authentic momentum with white squatter groups appearing and suburbia assuming a multi-coloured hue, regulated by taste, preference and affordability.

The new generation still go to work every day. They meet as colleagues at enterprise level, but now relate differently. There is a different work ethic now – one which is sensitive and tentative. It is often volatile as it engages in redress and constant restitution. Two decades later the abomination of apartheid is gone, but its residue is very evident and prominent in the hearts and minds of everyone.

So, the work ethic of 'the good old days' was founded on conservative values such as *moral* heritage, which saw the rise of the white bosses. These managers and entrepreneurs had come through depressions, droughts, world wars, and the legacy of the Anglo-Boer War. They had been injured and they also remembered. They subsequently enjoyed preferential treatment and opportunities as nepotism and cronyism favoured the *family*. Nothing has changed. Governments still do this because they are sanctioned by majority rule, they do it without relegating buddies or excluding anyone from the fold.

Where does this place modern human resource management (HRM), and particularly those individuals heading up the function? It places them right in the middle of an admixture of disciplines, with sociology and law assuming greater prominence and situational significance than psychology. In fact, applied behavioural science is the HR imperative now, as we seek to position an integrated, harmonious society at work.

Human resource management and leadership have moved beyond the mechanistic and systemic dimensions only. These are easy administrative tasks which can all be outsourced. They only constitute functional relevance and contain very little (if any) professional uniqueness. Procuring people, employing and deploying them, getting them skilled and competent, remunerated and fitting them into a structural design and system are all relatively easy activities, compared to cultivating a corporate soul and religion within which all people can be happy. The confluence of different peoples at the workplace poses the greatest challenge to modern HR managers. This is as much an ideological challenge as it is anthropologically complex and historically fractious.

Normalising the iniquities of the past and businesses built on false economics, while exploiting the working masses and benefitting a few, must happen in our lifetime. There is a groundswell of compounding disenchantment which will not only challenge continuing exploitation, but will actually very soon dismantle those persistent vestiges of a wrongful past. Most of us did not create these tantalising issues, nor do we even believe in them, but we did inherit both their beneficial residue and their challenges. They now constitute a cardinal part of the HR role. This is our currency and we are not (yet) good at it!

Unless we succeed in influencing the corporate conscience to feel and believe differently about universal fairness, subtle exploitation will prevail – because clearly, real fairness, equity and equality will remain unaffordable. As an example, the absurd and obscene wage gap between South African executives and their workers at lower levels is not only morally unsustainable, but is tantamount to a red flag, initiating industrial warfare.

HR managers must graduate to the normative domains of their function, and through honest introspection, engage in self-assessment for relevance and uniqueness (see Figure 7.1).

As South Africa calls for normatively driven HR leadership, so, too, the education and training of HR debutantes must align with realities, and existing HR executive development programmes must focus on aspects of personal and professional uniqueness, because we are the HR generation of redress, restitution and repair. It is all happening in our lifetime and remains an inescapable corporate and public call to us, the 'Remedial Generation'.

We have to repair something we did not cause, yet most of us benefitted from. What we inherited we must fix by taking cognisance of the origins and effect of historical iniquities, but without lingering there. We must move on. We must move forward, and not replicate the abominations of the past. Part of the challenge of moving forward positively, is recognising and respecting the psychology of disenchantment which now manifests so profoundly.

The emergent unhappiness (and even anger) amongst *marginalised* whites is becoming a serious issue, as bitterness and resurgent racism prove. While representivity and inclusivity are morally justifiable, their application and consequences present serious challenges to emotional stability at all levels, and an unprecedented encounter for HR managers. Retaining a knowledge, skills and competence base, while aligning the human resource profile with the *fairness* demands of the moment, is a difficult balancing act. While employment equity, broad-based black economic empowerment (BBBEE) and even race ratios may be met, the shareholders and investors fundamentally have one need only – a solid return on investment.

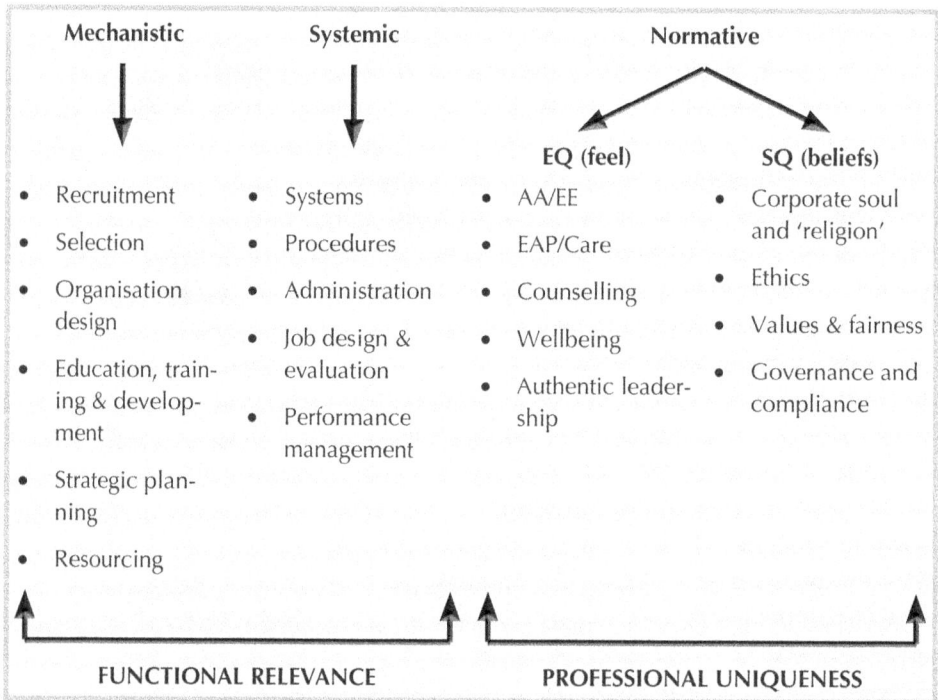

Mechanistic	Systemic	Normative	
		EQ (feel)	SQ (beliefs)
• Recruitment	• Systems	• AA/EE	• Corporate soul and 'religion'
• Selection	• Procedures	• EAP/Care	
• Organisation design	• Administration	• Counselling	• Ethics
• Education, training & development	• Job design & evaluation	• Wellbeing	• Values & fairness
	• Performance management	• Authentic leadership	• Governance and compliance
• Strategic planning			
• Resourcing			
FUNCTIONAL RELEVANCE		**PROFESSIONAL UNIQUENESS**	

Figure 7.1: Applied behavioural science as HRM

The current generation of HR practitioners will have to find the common ground of logic and pragmatism between our abominable past and our uncertain future. As the statutory prescripts insist on legally regularising the iniquities of the past by virtue of legislation emanating from the Department of Labour and the Department of Trade and Industries respectively, we are actually not able to normalise our volatile human resource situation. If we continue to confuse colour with competence through the statutory imposition of employment equity, affirmative action and BBBEE codes, then we are actually pandering to politics, not productivity. By continuing to do this, we are actually slavishly formulating another wrong, and two wrongs don't make a right: it actually makes things more wrong!

If we engage in sport with our eyes focused only on the scoreboard, then patently we are missing the game. Likewise, we dare not compromise the rudiments of practical economics, leadership and business practice by being politically correct, yet industrially and commercially defunct. Ours is the HR generation which has to find that common ground where morality and materialism connect harmoniously. For the moment, the passion and pain of South Africa are undeniably ruled by race, colour and gender.

The unique demographics of organisations now constitute their identity and their attractiveness, not the conventional principles of efficiency and profitability. The rate at which we are closing the wage gap, elevating females to top management and accelerating black wealth creation, are actually the priorities that matter. That is, if we are honest enough to admit it, and courageous enough to take a stand within the volatile organisational culture. What happened at Marikana is but a foretaste of things to come, if the human resource masses continue to experience a sense of exploitation and deprivation.

How do we authenticate HR leadership as we approach the third decade after the *normalisation* of South Africa in 1994? Let me not lecture on this subject, nor provide a list of universal philosophies. I would sooner turn my gaze inwards and end as I began, by admitting to myself, and publicly, personal challenges and specific competency acquirables:

- I must revisit, acknowledge and admit my own paradoxes and ambivalences and *sort them out*;

- I must acknowledge that two wrongs don't make a right. It creates more wrong. Therefore I must not allow negative trends and tendencies to take hold;

- I am the custodian of a better future. Therefore, I am a transient man and must assist people to relinquish *stuff* which is merely a burden, and help them *get on with it*;

- I have to *demote* myself from being an irrelevant HR executive to becoming a behavioural scientist who can influence and reshape the minds and hearts of other executives;

- Organisation renewal remains a great challenge. As HR practitioner I have to institute moral reform and inculcate a new order and era of thinking and feeling about people – our own people first. No, the customer is *not* king. Our *family* is supreme. Get that right;

- Short of instituting an organisational Truth and Reconciliation forum where people can purge personal and organisational toxicities, employees have to release the bondages which render them morally and emotionally incarcerated. Purge the pus! Liberate the real *you* and rehumanise the entire workplace.

Perhaps, in the fullness of time, a subsequent generation might remember and say: once upon a time, there was a humble HR practitioner who aspired to serve and service humanity ....

PART III: Dealing With the Challenges

CHAPTER 8: Talent Management Challenges in Emerging Markets*

Steve Bluen

Introduction

The projected growth of the BRICS (Brazil, Russia, India, China, and, latterly, South Africa) countries is impressive: Hewlett and Rashid (2011) predict that it will become the world's largest economy by the 2020s. It is not only the BRICS that have posted impressive economic growth.[1]

Other regions such as the Association of Southeast Asian Nations (ASEAN) and Africa have also grown tremendously over the last decade and indications are that they will continue in the future.

The ten countries of ASEAN represent a collective market of 620 million people, significantly larger than that of North America, Latin America and the Caribbean, the Eurozone, or the Middle East and North Africa. They are home to a young, large, and growing labour pool, as well as a growing and increasingly consumption-oriented middle class. The ASEAN countries posted a combined GDP of over $2.2 trillion in 2012 – larger than Russia's GDP and almost the same size as Brazil's – and many economists expect that number to double by 2020. ASEAN's five core countries – Indonesia, Malaysia, the Philippines, Singapore, and Thailand – have been growing as fast as any other regional grouping in the world over the past five years.[2]

As far as Africa is concerned, sub-Sahara's GDP growth averaged just over 5% since 2000 – even countries which are not rich in resources boomed. The region attracts private capital of about USD 50 billion a year.[3]

By 2050, whereas 97% of the 438 million people joining the global workforce will come from developing countries, the workforce in developed countries will have shrunk by 11 million, with emerging economies having grown by 1.7 billion.[4] Multinational companies (MNCs) have been expanding their presence, particularly into emerging markets.

These developments yield important talent implications. For example, in a 3-year period, IBM hired more than 90 000 people in Brazil, China and India.[5] Attracting, retaining, developing and deploying that amount of skilled and managerial talent over such a short period of time create exactly the kinds of challenges facing MNCs

---

* This chapter was originally published in Bluen, S. (2013). *Talent management in emerging markets*. Johannesburg: Knowres Publishing.

operating in emerging markets. Not least of these is the need to develop dynamic, world-class talent management approaches if they are to remain competitive. "While companies are facing significant talent management challenges in several regions of the world … the challenges are most acute … in the emerging markets such as the BRIC economies of Brazil, Russia, India, China and the economies of Central and Eastern Europe."[6]

The focus of this chapter is to describe the challenges inherent in managing talent in emerging markets and the responses MNCs have adopted to address those challenges. Before focusing on emerging markets, some of the dynamics of talent management per se are outlined. The situation becomes increasingly complex when managing talent globally, and the challenge becomes even greater when the MNC's global footprint extends to include emerging markets. To address these challenges, a framework for managing talent in emerging markets is proposed, and issues associated with each element of the model are discussed in turn. Finally, some learnings for managing talent in emerging markets are proposed.

Increasing Talent Management Complexity: from Local to Global to Emerging Markets

The challenge of managing talent in a single (domestic) business unit is exciting. An indication of the scope of single-country talent management challenges is presented in Table 8.1.

Table 8.1: Talent management challenges facing an organisation operating in a single country

Talent focus area	Key questions
Business strategy alignment	What is the five-year business plan, and how does it shape the talent strategy? Do we have a compelling talent management business case? Do we have the right talent mix and bench strength to achieve the business plan?
	Are our desired talent pools aligned to the business strategy?
Succession planning	What are the vacancy and labour turnover rates and the resultant positions needing to be filled?
	Is there suitable talent to fill the vacancies – either from within (internal cover and the multiple knock-on effects that such moves will create) or externally in the market?
	On average, how long do we take to fill each vacancy, especially those that are critical to the business's operations? How can we shorten this time to fill?

→

Talent focus area	Key questions
Succession planning (continued)	What does the talent mix look like? Do we have enough high-flyers to lead the company in the future?
	Who are the engine room and the negatively plateaued people, respectively? What engagement, advancement and development plans are to be made for each person within these categories?
Attraction and selection	What can we do to ensure that we recruit a disproportionate number of high-calibre talent into the organisation?
	Do we recruit people only to fill vacancies or does the company encourage recruiting people for potential, even if there is no vacant position for them to fill?
	Similarly, do we choose people who have skills required to fill current jobs or do we rather opt for talent with high potential when making selection decisions?
	How do we hone selection and promotion tools and skills to ensure culture fairness and enhance the predictive validity of talent decision making?
Retention and engagement	How do we engage each person individually (rather than adopting a generic engagement plan) so that they are motivated (a) to perform optimally over time, and (b) to remain engaged and committed to the business?
	Who are the restless people – the flight risks (the notoriously difficult task of predicting propensity to leave the business)? Can we accommodate their needs? Who require moves into other jobs? Who are likely to be promoted, and are they ready to take on the additional responsibility? What can be done to speed up this readiness?
Development	Is our career development approach mutually beneficial to employees and the company?
	Does the company have a learning and development plan in place to meet our current and future skills and leadership needs?
	Who needs to be trained, coached or mentored? What is the nature of those learnings and how do we reduce time-to-competence?

→

Talent focus area	Key questions
Development (continued)	Does everyone have an individual development plan agreed with their manager that is aligned to their competency and performance gaps, management/leadership capability needs and career paths?
	Do we deliberately move high-potential people across functions, regions or geographies as a form of accelerated development?
Managing performance	How do we ensure that the high-calibre people we have attracted, retained and developed perform optimally?
	Are the talent management and performance management approaches dovetailed and mutually supportive?
Reward and recognition	What, how, and at what market level, do we set competitive remuneration levels? What changes are needed to make the benefit structures competitive, yet affordable to the company?
Diversity	How do we maximise transformation to truly embrace diversity?
	How do we ensure that our diversity efforts go beyond headcount targets to transform the culture of the business?
Organisational culture	How do we create a total employment offering and market an employee value proposition that renders the business a true employer of choice – as perceived by existing employees and by aspirant employees in our target market?
	How can we turn this organisation into the most desirable place to work?
Talent information system	How do we run a talent management system that provides all users with real-time, consistent and accurate data upon which to make talent decisions?
Talent review and evaluation	Have we selected the appropriate talent key performance indicators (KPIs) that drive business performance?
	How do we optimise our talent KPIs?
	Does meeting talent KPI targets enhance business performance?

→

Talent focus area	Key questions
Line management's talent role	How do we enrol the chief executive officer (CEO), the Board and all line managers to fulfil their crucial roles in making talent management effective? How do we make them competent to fulfil these roles effectively?
The human resource (HR) function's role in talent management	How do we substantiate a budget to implement the answers to all these questions and develop an effective talent team to achieve the desired results? Does our talent strategy simultaneously meet business needs and conform to best practice?
Talent management's impact on business performance	Ultimately, are we doing all that we can to attract, retain and develop a disproportionate amount of high-calibre talent that will enable the business to achieve its strategic objectives and win in the marketplace?

Given the multiple moving parts, inevitable uncontrollable factors, and unpredictable changes, the dynamism inherent in talent management in a single business unit makes it an extremely exciting and challenging endeavour.

The situation becomes far more complex, though equally strategically important, when managing talent globally. Global talent management is crucially important for three reasons:[7] First, internationally competent business leaders represent a key component of global business success. Secondly, until recently, it has been extremely difficult to attract and retain suitable leaders to run international operations. Thirdly, given the complexities associated with international operations, talent management is more complex in global companies than in domestic firms. Indeed, the consequence of not deploying the right talent in the right places is a leading threat to MNCs. A quarter of the CEOs surveyed in the latest PricewaterhouseCoopers (PwC) CEO Survey[8] said they were unable to capitalise on market opportunities or had to cancel or delay strategic initiatives because of talent constraints, including: talent-related expenses rising more than expected; inability to innovate effectively or pursue market opportunities; cancelling or delaying key strategic initiatives; inability to achieve growth forecasts in overseas markets; and falling production and service-delivery quality standards. Thus, global talent management is a major strategic priority for CEOs. It is not surprising, therefore, that CEOs rated developing talent pipelines (and meeting with customers) as their most important priorities.[9] The reason for talent being so important is that the talent shortage is global and not local. There are no hidden pools of talent that companies can access to solve the problem. The full extent of the strategic importance of global talent management has been articulated by several leading academics in the global talent field.[10] These are summarised in Table 8.2 below.

Table 8.2: why global talent management is an increasingly important strategic issue for multinational corporations[11]

Trend	Implication
The critical importance of global talent management is recognised	The success of MNCs is closely linked to how well they identify, manage and adapt to the many global talent challenges they face. To achieve this, they need to understand the environmental forces shaping talent management.
Competition for talent is now global	Competition for talent has moved from country to regional and global levels: talent resides throughout MNCs' global operations. This requires a global talent management focus if MNCs are to remain competitive. This is becoming increasingly difficult, as MNCs compete in the same, limited talent pools where demand greatly outweighs supply. Consequently, MNCs have to become more attractive and develop compelling employee value propositions to attract and retain talent.
Global talent management is becoming more pervasive	With the rapid growth of both MNCs and the internationalisation of small and medium-sized businesses, global talent management appears increasingly on the strategic agendas of smaller organisations – not just the MNCs.
Knowledge-based economies require more highly skilled talent to fulfil more complex roles	The shift from product-based to knowledge-based economies and the dominance of the service sector have shifted the talent challenge to high-value people with higher cognitive abilities, which are typically in short supply. Furthermore, regarding global talent, cross-cultural competencies are required to perform effectively, yet they are relatively scarce.
The critical importance of MNC leaders is recognised	The success of MNCs in increasingly competitive environments depends heavily on the quality of their globally competent leaders.
The shortage of suitable international managers is a key constraint on MNC performance	The talent demand–supply gap is growing. The lack of suitable global managers has become a significant constraint on companies' abilities to implement global strategies. In particular, a shortage of leadership talent has been identified as a major obstacle MNCs face when attempting to operate globally.

$\longrightarrow$

Trend	Implication
Increased cultural and geographical talent mobility	Increased globalisation, lower emigration barriers, and immigration and intercountry disparities in real wage rates have led to greater international talent mobility. This is most apparent amongst professionals and highly skilled workers, giving rise to brain drains in many countries.
Emergence of the truly global elite	Increasingly, people with special talents have no allegiance to country or region and happily cross geographic and cultural boundaries. Owing to their global connections and world-views, they relate better to people with similar skills than to people with the same national or ethnic origins. It requires a different talent management approach to attract and retain them.
Downsizing, due to the global recession, affects trust	Globally mobile talent is increasingly trading security for flexibility, becoming less dependent on a single employer. Lowered trust levels mean that the psychological contract of trading loyalty for job security is being replaced: global employees are increasingly free agents who come and go as they wish and are responsible for their own employability, learning and career development.
Retaining global talent is key	Talent raiding has emerged as an aggressive attempt by some companies to hire employees from competitors. Retention of top-level global talent is a key challenge, particularly when embarking on mergers and acquisitions or joint ventures.
Reverse migration has increased	In an attempt to reverse the brain drain, countries are encouraging returnee immigrants, who have very marketable international experience and networks, to come home. This represents a valuable talent pool from which companies can recruit.
However, repatriation is a major cause of labour turnover	Repatriation is a major cause of labour turnover and needs to be addressed, given the valuable experience expatriates possess. Global assignments themselves are used as a means of attracting, retaining and developing talent.
Demographics influence global talent management	Demographic factors that will influence talent availability and recruitment approaches in future include the following:

Trend	Implication
Demographics influence global talent management (continued)	• Declining birth rates and longevity are reshaping age distributions. In certain developed countries, by 2025, the number of people aged 15 to 64 is expected to fall by 7% (Germany), 9% (Italy) and 14% (Japan). Thus the workforce rate is declining in the developed world. At the same time, the populations in emerging markets are increasing and getting younger. • Companies are required to manage two generations (Generation X and Y) of employees with differing needs. • The baby-boomers are ageing and approaching retirement. • With China's one-child policy, gender imbalances (more men than women) are apparent in the Chinese workforce.
Managing diversity is becoming increasingly important	As talent pools globalise, the levels of gender, ethnic, cultural and generational diversity increase, requiring MNCs to manage diversity effectively if they are to succeed.
HR is fulfilling an increasingly important role in MNCs	There is an increased recognition of the role HR fulfils in the success of MNCs. Given the intensification of global competition, HR's role in planning and forecasting talent needs across the firm's multiple locations, ensuring a ready supply of globally competent leaders to run MNCs and facilitating international learning and innovation, is acknowledged.

Leisy and Pyron (2009) highlight the global talent challenges involved when they observe that, to compete globally, MNCs need to adopt certain meta talent management processes, including the following:

• Effectively manage a dynamic and diverse workforce that is dispersed throughout the world,

• Comply with a maze of ever-changing tax, immigration and other laws and regulations,

• Maintain accurate and responsive HR data reporting,

- Address significant business and talent management differences between mature versus emerging markets,

- Deal with rising global labor costs in the face of a diminishing supply of skilled and semiskilled labor in emerging markets,

- Ensure that talent management programs are integrated and consistently applied to allow employees worldwide to be fully utilized, develop their careers and feel a part of one organization,

- Identify, develop and retain future business leaders around the globe,

- Maximize consistency, where appropriate, of worldwide HR policies and employee benefit programs.[12]

The challenges of global talent management are indeed daunting and more complex than those confronting talent managers operating in one (familiar) country. The task at hand becomes even more complicated when managing talent in emerging markets. In addition to the talent challenges discussed thus far, managing talent in emerging markets has unique challenges that need to be addressed. These can be narrowed down to five dynamics:

1. **Sourcing talent in emerging markets: from cheap labour to skilled and managerial talent pools.** Emerging markets have traditionally been viewed as a source of cheap labour. Given the global shortage of skills, emerging markets are being regarded as sources of skilled, professional and managerial talent, which adds to the complexity of the challenge.[13]

2. **Rapid development has absorbed skilled talent in emerging markets.** At the same time, developing countries, such as BRICS (Brazil, Russia, India, China and, to a lesser extent, South Africa), have grown so fast that there are insufficient skilled people to fill all the burgeoning positions opening up, especially in skilled and leadership roles. In fact, emerging-market MNCs are sourcing talent in developed countries. As Ren Jianxin, President of China National Chemical Corporation (ChemChina), observed: "Twenty-five years ago, ChemChina was spun off from China National Bluestar with a staff of just seven. Now we employ 160,000 people. We employ many people from Western countries, including at the management level. ... we work with leading human resource consultancies to recruit more Western professionals."[14]

3. **Divergent education levels reduce the number of graduates suited to work in MNCs.** The skills shortage is exacerbated because of the education-technology lag. Also, although tertiary institutions have mushroomed in emerging countries, they do not produce enough of the right calibre of graduates to fill skilled and leadership positions in MNCs.[15]

4. **Problems with employing expatriates in emerging markets.** MNCs have addressed the talent gap by recruiting expatriates to fill senior roles in emerging countries. This, in turn, creates its own challenges. Factors such as political instability, corruption, high crime rates, poor governmental or societal infrastructures, hostile commercial and labour laws, and 'foreign' cultures, customs and practices reduce the attractiveness of emerging-market countries as expatriate destinations.[16] In the 2011 Brookfield GRS Global Relocation Trends Survey, the four countries rated as the most difficult for international assignees were: 1st China, 2nd India, 3rd Russia and 4th Brazil.[17] Furthermore, expatriate cost to company is extremely high – estimated to be between three and four times the person's home salary.[18] Expatriate failure rates are also high (between 10 and 80%), and MNCs are poor at repatriating them post-assignment.[19] Pattie, White and Tansky (2010) report that 27% of repatriates leave their MNC in the first year of returning home, and a further 25% leave the following year. To overcome these problems, MNCs have adopted alternate forms of employment arrangements to meet their talent requirements (eg short-term assignments, commuter assignments, international business travel, and virtual assignments).[20]

5. **Challenges associated with hiring local talent in emerging markets.** MNCs are hiring increasing numbers of high-potential local talent to fill senior positions.[21] Hiring local talent creates its own challenges: to supplement education and competence gaps, MNCs offer extensive training, education and corporate university programmes.[22] Because suitably trained local employees with the MNC-relevant skills are in such short supply, they command excessively high salaries, further increasing the costs of doing business in emerging countries.[23] Also, local professionals and executives working in MNCs are highly marketable and therefore easily poached by other MNCs, exacerbating the vicious cycle of salary escalation. A 2010 survey of 2 200 Chinese managers found that, over 18 months, two-thirds had received a compelling job offer and 46% had moved jobs with increases in pay of greater than 30%.[24]

Not only are the talent management challenges different in emerging markets, but fit-for-purpose solutions are also required. Ready, Hill and Conger (2008) identified the following four factors that differentiate successful from the less successful MNCs operating in emerging markets:

1. *Brand*: Employees in emerging countries are beginning to think beyond making a living to making a future. A company with a desirable brand implies personal advancement and the chance of global mobility.

2. *Opportunity*: Besides the regular connotations of opportunity (such as challenging work, development, competitive pay, and challenging assignments), opportunity in the developing world implies accelerated career tracks to senior

positions, ensuring that their skills and experience develop in line with the rapid rate of growth in their markets.

3. *Purpose:* Local employees value companies with a game-changing business model – where they can be part of redefining their nation and even the world economy. Given that many have experienced poverty first-hand, they also value MNCs that focus on helping the less fortunate.

4. *Culture*: Four aspects of culture are important to local employees: an authentic brand promise; reward and advancement based on merit – that they were born in the developing world should not limit their global opportunities; receiving individual recognition and being part of a team; and a talent-centric culture.

To help structure the myriad of issues involved, a model of talent management in emerging markets is presented (see Figure 8.1), and the challenges and responses associated with each element of the model are discussed. While the components of talent management models are similar across developed and emerging markets, distinctive contextual factors, evident in emerging markets, pose unique challenges for MNCs that require creative responses. These challenges and responses form the content of this chapter.

A Framework for Managing Talent in Emerging Markets

With the exception of three components of the model, namely **localisation**, **expatriates** and **local employees**, the talent management model presented in Figure 8.1 could be applied in most settings. However, it is the distinctive contextual factors evident in emerging markets that pose unique challenges for MNCs and that require creative responses.

For a talent management strategy to be effective, it must cater specifically for the talent needs emanating from the broader business strategy. Similarly, the success of the talent strategy is measured by the extent to which the business has the right talent to meet its strategic business plans across its global footprint. The links between the business and talent imperatives are reflected in the model, where the business strategy informs and shapes the talent strategy and the output of the talent strategy impacts business performance. This firmly locates the talent strategy within the broader business context.

The talent strategy is divided into three components, namely the core talent management value chain, underpinning processes, and key role players. The core talent management value chain comprises those sequential elements traditionally associated with the talent management process, namely succession planning, attracting, selecting and on-boarding, engaging and retaining, developing, managing performance, and rewarding and recognising talent. Underpinning the core talent management value chain are several processes, including diversity and localisation, organisational culture, talent reviews and evaluations, and talent information systems. These processes support the talent management value chain.

While the HR function is the custodian of talent management, there are several other key role players in any emerging-market talent management approach, namely business leaders, especially those heading up MNCs in the host developing countries, expatriates and local employees operating in those countries. Set out below are some of the challenges associated with each component of the model and how they can be addressed.

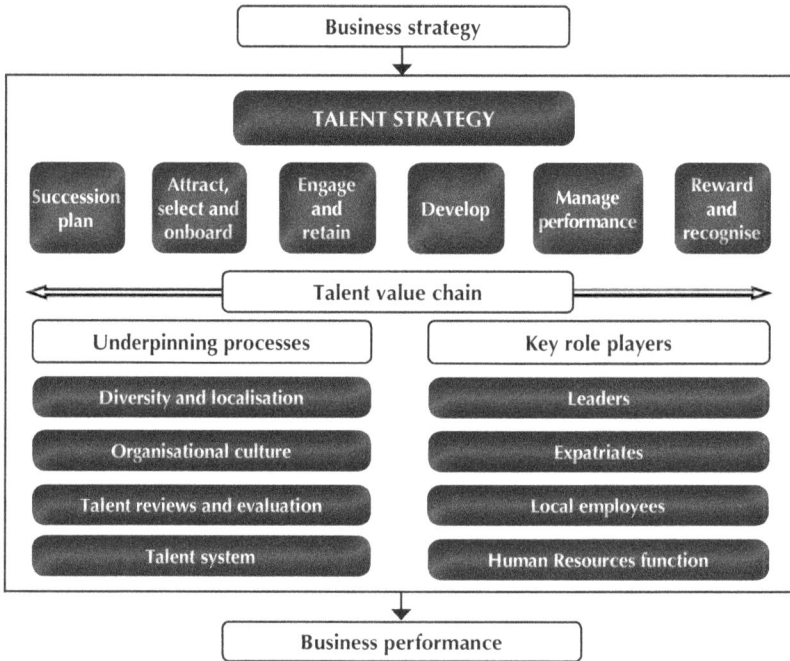

Figure 8.1: talent management in emerging markets

Linking the Talent Strategy to the Business Strategy

Challenges. The first, and arguably the most important, rule is that the sole purpose of the talent strategy is to support the business strategy by providing the right quantity and quality of people to implement the business strategies effectively across the global footprint, thereby maximising the MNC's competitive advantage. In their survey of 340 global leaders, Ernst and Young (2010) found that companies whose talent management programmes were aligned with their business strategies delivered a return on investment that was, on average, 20% higher over a 5-year period than companies without such alignment. While talent management should embrace functional excellence and conform to best practice, it has no purpose outside of attracting, retaining and developing people in line with business needs.

> HR Professionals need to know the strategic needs and directions of the firm and the important characteristics of the firm in order to craft a talent strategy, i.e., a strategy that identifies the important global talent challenges and identifies the global talent management initiatives that will effectively manage them.[25]

So, the first challenge is to shape the talent strategy in line with business needs and create a compelling business case for talent management. Once the business case has been accepted, the resources necessary to implement a talent strategy can be substantiated and implemented. A clear financial commitment to implementing the talent strategy is important, since the strategy can be costly and time-consuming, especially if it entails recruiting for potential, regardless of available vacancies. Also, during economic downturns, talent-related expenses, such as training, recruiting and, ultimately, retrenchments, are prime cost-cutting targets.[26] Armed with a sound business case, short-term cost-cutting measures might be avoided when the broader, longer-term business implications are considered.

Solutions. Talent pools represent a significant connection point between the business strategy and the talent strategy.[27] Strategically appropriate talent pools are shaped by asking questions such as, "Are our investments aimed at the talent areas that are most critical to the strategic success of the organization?"[28] Once the talent pool has been defined to meet organisational success, the talent strategy to attract, retain, and develop people to fill that talent pool will be aligned with the corporate strategy.

The shortage of suitable and available talent to fill senior positions in emerging markets is well documented.[29] Also, the success of MNCs in competitive environments depends heavily on the quality of their globally competent leaders.[30] Facts such as these represent a strong motivation for a compelling talent business case. Simply stated, without attracting, retaining, developing, deploying and motivating the right number and calibre of people, MNCs will not meet their global aspirations.

South African Breweries (SAB) provides a good example of linking the talent strategy closely to the business plan. In the early 1990s, when SAB started globalising, a component of the business model was to acquire businesses, initially in developing countries, and to send in hand-picked expatriates to run the acquired operation. To do so, the South African operation had to provide talent to fill global positions while continuing to perform optimally, that is, it had to have sufficient bench strength to meet local and international demands. The size of this challenge was impressive: some 200 executives – 40% of the senior management ranks – were expatriated over a 10-year period. To become an effective talent nursery, a strong talent business case was articulated and implemented.[31]

Emerging-market Talent Strategy: Core Value Chain

Having outlined the importance of linking the talent strategy to the business strategy, the focus turns to the talent strategy itself. In this section, emerging-market talent challenges and solutions pertaining to each of the elements of the talent core value chain are discussed.

(i) Succession Planning

Succession planning in a single business entity is difficult enough, given the number of 'moving parts' involved. The process becomes that much more complex when operating in multiple sites across the world, and, particularly, when some of those operations are located in emerging markets. This succession planning section is divided into internal and external components.

(a) Internal Environment

Challenges. A key planning feature is to achieve the right balance and calibre of people assigned globally across the MNC, especially when faced with a scarcity of talent. There needs to be a match between the strategic importance of the role in question and the candidate being sent to fill the position. This matching needs to be evaluated in relation to all other similar roles and people across the MNC, culminating in the right people being placed in the right jobs across the company and avoiding 'robbing Peter to pay Paul' scenarios. Also, the MNC must include all relevant host-country local employees when making succession plans, rather than focusing solely on home-country talent, which can create an unacceptable, two-tier talent system, deprive local talent of deserving career opportunities, and prevent the MNC from accessing a valuable source of high-potential talent.

To implement a global succession planning system, the MNC needs to calibrate all relevant jobs in terms of size, complexity and strategic importance, and all people within the global talent pool in terms of their experience, capability, potential to take on increasingly complex offshore roles, and emotional and cultural intelligence to operate effectively in emerging markets. This is a huge task if it is to be done accurately. Also, because of the problems associated with employing expatriates, the number of expatriates deployed needs to be kept to a minimum.

Solutions. The traditional approach of succession planning, which assumes stable environments and long-term career plans, is too linear to address the volatile and unpredictable nature of global talent management.[32] Instead, MNCs are increasingly using talent pools, comprising "high-potential and high-performing incumbents that the organisation can draw on to fill pivotal positions."[33] Central to the talent pool approach is selecting for talent (rather than only recruiting to fill vacancies), and placing people where and when the need arises.[34] This also presupposes people within the talent pool are sufficiently flexible to take on varied roles in diverse locations and still thrive. Another issue is who owns the global talent pool?

Traditionally, in decentralised operations, business unit leaders control their talent. This has deleterious consequences for talent management, because local leaders resist 'losing' their high-potential employees. However, given the strategic importance of deploying the best possible talent to take on key global assignments, increasingly MNCs are adopting a centralised approach to talent pool ownership. The solution is to define clearly which positions fall within the global talent pool and agree on guidelines by which people within the pool are attracted, developed, retained and deployed.

(b) *External Environment*

Challenges. The war for talent has morphed over recent years: talent within the developing world must be taken into consideration when conducting succession planning.[35] With emerging countries clearly representing the growth engine of the world, the demand for top talent has never been greater. The problem has been aggravated because of years of 'corporate imperialism' which ignored the option of fostering local talent and failed to develop local talent pipelines. Now the MNCs have limited local resources to recruit.[36]

Despite recent increased unemployment, a scarcity of high-level knowledge talent exists in emerging markets, and the demand and competition for such talent remains high.[37] McKinsey's (2005) study on China's looming talent shortages predicted that Chinese companies wanting to globalise would need 75 000 leaders who could work in global settings in the next 10 to 15 years, yet the current supply of such leaders is only 3 000 to 5 000. The serious shortage of Chinese professionals and managers is caused mainly by problematic training and education facilities.[38] Although higher education, which was seriously disrupted during the Cultural Revolution (1966-1976), has subsequently mushroomed, it still cannot keep pace with China's rapid economic development.

A curious factor exacerbating talent shortages is spatial immobility of labour. Many African countries would rather hire overseas expatriates than recruit from other African countries, even if they pay up to a 500% premium instead of recruiting comparable and competent Africans.[39]

One of the key challenges is the quality of education in most emerging countries. According to Accenture (2011), there are 33 million university-educated young professionals in the developing world as opposed to only 14 million in the developed world. South Korea produces as many engineering graduates as the United States, despite having one-sixth of the population. China produces more graduates annually than the United States of America, Japan and France combined. But only a small percentage of developing-world graduates are suitable for working in MNCs. For example, India produces 300 000 information technology (IT) engineering graduates annually, and the United States only 50 000. However, in the United States and India combined, only about 35 000 graduates are suitable for employment in the target jobs.

Failure to produce suitable emerging-market graduates to meet MNC needs causes skills shortages.[40] McKinsey (2005) found that less than 10% of Chinese candidates were sufficiently qualified to fill professional positions (eg engineers, accountants, medical staff), reflecting a major problem in the Chinese education system: an overemphasis of theory at the expense of practical application, independent and critical thinking, and teamwork. HR professionals in emerging markets such as China, Hungary, India and Malaysia report huge variations in the skill and suitability levels of their graduates. Poor English skills, dubious qualifications and cultural issues (eg a lack of teamwork experience, and a reluctance to take the initiative or assume leadership roles) were frequently mentioned problems.[41] Similarly, HR professionals said they would consider hiring only 10 to 25% of India's roughly 14 million university graduates, because the majority lacked the necessary training, language skills and cultural awareness to work for MNCs.[42] Also, African and South American companies were falling behind in developing new technology skills that allowed for participation in the global economy.[43]

Solutions. Emerging-market MNCs that cannot find sufficient local talent are recruiting globally. For example, the recruitment programme of Alghanim Industries, a Kuwaiti-based conglomerate, targets hiring people familiar with the corporate world and comfortable with working in a diverse workforce comprising 49 different nationalities.[44] The booming market of international search firms is further evidence of the trend that MNCs are increasingly engaging in truly global talent searches to recruit top-level leaders.[45]

A neglected source of talent is women. Women are an obvious solution to the dire shortage of top talent in emerging markets.

> Educated women represent the vanguard of talent management. Just as developing markets can bolster a company's bottom line, the lessons learnt in attracting, sustaining and retaining the best and brightest women in those markets can enhance and strengthen an organization's operations worldwide.[46]

(ii) Attraction, Selection and On-boarding

Challenges. Top talent is often not prepared to move to emerging-market locations.[47] Because high-potential employees are in demand, they can choose their assignments and avoid high-risk locations.[48] Different emerging markets pose different risks. For example, political instability has detracted from successful talent management in the Middle East, causing increased employee anxiety, distraction and negative talent flows. This is best illustrated by the instability prevalent in Iraq since 1980, causing mass migration of Iraqi talent to other countries, greatly depleting the Iraqi economy. A survey of 587 Middle East CEOs found that the CEOs perceived domestic political instability and global terrorism as the most serious threats to the business environment and to regional growth.[49]

A selection challenge in emerging markets concerns nepotism in candidate selection.[50] For example, *Waiko-ni-Wako* (a tendency to hire relatives and people from one's own tribe or province) is rife in Zambia, while, in certain cases, getting hired in the Ivory Coast depends more on who you know than what you know. Managers feel morally obliged to help community members who are less fortunate than themselves. The 'as-man-know-man' practice in Nigeria relies on networks to influence selection decisions.[51]

A key selection consideration is '**horses for courses**'. People who perform well in their home countries do not necessarily excel in developing countries, and vice versa. As Douglas Oberhelman, Chairman and CEO, Caterpillar Inc., says:

> Chinese leadership and needs are so different to those in India, Brazil, Canada and Belgium. Talent has to be regionally directed, and that's what we're working on. Frankly, it's a bigger challenge, because as we're new to some of these places and our growth is strong, we're having trouble teaching what we want our leaders to do and know.[52]

Besides the normal technical and managerial competencies associated with the job, expatriate competencies required in developing countries typically include high levels of resilience, resourcefulness, independence, cultural fluency and sensitivity, political astuteness and statesmanship, being able to interact authentically with people at every stratum of society, and embracing diversity. In addition, given the nature of an expatriate assignment, especially when the destination is in a country that is very different from the home country, the selection choice extends beyond the incumbent to considering the suitability of the partner and family.

Another challenge concerns on-boarding expatriates. A third of new hires leave a firm within their first two years.[53] However, a well-structured on-boarding programme can reduce turnover, increase productivity, and increase a company's attractiveness to potential employees. On-boarding addresses four needs, namely organisational culture mastery, emerging interpersonal networks, early career support, and strategy immersion and direction.[54] Given the differences in all facets of life confronting expatriates in developing countries, the need for familiarisation with both the company and the country is a key requirement for successful adjustment of expatriate families. Similarly, local employees joining a foreign MNC need on-boarding to understand the culture, customs and practices of the company in order to perform effectively.

Solutions. Market mapping, which entails benchmarking talent within a given market outside of one's own company, is a useful means of identifying talent in a host country. It has been used successfully to identify appropriate senior-level skills in new markets or where MNCs are setting up operations in new countries and do not want to alert their competitors to their intentions.[55]

To address home-country employees' reluctance to accept emerging-market assignments, an emerging trend in global companies is for the CEO and executive team to 'own' the top talent pool.[56] Top talent pool members receive increased exposure and development and are groomed to take on increasingly senior leadership roles. In return, they are expected to accept assignments in diverse environments. Successful performance in emerging-market roles serves as a stepping stone to advancement in the group. By centralising the top talent pool, companies are able to deploy resources appropriately and fairly across all their global operations, including the traditionally least popular ones, and thereby optimise person–job fit wherever they operate.

Regarding unacceptable labour practices such as nepotism, the MNC needs to ensure that the relevant HR policies and practices are adhered to in host countries. This should eliminate unacceptable practices and ensure that the MNC gains and sustains a global competitive advantage.[57]

As regards on-boarding expatriates, certain companies specifically focus on assisting people embarking on an expatriate assignment into emerging markets. They offer immersion programmes into all aspects of host-country life, including culture, history, geography, politics, eating patterns, and general customs and practices. This greatly helps with expatriate family adjustment to their new environments.

(iii) Engagement and Retention

Challenges. Exacerbating the skills shortage problem, emerging markets are particularly susceptible to losing talent to developed markets. For example, over 75% of graduates in high-tech-related subjects from China's top two universities, Tsinghua University and Beijing University, have gone to the United States since 1985 – a trend that is replicated at other leading Chinese universities.[58] In India, IT and business process outsourcing sectors recorded a 30 to 45% labour turnover even during the 2008 to 2009 economic downturn – businesses need IT professionals to provide software and systems solutions to replace laid-off workers.[59] Nigeria lost 10 694 tertiary-institution academics between 1986 and 1990; in 2007, approximately 36% of tertiary-educated Nigerians emigrated; and, in 2000, 20% of tertiary-educated Ugandans emigrated. The brain drain was also evident in Gambia (65%), Somalia (59%), Eritrea (46%), Mozambique (42%) and Sierra Leone (41%).[60] The continental brain drain from Africa was caused by attractive, developed-market offers for African high-potential employees, as well as political and socioeconomic factors. As local conditions worsened due to military rule or civil war, many educated Africans sought refuge abroad.[61]

Poaching is another retention challenge. Schuler et al. (2011) explain one of the causes of poaching in some developing countries: many MNCs have been expanding and relocating to developing countries. For example, in 6 years, Accenture's Indian staff complement increased from 250 to 35 000. By 2008, as a consequence of MNCs moving rapidly to India, its skilled labour supply was almost totally employed. Now MNCs moving to India need to attract workers away from their existing employers.[62] Because there is such a demand for high-level talent, the short-term solution of poaching senior managers with lucrative pay offers is rife in emerging markets. Bohara (2007:31) offers an alternate explanation for high labour turnover rates in India:

> ... for decades, multinationals have hired Indian nationals to run the business 'in country' with no expectation that these managers' own aspirations and skills might take them from a local leadership role to a position of power in the home office. Now in India, talent repays this treatment by moving from company to company and making no promises for long-term commitment.

Once again, this highlights the need for global talent management to incorporate high-potential, host-country talent into the MNC's international succession plans.

Remuneration is the main reason for labour turnover in China.[63] Other reasons include career advancement, unhappy relationships with management, poor culture fit, and seeking better benefits, training and personal development. Similarly, labour turnover is increasing in the Middle East, caused by factors such as diversification of the economy, leading to increased job opportunities, workforce mobility, and a shortage of skilled labour because expatriates are moving elsewhere.[64] Retention of skilled labour has become the most critical talent issue facing MNCs in the region.

Solutions. Greater engagement leads to greater performance and retention.[65] However, in a survey of over 11 000 workers worldwide, only 31% were engaged and only 61% said they planned to remain with their organisations.[66] Regarding scarce skills, because it is a sellers' market, global companies are making longer-term talent investments with increased financial incentives to attract and retain top talent.[67] Profit-sharing and stock option schemes are an effective means of retaining professional and managerial staff in China, suggesting that the new materialism has overtaken traditional cultural forces promoting egalitarianism and altruism.[68] MNCs operating in China, such as Citigroup, GE and HSBC, compete fiercely with local Chinese businesses for talent. They have tailored their employment value propositions, emphasising opportunities for real decision making, career development, housing, and education and learning. A survey of 113 Russian companies revealed that companies with formalised employer brands reported lower labour turnover rates and invested more in learning and development than companies with no employer brand.[69] Thus, crafting a formal employer brand/employment value proposition helps reduce labour turnover in developing countries. Factors typically associated with retention in the developed world (ie intrinsic and extrinsic rewards, managerial support, professional development practices, and performance management practices) increased satisfaction with, and pride in, the organisation, which, in turn, were inversely associated with propensity to leave the organisation.[70]

One way of retaining emerging-market, high-potential employees is to offer them aspirational jobs with attractive rewards and opportunities for advancement that most local employers overlook. In emerging markets, the war for talent is so fierce that the temptation to overpromise and underdeliver must be avoided.[71] Instead, companies that succeed in retaining talent ensure that they meet their promises. "[M]any of the people we interviewed were seeking a culture that would support the promise of an accelerated career path with growth opportunities for everyone, a commitment to meritocracy, and custom career planning."[72]

(iv) Development

Challenges. A study of 260 MNCs revealed that most MNCs adopted haphazard or ad hoc approaches to succession planning and development.[73] It concluded that MNCs have a long way to go before they fully embrace the need to strategically manage key employees. At least two specific development challenges face MNCs operating in emerging markets. First, expatriates need to develop the competencies necessary to operate effectively in host countries. Secondly, local employees need to develop technical and managerial skills to perform effectively in MNCs.

Although there is a burgeoning tertiary-education industry across the developing world, many tertiary qualifications are not suited to the needs of MNCs.[74] Poaching exacerbates an MNC's appetite to train local people. Chinese organisations are wary of investing in development for fear of losing trained staff. This results in underresourced training efforts, which detract from the availability of suitably competent local talent.[75]

Career development poses unique challenges for MNCs in emerging markets. Compared with employees remaining in their home countries, expatriate career paths are less clear and potentially produce higher levels of insecurity, especially if there are no post-assignment job-placement guarantees. Also, being far away from home base, expatriates may develop a sense of alienation from the company. For local employees, career development is equally important. High-potential employees want to know that they have a future with the company beyond local borders and that they will not be disadvantaged in their career progression because they come from a developing country.[76]

Solutions. One way of preparing managers for overseas assignments is to send them to business schools located in host countries before they commence the assignment, to familiarise them with the local markets. Some Chinese MNCs are sending their top managers to executive development programmes offered by their companies or business schools to give them a broader, global understanding beyond their company-specific knowledge and experience.[77] Chinese employees are also sent abroad to widen their knowledge and to understand the global business better. Some Western companies operating in China (eg P&G and Motorola) have created management development programmes to grow Chinese talent (Cooke 2011). Microsoft offers development programmes (such as rotation to the United States) and recognition programmes such as being selected as a 'Silk Road Scholar'[78], which appeal to Chinese employees.[79]

Action learning has emerged as a popular form of leadership development to familiarise leaders with business practices in emerging markets.[80] Business schools, such as the Gordon Institute of Business Science, have shifted the focus of general manager development to cater specifically for operating in emerging markets. As such, these programmes cultivate managerial competencies specifically for managing in emerging markets.

Regarding the development of local talent, learning and development opportunities are important talent attractors for local employees keen to climb the corporate ladder. MNCs are attractive to Chinese employees who have strong career aspirations and are seeking development opportunities.[81] Huawei, which has a strong learning and development focus, established the Huawei University in 2005, offering tailored training to employees and customers. New employees receive up to six months' induction training there. Mentoring is used to develop junior professionals. Selected overseas employees are sent to Huawei headquarters to understand its strategies, processes and culture, and disseminate these upon returning home – a further example of leadership development for local talent.[82]

Standard Chartered Bank China developed a 'raw talent superhighway' programme comprising six components. It represents a good example of developing local talent:[83]

1. *Selection*: Once specific skills required are identified, Standard Chartered Bank investigates nonbanking industries with similar expertise and aggressively recruits employees from those industries by offering greater opportunities for career advancement.

2. *Induction and orientation*: Standard Chartered Bank offers intensive induction for new hires to acculturate them and explain the importance of company values and ethics, central in the financial service industry.

3. *Technical training*: The bank includes a five-day 'boot camp' that delegates have to pass before being exposed to the bank's customers.

4. *Professional and management development*: New recruits undergo intensive training in English-language skills, communication and listening skills, and business etiquette. They receive career guidance and are exposed to networking sessions to understand the bank's different career paths. The bank also offers an Asian best-practice management development programme and an extensive suite of e-learning programmes to ensure learning and development are

accessible to all. Standard Chartered Bank has also established partnerships with Chinese universities to enhance recruitment and to offer employees ongoing professional development.

5. *Stretch assignments and deployment*: Standard Chartered Bank's talent motto of 'Go places…' tells employees that, if they do well, their careers will progress rapidly. It also emphasises that the bank is a global company with international opportunities. Chinese high-potential employees are often moved globally, including to the company headquarters in London.

6. *Personal development and performance management*: The bank's culture is both nurturing and performance-driven. High performance standards are consistently maintained. Katherine Tsang, CEO of Standard Chartered Bank China, says, "We deal with problems openly and honestly, and that has led to the creation of an authentic and trust-based culture."[84]

Standard Chartered Bank's holistic approach to talent attraction, retention and development has created many positive consequences, one of which was to reduce attrition by 3% in a year.

Latin American beverage company, FEMSA, has adopted an innovative development-multiplier plan. FEMSA's José Antonio Fernández Carbajal says, "We train people by moving those with useful skill sets to train clusters of employees, who in turn train other clusters. Knowledge is disseminated firsthand and spreads fast."[85]

An effective approach to expatriate career development is to appoint a home-executive sponsor for each expatriate, who contacts the expatriate regularly. Once a year, they have a formal career discussion, which forms part of the MNC's career development process. Also, by including expatriates in ongoing key events (eg conferences, leadership forums), the MNC ensures that expatriates remain in touch with the organisational culture and feel part of the larger company. Lenovo, which acquired IBM's personal-computer operations and is strongly rooted in China is a good example of how to approach career development in emerging economies.[86] CEO Bill Amelio describes the company as 'a stage without a ceiling for every employee – worldwide'.[87] Lenovo provides methodical development for its employees, in line with their career aspirations: career maps are created for every member of the high-potential talent pool. Competence gaps are identified and steps are taken to close those gaps. Central to Lenovo's talent-tracking process is that the career maps are linked to key positions across the globe and accountability for the entire process rests with Line Management and not HR.

(v) Managing Performance

Challenges. Managing performance is particularly susceptible to cultural interpretation and cross-country differences in custom and practice. Consequently, MNCs need to take care not simply to export their home-developed performance management approaches to host countries. For example, when SAB entered Tanzania, it exported its customer-focused goals approach to performance management. This approach experienced initial problems, despite being extremely successful in South Africa. Only once the programme was adapted to meet local needs and the logic in the broader company context was carefully explained did performance management gain traction in Tanzania. In China, performance appraisals display the most enduring influence of Chinese culture, which respects seniority and hierarchy, and values social harmony.[88] Chinese performance appraisal systems are reward-driven, focusing retrospectively on the person's performance. Conversely, Western appraisal systems adopt a developmental approach, focusing prospectively on individual performance and organisational goals. The challenge is to create a blend of the two approaches that achieves the desired performance results whilst maximising employee engagement.

Solutions. If performance management is to be effective in emerging markets, first, it needs to be adapted to local circumstances, and, secondly, it needs a strategic focus. The goals set must be linked to corporate objectives. It also needs to adopt a developmental approach by evaluating employees against their current job competencies and those required in future positions.[89]

One way of managing expatriate performance is to adapt the performance management system to take account of the host context.[90] This entails factoring in the impact of exogenous factors on business performance (eg currency fluctuations), clearly articulating the expatriate's goals, ensuring that performance evaluations measure the same things across countries, and determining the people best placed to evaluate the expatriate's performance.

(vi) Reward and Recognition

Challenges. Salaries of managers and highly skilled employees (locals and expatriates alike) are generally inflated in emerging markets. Because the demand for local, high-potential employees greatly outweighs the supply, salaries are excessively high.[91] Alternatively, expatriates, typically paid according to market conditions in their home countries, plus various expatriate premiums, receive much higher salaries than their local counterparts, who are paid in line with local market forces. This represents a source of injustice and frustration for local employees.[92] However, if companies do not offer expatriates competitive packages, they will decline the assignments, especially in less attractive destinations. Also, to attract employees to accept international assignments, MNCs often tailor packages to meet individual employee demands.[93] Conversely, to cater for the increased numbers of expatriate assignments, MNCs have begun to standardise their expatriate pay approach. Dynamics such as these pose remuneration challenges for MNCs eager to attract and retain the best available talent without paying too high a premium.

Solutions. The goal of an expatriate package is to keep employees 'whole' – where the expatriate does not experience an overt gain or loss when all elements of the package are combined.[94] To attract suitable talent, MNCs offer expatriates remuneration allowances to keep their sense of wholeness. These include host-country cost of living, healthcare, housing, foreign taxes, children's education, and hardship allowances.[95] These factors account for the unduly high packages earned by expatriates.

Another issue is the choice of a suitable expatriate remuneration approach. Three options have been identified by Sims and Schraeder (2005). The **balance sheet approach** aims at ensuring that the expatriate acquires equivalent purchasing power abroad to maintain home lifestyle. The **host country-based approach** curtails the spiralling costs of expatriate pay. It estimates what competitors are paying and the pay levels of local employees in comparable jobs, sharply restricting traditional allowances mentioned above. This approach also sends a message that doing an expatriate assignment is a prerequisite for upward advancement in the MNC. The **international headquarters approach** assumes all expatriates come from the same home headquarters and are paid on the same balance sheet programme. Gillette used this approach successfully when entering China.[96] Thus the balance sheet approach would address the issue of individual tailoring, the host-country approach deals with local employee resentment, while the international headquarters approach addresses the need for standardisation.

An unduly high salary demand by local, skilled professionals in China has caused some MNCs (eg FedEx, TNT and HSBC) to adopt a 'China plus one strategy' – maintain some presence in China, while moving operations to lower-wage countries such as Vietnam and Bangladesh.[97]

Emerging-market Talent Strategy: Underpinning Processes

Having outlined some of the challenges and solutions associated with the core talent management value chain, the focus shifts to issues associated with the processes underpinning talent management in emerging markets.

(i) Diversity and Localisation

Challenges. MNCs need to manage employees with dissimilar cultures, races, ethnicities, nationalities, religions, genders and generations, and all instances of prejudice need to be eradicated. Hewlett and Rashid (2010) collected data from 4 350 degreed men and women in Brazil, Russia, India, China and the United Arab Emirates and found that women in emerging markets were ahead of the curve regarding education, levels of ambition, and organisational commitment. However, several factors led them to be underleveraged. Problems included social disapproval of women travelling alone, the escalating crime rates which presented a harsh reality for professional women in emerging markets, and the triple whammy of gender, ethnicity and cultural bias. Between 25% and 36% of respondents from Brazil, China and the United Arab Emirates and 45% of the Indian respondents said that women were treated unfairly because of their gender. Another gender problem was work–home role conflicts, interestingly from the older generation, rather than childcare issues. In India and China, filial piety underpins the cultural value system, and daughterly guilt and responsibility are a far greater burden than maternal guilt. As one highly qualified Emirati woman explained, "It is part of the expectation of what children do in the Arab world. We take care of our parents when we grow up."[98]

There is very little evidence of diversity management or the existence of diversity policies in Chinese organisations. Where they are in place, they take the form of conflict avoidance rather than being a value-add to the business. Similarly, in the Middle East, women and foreign labour are still discriminated against, and Westerners and citizens are on a higher pay scale than people from emerging markets.[99]

Regarding localisation, there are many sound reasons why MNCs should employ local talent rather than relying on expatriates. These include the high expatriate costs to company, the reluctance of expatriates to accept assignments, especially in unfamiliar emerging-market destinations, language, custom and practice difficulties, and the expatriate's lack of a deep understanding of local conditions. Also, much goodwill is generated when MNCs appoint local people, especially into leadership positions. However, as outlined previously, it is difficult to find suitable local talent to fill senior MNC positions. Also, once on assignment, many expatriates are reluctant to forego the high salaries they earn, especially when their post-assignment career paths are unclear. Thus the requirement that expatriates find local talent to mentor, develop and ultimately replace them is often unmet, and localisation remains a challenge.

Solutions. Regarding diversity, simply stated, there is no room for unfair discrimination in any organisation. That is especially true in MNCs operating in emerging markets where, typically, local people have endured many forms of hardship and do not need additional adversity in the form of discrimination imposed on them by foreign MNCs. A fundamental (expatriate or local) managerial selection criterion is, therefore, the absence of any discriminatory biases. MNCs must ensure that the policies and practices of their headquarters and all their subsidiaries are free from any form of prejudice. These policies also need to adhere to relevant host-country laws. For example, owing to pressure from civic rights organisations, some Middle Eastern governments have introduced laws to protect and ensure the dignity of all employees, which heralds a new talent-friendly approach to people management in the region.[100]

A host country-specific employment equity strategy, which conforms to local laws, customs, practices and context, needs to be developed in each MNC subsidiary. It must go beyond eliminating unfair discrimination to embrace diversity and ensure that the potential value-add of employing diverse people, each with their own contributions, is realised.[101]

To overcome the gender problems and capitalise on the wealth of female talent, Hewlett and Rashid (2010) propose four solutions. First, MNCs should find talent early by recruiting women directly from universities. For example, the Google India Women in Engineering Award was launched and has been successful in attracting and retaining female engineering talent. Secondly, MNCs need to help top, emerging-market women to build networks and relationships and feel valued. GE is piloting a talent-spotting and mentoring programme in the United Arab Emirates to help women connect with one another across the company. Thirdly, give women international exposure to increase their chances of breaking through the glass ceiling in MNCs. In emerging markets, this works best when companies back it up with flexibility and support to reduce the burden on families and spouses. Fourthly, help professional women to build ties to clients, customers and communities in emerging markets. This helps establish a broad support system dealing with the conflicting work–home demands. It also helps women succeed in business.

Key to adopting a successful diversity strategy is to ensure that it has a sound business case. As Rohana Rozhan, CEO of ASTRO Malaysia Holdings states, "Diversity is part and parcel of everything we do because to succeed, ASTRO's workforce must directly reflect its market place."[102]

Regarding localisation, targets need to be set and met in much the same way that expatriates are required to deliver on any other performance target. Procter & Gamble, which focuses its growth in emerging markets, provides a useful approach to hiring local talent which ultimately feeds its global leadership pipeline. It has built a global talent supply chain process, which is coordinated globally but executed locally. Regular hiring and promotions are managed locally in the emerging markets, but high-potential prospects and key stretch assignments are identified globally. Hiring local, high-potential employees translates into creating a diverse talent pool for the entire group. At country leader level, there are about 300 executives who come from 36 countries. The leadership (ie top 40) comes from 12 different countries.[103]

Similarly, Hartmann, Feisel and Schober (2010) investigated how seven foreign MNCs operating in China attracted, retained and developed local talent. They found that, in most cases, the MNCs transferred their home-developed talent management practices directly to their Chinese operations. For example, high-potential employees were identified using standard performance appraisals. Round-table discussions were held by executives to determine the high-potential talent pools. Development either consisted of attending internal or external programmes. A common feature was the reliance on overseas assignments to integrate high-potential employees into the broader MNC network and to transfer organisational culture and strategy.

One way in which both diversity and localisation challenges can be addressed is to adopt a far more host-country orientation in selecting, developing, promoting and deploying local talent instead of trying to emulate the MNC's headquarters within the host country. In this way, diversity can be truly embraced, local talent can be engaged, and an organisational culture can be forged that includes the best of both worlds.

(ii) Organisational Culture

Challenges. One of the major challenges facing MNCs in emerging markets is dealing with diverse cultures. Although many MNCs have strong, high-performing cultures, they cannot expect to translate their culture automatically into an emerging-market host operation.[104] Instead, they need to respect the local culture and work within it to move the organisation forward. Cultural differences must be taken into consideration if they are to be successful in their host countries.

    Solutions. Presumably, the MNC's culture is one of the features that made it successful in the first place. The challenge, then, is to take the key elements of that culture and infuse them into the host-country operation whilst simultaneously taking account of local cultures, customs and practices. Ultimately, the challenge is to develop a new organisational culture that builds on the best of both cultures and provides a talent-centric environment where high-potential employees thrive knowing that they are critical to the MNC's success.[105] Moreover, culture has an important role to play in effective talent management. If the MNC can create a welcoming culture that embraces all employees, it is likely to succeed in talent management. As Armando Garza Dada, Chairman of the Board of Directors, Alfa SAB de CV, Mexico, commented, "Our capacity to attract, retain and manage executive talent does not depend on the compensation package, but rather on our ability to create a sense of belonging to an organisation that offers a long-term relationship and a professional development opportunity.".[106]

(iii) Talent Analytics

Challenges. Because talent management has become such an important issue, it is imperative to move beyond instinct and gut feel when making talent decisions. Companies that are not using workforce analytics appropriately risk losing their competitive talent edge.[107] In the PwC (2012) Survey, two-thirds of the CEOs in their sample consistently implementing new approaches to solve their talent shortages, are seeking relevant data and analysis from talent managers to make informed investment decisions around people. Schweyer (2004) notes:

> If you do proper workforce analytics and planning then you know who to recruit, who to develop, who to redeploy and where to redeploy them, whether you should hire someone externally or promote someone from within, and whether you should look for a contingent worker, contractor, or full-time worker. Workforce planning analytics can help you make the best talent management decisions and align those with your corporate objectives.[108]

The importance of conducting detailed talent analytics in MNCs operating in emerging countries cannot be overstated. The challenge of gathering and analysing the necessary data is immense, especially considering the number of employees involved and the differing geographies, maturities, organisational structures, targeted jobs, talent pools and performance and potential levels to be considered in such an analysis. However, Lewis and Heckman (2006) caution that, to make informed talent decisions, companies should avoid simply collecting tables of talent data without first adopting a conceptual model to guide the choice of data collected and the manner in which it is interpreted.

Solutions. As MNCs become more global, complex, advanced analytics are being increasingly used to make informed talent-related decisions.[109] Typically, talent reviews, containing all the relevant analyses, are cascaded up the organisation to successively senior levels and appropriate decisions are made at each level in the MNC.

Boudreau and Ramstad (2004) provide a useful framework for ensuring that valid talent conclusions are reached. Their 'LAMP' model describes:

- *Logic:* A rational talent strategy, linking talent pools to the MNC's competitive advantage, to generate meaningful talent questions.

- *Analytics:* Once the logical structure is in place, the right analytics can generate insights into organisational issues. Analytics goes beyond statistics and research design, and requires savvy to ask the right talent questions and answer them intelligently.

- *Measures:* The challenge of measures is to balance precision and usefulness – sufficient data that is timely, reliable and available.

- *Process:* A change management process is needed to implement the talent decisions taken.[110]

Advanced analytic tools and techniques, such as predictive modelling, allow organisations to predict into the future and thereby enhance talent management decisions.[111] Successful MNCs are using modelling to anticipate future talent supply and demand locally and globally. They are measuring recruiting effectiveness not just to forecast who will be hired, but to predict which recruits are likely to rise to leadership over time. Also, because people leave companies for various reasons, by using multivariate predictive modelling, companies can identify key employees who may be flight risks and use the insights to develop tailored plans to retain them.[112]

(iv) Talent Information Systems

Challenges. One way of driving talent analytics is to adopt an enterprise-wide software system. It should provide real-time data that can be mined to gain talent insights upon which informed talent planning and decision making can be based. The logistical challenges associated with designing, implementing and maintaining one standard system across multiple geographies, organisational maturities, languages and bandwidths are immense. Also, not all HR measures are standardised across every business in an MNC, which leads to incomplete or unstandardised data rendering cross-boundary comparisons unreliable. Furthermore, when operating a global IT system, it is extremely cumbersome to effect changes in one business without seriously impacting the entire group.

    Solutions. Because of the size and complexity of designing and implementing a global, enterprise-wide talent system, a comprehensive, structured and detailed change management approach should form part of the design, build, implement and anchor phases of the initiative.[113] However, there are alternative solutions to enterprise-wide systems. MNCs can use their existing systems, but with better integration. On the other hand, MNCs can jump-start their IT talent efforts by using cloud technology to host their reporting and analytics infrastructure, which provides analytics support based on industry best practices, thereby saving costs, time, capital expenditure and internal support requirements.[114]

Emerging-market Talent Strategy: Key Role Players

Talent challenges and possible solutions regarding the third component of the talent management strategy, namely the key role players, are now discussed.

(i) Leadership

Challenges. Arguably the most important factor determining the success of talent management (and, indeed, the success of MNCs) in emerging markets is the availability of suitable leaders for host-country operations. The shortage of leadership talent is the major obstacle MNCs face.

> … Demographic shift – notably the impending retirement of baby boomers – along with changing business conditions, such as significant growth in largely unfamiliar markets, like China, have combined to produce something of a perfect storm. Leadership development has become a much more strategic process …[indeed]… companies have been forced to pass on hundreds of millions of dollars of new business because they didn't have the talent to see their growth strategies through to fruition.[115]

Leaders require distinct qualities and competencies and a desire to manage in culturally and geographically distant countries.[116] Specifically, they need several forms of capital – **cognitive capital:** understanding how knowledge needs to be disseminated across the global footprint; **social capital:** making the necessary connections to perform boundary-spanning roles effectively; **political capital:** the legitimacy to be regarded as a credible leader in foreign countries; and **human capital:** the competency to operate in diverse cultural contexts. However, when selecting leaders, MNCs often focus solely on technical capabilities at the expense of other core capabilities. MNC leaders also need to develop local knowledge in their host countries.[117] This includes information about the local economy, politics, culture and business customs, local demands and tastes, ways to access local labour pools, distribution channels, infrastructure raw materials, and other factors required to conduct business successfully in the host country.[118] Caliguiri (2006) identified 10 tasks that global leaders of MNCs need to perform. These are: work with colleagues from other countries, interact with external clients from other countries, work with internal clients from other countries, speak different languages, manage employees of different nationalities, develop a strategic business plan on a global basis for their business unit, manage a globally linked budget for their business unit, negotiate in other countries or with people from other countries, manage foreign suppliers or vendors, and manage risk on a worldwide basis for their business unit. To do this effectively, global leaders need specific knowledge, skills and abilities, and personality characteristics.

Solutions. Given the capabilities expected of MNC leaders, it is essential that the right criteria are adopted when selecting and developing leaders for global assignments. For example, cultural intelligence is an important selection factor when intercultural effectiveness is required. Intercultural effectiveness is defined as "a set of cross cultural capabilities that describe a person's capacity to function effectively in culturally diverse settings".[119]

Sheehan (2012) found significant positive relationships between management development and perceived subsidiary performance in a sample of 143 Polish, Czech Republic and Hungarian subsidiaries of United Kingdom-based MNCs. The most effective means of developing global leaders is by giving them long-term international assignments, sending them on executive development programmes, and selecting them as members of international, cross-functional project teams.[120] Ruddy and Anand (2010) note a 70-20-10 rule for developing global leaders: 70% development via job experience, 20% through coaching and mentoring, and 10% through formal training. The high levels of independence and increased job responsibility inherent in overseas assignments contribute to their growth and career success: executives with overseas experience are more marketable, are promoted more often, perform better, and get paid more than executives with only local experience.[121] However, exposure to cultural diversity and international assignments does not necessarily enhance learnings. Instead, all four components of experiential learning (ie concrete experiences, reflective observation, abstract conceptualisation, and active experimentation) are necessary for learning to take place. It is the **quality** of the travel experience rather than the **quantity** of travel that aids global leadership development."[122]

(ii) Expatriates

Challenges. Three reasons for using expatriates are: (a) to fill positions where suitable local talent is not available; (b) to develop managerial competence; and (c) to ensure knowledge transfer across business units.[123] However, expatriate failure rates have been reported at anywhere between 10% and 80%.[124] The main reason cited is the inability of the expatriates and/or their families to adjust to the host-country culture. It has been estimated that each expatriate failure costs the company over $1 million: taken collectively, expatriate failures cost United States firms about $2 billion per year.[125] A key challenge, then, is to ensure that expatriates succeed, and one way to do this is to closely manage the performance of each expatriate. This depends largely on his or her competencies, which include technical abilities, personal adaptability to foreign cultures, and familiarity with the host country.[126]

Collings et al. (2007) identify several challenges associated with the use of expatriates. First, **limited availability of suitable international managers** to run overseas operations curtails the implementation of global plans. Factors contributing to this challenge include complications arising from dual-career couples – partners are often prohibited from working in host countries, thereby retarding their career growth. A further supply-side challenge is the failure of MNCs to implement an effective talent management approach. Expatriates' willingness to move to emerging markets where they may be most needed is becoming increasingly rare. The three countries with the fastest-growing, new expatriate destinations, namely China, India and Russia, are also the three countries with the highest levels of difficulty for project managers and expatriates: 21% of firms reported that China had the highest assignment failure rates.[127] Secondly, **expatriate costs are exorbitant**. Interestingly, although it is estimated that the cost of an expatriate is between three to four times the person's home salary, little is known of the exact benefits of employing expatriates: return-on-investment analyses are scarce. The third challenge is the **mushrooming demand for expatriates**. The growth of foreign direct investment in developing countries has created a demand for global managers with the competencies to operate in these distant markets. Because of the shortage of talent within these markets, particularly shortages of qualified, local senior executives and the strategic roles these managers play, the use of expatriate managers in emerging markets has become inevitable.[128] Fourthly, **expatriate failure** (where expatriates terminate assignments and return home prematurely) is prevalent. The high costs associated with expatriate failure, both direct (eg salary) and indirect (eg loss of market share, reputation damage in host country) suggest that far more attention should be paid to preventing such failures. This leads to the fifth challenge, **expatriate performance**. Factors impacting on performance include technical expertise, self and family adjustment to the host culture, environmental factors (eg politics, stability and cultural distance from one's home culture), support provided by the home country, and peculiarities of the host environment. The final set of challenges identified by Collings et al. (2007) is **the changing nature of careers in the international context**. Increasingly, international assignments are viewed as a means to an end – developing competencies that increase individual employability and marketability, rather than limiting career progress to the MNC in which they work.[129] Also, there is a growing trend for self-initiated foreign work experience rather than being sent on international assignments by the MNC. These self-initiated foreign workers are self-financing and take responsibility for establishing themselves in their host environments.

A further problem is poor retention of repatriates (ie repatriated expatriates). By disseminating useful knowledge and new perspectives gained on assignment, international experience acquired by repatriates is invaluable.[130] However, repatriation is typically poorly handled. Over 30% of companies do not discuss repatriation with expatriates at all, and over 40% only discuss their homecoming less than 6 months before the assignment ends. Less than 37% do any form of career planning with repatriates, and only one-third of MNCs have a strategy to address the problems that expatriates encounter when returning home. Many MNCs have no policies or programmes to assist repatriates with their careers. Consequently, it is not surprising that repatriate labour turnover is high. The 2010 Brookfield GRS Global Relocation Trends Survey found that 61% of expatriates left their companies within 2 years of completing their overseas assignment.[131]

Approximately two-thirds of expatriates are accompanied by their partners, children or both, which places the stress of cross-cultural relocation, education and social development of their children on them and their families.[132] Also, over half the expatriate families are dual-career couples, which further adds to the stress of the family – especially when the partner is expected to give up his or her job and be unemployed in the host country.

Given the myriad of challenges associated with the expatriation process, it is surprising that many companies have failed to address the issue of globalisation effectively in their talent management programmes. Ernst and Young (2010) found that 63% of their respondents stated that their organisations lacked standard policies for managing the careers of international assignees, and 47% said their MNCs placed little or no importance on helping repatriates reintegrate into the organisation.

Solutions. To address cultural-adjustment problems, MNCs provide expatriates and their families with cross-culture training, the benefits of which have been widely acknowledged.[133] To overcome difficulties of employees rejecting overseas assignment offers, companies have adopted several alternate approaches. These include (a) hiring **self-initiated movers**; (b) hiring **host-country nationals** – specifically those who have worked for other MNCs and who have global experience and networks; (c) hiring **third-country nationals**, who are particularly valuable when MNCs wish to transfer common standards across diverse countries. This approach has been embraced by Adidas, where over 50% of its internationally mobile talent comprises third-country nationals. Adidas aims to increase that number by 20% as part of a strategy to build its employer brand.[134] Another approach is to hire **already-acculturated talent (inpats)** – expatriates from emerging countries who have worked in developed countries. Inpats are increasingly being used as a source of international management for at least three reasons: first, to create diverse strategic perspectives; secondly, because of the rise of emerging-market assignments, which are unattractive to traditional expatriate pools; and, thirdly, owing to the growing need to provide career opportunities for high-potential employees.[135] Other alternatives to expatriation include short-term assignments, commuter assignments, international business travel and virtual assignments that overcome many of the challenges facing traditional international expatriation.[136]

To address high levels of repatriate labour turnover, Bolino[137] (2007) proposes MNCs adopt three support practices:

- *Career development plans* entail career planning to ensure career progression has been enhanced (rather than sidetracked as many repatriates feel), repatriate agreements and skill utilisation (where repatriates are formally assigned meaningful jobs commensurate with their seniority that use their experience acquired overseas), and formal recognition of the value of international experience.

- *Connectivity mechanisms* include regular home visits and home-office communications. They help keep expatriates abreast of home-country corporate changes. Developing and retaining a meaningful relationship with someone in the home country also assists with repatriate success.

- *Repatriation assistance* includes pre-return repatriate training to familiarise expatriates with the challenges they will face upon homecoming and updating them with any technical or structural changes that have occurred in their absence. Logistical support includes identifying houses, helping select movers and providing family support.[138]

Expatriate success is positively associated with family adjustment in the host country.[139] Employer support for expatriates' spouses increases overall family adjustment, reduces premature assignment withdrawal, and increases the spouse's willingness to accept long-term global assignments. Cole (2011) found that the most valuable form of spousal support was assistance with networking regarding employment opportunities in the host country. Hiring existing expatriate spouses to assist newly arriving spouses also assists with the settling-in adjustment period. Another important form of support is assistance with finding and creating an appropriate social network, which enhances the psychological wellbeing of the expatriate spouse.[140]

Finally, there are six domains in which immigrants need to acculturate in order to adjust effectively. These include politics and government, work, the economic domain (including consuming goods and services), family relations, social relations, and ideology, which includes ways of thinking, principles and values, as well as customs and religious beliefs. However, most MNCs do not focus on all of these domains in attempting to help expatriates adjust to their host-country environments.[141]

(iii) Local Employees

Challenges. MNCs are increasingly moving away from using expatriates, favouring local talent instead.

> The use of expatriates to turn a business around or to open a new market is declining, mostly because of the cost involved and the limited success of expatriates in these assignments…Allan Church from Pepsi said, "We are having more success with local home-grown talent than with expatriates, as they are better at managing within the local business culture. Expatriates often take three to five years to make an impact on the people they manage and then they move on again."[142]

Similarly, Petr Šulc of the Czech pharmaceutical company, Zentiva, commented, "Strong local management is very important. We cannot do business in a country from outside that country, and it cannot be done by someone who has no experience, contacts or knowledge of the markets."[143] Notwithstanding this recognition of the importance of hiring local talent, in emerging markets, local talent that meets the stringent criteria of MNCs is scarce – either because of poor education or because high growth in those economies has given rise to a shortage of available talent. This poses a major challenge for MNCs.

Solutions. Ways of addressing local talent issues have been discussed under various headings throughout the chapter.[144] These include setting localisation targets to ensure that localisation takes place, sending local employees on accelerated learning and development experiences, sending local, high-potential employees on overseas assignments, deploying them across the MNC's global footprint, and generally providing them with attractive career opportunities.[145] One approach to ensuring a seamless transition to local leadership is tasking expatriates with identifying, developing and supporting local, high-potential employees to take over from them. As Louis Camillleri, Chairman and CEO, Philip Morris International, Switzerland, said, "Ultimately, you can't rely solely on expatriates to run a local business forever. They certainly have an important role to bring our affiliates in given countries up to certain standards, but they also have the critical role of transferring knowledge and expertise so that those businesses can stand on their own. The goal is that those affiliates are eventually run by country nationals."[146] Similarly,

> …because the competition for all kinds of talent is truly worldwide, leaders have to solve the global talent problem in their own countries. We cannot outsource our way out of this shortage. Those days are over. Countries like India that in the past have

provided resources for outsourcing are now experiencing their own talent shortages. Nor will immigration solve the problem, because countries like China, once sources of skilled talent, are now luring their expatriate workers home to take advantage of higher wages and a growing economy.[147]

Indeed, Jeffrey Joerres (2011), CEO Manpower at McKinsey, states that the era of employing Western expatriates in emerging markets is ending. Instead, he proposes adopting a '**reverse expatriate**' strategy. Reverse expatriates are local managers who are selected to lead the local subsidiary of an MNC. They are sent on a developmental immersion into the MNC's established operations for several months. He cites numerous examples where this growing practice has been tremendously successful and concludes that "any multinational that really wants to grow in emerging markets should think hard about implementing a reverse-expatriate strategy of its own".[148]

There are over 20 million people of Indian origin who live overseas, and the Chinese diaspora is greater than 35 million, which represents a valuable source of local talent.[149] Many MNCs are wooing these people back home by going to overseas recruitment fairs and by maintaining links with overseas-based executives.

Some companies are focusing longer term on increasing the market readiness of talent by providing secondary schooling for local children. Embraer, the Brazilian aircraft manufacturer, runs a school for underprivileged children. It is also creating physics laboratory stations that enable the curriculum's engineering module to be replicated across multiple schools.[150]

(iv) HR Function

Challenges. For many HR organizations, emerging markets used to be the last thing they focused on. Now it's becoming the first. … In fact, a recent Deloitte and Forbes Insight Survey highlighted the competition for talent that is occurring globally and in emerging markets as the most pressing talent concern today.[151]

The complexity of talent management facing MNCs in emerging markets is great. The challenges facing corporate HR functions of MNCs focus on effectively managing two key issues: increased global competition for highly skilled talent, and new forms of international mobility needed in emerging markets.[152] Regarding **talent competition**, Farndale, Scullion and Sparrow (2010) identify three issues: first, to remain competitive, MNCs are demanding increasingly high skills levels and qualities in staff. Secondly, because there is insufficient senior talent to meet these demands in traditional talent pools, MNCs are broadening their search to wider talent pools across the world. Thirdly, to remain competitive, MNCs are extending their pipelines and are increasingly forward planning to recruit ahead of the curve. Marijn Dekkers, Chairman of Bayer AG says, "what is changing is that among Western companies, the ability to hire, develop and retain talent in the emerging economies has become a major point of competitive differentiation".[153]

Regarding the second issue, **international mobility needed in emerging markets**, Farndale et al. (2010) use China and India as examples to demonstrate that local talent in these countries is not meeting the rigorous demands of MNCs. Retention of knowledge workers in emerging markets is a further issue facing MNCs. The need to improve employee engagement and retention in emerging markets is an HR priority. Because of the shortage of local talent and the reluctance of individuals to be mobile, the consequence for HR is to develop alternate methods of sourcing international talent beyond expatriates.[154]

MNCs' changing global business models represent a major challenge for HR. Historically, MNCs adopted an international or federal model, where operations in the rest of the world were subordinate to the MNC's home market. Alternately, the entrepreneurial (or multidomestic) model has been embraced, where multiple geographies are all treated separately.[155] Many MNCs are increasingly moving to a third model, where the businesses are globally integrated and the MNC's home market is treated as one of many global markets. This shift represents one of the most significant transformations an MNC will ever make, and HR's role in this process (especially regarding the far-reaching talent implications) is central.[156]

Solutions. Common HR outputs in MNCs include focusing on the top talent across the company, developing core management capability by accelerating development of senior leaders, conducting proactive succession planning, and developing a pool of highly competent global managers.[157] Farndale et al. identify four key HR roles:

- *Champions of process* to oversee the global implementation of a talent management strategy that ensures the MNC's talent base is fit for purpose.

- *Guardians of culture* to oversee the implementation of values and systems when developing a talent management culture and employer brand globally. MNCs entering emerging markets may take an expedient approach to implementing global best practice, especially in least-developed countries where labour standards are low and employment regulation enforcement is weak.[158]

- *Network leadership and intelligence* to be in touch with the latest trends in the internal and external labour market and to possess the leadership to act upon those trends.

- *Managers of internal receptivity* to fulfil a role in managing expatriates' careers and ensuring that they are looked after in the process.

To perform these roles, HR needs to shift to a capability-driven perspective, focusing across the MNC to participate in mutual sharing of talent, which, in turn, reflects a move towards a more centralised approach to global talent management.[159]

As globalisation increases, MNCs will need direction and support from HR to develop global talent strategies that provide new skills in new places and to create a leadership pipeline that can be rapidly deployed to capitalise on global opportunities as they arise.[160] Also, MNCs will need HR's help to manage increasingly complex and diverse workforces with vast differences in nationality, culture, socioeconomic background, lifestyle and education, in addition to the traditional diversity factors of gender, race, ethnicity, religion and generation.[161]

Ultimately, HR is the custodian of the entire talent management strategy. As such, HR needs to design and implement the processes, competencies, and innovative solutions to all the talent management challenges identified throughout this chapter. The measure of HR's success is the extent to which it is able to shift the notion of talent being an inhibitor of global expansion to a competitive advantage that is widely regarded as a cornerstone of the company's success across the world.

Business Performance

This leads directly into the last stage of the model, the impact of the talent management strategy on business performance. If the MNC meets all the challenges associated with talent management in emerging markets, then the company will have become successful in attracting, retaining and developing a disproportionate number of high-calibre, diverse people with the right skills and motivation that can be deployed in the right place at the right time and right price to enhance the corporate culture and contribute meaningfully to the MNC's performance.

Conclusions

Managing talent in emerging markets poses certain challenges. However, with the right creativity and compassion, these can be addressed in a way that enhances the MNC's competitive advantage. From the preceding analysis, several learnings accrue for MNCs on how to manage talent in emerging markets:

1. The sole purpose of a talent strategy is to support the MNC in achieving its strategic goals. Therefore, it needs to be derived from the corporate business plan and must be measured in terms of its contribution to the achievement of company goals.

2. Because there are so many moving parts involved in global talent management, it is important to adopt a systemic, holistic approach that includes the overarching corporate strategy, all the components of the talent value chain, the underpinning processes, and the key role players.

3. Critical to this is the need to attain relevant, accurate and current information on all people in the defined talent pools upon which informed, talent-related decisions can be made. The existence of an enterprise-wide IT system that provides real-time talent data helps streamline talent management across multiple geographies.

4. The adoption of a global talent pool of senior executives, managed centrally in the MNC's headquarters, provides the best approach to dealing with the selection, retention, development and deployment of people to lead the various businesses across the globe.

5. Because the challenges facing MNCs in emerging markets are so different from home-country jobs, the criteria for success and subsequent selection, on-boarding, retention, development and promotion of both expatriates and local talent need to be tailored to meet each host country's explicit needs.

6. Because the circumstances of each of the talent pool members operating in an emerging-market MNC is unique, a 'one size fits all' approach needs to be replaced with an individually tailored talent management approach that caters to their specific needs and family circumstances.

7. Because of the dramatic changes in global talent dynamics, MNCs need new and innovative approaches to resourcing their operations. These include finding appropriate ways of sourcing and developing talent across the world (in particular local, high-potential talent in host countries), adopting alternative approaches to the traditional expatriation process, and optimising the skills and experiences of repatriates as well as local, high-potential employees when they move from host to home countries.

8. Besides the regular leadership criteria, specific characteristics of successful MNC leaders in developing countries include high levels of emotional and cultural intelligence, resilience, political astuteness, ethics, the common touch, an absence of any prejudice, and a strong and supportive family structure.

9. The MNC operating in emerging markets has an opportunity to be a good corporate citizen that goes way beyond making financial gains. By imparting lessons learnt from the home country and being receptive to the culture, customs and practices of the host country, the MNC can benefit from the best of both worlds. Local talent and the broader community thrive as a result of the employment, development, advancement and global opportunities that the MNC brings. At the same time, the MNC benefits from the unique skills, culture, diversity and creativity that local talent brings to the workplace, not only in the local environment, but also globally.

10. At the heart of any talent management approach is the key relationship between an individual employee and his or her manager. If that relationship is poor, then talent management will suffer, no matter how good the systems and processes. As well-known authors Buckingham and Coffman[162] observed – people join companies, but they leave their managers. "The manager creates the connection between the employee and the organization, and as a result, the manager-employee relationship is often the 'deal breaker' in relation to retention."[163]

11. Finally, there is no single silver bullet for success in talent management. Instead, if an MNC wants to be competitive in attracting, retaining, developing and deploying high-calibre talent, it needs to create the right environment and to adopt a total employment offering that will be attractive to its target talent pools. This is as applicable to a small business operating in a single town as it is to a global MNC.

Endnotes

1   Hewlett and Rashid (2011).
2   Brooks (2014).
3   Crous & Attlee (2014).
4   Accenture (2008).
5   Schuler, Jackson & Tarique (2011).
6   Farndale, Scullion & Sparrow (2010:161).
7   According to McDonnell, Lamare, Gunnigle & Lavelle (2010).
8   PwC (2012).
9   15th Annual CEO Survey (PwC 2012).
10 Some of the prominent writers on global talent management include: Collings, McDonnell & Scullion (2009); Collings, Scullion & Morley (2007); Farndale, Scullion & Sparrow (2010); Hewlett & Rashid (2010); McDonnell & Collings (2011); Ready, Hill & Conger (2008); Schuler, Jackson & Tarique (2011); Scullion & Collings (2011); Scullion, Collings & Caligiuri (2010); Tarique & Schuler (2010).
11 Table 8.2 is adapted from: Schuler, Jackson & Tarique (2011); Scullion & Collings (2011); Scullion, Caligiuri & Collings (2008); Tarique & Schuler (2010).
12 Leisy & Pyron (2009:58-59).
13 Deloitte (2012); Manning, Massini & Lewin (2008).
14 PwC (2012:10).
15 Deloitte (2012).
16 Farndale, Scullion & Sparrow (2010).
17 Mercurio (2011).
18 Collings, Scullion & Morley (2007).
19 Sims & Schraeder (2005).
20 Collings et al. (2007).
21 Guthridge, Komm & Lawson (2008).
22 Accenture (2008); Cooke (2011); Ready, Hill & Conger (2008).
23 Farndale et al. (2010).
24 PwC (2012).
25 Schuler et al. (2011:513-514).
26 See Sheehan (2012).
27 Boudreau, Ramstad & Dowling (2002).
28 Boudreau et al. (2002:17).
29 For example: Elegbe (2010); Li & Scullion (2010); McKinsey (2005).
30 Schuler et al. (2011); Scullion & Collings (2011).
31 See chapter 9 outlining the SAB talent case.
32 McDonnell & Collings (2011).
33 Collings & Mellahi (2009:307).
34 McDonnell & Collings (2011).
35 Deloitte (2010).
36 Hewlett & Rashid (2011).
37 Li & Scullion (2010).
38 Ke, Chermack, Lee & Lin (2006).
39 Elegbe (2010).
40 Farndale et al. (2010).
41 Guthridge, Komm & Lawson (2008).
42 Holland (2008).
43 Scullion & Collings (2011).
44 Ali (2011).
45 Accenture (2008).
46 Hewlett & Rashid (2011:12).
47 Scullion & Collings (2011).
48 Farndale et al. (2010); Yeung, Warner & Rowley (2008).
49 Ali (2011).
50 While nepotism occurs throughout the world, it poses a selection challenge in emerging markets and, therefore, is mentioned in this chapter.
51 Elegbe (2010).
52 PwC (2012:26).
53 Stein & Christiansen (2010).
54 Stein & Christiansen (2010).
55 Sparrow & Balain (2008).
56 SABMiller (2011).
57 Schuler et al. (2011).
58 Cooke (2011).
59 Tymon, Stumpf & Doh (2010).
60 See Elegbe (2010).
61 Elegbe (2010).
62 Schuler et al. (2011).
63 According to Cooke (2011).
64 Ali (2011).
65 Corporate Leadership Council (2004).
66 BlessingWhite Research (2011).
67 Deloitte (2010).
68 Cooke (2011).
69 Kucherov & Zavyalova (2011).
70 Tymon et al. (2010) investigated retention and labour turnover in a sample of 4 811 professionals employed in 28 Indian firms.

71 Ready et al. (2008).
72 Ready et al. (2008:6).
73 McDonnell, Lamare, Gunnigle & Lavelle (2010).
74 Accenture (2011).
75 Cooke (2011).
76 Ready et al. (2008).
77 Dietz, Orr & Xing (2008).
78 This is analogous in Western tertiary education to being selected as a Rhodes Scholar.
79 Schuler et al. (2011).
80 See chapter 5 on in-market action learning.
81 Cooke (2011).
82 Cooke (2011).
83 See Ready et al. (2008) who outline the Standard Chartered Bank China case in detail.
84 Ready et al. (2008:8).
85 Accenture (2008:27).
86 See Ready et al. (2008) who outline the Lenovo case in detail.
87 Ready et al. (2008:3).
88 Cooke (2011).
89 McDonnell & Collings (2011).
90 Collings et al. (2007).
91 Farndale et al. (2010).
92 Leung, Zhu & Ge (2009).
93 Warneke & Schneider (2011).
94 According to Sims & Schraeder (2005).
95 Sims & Schraeder (2005).
96 Expatriate pay in emerging markets is a complicated topic that requires much elaboration to cover properly. See Mark Bussin's chapter in this book (chapter 6) for a detailed explanation of how to meet the challenges in this field.
97 Schuler et al. (2011).
98 Hewlett & Rashid (2010:103).
99 See Ali (2011) and Cooke (2011).
100 Ali (2011).
101 This, in turn, poses additional challenges for MNCs operating in countries that have discriminatory laws (eg laws discriminating against women) or where an informal caste system is still in place.
102 PwC (2012:24).
103 Ready & Conger (2007).
104 As noted by Fealy & Kompare (2003).
105 Several authors who discuss features of talent-centric cultures have been cited elsewhere in the chapter. See: Farndale et al. (2010); Hartmann et al. (2010); and Ready et al. (2008).
106 PwC (2011:10).
107 Deloitte (2011).
108 Cited in Lewis & Heckman (2006:147).
109 Deloitte (2012).
110 See Lewis & Heckman (2006:148).
111 Deloitte (2012).
112 Deloitte (2012).
113 For example, see John Kotter's (1995) eight-stage change model that could be applied to, and adapted for, a global talent system implementation project.
114 See Deloitte (2012).
115 Ready & Conger (2007:2).
116 Farndale et al. (2010).
117 As argued by Shenxue & Scullion (2010).
118 See Makino & Deklios (1997), cited in Shenxue & Scullion (2010:191).
119 Ng, Van Dyne & Ang (2009a:99).
120 Ruddy & Anand (2010).
121 Pattie, White & Tansky (2010).
122 As cautioned by Ng, Van Dyne & Ang (2009b).
123 See Edström & Galbraith, as cited in Collings et al. (2007).
124 Okpara & Kabongo (2011).
125 Sims & Schraeder (2005).
126 Shenxue & Scullion (2010).
127 Farndale et al. (2010).
128 Shenxue & Scullion (2010).
129 This is aligned to the notion of a boundaryless career: building market value through transfer across boundaries, rather than pursuing traditional organisational careers.
130 Pattie et al. (2010).
131 Reif (2011).
132 Cole (2011).
133 Okpara & Kabongo (2011).
134 Farndale et al. (2010).
135 Farndale et al. (2010).
136 Collings et al. (2007).
137 See Pattie et al. (2010) for a full discussion of the career-development practices proposed by Bolino.
138 Pattie et al. (2010).
139 Cole (2011).
140 Cole (2011).
141 See Haslberger & Brewster (2008).
142 Ruddy & Anand (2010:587).
143 Accenture (2008:25).
144 See Richard Forbes's chapter (chapter 7), which outlines a variety of approaches to managing local talent in emerging markets effectively.
145 See Ready et al. (2008).
146 PwC (2011:12).
147 Gordon (2009:viii).
148 Joerres (2011:2).
149 Accenture (2008).
150 Accenture (2008).
151 Deloitte (2011:10).
152 Farndale et al. (2010).
153 PwC (2012:20).

154 See the section on expatriates above for a detailed account of this.
155 Deloitte (2012).
156 Deloitte (2012).
157 Farndale et al. (2010).
158 It is common for Chinese workers to be asked to work overtime at short notice – paid or unpaid (Cooke 2011).
159 Farndale et al. (2010).
160 Deloitte (2012).
161 Deloitte (2012).
162 Marcus Buckingham and Curt Coffman of the Gallup Organization, coined the phrase in their in-depth study of great managers across a wide variety of situations in the best-seller 'First, break all the rules: What the world's greatest managers do differently'.
163 Lockwood (2007:5).

References

Accenture. (2008). *Multi-polar world 2: the rise of the emerging-market multinational.* Retrieved August 30, 2014 from www.accenture.com/forwardthinking

Ali, A.J. (2011). Talent management in the Middle East. In H. Scullion and D.G. Collings (Eds.), *Global talent management.* New York: Routledge.

Andors, A. (2012). Hidden in plain sight: In the war for talent in fast-growing markets, local women are the not-so-secret weapon. *HR Magazine*, January, 34–35.

Bhatnagar, J. (2007). Talent management strategy of employee engagement in Indian ITES Employees: Key to Retention. *Employee Relations, 29*, 640–663.

BlessingWhite Research. (2011). *Employee engagement report, 2011.* Princeton, NJ: BlessingWhite, Inc.

Bohara, A. (2007). Managing talent in a global work environment. *Employment Relations Today,* Fall, 27–35. Retrieved August 30, 2014 from www.interscience.wiley.com

Boudreau, J.W. & Ramstad, P.M. (2004). *Talentship and human resource management measurement and analysis: From ROI to strategic organizational change.* Working paper G 04-17 (469). Los Angeles: Center for Effective Organizations, University of Southern California.

Boudreau, J.W., Ramstad, P.M. & Dowling, P.J. (2002). *Global talentship: Toward a decision science connecting talent to global strategic success.* Working paper. Ithaca, NY: Center for Advanced Human Resources Studies, Cornell University.

Brooks, K. (2014). Indonesia and the Philippines: A tale of two archipelagoes. *Foreign Affairs, 93*(1) (January-February), 37.

Buckingham, M. & Coffman, C. (1999). *First, break all the rules: What the world's greatest managers do differently.* USA: Simon & Schuster.

Caliguiri, P. (2006). Developing global leaders. *Human Resource Management Review, 16*, 219–228.

Cole, N.D. (2011). Managing global talent: Solving the spousal adjustment problem. *The International Journal of Human Resources Management, 22*(7), 1504–1530.

Collings, D.G., McDonnell, A. & Scullion, H. (2009). Global talent management: The law of the few. *Poznan University of Economics Review, 9*(2), 5–18.

Collings, D.G. & Mellahi, K. (2009). Strategic talent management: A review and research agenda. *Human Resource Management Review, 19*, 304–313.

Collings, D.G., Scullion, H. & Morley, M.J. (2007). Changing patterns of global staffing in the multinational enterprise: Challenges to the conventional expatriate assignment and emerging alternatives. *Journal of World Business, 42*, 198–213.

Cooke, F.L. (2011). Talent management in China. In H. Scullion and D.G. Collings (Eds.), *Global talent management*. New York: Routledge.

Corporate Leadership Council. (2004). *Employee engagement: Framework and survey – Corporate Leadership Council*. Washington, DC: Corporate Leadership Board. Retrieved August 30, 2014 from ww.corporateleadershipcouncil.com

Crous, W. & Attlee, Z. (2014). *African human capital and labour reports*. Rosebank: Knowres Publishing.

Deloitte. (2010). *Talent edge 2020: Blueprints for the new normal*. Retrieved August 30, 2014 from www.Deloitte.co/us/talent

Deloitte. (2011). *Human capital trends 2011: Revolution/Evolution*. Retrieved August 30, 2014 from www.Deloitte.com

Deloitte. (2012). *Human capital trends 2012: Leap ahead*. Retrieved August 30, 2014 from www.Deloitte.com

Dietz, M.C., Orr, G. & Xing, J. (2008). How Chinese companies can succeed abroad. *McKinsey Quarterly*, May.

Edström, A. & Galbraith, J.R. (1977). Transfer of managers as a coordination and control strategy in multinational organizations. *Administrative Science Quarterly, 22*, 248–263.

Elegbe, J.A. (2010). *Talent management in the developing world: Adopting a global perspective*. United Kingdom: Gower.

Ernst & Young. (2010). *Managing today's global workforce: Elevating talent management to improve business*. United Kingdom: Ernst & Young Global Limited.

Farndale, E., Scullion, H. & Sparrow, P. (2010). The role of the corporate HR function in global talent management. *Journal of World Business, 45*(2), 161–168.

Fealy, L. & Kompare, D. (2003). When worlds collide: Culture clash. *Journal of Business Strategy, 24*(4), 9–13.

Gordon, E.E. (2009). *Winning the global talent showdown: How businesses and communities can partner to rebuild the jobs pipeline*. San Francisco: Berrett-Koehler Publishers.

Guthridge, M., Komm, A.B. & Lawson, E. (2008). Making talent management a strategic priority. *McKinsey Quarterly*, January, 49–59.

Hartmann, E., Feisel, E. & Schober, H. (2010). Talent management of Western MNCs in China: Balancing global integration and local responsiveness. *Journal of World Business, 45*, 169–178.

Haslberger, A. & Brewster, C. (2008). The expatriate family: An international perspective. *Journal of Managerial Psychology, 23*(3), 24–346.

Hewlett, S.A. & Rashid, R. (2010). The battle for female talent in emerging markets. *Harvard Business Review*, May, 101–106.

Hewlett, S.A. & Rashid, R. (2011). *Winning the war for talent in emerging markets: Why women are the solution*. Boston, MA: Harvard Business Review Press.

Holland, K. (2008). Working all corners in a global talent hunt. *The New York Times*, February 24. Retrieved August 30, 2014 from http://nytimes.com/2008/02/24/jobs/24mgmt.html

Joerres, J. (2011). Beyond expatriates: Better managers for emerging markets. *McKinsey Quarterly,* May, 1–4.

Ke, J., Chermack, T.J., Lee, Y.H. & Lin, J. (2006). National human resource development in transitioning societies in the developing world: The People's Republic of China. *Advances in Developing Human Resources, 8*(1), 28–45.

Kotter, J. (1995). Leading change: Why transformational efforts fail. *Harvard Business Review,* March-April, 59–67.

Kucherov, D. & Zavyalova, E. (2011). HRD practices and talent management in companies with an employer brand. *European Journal of Training and Development, 36*(1), 86–104.

Leisy, B. & Pyron, D. (2009). Talent management takes on new urgency. *Compensation and Benefits Review, 41*, 58–63.

Leung, K., Zhu, Y. & Ge, C. (2009). Compensation disparity between locals and expatriates: Moderating the effects of perceived injustice in foreign multinationals in China. *Journal of World Business, 44*, 85–93.

Lewis, R.E. & Heckman, R.J. (2006). Talent management: A critical review. *Human Resource Management Review, 16*, 139–154.

Li, S. & Scullion, H. (2010). Developing the local competence of expatriate managers for emerging markets: A knowledge-based approach. *Journal of World Business, 45*, 190–196.

Lockwood, N.R. (2007). Leveraging employee engagement for competitive advantage: HR's strategic role. *SHRM Research Quarterly,* 1–11.

Makino, S. & Deklios, A. (1997). Local knowledge transfer and performance: Implications for alliance formation in Asia. *Journal of International Business Studies, 27*, 905–928.

Manning, S., Massini, S. & Lewin, A.Y. (2008). A dynamic perspective on next-generation offshoring: The global sourcing of science and engineering talent. *Academy of Management Perspectives,* August, 35–54.

McDonnell, A. & Collings, D.G. (2011). The identification and evaluation of talent in MNEs. In H. Scullion & D.G. Collings (Eds.), *Global talent management.* New York: Routledge.

McDonnell, A., Lamare, R., Gunnigle, P. & Lavelle, J. (2010). Developing tomorrow's leaders – Evidence of global talent management in multinational enterprises. *Journal of World Business, 45*(2), 150 160.

McKinsey. (2005). *Assessing China's looming talent shortages.* Boston: McKinsey Consultants.

Mercurio, V. (2011). Brazil: A mobility road map for an emerging market. *Strategic Advisor, 7*(64), June, 1–4.

Ng, K., Van Dyne, L. & Ang, S. (2009a). Beyond international experience: The strategic role of cultural intelligence for executive selection in IHRM. In P.R. Sparrow (Ed.), *Handbook of international human resources management: Integrating people, process and content.* Sussex, United Kingdom: Wiley.

Ng, K., Van Dyne, L. & Ang, S. (2009b). Developing global leaders: The role of international experience and cultural intelligence. *Advances in Global Leadership, 5*, 225–250.

Okpara, J.O. & Kabongo, J.D. (2011). Cross-culture training and expatriate adjustment: A study of Western expatriates in Nigeria. *Journal of World Business, 46*, 22–30.

Pattie, M., White, M.M. & Tansky, J. (2010). The homecoming: A review of support for repatriates. *Career Development International, 15*(4), 359–377.

PwC. (2011). Growth reimagined: The talent race is back on. *14ᵗʰ Annual Global CEO Survey 2011*. Retrieved August 30, 2014 from www.pwc.com/ceosurvey

PwC. (2012). Delivering results: Growth and value in a volatile world. *15ᵗʰ Annual Global CEO Survey 2012*. Retrieved August 30, 2014 from www.pwc.com/ceosurvey

Ready, D.A. & Conger, J.A. (2007). Make your company a talent factory. *Harvard Business Review,* June, 1–10.

Ready, D.A., Hill, L.A. & Conger, J.A. (2008). Winning the race for talent in emerging markets. *Harvard Business Review,* November, 1–10.

Reif, C. (2011). Repatriation the right way. *Strategic Advisor, 7*(60), 1–4.

Ruddy, T. & Anand, P. (2010). Managing talent in global organizations: A leadership imperative. In R. Silzer and B.E. Dowell (Eds.), *Strategy-driven talent management.* San Francisco: Jossey-Bass.

SABMiller. (2011). Global Model for Talent Management (TM) 2011. Unpublished internal company document.

Schuler, R.S., Jackson, S.E. & Tarique, I. (2011). Global talent management and global talent challenges: Strategic opportunities for IHRM. *Journal of World Business, 46*, 506–516.

Scullion, H. & Collings, D.G. (2011). Global talent management: Introduction. In H. Scullion and D.G. Collings (Eds.), *Global talent management.* New York: Routledge.

Sheehan, M. (2012). Developing managerial talent: Exploring the link between management talent and perceived performance in multinational corporations (MNCs). *European Journal of Training and Development, 36*(1), 66–85.

Shenxue, L. & Scullion, H. (2010). Developing the local competence of expatriate managers for emerging markets: A knowledge-based approach. *Journal of World Business, 45*, 190–196.

Sims, R.H. & Schraeder, M. (2005). Expatriate compensation: An exploratory review of salient contextual factors and common practices. *Career Development International, 10*(2), 98–108.

Sparrow, J.P. & Balain, S. (2008). Talent proofing the organization. In C.L. Cooper and R. Burke (Eds.), *The peak performing organization.* London: Routledge, 108–128.

Stein, M.A. & Christiansen, L. (2010). *Successful onboarding: A strategy to unlock hidden value within your organization.* New York: McGraw Hill.

Tarique, I. & Schuler, R.S. (2010). Global talent management: Literature review, integrative framework, and suggestions for further research. *Journal of World Business, 45*, 122–133.

Tymon, W.G., Stumpf, S.A. & Doh, J.P. (2010). Exploring talent management in India: The neglected role of intrinsic rewards. *Journal of World Business, 45*, 109–121.

Warneke, D. & Schneider, M. (2011). Expatriate compensation packages: What do employees prefer? *Cross Cultural Management: An International Journal, 18*(2), 236–256.

Yeung, A.K., Warner, M. & Rowley, C. (2008). Growth and globalization: Evolution of hman resource practices in Asia. *Human Resource Management, 47*, 1–13.

CHAPTER 9: Leadership in the Emerging World

Amanda Glaeser

In the face of turbulence and change, culture and values become the major source of continuity and coherence, of renewal and sustainability. Leaders must be institutional-builders who imbue the organisation with meaning that inspires today and endures tomorrow. They must find an underlying purpose and a strong set of values that serve as a basis for longer-term decisions even in the midst of volatility. They must find the common purpose and universal values that unite highly diverse people while still permitting individual identities to be expressed and enhanced. Indeed, emphasising purpose and values helps leaders support and facilitate networks that can respond quickly to change because they share an understanding of the right things to do.

– Rosabeth Moss Kanter (2010)

Introduction

This increasingly complex world, which is faced with continuously changing conditions, creates a compelling argument for leaders, both collectively and individually, to develop new ways of thinking about leadership. Dealing with the obvious issues is no longer adequate – what is required are anticipating and preparing people for the future, and thinking not only horizontally but also vertically, in order to grasp new leadership practices aimed at bringing about quantum change.

In *The emerging markets century* (2006), Antoine van Agtmael posits that many new challenges face the new breed of world-leading companies entering the markets – companies which are catching their Western and more established competitors off guard. How have corporate giants like IBM, Shell, Ford and Sony made it onto the endangered list? What in their development and leadership placed them in this situation?

Emerging economies are growing, while developed countries and their businesses are taking strain.

In South Africa, success stories are tempered by wide-spread criticism of leadership and development initiatives. The thin layer of active leadership in the social sector attracts the most heat – and the most criticism – for being inefficient. Human and intellectual capital development pose a challenge for academic institutions. Diversity continues to be hampered by old-school mindsets and practices, resulting

151

in South Africa not fully utilising the diversity of talent that its multicultural society has to offer (Ramphele, 2012). In addition, South Africa is home to four major race groups and 11 official languages, which can present further obstacles to total integration.

Leadership is generally defined as the ability to direct followers towards an appropriate goal. This implies the capacity to envisage an ideal future (Ngubeni, 2012) and to back it up with a sound knowledge base. According to the Centre for Knowledge Societies, emerging economies are defined as those 'regions of the world that are experiencing rapid informationalisation under conditions of limited or partial industrialisation' (Wikipedia, 2013), in addition to being depicted as markets in-between non-traditional user behaviour, witnessing the rise of new interest groups in products or services. Rapid growth and industrialisation have made India and China the biggest emerging economies to date. The general understanding is that a growing economy moves from low agricultural productivity to high industrialised productivity.

South Africa, which is considered to be part of the developing world, is a young democracy with 46 years of racial discrimination behind it. Despite its historical legacy, it is a market characterised by both high potential and high complexity: having emerged from its history of segregation (apartheid), it now straddles both the developed and the developing worlds. South Africa is classified as an upper middle-income country, together with Mexico, Malaysia, Algeria, Brazil and others.

In an address, the Rector of the University of the Western Cape, Professor Brian O' Connell (2013), referred to the challenge of making sense of a world in which 85 per cent of its citizens live under emerging world standards, while the remainder live in a developed world which still dominates as the model to aspire to. People in developing economies expect the same resources to be available to them, to the same high standards enjoyed by the privileged 15 per cent of the world's population.

South Africa's inclusion, late in 2011, in BRICS (Brazil, Russia, India, China and South Africa), hailed as the new emerging power group, made it subject to criticism. Some argue that this happened as a result of lobbying; that South Africa may not have been the best choice, given the stronger and bigger economies of countries such as Indonesia, Turkey, Mexico, Nigeria and South Korea.

Context for new leadership paradigms in emerging countries

> There are no rules here – we're trying to accomplish something.
>
> – Thomas A. Edison

The future is disorder, and Western well-developed and accepted thinking models can no longer control disorder with force. Like the wind, the Internet cannot be 'boxed in'. Information is available to the masses, liberating them from mind control. The birth of new forms of organisations and leadership has begun.

This shift is all about including the so-called 'soft' issues in leadership thinking. Failure to do so will result in the collective energy tipping between chaos and order, as is evident in recent events in emerging countries such as Egypt, Bahrain, Tunisia, Libya, Syria and Cyprus. These events indicate a shift in people's expectations for a different kind of formal leadership. A 12-year-old girl in Pakistan challenged the authorities to allow girls to also receive schooling, thereby targeting power and authority in an attempt to change, and to establish a different leadership model. New expectations have seen nations demanding to be included, to be heard. They are calling for desired values to become more visible as tangible proof of what 'the people' deem to be important.

The actions of the youth, in particular, embody feelings of a release of the old, and an outreach towards a new way of being: they want to be part of the action, they want to satisfy their needs. This signals a different world view from that of the older generation, and sends a clear message to current leadership. Leaders must now prioritise connectivity as well as relationships. Such extreme (some would say, revolutionary) actions represent a shift which is aimed at accommodating contestation from people across society. They want to establish an agreed culture, while raising awareness of issues relating to diversity and community, and they call on their leaders to inculcate those values that will help to form an integrated nation. Diversity in itself is already a challenge, made all the more daunting with the inclusion of different generational worldviews and issues such as ethnicity, culture, religion, gender and values. Such differences demand attention. There is no natural integration amongst different communities living together, therefore the focus should fall on providing active support for education which is aimed at integration. The aim should be to optimise positive energy to co-exist and to establish collaboration as a key cultural behaviour. This culture is very evident in China, and despite Chinese ideology differing so vastly from Western ideology, we can all learn from how they interact with people.

The big question, according to Valoida (2013), is the issue of inequality and how to address the 'precariat', i.e., those people with no or few prospects, so as to enable them to join the mainstream economy. Valoida (2013) concedes that there are no clear solutions, mainly because leaders are locked in current paradigms. In the main, current leadership responses can best be described as technocratic, myopic and contained within current policy parameters.

Looking at the South African context as an example of an emerging economy, there is a complex set of variables to take cognisance of: a history of colonialism and oppression saw black people not only being disadvantaged, but losing their normative heritage as a result of dominant Western norms. Yes, South Africa is a 'hot pot' of cultures, but the reality remains that the people of this nation constructively seek to 'build the country together' in the face of existing weaknesses. South Africa has much it can share with the world as a result of its unique experiences, diverse population and history of dealing with complex structures and changes. Nelson Mandela's conscious leadership is evidence of how the presence of a contextually aware leader can bring about positive change.

When such success stories exist, the question arises how international models can be balanced with local realities and successes. Will an international intervention add value if there is no understanding of the DNA of a country, and no knowledge of what drives its people and their passions?

There is a need to reflect on history and cultural norms to prevent business and changing social conditions from alienating people from their traditional roots. Leaders need to contemplate the unintended consequences of such 'liberations'; for example economic projects in countries may clash with those cultural values a community aspires to. This is pertinent in South Africa, where traditional leaders still have a place within communities as leaders of subjects who often have no other source of income, and no alternative place to live (Butler, 2007).

Capitalism cannot, however, be viewed as all bad. Sisodia (2013), for instance, sings its praises for ending poverty and creating values beyond what other institutions, such as governments and religion, have been able to achieve. An example is China changing its economic strategy in the early 1990s, which has resulted in Chinese people being ten times richer than before. World-wide, poverty levels are decreasing.

Social order can be fragile, and can break down at any time – as is happening in countries across the world. Risk identification should form part of regular analytical forecasting in terms of general public pressures, ethnic disputes, labour unrest and political trends. The ultimate goal is to determine how we can build social cohesion and social development together, while meeting demands for economic growth. The context in which this cohesion needs to be built is subject to an ever-shifting and unpredictable economic environment. Such turbulence tends to keep the focus on economic growth, as opposed to including greater social capital growth. However, in the current economic climate, emerging countries are showing signs of growth despite the worldwide economic downturn. This is a result of emerging markets connecting directly with one another, as opposed to retaining a dependence on European and Western markets. The inherent ability to deal with chaos and not be dependent on a controlled and mechanised existence, allows the emerging world greater flexibility and invites new thinking amidst challenging and unpredictable times. What is important is not to allow rigid paradigms to block new thinking. Emerging market leaders are responding more imaginatively to unpredictable and chaotic markets, possibly because their patterns of thinking are less conditioned than those of leaders in established countries. What comes to mind is how the Vietnam War dynamics could not be predicted by intelligent analysis and planning only. In fact, because of the passion and commitment of the Vietnamese people, who thought in unconventional ways, their strategies were not predictable and came as a surprise to first-world mindsets such as the United States.

Robert McNamara, Head of the American defence force during the Vietnam War, in reflecting on his hyper-rational approach, admitted that he misjudged the importance of the intangible and the irrational in human affairs. Leaders in 'less sophisticated worlds' are willing to act, even if it entails making mistakes. Rationality alone will not save the day (Rosenweig, 2010).

In South Africa, the following question needs to be asked: Why do so many South Africans choose to be unemployed? Is the system not conducive to people creating enterprises to generate a living? According to Valoida (2013), the informal economy in South Africa is small compared to that of other emerging countries, and this makes South Africa something of an oddity. Perhaps the country has too many big retailers dominating markets – most likely the unintended consequence of limiting entrepreneurial opportunities.

Abbott (2011) posits that it is generally accepted that South Africa has dominant businesses, and this state of affairs reduces competition. Such market domination highlights the need for serious economic structural reform (Valoida, 2013). To achieve this, it is surely time to consider applying the same ingenuity which leaders in so many emerging markets are now showcasing.

The economic results tell a story

The McKinsey Global Institute (2010, p. 15) reports as follows:

> Developing countries are growing their economies, against the odds. The GDP growth from 2000 to 2008 indicated the following trend: Emerging Asia 8,3 per cent; Middle East 5,2; Africa 4,9; Central Eastern Europe 4,8; Latin America 4,0; the world grew at 3 percent; whilst the established developed markets of developed economies grew by only 2 percent. Developing nations are increasingly connecting with one another (South-South exchanges), to the extent where trade between them is as high as 50 percent of the total world trade. Western Europe trade shrank from 51 percent to 28 percent.

The BRICS conference held in 2013 in Durban, South Africa, reported the following percentages of growth for 2012: Brazil – 39 per cent, Russia – 10 , India – 25, China – 48, South Africa – 3 (the tourism sector grew by ten per cent) (e-tv News Report, March 2013). This international collaboration is not always without its tensions: China, for instance, has begun competing in the same markets as other BRICS countries, and is therefore moving into sensitive territories. The fact that it has strengthened ties with Latin American nations is viewed with some suspicion, and its fabric trade in African prints has been condemned as nothing but cheap reproductions. This, and other tariff-related practices, has seen the textile industry in South Africa shrink, leading to more unemployment due to the loss of an estimated 300 000 jobs (Brink, 2013).

India, on the other hand, is positioned as excelling in the services industry, and is the country of choice when it comes to call centres. This confirms that while BRICS nations are partners, an element of fierce competition exists amongst them. This situation does not bode well where the strategy of developing countries (BRICS nations in particular) is to reduce dependency on trade with Western countries. Certain studies have focused on what can be described as 'China's economic colonisation of Africa' (see Watts, 2008), claiming that China's engagements with Africa are skewed towards benefitting Beijing. Africa offers a high return on investments, and China's trade with Africa was estimated at $220 billion in 2012 – which represents an annual growth of 25 per cent from the previous year (Delano, 2013). Establishing commercial equilibrium amongst the BRICS countries requires sensitive management if positive relationships and balance are to be maintained.

The key demand is still for everyone to identify with a higher purpose, not just basic survival needs, which is the main context for all to work with and to strive for. In this context the desired outcomes of leadership are direction, alignment and commitment. Leadership is about conscious business aimed at leading the organisation's culture beyond profit and shareholder satisfaction; it requires leadership which leads to a conscious culture of producing results, but is also aimed at attaining a higher purpose, namely improving and nurturing the world we live in (Mackey, 2011).

This view resonates with Dave Ulrich's (2012) human resources concept of working from the outside in, to ensure that the company's stakeholder needs to form part of its strategic thinking. It is by considering the outside world that value-add to all stakeholders is optimised. Appreciation for emerging context should see strategic planning moving away from traditional and established mindsets (Porter & Kramer, 2011). Leadership matters when organisations build progress in a way that benefits all stakeholders, including specifically the community and the environment.

This new leadership paradigm requires not only a mindset change, but also seeks leadership capacity that is not readily available. It requires an innate desire to not only focus on the economic health of a country, but also on an active, social capital-building plan – a process through which citizens will accept the role, beyond equal opportunities, of working on overcoming the limiting views of the past. The result must be social cohesion, with a deep understanding of those transformational requirements that will lead to a new humanity. The formula for an accomplishment of this nature may well be found in the wisdom of social capital thinking: 'Social capital is shared norms or values that promote social cooperation, instantiated in actual social relationships' (Fukuyama, 2002, p. 27). Social capital has a heterogeneous nature, with qualitative dimensions of social relationships, which includes a pervasiveness that can have either a positive or a negative effect on a social system. An example of a culture that seems to have achieved social capital as a core competence is China: investing in relationships is what the Chinese people do; their model is dependent on teamwork, cooperation and trust. They invest in relationships, they view partnerships as first priority, and only afterwards do they focus on other matters. When they were faced with the Asian crisis in 1997 they 'recycled' their human capital into other sectors, with the intention of preserving the jobs, security and dignity of their people. As a result, they recovered in record time from this economic setback. Many see China as positioned to be the next country to lead the world (Ngubeni, 2012). China puts people first and rarely treats them as dispensable (Turley, 2012). This comes with the understanding that their context is very different from that of Western nations. The end of the Soviet Republics and Chinese economic reform are indications that a new form of capitalism is eminent – a new economic model that is 'softer' than capitalism and signals a version of social market economics. It is also argued that pure capitalism cannot alleviate the poverty that exists in the world. The notion of 'liberal capitalism', introduced by Allen and Thomas (cited in Abbott 2011) sees the incorporation of benefits into all facets over which the business world exerts some influence.

India is viewed as putting people central to its operations, by placing motivating and developing employees above shareholders' interests with a view to ensuring long-term sustainability. Engaging employees by creating a sense of social mission, openness and good communication is a focus of India's organisational cultures (Cappelli, Singh, Singh & Useen, 2010).

Table 9.1 provides generic indicators of sources where social capital can be actively enhanced.

Table 9.1: Formal and informal sources and indicators of social capital

Formal and informal social capital	Indicators of socal capital
Structures and governance	A positive sense of culture and climate
Policies and procedures	Support for and adherence to processes
Informal relationships	Sense of community, affinity
Network ties	Disclosive communications
Personal and emotional ties	Social trust
Shared language and codes	Collaboration
Myths and rituals	Informal coordination, self-organisation, reduced opportunism

Adapted from Lengnick-Hall and Lengnick-Hall, 2003

It is important to note that the median ages of people on the planet are rising. This creates a different set of values, shifting from 'me', towards meaning and a desire for 'value-add'. In addition, the rise of feminine values contributes to a better sense of what is right and wrong, and of people being more conscious of, and desiring, harmony – also with nature (Sisodia, 2013).

The emerging world has become the research and development terrain for many Western companies, thus the frontiers of innovation can often be found in such locations. This requires leaders in the emerging world to keep an open mind, while gaining maximum benefit from those ventures launched in their countries, which are funded by developed nations. While lessons can be learned from the developed world, Holger Dragman (cited in Ngubeni, 2012) urges developing countries to develop their own sustainability models and to align them to targeted needs within their societies.

The concept of ensuring shared value to enable local development is paramount to guaranteeing that all stakeholders benefit – not only the community, but also the business as a partner to others – this, as opposed to organisations solely having a profit focus. Such thinking enhances the well-established capitalism model and applies equally to advanced economies and developing countries; its essence is to better connect the profit goal with societal benefits. It is about new ways of serving and improving the world in a congruent manner, so that all involved will benefit!

Research evidence on sustainability needs indicates that humans currently use 30 per cent more resources than what the earth is capable of producing (Ulrich & Ulrich, 2010). The ethical focus should therefore be not to compromise the future while meeting the needs of present realities. This paradigm requires holistic thinking as opposed to 'balance sheet' thinking, which is driven by time constraints aimed at meeting targets. The profit motive and insufficient time to think are often barriers to new world views emerging. Conscious capitalism builds on the foundation of capitalism as a healthy model, but it allows for the introduction of compassion, collaboration and value creation.

Nations are serious about achieving goals, investing in talent and leadership development and creating new business models, if the people involved are allowed enough time to think. It is also imperative for strategic teams to welcome young members, as this helps to maintain a balance between old paradigms and forward-thinking. Past experiences must not be an obstacle to a better future.

A further dilemma may well be that many sitting around the boardroom table are steeped in traditional leadership thinking (including that of Western MBA schools) which sees them dominating decision-making, rather than actively being open-minded and pursuing the unique local realities of a country. Valoida (2013) proposes that socially engaged and aware young people can adapt to complex local social conditions: their fresh insights may address issues of unemployment better than narrow business models do. Mills (cited in Abbott, 2012) states that each country must forge its own developmental path: selectively taking lessons from other countries is not a formula for success, rather, peoples' own unique ability to transform and modernise themselves must be recognised. This status quo, accompanied by a leadership gap where inadequately prepared people are often found in key roles, exacerbates the leadership challenges facing society. Graph 9.1 indicates the scale of the problem: not enough able leaders are available. This, combined with a projected growth in employee numbers, presents countries with the significant challenge of implementing fast-track leadership development programmes (see Graph 9.2, showing staff growth between 50 and 70 per cent for growing economies).

A further barrier to relevant leadership development is the fact that stereotypical Western executives are held up as role models – their hard-nosed attitudes and behaviours seem to be the norm. This homogenous view needs to be balanced with local realities.

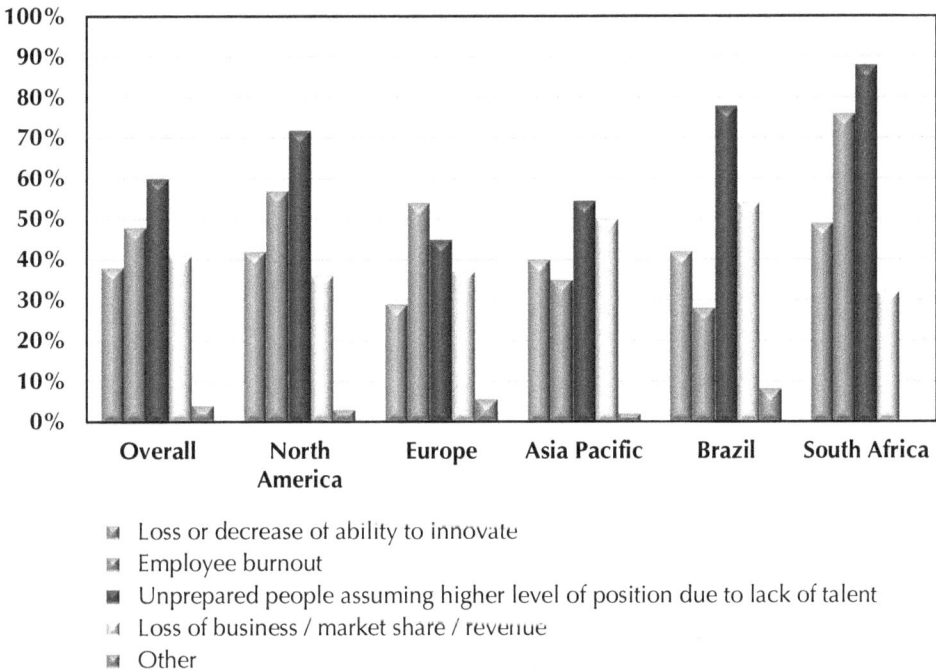

- Loss or decrease of ability to innovate
- Employee burnout
- Unprepared people assuming higher level of position due to lack of talent
- Loss of business / market share / revenue
- Other

Graph 9.1: The main challenges to leadership development
Source: CPP Inc., 2008

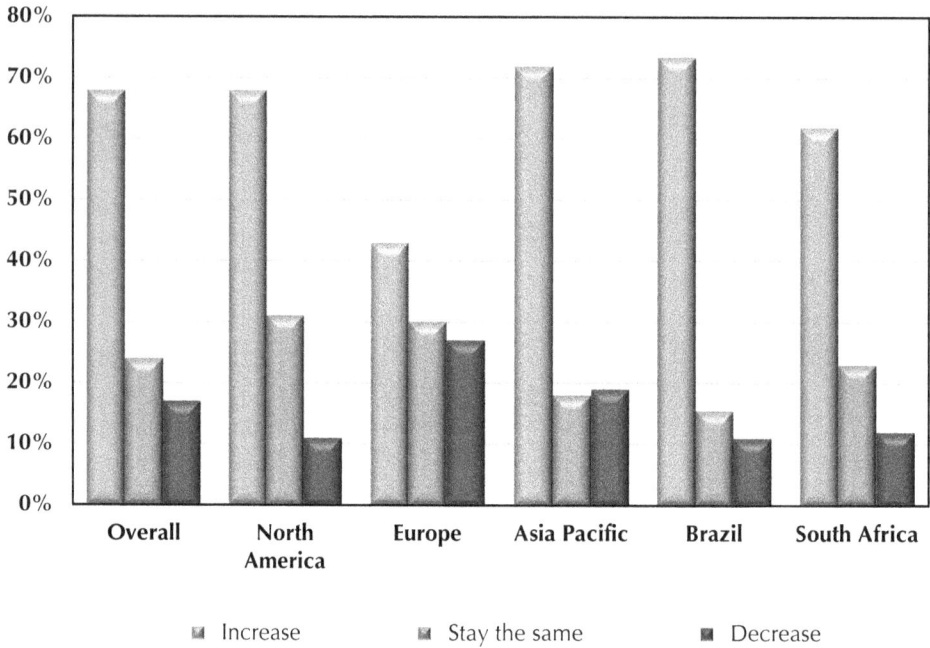

Graph 9.2: Expectations of employee growth over the next ten years
Source: CPP Inc., 2008

The story of Japan contains many leadership lessons, for instance, what gets you to the top will not keep you there. In the past this allowed for very little diversity, and what organisations deemed would fit their company was viewed from their own narrow perspectives. Leaders therefore showed very little interest in local contexts when doing business outside Japan; they did not allow many foreign markets to make inroads into Japan, which resulted in ignorance regarding the way other countries do business. The Japanese workforce did not oppose company authorities and they showed a preference for homogeneous teams (especially at the top). This contrasts sharply with the situation in BRICS countries, where homogeneity is not problematic. Leaders are needed who can represent all cultures as well as diverse thinking (Black & Morrison, 2010).

Current leadership development practices

Responses to new, evolving needs and environmental changes are forcing leaders to move away from tradition and to start thinking more about being adaptive. At the same time they need to maintain executive direction; i.e., allow for greater inclusiveness in order to create opportunities for people and groups to influence specific issues. Fast tracking the development of new leaders has become a priority for both organisations and societies. In this regard, the top five practices as prioritised/selected by organisations to develop leaders, are the following:

- Participation in cross-functional international teams: 22 per cent;
- International assignments (two years): 20 per cent;
- Internal development programmes: 17 per cent;
- Short-term international assignments (six months): 17 per cent;
- Mentoring and/or coaching: 14 per cent.

These leadership development practices may well have limitations for emerging markets which may be subject to different realities. India has identified the following leadership skills as critical, in order of priority, for the country's development (Cappelli et al., 2010):

- Articulate a path to the future by thinking strategically and directing change;
- Be inspirational, accountable and entrepreneurial;
- Support talent selection and development;
- Support best organisational structures and core values;
- Understand competitors, markets and outside relations.

These requirements are impressive, since they are quite generic and align with the general needs put forward by the literature. The necessary differentiation may well lie in the application of these requirements, to different cultures and in different scenarios. Alternatively, it may not yet be easy to use the terminology that will identify the less tangible competencies of leaders in a changing world.

A distinction can be made between *problem solving*, taught in formal leadership development programmes, and *problem finding*, which can only be acquired through actual work experience. Success is not only the ability to analyse data, but also the ability to scan environments for intangible clues about potential problems. Leaders must be able to find meaning by detecting changes in their methods of operating, and identifying people behaviours and competitor actions long before these manifest on reports and in financial statements. Livingston (2009) claims that formal leadership development falls short in its ability to teach problem finding, thus the perceptual skills to anticipate problems is lacking. In the words of Peter Drucker (1964): 'Not how to do things right; but to find the right things to do.'

Psychologists label the former 'respondent behaviour', i.e., the ability to score high marks in examinations, but it does not necessarily result in practical application. The latter, known as 'operant behaviour', implies the finding of opportunities, initiating action, and following through to obtain the desired results. An example in this instance is to refer to the question on everybody's lips: What happened to Japan? Often a leader's or country's biggest strength becomes its biggest weakness. To avoid making the same errors as the Japanese did, it is imperative not to become overly reliant on protected domestic markets, but to find new business models and steer clear of homogeneous leadership.

Another challenge is the generational differences posed by Generation Y employees (born between 1981 and 1999), whose work values tend to differ from those of the Baby Boomers (born between 1941 and 1959) who still occupy senior roles in the workplace. This necessitates a review of the work policies, learning methods and practices that appeal and motivate different groups of employees. The in-between Generation Xers (born between 1960 and 1980) pose even more challenges due to their diverse nature: they have a particular history relative to economic hardships and single parenting – phenomena which peaked during that period (Erickson, 2010).

On reflection, the question is whether learning specialists are able to provide leadership development programmes that can offer a level of learning to challenge young leaders in more context-appropriate and open-minded ways.

Frameworks for current and future leadership paradigms

Leadership is mostly about change and transformation, dealing not with incremental change efforts but with movement from one leadership logic to the next (McGuire & Rhodes, 2009). Transformation cannot be achieved by conventional thinking; it is very much about implementing and maintaining *new* ideas so as to advance to the next level of new logic. This style is often used to describe young, dynamic leaders who convincingly direct change in themselves, in other individuals, and in groups and organisations. Success is measured in terms of a leader's ability to 'fit' where required. A leadership style therefore needs to fit not only the individual but also the organisation, in order to be authentic (Ngozo, 2012).

Table 9.2 indicates the shifting competencies for effective leadership over time. Mankind is evolving to an uncertain point and without clarity on how to gain commitment to one another, or how to attain a shared vision and mission. Therefore, the result may well be an undesirable future.

Table 9.2: Shifting paradigms which leaders need to embrace

Shifting paradigms leaders need to embrace		
INDUSTRIAL Age	**INFORMATION Age**	**CONSCIOUSNESS Age**
Change	Transformation	Evolution
Focus on: Quality of product	**Focus on:** Intellectual capital	**Focus on:** Cultural capital
Quality Skilled labour Productivity Efficiency Mass marketing	Knowledge Learning Personal growth Empowerment Customer satisfaction	Ethics and values Vision and mission Values alignment Whole system change Customer collaboration

Source: Barrett, 2006

Leaders need to deal with the ambiguity of global and local effectiveness and to acquire the capability to deliver cultural capital (see Table 9.2). The growing divide between the developed and the developing worlds, where the latter focuses on progress and building domestic demands (the specific social, economic and political needs of a country), creates the leadership challenge to be relevant, 'new' leaders. Knowledge, skills, values and behaviours must be fit for purpose, and generalisations must be referenced in moderation. More thinking is therefore critical to source the ingenuity required for the demands of a non-linear time.

It is widely claimed that consciousness influences human performance, and we have witnessed this notion becoming mainstream in terms of creating new mindsets. First, the concept of conscious leadership implies that leaders must be aware, i.e., to think and feel on different levels of being – something which is not a new concept, given the numerous theories around levels of leadership functioning (Elliot Jaques, Jim Collins, Richard Barrett, etc).

What is unique, however, is the sense of transcending levels of self-awareness and mechanistic business principles, and moving into the realm of why it is imperative to care about the whole. Barrett (2012) expands on the need to understand a new basis for decision-making: leaders and organisations need to be more flexible and more adaptable, while also reflecting on their shared human values.

Figure 9.1 depicts the seven levels of consciousness, a framework for full-spectrum thinking pertaining to how to be a leader within diverse and complex settings. Figure 9.1 also indicates how leaders should ideally develop in order to shift from the self and an overly economic focus, to creating meaning for both the self and others. Lastly, it offers a leadership paradigm of stewardship that will make a difference to all. This is an inclusive paradigm in which all aspects are critical, and where no hierarchy of levels exists. Success means all seven levels are incorporated into the leader's thinking, to produce optimum results.

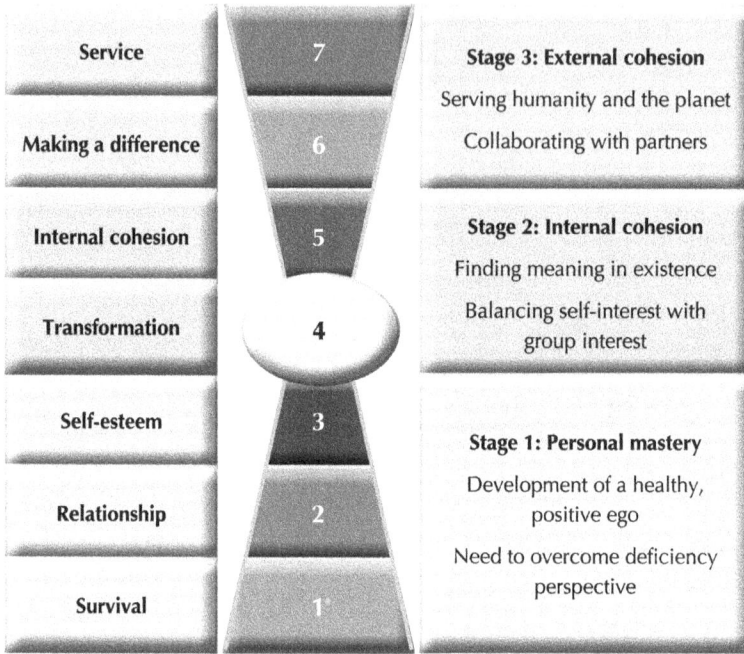

Figure 9.1: Principal focus of the three stages of leadership development
Source: Barrett, 2006

Leadership should be synonymous not only with profits, but also 'communityship' (Mintzberg, 2004). Due to workplace pressures thoughtful thinking becomes a luxury, while slowing down and reflecting are critical imperatives in ensuring that leaders remain connected and committed to the issues at hand. Opportunity and crisis create new leadership paradigms and a trend in developing nations is to revert back to family-style leaders, especially in Brazil, India, Mexico and Turkey. China, on the other hand, positions the state as a family surrogate (Raman, 2009). This practice creates risks and is not deemed ideal, but it has brought back the leadership model of being part professional and part family in terms of business practices, necessitating conscious attempts to reintroduce the concept of caring. This resonates with the Maslow model, as enhanced by Barrett (2012), which demonstrates the importance of including the collective context.

This significant leadership consciousness model, which speaks to the issues under discussion here, emphasises the notion of conscious leadership, which elevates leadership practices from specific needs to a full spectrum and collective focus. Barrett (2012, p. 255) defines consciousness as 'awareness with a purpose'.

Figure 9.2, like Figure 9.1, depicts the full spectrum of seven levels of consciousness which incorporate both the rational and the emotional aspects of being a leader. The intention is that not one single level, but rather all seven levels should carry equal importance in a leader's work and social endeavours. This concept challenges leaders to move away from focusing only on economic motives (something economists would no doubt challenge!) to include the marginalised in good citizenship and economic activities, to create a coherent alternative to fill this vacuum that exists for large numbers of people, and therefore to be able to deal with multiple situations at many different levels.

Things look bleak when an economy is in a downward spiral, yet the situation creates scope for new ideas. What is called for, are innovation and experimentation, with active participation from political and academic stakeholders (Valoida, 2013).

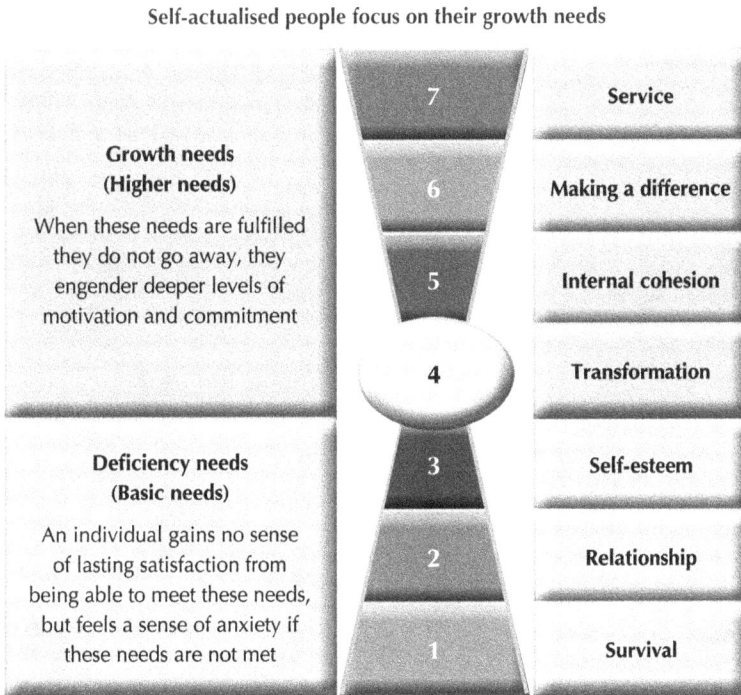

Self-actualised people focus on their growth needs

Growth needs (Higher needs) When these needs are fulfilled they do not go away, they engender deeper levels of motivation and commitment	7	Service
	6	Making a difference
	5	Internal cohesion
	4	Transformation
Deficiency needs (Basic needs) An individual gains no sense of lasting satisfaction from being able to meet these needs, but feels a sense of anxiety if these needs are not met	3	Self-esteem
	2	Relationship
	1	Survival

Figure 9.2: Deficiency needs and growth needs
Source: Barrett, 2006 (slide show)

Leaders can only develop and enrich people and situations if they function from a growth needs perspective. This requires the leadership focus to be on the needs articulated by workforces; to professionalise leadership in the context of being locally appropriate (country-specific) but not to be ignorant of the international world. In addition, such a leader should fuse the emotional component with rational management, where the rational tends to be an overly strong traditional Western norm.

Another supporting paradigm for these challenges is Theory U: Leading from the emerging future (Scharmer, 2005). Scharmer (2005, p. 3), argues that we need to allow a new social presence to arise: 'The spontaneous rise of social fields that embody this heightened collective awareness and action is one of the most significant developments of our time.'

A leadership blind spot needs to be addressed by paying attention to people's approaches to work. The premise is that what and how leaders do things, is directed by the 'inner place' from which they operate. That place where the quality of their attention is seated, provides leaders with a sense of where their actions stem from; it includes a sense of future possibilities, not only past and present experiences, and allows them to observe reality with fresh eyes.

Figure 9.3 illustrates the process of paying attention and sensing the future. The process is enhanced if it is a participative group endeavour.

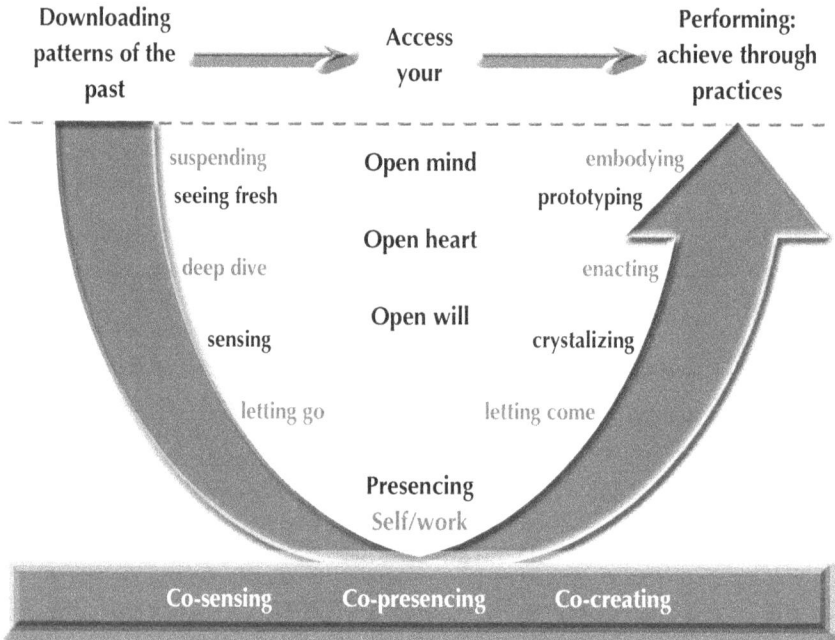

Figure 9.3: Theory U: Leading from the emerging future
Source: Scharmer, 2005, p. 11

Fred Kofman (cited by Mackey & Sisodia, 2013, p. 194) posits that this type of all-inclusive and humanistic leadership energy leads to 'peace and happiness in the individual, respect and solidarity in the community, and mission accomplished for the organisation'.

Development and change challenges for new leadership paradigms

Mackey and Sisodia (2013) believe conscious leaders have the following capabilities as part of their profile: they have high analytical, emotional, spiritual and systems intelligence; combined with integrity and the capacity to love and care; as well as a servant leadership orientation. This translates into concepts such as emotional, spiritual and systems intelligence, yet none of this can be attained at the expense of a high analytical intelligence (e.g., high IQ). Systems intelligence involves the ability to 'feel' the system, i.e., an interconnectedness and oneness with the organisation. This includes being able to contribute to the creation of such a system. Conscious leaders not only make a positive impact, they are also able to embed a sense of purpose that creates meaning for others. This, according to Mackey and Sisodia (2013), leads to a conscious culture where accountability, trust, caring, transparency, integrity, loyalty and egalitarianism prevail.

Operating processes in emerging countries tend to require a more agile mindset, rather than a strict project-type methodology; often a zero-based thinking approach is more appropriate for accommodating local needs.

Balancing choices with consequences in the context of creating a better world (which implies better leaders) is becoming an important business principle. Great leadership today has a new meaning: capital without conscience is no longer an acceptable concept, and this has resulted in conscious leadership becoming the new currency in leadership thinking (Mackey & Sisodia, 2013). New awareness entails tapping into this human transcendence, rather than merely focusing on the self, to arrive at a mindset where everybody who can add value is included. This creates an adaptive system with self-organising principles at its core. The result is that agreed values are upheld by teams, and that co-created processes are 'hardwired' to give results in an interdependent system. Being dependent on an individual leader becomes less of a neccesity.

Furthermore, a leadership culture needs to be established which implies collective learning amongst leaders in the workplace, in addition to finding practices to both sustain and renew the collective leadership culture. This ensures an open system which can meet the demands of emergent change. The paradigm of what is 'normal' may well be very different in different scenarios, and making sense of new, local or emerging realities must occur outside of existing paradigms.

Organisations struggle with leadership development. Often it is the top performers in a specific discipline who are promoted, after which they are mostly left to their own devices and expected to survive. From the literature it is clear that the challenge is to develop leaders who can work contextually with their own specific country and organisational issues. New competencies that will break old patterns are needed to address challenges with new models of thinking that are fit for purpose within a specific scenario. One of South Africa's critical high-level issues requiring new leadership thinking is the country's rating, in position 110 out of 182 nations, on the Human Development Index in terms of quality of education. The situation calls for new education strategies which will raise the country above the world average. To do so, poverty levels and issues of inequality need serious leadership attention.

If we follow the logic of businesses having the ability to add value not just to business but also to societies, leaders at all levels must be made aware that they need to make a full-spectrum difference, as per the Barrett model of levels of being.

When Jakes Gerwel (former personal assistant to Mandela) was interviewed by Higgins in 2012, he emphasised the importance of the social sciences retaining a balance with the non-human sciences (engineering, natural, chemical, medical sciences, etc). Values and good people practices need to remain part of the modern debate. We need to retain Mandela's sense of collective leadership by keeping in mind the importance of individuals needing to feel engaged, before being able to relate to, and participate, with the collective. Gerwel (2012) reflected on how Mandela was always able to make decisions for the future by 'looking back' to the present. Madiba's ability to envisage the impact which decisions would have on the future was a leadership strength that assisted South Africa greatly during turbulent times. Mandela also believed that humans are essentially good, and this is what creates the connectedness and unity which help people build a country (Higgins, 2013).

It has been said that leadership equals energy, and that a leader's mindset pervades the culture of his/her people. The 'U model' (Scharmer, 2005 – see Figure 9.3) is an example of a thinking process which leaders can utilise to develop a relationship with the future, while being wholly in the present.

The more generic, tangible competencies still apply. However, the difference may well lie in the intangible capacity of an individual, such as being able to read the signs for a unique leadership style or insight, in respect of the appropriate direction to take in a given situation. The model on leadership consciousness is a great aid in this regard – it helps the leader to establish which level of the organisation s/he is dealing with, as well as how to create higher levels of awareness amongst people in a particular system. This implies that we need to develop training methodology and media to establish those competencies which will support analysis and judgement in a specific context, before taking the appropriate action.

A first challenge is to identify the best people for leadership roles. More often than not, it is those individuals with a high need for control and power who get noticed and are earmarked for critical roles, while other (more capable) people do not compete or do not desire those responsibilities because they are under-appreciated: Griffin (2009) differentiates between 'reluctant' and 'unknown' leadership talent. Potential leaders in these instances can be highly successful if developed through encouragement, inclusion and personal coaching.

Generally it is important to gain self-insight into balancing ambition, control and power with existing social needs. Multi-rating feedback for individuals helps to eliminate blind spots and this, in turn, leads to continuous improvement.

The case of individualising leadership development relative to matching person needs with role profiles is also a consideration for success.

Attention and time out to think bring greater awareness, which can lead to higher consciousness in terms of decision-making in specific contexts. The use of surveys is a powerful way in which to grasp context, as provided by people already in a system.

Processes to help access the tacit knowledge that exists in oneself and in others help to create greater awareness of what is effective. The challenge is to source a core inner place where behaviour comes from. Arguably, this can only be done through effective learning from experience (one's own and that of others). This is possible through co-creation and collective thinking which, in themselves, are new competencies that cannot be taught or practised adequately. The challenge is to understand the place we as leaders act from, rather than putting too much emphasis on what we do. This makes leadership personal and also inherently collective, it makes sense within leaders and in their relations with one another; it fuses deep thinking and interaction with emerging concepts at inception.

Aggregated thinking accesses tacit territory and may lead to the sensing power where the collective transcends the individual, to arrive at a deeper level of awareness. The creation of learning communities is an example of this process.

Diversity management as a competency is critical to ensure optimal contributions to prevent a singular view from forming too early in a process of developing a strategy for different and sometimes unknown contexts. Local people must form part of the 'think tanks' that are planning new ventures.

If goodwill triumphs (along with being courageous, decisive and ethical), leaders should create an energy that can bring forth ingenious ideas, for and from people, and so be part of adding value that affects them directly. This will help to advance the previously disadvantaged, it will help grow talented people and foster democracy and inclusion, make work more meaningful, encourage socioeconomic literacy, bring about greater social engagement, and lead to internal alignment and optimum productivity. It is therefore about optimising those contributions which can play a role in alleviating poverty and looking at the 'softer' version of capitalism. This offers value-add to all stakeholders, while still delivering business results.

A view on leadership in South Africa

In many ways, South Africa is a unique country. As such, one can expect to find unique leadership needs. Vusi Gumede (2013) posits that a focus on Afrocentricity and indigenous knowledge is critical, considering the country's colonial past. He warns that new trends may signal similar shifts, such as economic domination on the part of certain countries, except these will manifest in unexpected formats.

Gumede (2013) calls for full consciousness of what is happening, without being critical of the West. He also reflects on how divided Africa remains despite efforts to create unity. The effective management of diverse issues calls for a leader who can bring about integration in respect of those issues people agree on. Such communalism is a positive force in overcoming the challenge of functioning in concert, as a single body. We need new economic models now that the old models have failed us. A paradigm which embraces more robust thinking, is needed. In Gumede's view, Africa should reject advice from the West in favour of greater African cohesion, as this is a critical mindset for future success (Gumede, 2013).

Conclusion

The power to unleash global growth may well lie in the connection between societal and economic growth (Porter & Kramer, 2011). The dominance of business in our everyday lives places a responsibility on organisations to take better care of the whole. Taking responsibility and moving towards a paradigm of conscious capitalism will entail a new way of thinking for many workplaces (Harman cited in Barrett, 2012). Values-based decision-making is about chiselling out a new-era workplace in which conscious capitalism is an emerging force. The challenge to leadership is to follow the pioneers in creating a new model of co-existence. Indications are that the leadership challenges facing developing countries (and our collective future) include the following: embracing diverse peoples in order to optimise new thinking (demonstrate a commitment to manage diversity); creating a collaborative culture that builds alliances and is experienced as partnerships; ensuring that communication is frequent, open and multidimensional, and that value-add thinking includes the community in which the business functions; creating integration amidst differentiation in order to brand and operate a business; dealing with paradoxes; constantly redefining work and structures so that they have agility and flexibility as a cultural norm; having the courage to deal with uncertainties; balancing money and meaning; and including intuition in any analysis.

The leadership competence would be to have flexibility combined with order; meaning that the organisation can change direction without losing its essential core, and give direction without confusing authority with authoritarianism. Growing requires skill in dealing with bigger and more complex 'problems', thus incorporating higher levels of thinking; as the system matures, being able to deal with issues at a next stage of growth will become imperative.

The congruence of co-existing will create a new direction for the future. This should be a priority focus for any leadership which envisages the establishment of a new order, a place where local differences and global realities all form part of a vision and strategy for a connected people who are working towards continuous progress.

The culture of an organisation is experienced through the values of the leadership; co-created values that are lived day to day will enhance both trust and social capital. In turn, this will reduce operational effort and costs. Building the concepts of cultural capital into processes, with the purpose of engaging employees as participants as well as partners, will propel workplaces into a position of purposeful consciousness. All of this is only possible if leadership – personally and within their environments – achieve internal stability and external equilibrium, i.e., if they integrate themselves into elements of the organisation and the societies they operate in.

The seven levels of full-spectrum consciousness signal a shift from 'I' to 'we' (Barrett, 2012). It is not just about what, how and why, but also about caring for the world. When leadership practices are in sync with what external communities and stakeholders expect, organisations will thrive. Organisations *can* ensure the wellbeing of people and they *can* also transform the world – a world in which people engage fully to create an ideal existence, where everyone achieves extraordinary levels of being.

> Greatness is not a function of circumstance. Greatness, it turns out, is largely a matter of conscious choice and discipline.
>
> – Jim Collins

References

Abbott, P. (2011). *Human resources management in the South African socio-economic context*. PhD dissertation, University of Johannesburg, Johannesburg.

Arthur, W.B., Day, J., Jaworski, J., Jung, M., Nonako, I., Scharmer, C.O. and Senge, P. (1999-2000). *Illuminating the blind spot: Leadership in the context of the emerging world*. McKinsey Society for Organisational Learning (SoL) Leadership Project. Retrieved September 2, 2014 from http://www.dialoguonleadership.org/Whitepaper.html

Barrett, R. (2006). Newsletter sent to the author by Cultural Transformation Tools (CTT). Retrieved September 2, 2014 from http://valuescentre.com/resources

Barrett, R. (2012). *The values driven organisation: Unleashing human potential for performance and profit*. London: Routledge.

Black, J.S. & Morrison, J. (2010). A cautionary tale for emerging market giants. *Harvard Business Review, 88*(9), 99–102.

Brink, B. (2013). Protection: A hole in the tariff walls. *Debate, 2*, Summer, 1.

Butler, M. (2002). *Traditional authorities: Know where to land*. Unpublished research paper for the Association for Rural Advancement.

Cappelli, P., Singh, H., Singh, J.V. & Useen, M. (2010). Leadership lessons from India. *Harvard Business Review*, March, 90–98.

Collins, J. (2005) *Good to great and the social sectors: A monograph to accompany 'Good to great'*. New York: Harper Collins.

Davies, M. (2013). South Africa needs to justify its inclusion in BRICS. *Sunday Times*, March 17, 14.

CPP. (2008). *Global human capital report: Workplace conflict and how businesses can harness it to thrive*. Unpublished document.

Delano, R. (2013). Sunrise in Africa. *Opportunity*, 22–24.

Drucker, P. (1964). *Managing for results*. New York: Harper & Row.

Edison, T.A. (n.d.). Famous Edison quotes. Retrieved September 3, 2014 from http://www.thomasedison.org/index.php/education/edison-quotes/

Erickson, T.J. (2010). The leaders we need now. *Harvard Business Review, 88*(5), 55–66.

Fukuyama, F. (2002). Social capital and development: The coming agenda. *SAIS Review XXII, 1*, Winter-Spring, 23–37.

Griffin, N.S. (2009). Personalise your management development. *Harvard Business Review on developing high-potential leaders.* Boston, MA: Harvard Business Press, 79–96. Retrieved September 4, 2014 from http://hbr.org/2003/03/personalize-your-management-development/ar/1

Gumede, V. (2013, April 19–25). Time for Africa to go back to its roots. *Mail & Guardian*, 27.

Higgins, J. (2013, April 19–25). Gerwel: Class progress or class war? *Mail & Guardian*, 35–36.

Lengnick-Hall, M.L. & Lengnick-Hall, C.A. (2003). Human resource management in the knowledge economy. San Francisco: Berrett-Koehler.

Livingston, J.S. (2009). Myth of the well-educated manager. *Harvard Business Review on developing high potential leaders.* Boston: Harvard Business School Publishing, 119–148.

Mackey, J. (2011). What is it that I only I can do? *Harvard Business Review,* January, 118–123. Retrieved September 3, 2014 from http://www.hbr.org/2011/01/the-hbr-interview-what-is-it-that-only-I-can-do/ar/1

Mackey, J. & Sisodia, R. (2013). *Conscious capitalism.* Boston: Harvard Business School Publishing.

McGuire, J.B. & Rhodes, G.B. (2009). *Transforming your leadership culture.* Hoboken, NJ: John Wiley and Sons, Inc.

McKinsey Global Institute Report (MGI). (2010, June). *Lions on the move: The progress and potential of African economies.* Retrieved September 4, 2014 from http://www.mckinsey.com/insights/africa/lions_on_the_move

Mintzberg, H. (2004). *Managers, not MBAs.* San Francisco: Berrett Koehler Publishers.

Moss Kanter, R. (2010). *Adding values to valuations: Indra Nooyi and others as institution-builders.* Retrieved September 4, 2014 from http://blogs.hbr.org/2010/05/adding-values-to-valuations-in/

Ngozo, A. (2012/2013). Sustainable cities for a sustainable South Africa. *Titans*, 18–25.

Ngubeni, S. (2012). Last word. *CEO, 11*(9), 56.

O'Connell, B.P. (2013). Presentation at the University of the Western Cape, February.

Porter, M. & Kramer, M. (2011). Creating shared value. *Harvard Business Review,* January–February, 62–117.

Priestland, A. & Hanig, R. (2009). Developing first level leaders. In *Harvard Business Review on developing high potential leaders.* Boston, MA: Harvard Business School Publishing, 97–118.

Raman, A.P. (2009). The new frontiers. *Harvard Business Review,* July–August, 130–139.

Ramphele, M. (2012). *Conversations with my sons and daughters.* Parklands: Penguin Books, SA.

Rashid, R. (2010). The battle for female talent in emerging markets. *Harvard Business Review, 88*(5), 101–106.

Rosenweig, P. (2010). Robert S. McNamara and the evolution of modern management. *Harvard Business Review,* December, 87–93.

Scharmer, C.O. (2005). Theory U: Leading from the emerging future. Retrieved September 4, 2014 from www.ottoscharmer.com, 4–11.

Sisodia, R. (2013). Video clip at Conscious Capitalism workshop, CEBANO Consulting, Cape Town.

Turley, J. (2012). China, Africa's HR and success: The amazing power of valuing people. In J. Herholdt (Ed.)., *People management strategy in organisations*. Johannesburg: Knowres Publishing.

Ulrich, D. (2012). Presentation at the HR Value Creation Conference, Cape Town, December.

Uhlrich, D. & Uhlrich, W. (2010). *The why of work*. New York: McGraw Hill.

Valoida, I. (2013). Presentation made at the University of the Western Cape, March.

Van Agtmael, A. (2007). *The emerging markets century*. Retrieved September 3, 2014 from http://www.theemergingmarket century.com/

Watts, R. (2008). Enter the dragon! China's colonisation of Africa. *Leadership*, 38–41.

CHAPTER 10: Reward and Recognition

Mark Bussin and Elmien Smit (21st Century Pay Solutions Group)

Introduction

Encourage and reward your employees. Without them, you can do nothing.
They help you accomplish your goals; now help them accomplish *theirs*.

– Anonymous

This statement is remarkable in the sense that rewarding and recognising employees is still a contemporary issue. Many questions are asked in terms of remuneration, e.g.: Should companies pay executives for performance on the job or for their skills or hours of work? How are pay and promotions structured across jobs to induce optimal effort from employees? In this chapter the importance of rewarding leadership will be examined, and components of remuneration and total reward systems will be explained. The responsibility of Human Resource Management (HRM), how much to pay, total reward statements and reward challenges that HR staff are faced with today, will be explained.

The importance of reward and recognition

Most companies are faced with a reward challenge, which implies that they struggle to understand how to reward programmes which are well integrated with their business strategy, and easily adapt to market requirements.

The problem with reward programmes in many companies today is that they are missing one of the key pillars, which include remuneration, benefits (and, in particular), recognition and appreciation (*Entrepreneur*, 2013). In some cases the fundamentals are addressed, but are not properly aligned with the companies' other strategies.

Recognition and appreciation are essential parts of the remuneration programme. Employees like knowing whether their contribution is valued. Recognition involves acknowledging someone, in front of his/her peers, for specific accomplishments achieved, actions taken or attitudes exemplified through their behaviour (Brun & Dugas, 2008). Appreciation is based on expressing gratitude towards someone for their actions (Döös & Wilhelmson, 2009).

Having a reward programme is vital: without the key characteristics of good remuneration management, companies would lack a reliable structure for determining employee remuneration. Thus, equally vital are the design of a reward programme, how it is administered, and communicating a well-defined reward strategy which is supportive of the business strategy. Having an effective remuneration programme in place can help solve many of a company's HR issues.

Reward and remuneration

Organisational reward systems – both financial and nonfinancial – are key elements in a company's strategic approach to HRM, as these can influence a number of HR processes and practices aimed at attracting and retaining high-performing staff (Guthrie, 2007; Rubino, 2006). Research has shown that the types of reward offered to employees reduce labour turnover, have a motivational impact, and positively influence a company's organisational culture and bottom line (Guthrie, 2007; Marchington & Wilkinson, 2008; Nelson & Spitzer, 2003). Remuneration also matters because money spent on salaries, benefits and other forms of reward typically amounts to well over half an organisation's total costs. Reward and remuneration are therefore major determinants both of profitability and competitive advantage for a company (Torrington, Hall, Taylor & Atkinson, 2009).

In this chapter the following short definitions will apply:

- *Reward* – the combination of all types of reward, including financial and non-financial, direct as well as indirect, intrinsic and extrinsic, which are made available to employees;

- *Remuneration* – any payment in money or in kind, to any person who works for any other person or organisation. It typically includes the total guaranteed package, short-term incentives (STIs) and long-term incentives (LTIs). It is one of the components of a reward system. In some parts of the world, this is known as compensation and the terms are used interchangeably in this chapter.

The purpose of reward and remuneration

Employers utilise employee reward and remuneration to achieve the following organisational goals (Gilman, 2009; Torrington et al., 2009):

- *Recruiting high-quality employees and retaining their services in the organisation.* Prospective employees compare pay scales and will most likely choose jobs that offer a higher salary. Employees expect to be treated fairly by employers, and part of the perception of fairness is influenced by the equity (fairness) that exists in the compensation system.

- *Improving employee performance.* Employees expect to receive a certain level of remuneration for exerting a certain level (specified or determined) of discretionary effort. They also expect that such compensation will be fair. When the organisation recognises hard work and excellent performance, employees are more willing to exert higher levels of discretionary effort in the expectation that this will also be rewarded in future.

- *Ensuring fairness.* Employees expect congruence between their effort levels and the compensation they receive. They also compare their own efforts and rewards with those of their colleagues, as well as with employees in similar jobs in different organisations. When employees perceive incongruence between their effort levels and their compensation, or that of colleagues/other employees with whom they compare their situations, they experience dissonance and will react by changing their effort, their perceptions of the reward or the people to whom they compare themselves, or by leaving the organisation. Organisations establish fairness in the pay structure by ensuring internal equity through job evaluation and external equity through salary surveys.

- *Ensuring legal compliance.* Compensation consists of more than money. All countries have specific legislation and regulations that affect components of compensation, such as leave, overtime pay and minimum pay levels. Unions often have a profound influence on employee compensation, and applicable union agreements must be considered in determining a compensation strategy.

- *Controlling labour costs.* Employee remuneration is often one of the main cost items in an organisational budget. Ensuring a sustained competitive advantage means engaging the best talent, but ensuring sustained profitability means creating and implementing a compensation strategy that returns the best value for money. Labour costs are determined by taking into account the number of employees and the hours they work, the average cash compensation paid, and the average benefit costs (Milkovich & Newman, 2009). These three components can be controlled so as to keep labour costs affordable, although the increased use of a variable pay component may make the tight management of labour costs more difficult.

- *Motivating staff.* Reward and remuneration systems are often used to channel effort and enthusiasm in specific directions and to encourage particular types of employee behaviour that lead to improved organisational performance. People value and are motivated by different rewards for different reasons, and therefore reward systems must be diverse enough to accommodate different and changing employee needs. Reward systems must be comprehensive and based on realistic analyses of employee needs and work situations. Both intrinsic and extrinsic rewards influence an individual's motivation and job satisfaction (Weiss, 2001).

Studies show that nonfinancial reward initiatives which are aimed at strengthening employees' intrinsic motivation have a positive impact on performance (Peterson & Luthans, 2006). These nonfinancial rewards fulfil employees' need for challenge, responsibility, decision making, variety, social recognition and career growth, either alone or in conjunction with financial rewards (Armstrong & Murlis, 1994; Luthans, 2005; Odendaal, 2009). Additional research suggests that whereas financial and other tangible incentives such as pay, benefits and praise may be more motivating in the short term, in the long run, nonfinancial incentives such as challenging and interesting tasks are more motivating (Arnolds & Venter, 2007).

The impact of globalisation on remuneration

The emergence of the global marketplace has had a profound impact on the traditional ways in which work is managed and employees are remunerated, which raises the issue of global pay. More and more companies are doing business internationally, which implies that they have employees in various countries, but it also implies a squeeze on profits due to intensive local and global competition (Dessler, 2009). So far, there has been a strong perception that the ways in which pay is determined and delivered constitute a well-defined marketplace that reflects a common set of values unique to each country. This perception is, however, often not based on reality, since pay practices vary widely due to a number of variables such as the type of industry, geographical location, company size, location of the parent company, where a company is in its growth cycle, and the degree of creativity or risk-taking a company may exhibit in dealing with local, traditional pay practices and statutory requirements (Coleman, 1999).

A number of progressive multinational companies now view the global marketplace in the context of the company's own strategic plans and its response to competition on a global scale. Rather than focusing on each country individually, these organisations look at the global marketplace and seek to develop synergistic approaches that maximise the best remuneration practices and apply them to the highest degree possible in local markets. Ensuring quality of products and services, increasing market share and sustaining a competitive edge are core goals that trigger a high level of interest in creative approaches to remuneration (Coleman, 1999; Dessler, 2009; Torrington et al., 2009).

The reward system

Reward management is a key element in the strategic approach to HRM. The actual remuneration system may require adjustment to engender employee motivation, effort and performance. The total reward system, which is essential to effective reward management, is a significant part of the company's financial strategy (Marchington & Wilkinson, 2008).

Reward practices and criteria must be linked to the organisation's performance appraisal system. Weiss (2001, 117) stipulates the following criteria for an effective reward system:

- Rewards should be clearly defined and consistent with other rewards for comparable work and expertise;

- Employees should be informed about what exactly they are being rewarded for (e.g., quality, performance or innovation);

- Rewards should differentiate between different levels of performance;

- The criteria for giving rewards should be accurately and comprehensively communicated across organisations to ensure that employees perceive the rewards as being equitably distributed;

- The organisation's rewards must be comparable with those of the company's competitors;

- Rewards must fit individual needs, be high enough to provide personal satisfaction, satisfy high performers, be related to job satisfaction and performance, and fit other organisational requirements (management style, structure and strategy).

Reward strategy

The *reward strategy* of an organisation informs all employees of the direction the organisation wishes to take in terms of reward management. It also describes the types of reward being offered to support the implementation of the organisational strategy and accomplish organisational goals (Luthans, 2005). The strategy provides a well-reasoned and action-based framework for developing reward policies, practices and processes. It also differentiates between the components of total rewards and is based on the needs and values of the organisation and its employees. The reward strategy ensures that the organisation directs its reward investments appropriately, to achieve the greatest impact (Armstrong, 2006; Gross & Friedman, 2007).

The *total reward framework* evolves from the organisation's reward, HR and organisational strategy. Effective reward strategies positively influence employee behaviours by incorporating extrinsic and intrinsic motivators. Employees receive tangible and intangible rewards in return for their performance, while making a meaningful contribution to the organisation. As the organisation succeeds so does the employee, and vice versa (Luthans, 2005).

It is important that a reward system clearly states the company's *value proposition*, which is an analysis and quantified review of the benefits, costs and value an organisation can deliver to customers and other constituent groups within and outside the organisation. It is also a positioning of value, where *value = benefits – cost* (cost includes risk).

Value proposition statements are not communicated externally. Rather, it is the *messages* created out of the value proposition statement that are communicated externally. These can be used in a variety of ways, such as in marketing communications material or in sales proposals (Kaplan & Norton, 2004). In the context of reward, a company's value proposition is generally used to position value to prospective employees when recruiting new people, or for retaining and motivating existing employees. This is also sometimes called the *employee value proposition* (EVP). Examples of marketing messages, communicated as part of the EVPs of several well-known organisations, are shown in Table 10.1.

Table 10.1: Marketing messages communicated as part of employee value propositions

Organisation	Marketing message communicated as part of the EVP	Impact
McDonald's (Singapore)	'Every crew member can be a manager'	Empowers restaurant employees who wish to make McDonald's a long-term career, and communicates career path and longevity as employee benefits.
Kotak Mahindra Bank (India)	• Focus on results • Leadership • Active involvement/inclusiveness • Maximum challenge • Entrepreneurial creativity	The EVP is called 'the FLAME' and is designed to 'ignite the spirit within' employees. It communicates a workplace characterised by challenge, innovation and reward.
Hewlett Packard (global)	'Stretch Strive Succeed'	Communicates a workplace that is inspiring and challenging, and characterised by simplicity, clear direction and success.

Reward categories

WorldatWork, the largest global not-for-profit professional association dedicated to knowledge leadership in total rewards, defines this concept as containing five core reward categories (see Figure 10.1).

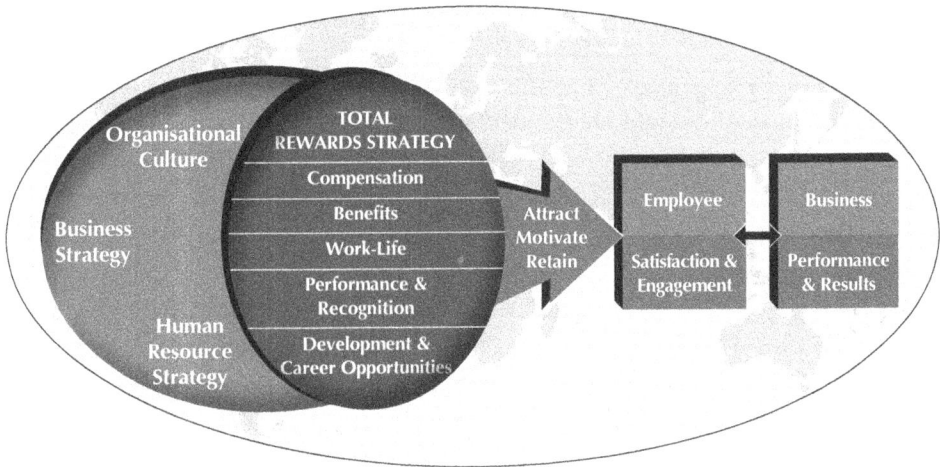

Figure 10.1: WorldatWork's Total Rewards Model
Source: WorldatWork, 2007, p. 7

The figure not only positions the total reward strategy within the context of the business, the HR strategy and the organisational culture, but also illustrates the five core categories of a total rewards framework which forms part of the company EVP:

- Remuneration (compensation);
- Benefits;
- Work–life balance;
- Performance and recognition;
- Development and career opportunities.

Attitudes to reward systems are changing. Employers have realised that remuneration is no longer used only as a currency in exchange for effort, time and skill, but such programmes are increasingly used to attract, retain and motivate (Gross & Friedman, 2007). It has also been proved that where reward processes are linked to key performance drivers in an organisation, employee morale, retention, engagement and productivity significantly improve.

Furthermore, governance and compliance with organisational policies and regulatory requirements are enhanced (Luthans, 2005; Torrington et al., 2009). This confirms that although there appears to be a need for more flexible reward systems that align to employee needs, these systems should still be governed by policies, guidelines and frameworks, and should not lead to total flexibility at the expense of regulation.

Drivers of reward strategy

Four considerations affect strategic reward and remuneration decisions: 1) organisational (business) strategy; 2) organisation product life cycle; 3) remuneration policy; and 4) employee reward preferences and needs.

Organisational strategy

The ultimate objective of the total reward strategy is to ensure that the company attracts and retains the right employees, and motivates them to work in support of the business plan, while also being legally compliant. Recognition for outstanding achievement is a crucial part of the process. The *right* total reward strategy can deliver the *right* amount to the *right* people at the *right* time, for the *right* reasons (Gross & Friedman, 2007).

Organisations can choose to follow various business strategies; most commonly used are the innovator, the cost-cutter and the consumer-focused strategies. These require diverse and even contrasting behaviours from employees, therefore the compensation strategies should vary in each case. A business that chooses an *innovative business strategy* must develop a total reward strategy that rewards innovative behaviour and decisions.

An organisation that follows the *cost-cutter approach* should focus on efficiency and emphasise productivity in compensating employees, while a *consumer-focused business strategy* should be supported by a compensation strategy that rewards employee behaviours that ensure customer satisfaction (Milkovich & Newman, 2009).

A reciprocal relationship exists between the business strategy and the total reward strategy. The organisational strategy informs the reward strategy, and the reward strategy enables employees to implement the business strategy by giving clear indications of the types of behaviour that will be rewarded. The *business plan* is used as a point of departure for developing the reward and remuneration strategy. This is followed by an assessment of how well the current, total reward system supports the objectives of the business.

Gaps and any areas that are overfunded, are identified. A pay or remuneration strategy which forms the basis of the total reward strategy is then developed. Next, the reward and remuneration philosophy is updated accordingly and aligned with the business strategy.

Organisation product life cycle

The industry or product growth rate or life cycle stage all have a significant impact on the remuneration strategy adopted. Figure 10.2 shows an example of industry maturity or product life cycle, and sets out common organisational strategies that are used in each of the stages.

Each stage has a preferred remuneration strategy attached to it (see Table 10.2 for the most appropriate for every stage).

Common business strategies used in specific life cycle stages			
Embryonic	**Growth**	**Mature**	**Aging**
• Start-up • Develop new product	• Acquire market share • Find new markets	• Consolidate position • Find and protect market niches • Become low-cost producers	• Reduce costs • Withdraw from unprofitable market segments

Figure 10.2: Industry maturity or product life cycle

Table 10.2: Common approaches to reward and remuneration in each life cycle stage

Embryonic	**Growth**	**Mature**	**Aging**
• Less emphasis on salary, benefits and perks • Attention to share options and long-term incentives	• Continued emphasis on long-term incentives, with increasing attention to ways to promote short-term results • Catch up with salary and benefits	• Most attention focused on keeping salary and perks competitive • Reduced concern for long-term incentives • Bonuses oriented to boosting productivity	• Benefits and salary are king • Very little attention given to long-term, growth-oriented incentives

Remuneration policy

The remuneration policy indicates how the remuneration strategy will be implemented. It guides management decisions and should therefore be informative enough to ensure effective decision making, yet flexible enough to allow for individual differences in pay, should this be necessary. Organisations can choose between several competitive pay-policy options. The *match policy* pays employees salaries which are on par with those of the competition. This approach ensures that the organisation's remuneration costs are approximately equal to those of the competition, and, therefore, its ability to attract and retain talented employees is similar to that of competitors. When an organisation pays more than competitors in the market, it follows a *lead policy*. This approach allows the organisation to attract and retain talented employees, but it increases labour costs. An employer who pays below the current market rate follows a *lag policy*. This may hinder the ability to attract and retain talent, except when the low basic salary is enhanced with other forms of compensation, such as share options or high-performance bonuses.

Typically, a remuneration policy will focus on the following:

- Statement of intent and philosophy;
- Employee value proposition;
- Purpose;
- Application and scope;
- Document control and versions;
- Philosophy of fixed or guaranteed pay (GP);
- Philosophy of variable pay (VP);
- Remuneration mix;
- Comparative benchmarking;
- Links to performance management;
- Communication and the extent of transparency allowed;
- Annual remuneration reviews;
- Remuneration committee scope and guidelines.

The total rewards strategy and framework are integral to an organisation's EVP (CLC, 2008). When the framework is designed, the components offered by competitor organisations should be considered, as well as the value employees attach to the respective components (Harris & Clements, 2007). A sound reward framework positively influences the EVP, enhances the employer's brand, and builds the organisation's reputation as an 'Employer of Choice' for current and prospective employees.

Employee reward preferences and needs

Employee reward preferences have received more and more attention over the past few years. As employers, we know that not all employees want the same things. The reward strategy needs to consider the extent to which employee requests will be considered, for example, more leave, less overtime, and greater flexibility.

Employers typically do a cost benefit analysis while considering the request. Introducing flexibility often comes with associated administrative costs. Experience shows that accommodating reasonable employee requests far outweighs the administrative costs of introducing flexibility.

Elements of remuneration

Once the mechanisms for determining rates of pay for jobs in an organisation have been settled, the pay or remuneration package should be constructed. An individual's pay will be made up of fixed (or guaranteed) and variable pay elements (see Figure 10.3). *Fixed or guaranteed pay elements* make up the regular weekly or monthly payments made to the individual, which do not vary other than in exceptional circumstances. These include basic salary and employee benefits. *Variable pay elements* can be determined by either the employer or the employee (Torrington et al., 2009), and include short- and long-term incentives.

Incentives

Short-term incentives (STIs) are applicable for up to one year (e.g., incentive target, discretionary bonus, and profit share), and are tied to the performance of the company, team and/or individual. The *incentive target* is a bonus related to the achievement typically of a financial target such as turnover or profit, as well as other objectives. The *incentive bonus* is typically a percentage of the total guaranteed package. The *discretionary bonus* is a discretionary amount that bears some relationship to the individual's performance. *Profit share* is a predetermined percentage of the organisation's profits, usually also dependent on the achievement of other objectives.

Long-term incentives (LTIs) are applicable for over one year (examples include share options, share grants, share purchases or long-term cash incentive schemes).

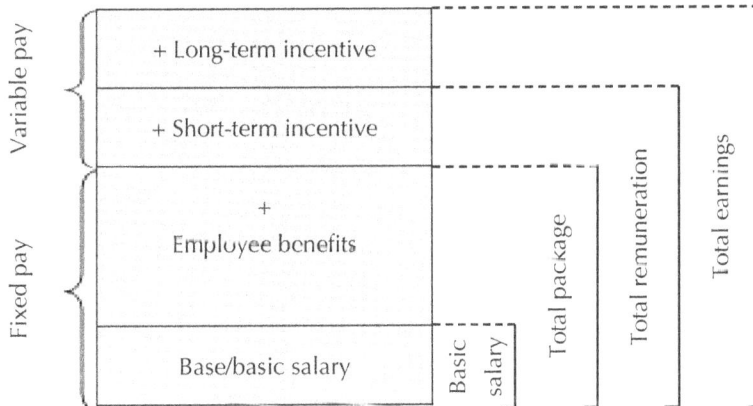

Figure 10.3: Typical elements of remuneration

Individual incentives reward individual performance (e.g., sales commissions and once-off bonuses). *Team incentives* focus on the performance of a work group or team. *Gain-sharing plans* are examples of a team incentive, used, for instance, when an employee team achieves specific goals such as reducing waste, reducing accident rates or improving productivity. *Organisational incentive schemes* reward employees based on the performance of the entire organisation, while *profit-sharing* and *employee share ownership* schemes are also common.

Best-of-breed organisations use both short- and long-term incentives in their remuneration mix. The primary purpose is to encourage the long-term viability of the company; executives are urged not to harm the company for short-term gains, because they would have too much to lose in the long term. A well-designed 'total earnings' scheme should prevent this from happening (Bussin, 2002a).

The link between the performance management system and remuneration is most commonly experienced in three ways. The higher the performance score,

- the higher the fixed pay increase;

- the greater the slice of the STI pie relative to the pool; and

- the greater the likelihood of receiving a larger amount of the share scheme pool and share top-ups.

Benefits

Benefits (fringe benefits) are indirect compensations that employees receive because they belong to the workforce of an organisation. These tend to be more prolific in emerging markets, and, in some countries, the tax treatment in this respect is still favourable. Benefits may be either cash or noncash additions to an employee's pay and must be taken into account in calculating the total package (see Table 10.3).

Table 10.3: Examples of cash and noncash benefits

Cash benefits	Noncash benefits
<ul><li>Car allowance</li><li>Entertainment allowance</li><li>Housing subsidy</li><li>Professional fees</li><li>Cell phone allowance</li></ul>	<ul><li>Vacation leave</li><li>Sick leave</li><li>Pension/provident fund contribution</li><li>Medical contribution</li><li>Group life assurance</li><li>Accident insurance</li><li>Housing loan</li><li>Educational assistance</li><li>Travel abroad</li></ul>

Where trade unions are recognised, any changes to conditions of employment must first be negotiated with them. Sometimes, organisations are subject to regulation through bargaining councils, which means their remuneration practices are prescribed by industry-specific needs. It is unlikely that an application for exemption regarding the total package structure will be successful.

How much to pay

There are various factors to take in account when designing a pay structure and pay range for a specific position in the company. A few examples will be examined in order to outline how fixed and variable pay play a part in the remuneration awarded to each position.

Remuneration levels, typically shown in percentiles, are defined as follows:

- *Lower quartile:* 75 per cent of the sample earns more and 25 per cent earns less than this salary level;

- *Median:* 50 per cent of the sample earns more and 50 per cent earns less than this salary level;

- *Upper quartile:* 25 per cent of the sample earns more and 75 per cent earns less than this salary level;

- *90th percentile:* ten per cent of the sample earns more and 90 per cent earns less than this salary level.

Below are examples of the remuneration packages offered for a human capital position in South Africa, according to 21st Century's RewardOnline Survey. Data like this are available for all emerging markets. Current South African data are shown for illustrative purposes.

Table 10.4: Example of remuneration for a Human Capital Consultant (D1)

Remuneration element	10th	25th lower quartile	50th median	75th upper quartile	90th
Basic salary	279 532	301 146	336 944	397 250	453 089
Fixed bonus/13th cheque	19 792	27 600	28 857	33 835	36 944
Total base salary	279 981	307 388	348 684	403 205	455 305
Car allowance	24 000	49 764	49 764	74 250	106 515
Housing benefit	14 760	16 200	16 200	90 657	99 546
Cell phone allowance	6 480	7 200	7 200	7 920	8 568
Sundry benefits	12 116	14 322	18 000	44 070	59 712

Remuneration element	10th	25th lower quartile	50th median	75th upper quartile	90th
Pension/provident fund contribution	30 773	38 313	58 223	63 333	68 374
Medical contribution	2 187	11 451	20 340	28 524	39 448
Group life assurance	2 041	2 310	4 081	8 236	10 470
Total guaranteed package	271 094	322 779	416 109	500 232	577 148
Short-term incentive	33 762	63 597	78 088	107 937	136 389

Table 10.5: Example of remuneration for a Human Resource Manager (DU)

Remuneration element	10th	25th lower quartile	50th median	75th upper quartile	90th
Basic salary	473 913	501 429	637 110	902 508	966 036
Fixed bonus/13th cheque	23 741	31 598	44 692	52 106	56 554
Total base salary	487 631	515 048	666 870	902 508	966 036
Car allowance	118 579	134 448	160 896	169 873	175 259
Cell phone allowance	6 000	6 000	6 000	6 000	6 000
Pension/provident fund contribution	24 700	28 370	48 287	63 730	124 081
Medical contribution	19 209	23 184	23 196	27 744	36 387
Group life assurance	1 138	2 613	11 709	20 798	22 260
Total guaranteed package	545 874	712 399	855 524	954 005	1 053 676
Short-term incentive	104 425	124 905	230 336	366 990	400 924

The percentiles can be used as guidelines for HR, line and remuneration management, when deciding on the remuneration of a specific position. The percentile is based on the level of responsibility, the scarcity of skills, the complexity of the business and the performance of the individual, for instance. Thus, the company could choose to pay at a higher percentile for an individual who exceeds expectations in terms of the above.

To gain a holistic picture of remuneration, the use of total reward statements has become very popular and is the focus of the next section.

Total reward statements

A *total reward statement* (TRS) is a personalised document that communicates the overall value of the financial rewards offered to employees. The TRS can also be used to reinforce the communication of less tangible benefits such as work–life programmes, learning and development, and flexible work arrangements.

Contents of a TRS

To provide individuals with a thorough and comprehensive view of their overall reward package, a TSR should contain details of both the tangible and the intangible rewards offered by the company. In addition to fixed and variable pay, each TRS needs to contain details about pensions, private medical insurance, life assurance, share schemes, company car, fuel, car insurance, taxes related to car possession/use (where applicable), laptop, mobile phone, gym membership, subsidised canteen, luncheon vouchers and anything else which is subsidised or costs the employer money.

The importance of a TRS

Some organisations used to prepare TRSs only for managerial and executive positions, or, more generally, for those individuals they were more interested in retaining. The benefit companies can derive from giving evidence of the perks offered to all employees cannot be overemphasised. It can be priceless in terms of developing, strengthening and endorsing the employer's brand, as well as helping employers to retain staff. Organisations develop TRSs for the following reasons:

* To attract, motivate and retain employees;

* To reinforce their brand and set them apart from other organisations;

* To raise awareness and appreciation by focusing attention on the benefits the organisation offers;

* To reduce the cost of benefits administration, by providing an employee with a self-service tool that results in fewer phone calls, thus enabling HR to focus more on strategic issues.

Who benefits from using a TRS?

The trend to use TRSs is driven by the many benefits both employers and employees can derive from them:

- Organisations that are cash-constrained could become more competitive by emphasising (or 'selling') the value of intangible rewards or benefits which employees find difficult to attach a value to;

- Organisations with high staff turnover due to perceived weakness/lack of desired reward elements can correct this perception;

- Organisations with large numbers of employees across multinational operations can realise their economies of scale by producing statements in bulk;

- Organisations can thoroughly identify all the benefits and reward design aspects across various geographical areas. Having recourse to statements helps corporations ascertain which source of data can make benefits management more straightforward in each of the countries concerned;

- Employees who are educated and informed about their reward package and have the tools to assist them with their own financial planning, benefit from using a TRS.

There are various reasons why certain big companies avoid using TSRs, including time, cost and resource constraints; when they actually offer very little in addition to basic salary; when the take-up rates of the current offering are rather low; or in cases where companies have just completed the process of acquiring/merging with another organisation. In the case of the latter, since the benefits structures and payroll systems of the companies concerned might differ, it is advisable to ensure that the offerings are comparable, before issuing TRSs.

Reward and recognition challenges

This section addresses some of the current remuneration issues facing CHROs, not only from the perspective of employers, but also that of HR managers and their continuing relevance. These challenges include setting executive pay levels, payment for hardship, minimum wages and the Gini coefficient.

Executive pay levels

Often, rewarding of the chief executive officer (CEO) and executives is more multifaceted than expected, and a strategic perspective on remuneration requires an exploration beyond just what the CHRO earns. The most common determinants of executive pay are the following:

- Organisation size – turnover, number of employees, value of assets;

- Organisational performance – profitability, return on investment, value-add;

- Executive-specific factors – age, experience, tenure, career path;

- Organisational structure – holdings, subsidiary or single unit company, capital or labour intensive;

- Job or position-specific factors – level of decision making, consequence of error, organisational level;

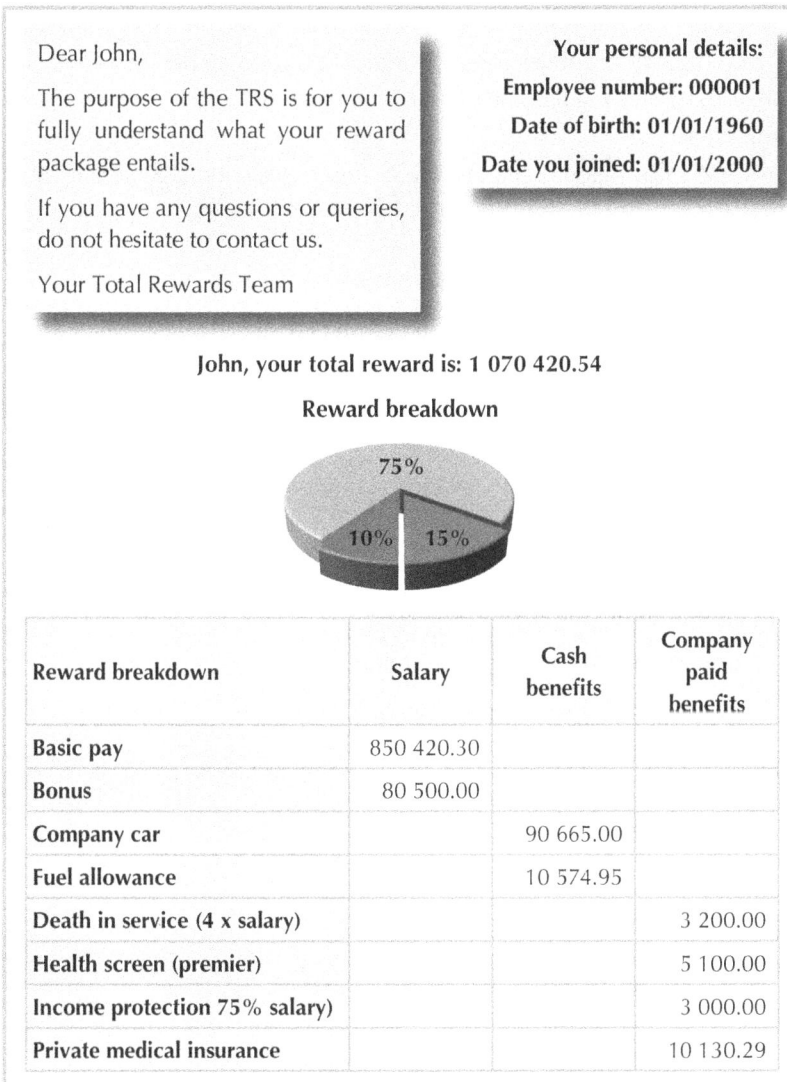

- Job complexity.

Dear John,

The purpose of the TRS is for you to fully understand what your reward package entails.

If you have any questions or queries, do not hesitate to contact us.

Your Total Rewards Team

Your personal details:

Employee number: 000001

Date of birth: 01/01/1960

Date you joined: 01/01/2000

John, your total reward is: 1 070 420.54

Reward breakdown

75%

10%   15%

Reward breakdown	Salary	Cash benefits	Company paid benefits
Basic pay	850 420.30		
Bonus	80 500.00		
Company car		90 665.00	
Fuel allowance		10 574.95	
Death in service (4 x salary)			3 200.00
Health screen (premier)			5 100.00
Income protection 75% salary)			3 000.00
Private medical insurance			10 130.29

Figure 10.4: Example of a total rewards statement

Deciding on the level of a job is an important indicator for determining where to benchmark it in terms of pay level. At *top management* levels, strategy and policy decisions are regarded as superior to any other decision-making in the company. These responsibilities and decisions give overall direction to the company. Top management decides on policy in all major areas of operation, such as finance, production, marketing and HR.

At *senior management* level the execution of policies and strategies is broadly planned or programmed within the limits of discretion set by top management. Senior management decides on the company's structures.

At *middle management* level the boundaries of decision-making for interpretive decisions are dependent on senior management's ideas (Phillips, 2009). The interpretive aspects come from making the best decision out of a spectrum of possible options, within the limits of discretion. Middle management decides on systems and procedures, rules and regulations, design manuals and interpretations not covered by existing rules.

Below is an illustration of the responsibilities of each management level (Bussin, 2007, p. 19).

Table 10.6: Top, senior and middle management responsibilities

F	Top management policy making/strategic intent
E	Senior management/general management strategy execution/long-term planning
D	Middle management/professional interpretive/probabilistic/tactical management
C	Skilled workers/advanced operational routine/process/systems/deterministic
B	Semi-skilled workers/operational automatic/operative/sub-system
A	Basic skills defined/primary skills

Figure 10.5 provides a schematic illustration of top, senior and middle management, and their respective grades. It also indicates the type of incentive best suited to each level.

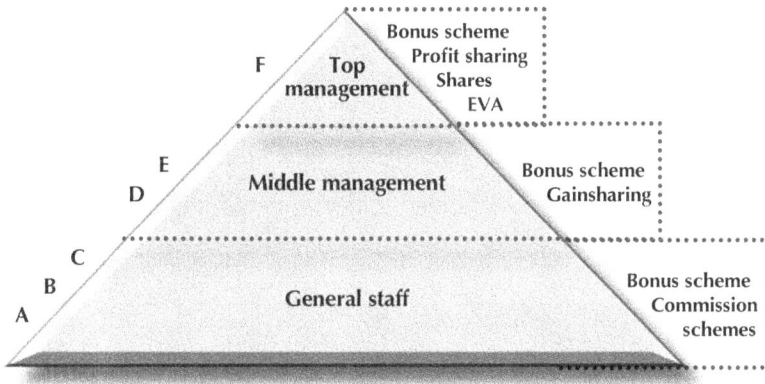

Figure 10.5: Typical incentive scheme applications
Source: Bussin (2007)

Payment for hardship

Hardship pay for expatriates is another remuneration challenge for HRM, as this forms part of the design and maintenance of an international remuneration programme. To be successful, HR practitioners must have knowledge of the laws (tax systems, rates), customs (attitudes towards remuneration) and environment (inflation and exchange rates, cost of living) as well as the employment practices of the different countries involved.

Company and individual purposes for expatriation

First, explaining what is meant by 'expatriate' will clarify why payment for hardship is necessary. An expatriate is a person working in a foreign country, either on a permanent transfer or on assignment (typically ranging from 30 days to three years, depending on the assignment). That person remains, however, a citizen of his/her home country.

Each organisation has a different reason for deciding to go global. Establishing the specific purpose is the first step in strategic international HRM. Once this has been done, the rationale for the remuneration strategy evolves from there. According to Mello (2011) there are various reasons why companies decide to become global players: 1) market opportunities in other countries may be better; 2) companies might achieve economies of scale by expanding the scope and volume of their operations in support of global initiatives; 3) they want to maintain competitive advantage; and 4) due to acquisitions it is possible that companies can be owned (or partially owned) by a foreign-based company. Other reasons include

- business or market development;
- the set-up, transfer, or integration of IT;
- management of an autonomous subsidiary;

- coordination or integration of foreign with domestic operations;
- a temporary assignment to a vacant position;
- the development of local management talent.

Although it is important for the company to have a purpose for entering the global market, there may also be an individual purpose for a global assignment. Reasons include developing an employee for a top management position, the possibility of developing interpersonal or technical skills and, possibly, if the spouse of an employee receives a global assignment, the opportunity for that person to follow their spouse/partner. Baruch, Steele and Quantrill (2002) take it a step further by explaining that the reasons why people are willing to relocate to a different country include being exposed to different opportunities, a better lifestyle, the wish to follow a specific career path, or to gain global experience which will make them more marketable.

Approaches to international assignment remuneration

Various different pay practices should be taken into account when designing an expatriate remuneration programme. However, three broad approaches to expatriate pay can be identified as the dominant philosophies:

- *Build-up method.* Here, the home-base salary is used as a basis, minus hypothetical tax, before building on this by adding an international premium, a cost-of-living index, and the exchange rate to deliver a net assignment package. The build-up method is used to maintain internal equity and equalise the impact of host country tax;

- *Local market approach.* This approach is selected if it proves to be better than the build-up option. It is used where a strong local market exists in the host country, and where the build-up method delivers less than the local market remuneration levels (e.g., if an expatriate is sent to a major first-world country such as the United Kingdom or United States);

- *Internationally mobile expatriate.* This approach is used by large, global multinational organisations with a large pool of permanent expatriates who move from one country to the next on assignments. The internationally mobile expatriate approach is used to put all expatriates on an equal footing, regardless of their nationality.

The context of hardship pay

Hardship refers to the relative difference an expatriate and his/her family are likely to experience, and the relative impact which moving between different locations may have on their lifestyle.

Hardship allowances refer to the pay an expatriate employee may receive for living and working in a potentially dangerous area, or where the lifestyle (e.g., language, customs, religion, quality of life) is so different that it makes it difficult to adapt to life in the new location. Along with hardship allowance, the employee may receive additional vacation time and other benefits, as stipulated in the contract.

Figure 10.6: Typical expatriate compensation components
Source: Mathis and Jackson (2003, p. 597)

This figure offers a holistic picture of where payment for hardship fits into the remuneration context. Typical factors that shape the notion of hardship within a country include the following:

- Economic, e.g., poverty levels and level of service provision;
- Political, e.g., freedom, or tolerance towards different points of view/lifestyles;
- Religious, e.g., freedom/tolerance towards different religions;
- Public service, e.g., provision of water, electricity, sanitation, work permits, etc.;
- Environment/climate, e.g., extreme weather;
- Personal safety, e.g., security/crime levels;
- Health, e.g., prevalence of disease and health standards;
- Education, e.g., standards, prevalence of international schools;
- Transportation, e.g., availability and reliability of public transport, cost of fuel and general road safety.

The ratings pertaining to hardship are classified into four main groups:

- 1- Minimal hardship
- 2- Some hardship
- 3- High degree of hardship
- 4- Extreme hardship.

In assessing how much to pay an expatriate, it is important to take into account the relative hardship in terms of quality of living, the difference in conditions between locations, and the relative level of difficulty that will be experienced in adapting to a new location.

Table 10.7: International hardship premiums by country

Country	Hardship rate	Salary premium as a percentage
USA	1	10
Italy	1	10
New Zealand	1	10
Argentina	2	20
Brazil	2	20
South Africa	**2**	**20**
China	3	30
Kenya	3	30
Mexico	3	30
Iran	4	40
Nigeria	4	40
Sudan	4	40

Source: Xpatulator website (Accessed 7 March 2013)

From this table it is clear that South Africa is rated average in terms of hardship, and that expatriates from other countries will typically be paid a 20 per cent salary premium. The US, New Zealand and Italy are rated as 'minimal hardship' countries, while China, Kenya and Mexico are deemed to entail a high degree of hardship. Expatriates to Iran, Nigeria and Sudan can expect to be faced with extreme hardship, and will typically be paid a 40 per cent salary premium for this.

Hardship is relative to both where the expatriate is relocating from (home country) and where s/he is relocating to (host country). This means that the hardship premium for any location is also dependent on the expatriate's home country. For example, an employee relocating from the US to Sudan (see Table 10.7) would experience far greater hardship than someone relocating from Nigeria to Sudan, or, for that matter, from the US to New Zealand. The most common approach is to apply the following formula to determine the hardship premium for an assignment:

Host hardship % – home hardship % = assignment hardship %

Of course it is possible to arrive at a negative premium. For example, an expatriate relocating from the Sudan to the US, using the above formula, would have an assignment hardship premium of -30 per cent. There are two main approaches to follow in such an instance: the first is to apply the negative percentage and pay the expatriate less for the 'privilege' of going to a location where the hardship rate is lower. The challenge is that few expatriates would relocate from their home location in order to earn less money. The second approach is to discount negative premiums – this ensures that the expatriate would not face a reduction in pay when moving to a location where the hardship rate is lower.

The Xpatulator website recommends using the following three types of calculations to determine expatriate pay which includes a hardship premium:

- *Salary purchasing power parity (SPPP)*. This calculator reports how much an expatriate would need to earn in another location, to compensate for a higher cost of living, hardship, and the exchange rate, in order to have the same relative spending power and therefore a similar standard of living as s/he would have in their current location;

- *Cost of living allowance (COLA)*. This calculator reports how much additional allowance (over and above the current salary) an expatriate needs to earn in another location, to compensate for the higher cost of living, hardship, and the exchange rate, in order to have the same relative spending power and therefore a similar standard of living as s/he would have in their current location;

- *Cost of living index (COLI)*. This figure represents the difference in cost of living between the two countries (home and host) involved in an assignment. For instance, the COLI for an assignee sent to France from Africa may be 1.6. This information is based on the difference in the price of a similar basket of goods/groceries and reflects the fact that living in France would be 1.6 times more expensive than living in Africa.

The role of HRM as well as the remuneration management team is essential in designing and maintaining expatriate remuneration. International remuneration is an area where a clear strategy and aligned practical policy are required to ensure attraction, fairness, equity, motivation and retention.

Minimum wages

For the past few years, the minimum wage has been a debated subject amongst policymakers and economists. A minimum wage can be referred to as the lowest hourly, daily or monthly wage employers are legally obliged to pay employees.

We believe an increase in the minimum wage will deliver benefits that outweigh the costs involved. Matthews (2013) argues that research generally shows that policies that increase the remuneration of low-wage workers significantly reduce turnover, boost worker effort, encourage employers to invest in employee training, and can increase the demand for goods and services – all of which helps to balance out any potential negative effects. Only a few jobs are lost when the minimum wage is increased. Once minimum wage earners receive an immediate increase, this extra income is pumped back into the local economy, which leads to higher overall employment.

Conservatively speaking, economists warn that a higher minimum wage leads to a reduction in employment, i.e., if labour becomes expensive, companies will 'purchase' less of it. As Krugman (1998) suggests, a better method for raising the living standards of low-wage workers would be to increase worker income through policies such as earned income tax credit, under which employees who earn less than a given amount receive money from the government, rather than paying taxes. The question arises why the minimum wage still presents a challenge, when better tools are available.

Who is responsible for determining the minimum wage?

Government acts, such as 'Conditions of Employment', typically give powers to the Minister of Labour to determine and set minimum conditions and terms of employment. More specifically, minimum wages are typically targeted at those in the workplace who are the most vulnerable. Weak sectors are those without unions, or with very little union activity, and they typically include

- domestic workers;
- contract cleaners;
- the private security sector;
- wholesale and retail staff;
- farm workers;
- the forestry sector;
- the taxi sector;
- learnerships;
- children performing advertising, artistic and cultural activities.

Minimum wages may differ across areas (city vs. rural). Other factors influencing the minimum wage are pay periods, job functions, years of experience and working hours. The minimum wage in South Africa, according to *Government Gazette* number 36076 (January 2013, p. 3) for the wholesale and retail sector is shown below.

Table 10.8: Area A – Minimum wage for the period 01/02/2013 to 31/01/2014

Job categories	Rand per hour	Rand per week	Rand per month	27 hours Rand per hour
Assistant manager	27.37	1 231.65	5 336.74	28.37
Cashier	15.96	718.20	3 111.96	16.35
Clerk	18.92	851.40	3 689.12	19.60
Displayer	19.65	884.25	3 831.46	20.35
Driver Gross vehicle mass (3 500kg)	14.41	648.45	2 809.73	14.93
Driver Gross vehicle mass 3 501 (9 000kg)	17.43	784.35	3 398.59	18.06
Driver Gross vehicle mass 9 001kg (16 000kg)	19.03	856.35	3 710.56	19.71
Driver Gross vehicle mass 16 000kg+	20.91	940.95	4 077.14	21.66
Forklift operator	13.85	623.25	2 700.54	14.35
General assistant/ trolley collector	12.69	571.05	2 474.36	13.14
Manager	30.01	1 350.45	5 851.50	31.08
Merchandiser	14.99	674.55	2 922.83	15.53
Security guard	12.90	580.50	2 515.31	13.37
Sales assistant	18.92	851.40	3 689.12	19.60
Sales person	18.92	851.40	3 689.12	19.60
Shop assistant	14.99	674.55	2 922.83	15.53
Supervisor	23.27	1 047.15	4 537.30	24.11
Trainee manager	25.14	1 131.30	4 901.92	26.04

Silva (1997) identifies three employer and HR department concerns in countries with legal minimum wages: 1) minimum wages tend to be fixed on unimportant considerations (e.g., political), or on inadequate data which should help define the level of wages; 2) such cases have an adverse effect on competitiveness in the global market and on employment creation, where the minimum wage is fixed above a certain level. Thus, employers and HRM see the minimum wage as a 'safety net' measure to uplift those living on the poverty line; and 3) increases in minimum wages are not matched by productivity gains, which would help to counterbalance increased labour costs.

HRM is expected to evaluate and adhere to legislation and regulatory acts, in terms of employment, staffing, assessments and remuneration, in order to create an equal, honest and trustworthy organisation which embraces diverse cultures and employees, skills and ideas.

In this ever-changing business world, increased globalisation creates major concerns as well as directives for employers and HRM to negotiate pay systems. Silva (1997) explains that these are aimed at

- achieving strategic company objectives;
- flexibility in terms of the variable component which could absorb downturns and reduce labour costs;
- encouraging improved performance;
- enhancing a worker's earnings through improved performance;
- reducing the incidence of redundancies in times of recession or poor enterprise;
- rewarding good performance without increasing labour costs;
- attracting competent individuals.

Gini coefficient

Poverty worldwide is nowhere near being reduced to minimum levels – in fact, global poverty is on the rise. In many countries income gaps are widening, rather than narrowing (Kingdon & Knight, 2006). The Gini coefficient (derived from the work of Corado Gini, an Italian statistician) measures the inequality of income distribution in a country or given society. It ranges between zero and one, and provides an objective measure of income inequality which allows countries to compare themselves to other nations, and to follow their past performance (Manson, 2009). What this means is that

- a coefficient of zero (0) indicates that income is equally shared among everyone, i.e., everyone earns the same;
- a coefficient of one (1) indicates that one person earns all the income, while everyone else earns nothing.

The following diagramme illustrates the notion of equality versus inequality, to show that the Gini coefficient ranges from 0 to 1.

Figure 10.7: Equality versus inequality

Most European nations and South Korea tend to have Gini indices between .24 and .32, whereas the US, Mexico and South Africa tend to have Gini indices above .40, which indicate that these countries have greater inequality. Table 10.9 shows this in greater detail.

Table 10.9: Gini coefficient: Global versus South Africa

Country	Gini coefficient
Denmark	0.24
European nations	0.26
France	0.32
South Korea	0.31
Japan	0.37
Russia	0.42
United States	0.45
Mexico	0.51
Brazil	0.51
South Africa	0.65

Source: The World Factbook, Distribution of family income: Gini index

The evolution of the Gini coefficient is beneficial in that it reveals trends, which can lead to improvements being made. Some find the Gini coefficient powerful in the sense that it is a useful tool for helping travellers and investors grasp the principal factors which characterise specific societies. The Gini coefficient also measures inequality by means of a *ratio analysis*, rather than a value which is not representative of the population. In addition, the Gini coefficient can be used to compare income distribution between different countries and across different populations, thus helping to identify trends. For instance, the coefficient for urban areas is more valuable to businessmen than that of rural areas. Therefore, it can indicate whether or not income distribution has changed within a country, and will help to determine whether income inequality has increased or decreased.

Further, 1) the Gini coefficient guarantees anonymity, in that it does not identify the highest and the lowest earners in a country; 2) it addresses scale independence, which suggests that it is not based on the size of a country's economy, or whether it is a poor or rich country; 3) it addresses population independence, i.e., it is not concerned with population size; and 4) it addresses the transfer principle, which suggests that if income is transferred from the rich to the poor, this will result in a more equal distribution.

Unequal income distribution especially plays a role in emerging markets, although the gap between rich and poor is growing worldwide. Certain factors contribute to the inequality of income distribution, including new technology, increased trade and immigration, and deregulation. Economists believe it is better to redistribute income after it is earned, than to tamper with those markets that are responsible for such unequal outcomes (Pearlstein, 2006). The figure below reflects a typical pay scale architecture.

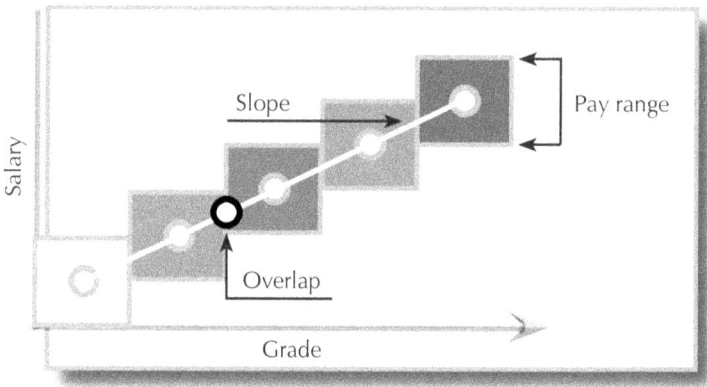

Figure 10.8: Typical pay scale structure
Source: Salary structuring, 21st Century Pay Solutions Group

Our research has shown that on average the pay slope for an emerging market is 1:80. This implies that in terms of remuneration, the lowest-level employee in a company receives 80 times less than the highest-level employee. This pay slope is thus indicative of a high Gini coefficient, which suggests a case of unequal income distribution.

Is it possible to flatten the pay slope and return to a more equal income distribution? As mentioned before, although certain factors cause such an unequal distribution, it is possible to address them by

- addressing issues related to new technology, increased trade and immigration, and deregulation;

- addressing child poverty;

- ensuring continuous training and development, and generating new skills and talent (to combat the issue of skills scarcity);

- providing workers with more bargaining leverage, by restoring workers' right to form a union and exercise freedom of speech;

- ensuring that executive remuneration packages are signed off by the company's shareholders;

- increasing productivity of employees at the bottom of the income ladder (see Pearlstein, 2006).

Combating unequal income distribution is not only the responsibility of government, but also of companies. Problems often hunt in packs, as the saying goes, and several aspects need to be addressed at the same time. In our view the list, in order of priority, is: education, which leads to jobs, which leads to housing, which leads to a reduction in crime, which has a positive effect on productivity, which then leads to higher salaries and wages for all.

Reward trends

Having a good idea of global remuneration trends can be very helpful in setting an organisation's remuneration strategy and preparing for what lies ahead. These trends reflect what leading organisations are currently doing or are contemplating doing in the future. Note that a trend does not necessarily represent good or best practice – it indicates only that a greater number of organisations are considering it. In addition, with the rapid increase in the application of Western HR practices in emerging markets, it is crucial to consider and investigate the impact of how non-Western employees react to those practices.

The following trends, where appropriate, can guide an organisation's remuneration strategy. Trends should, however, be aligned with the organisation's operational strategy, when implemented.

Global remuneration

Glopats (globally mobile expatriates) want to know that their remuneration is competitive, and that they will not be worse off (i.e., that hardship has been taken into account), that they can maintain their standard of living, and that their purchasing power parity (PPP) index will be upheld. Finally, they want to know that sufficient and adequate pension arrangements have been made. Organisations are therefore increasingly exploring 'global' retirement funds.

A real challenge facing some emerging markets is how to bring about a closer alignment between glopat pay and local employee pay. In some countries there are laws stating that the transfer of knowledge from the glopat to local employees should take place anywhere within three to five years. Work permits would theoretically not be renewed after this time frame, but in practice this is rarely achieved.

Retention of employees

Employee retention has been the single biggest driver of remuneration policy for the past five years. Currently, critical shortages are evident in the number of engineers, artisans, chartered accountants, information technology specialists, and inspiring leaders. Organisations have explored and implemented many different mechanisms from a remuneration point of view, and the following points cannot be emphasised enough:

- People join companies and leave managers;

- Twenty-five per cent of the decision to remain in an organisation is influenced by remuneration;

- Inspirational leadership continues to influence employees' decisions to remain in an organisation, especially if they perceive their remuneration as fair (Bussin, 2002b).

In developing markets, retention mainly refers to being retained in the country, rather than the company. Often this requires companies to work closely with government policy-makers to ensure that labour laws, tax laws and general labour relations laws are conducive to retaining skilled workers within the country. Being an 'investor-friendly' country also impacts employee perceptions about a good country to work in. Sometimes it is also a matter of safety – governments need to ensure that their countries are safe, and that citizens do not feel under threat.

Media scrutiny

Instances of exorbitant remuneration continue to grab media headlines. Remuneration reflects the values that guide employer decisions and influence the treatment of employees. It is a reflection of the organisation's image and reputation. A compensation manager must be proactive and knowledgeable about the accounting practices employed in the organisation. This is especially important where variable pay is based on organisational performance in terms of profit (Milkovich & Newman, 2009). Organisations need to ensure that their processes are extremely robust and can withstand any stakeholder scrutiny.

A strong and free press assists with governance. Governments should not underestimate the power of a free press, relative to investor friendliness and citizens' comfort levels.

Specialist career tracks

A fairly significant trend has evolved over the past few years: organisations are acknowledging that superb skills in, or knowledge of, a technical position should also ensure advancement in organisations. Dual career paths – one for management and one for technical personnel – now exist in some organisations. The benefit of this approach is that the knowledge and skills of top-performing technical people can be retained where they can be utilised more effectively and profitably by the organisation.

Employees who are technically above-average performers are not necessarily good management material, and it is in the best interests of the company to retain such employees where they can contribute to creating sustained competitive advantage for the organisation.

Greater flexibility

More than three-quarters of respondents to a recent survey (21st Century Pay solutions Group, 2013), which asked the question: 'Would you rather have a pay increase next year or more flexibility?' responded that they would prefer greater flexibility. There are a number of ways in which to introduce flexibility into compensation, two of which are discussed here.

- *Total guaranteed remuneration package.* This rests on three fundamental pillars: internal equity, structuring flexibility, and external market competitiveness. The total package concept is exciting and flexible, in that employees can choose (from amongst a number of options) those benefits that are best suited to their lifestyle. The benefit of the total package to the employer is that it contains and defines the total fixed cost of employment, and empowers employees to structure more competitive packages which are comparable to those of their peers.

- *Life cycle theory.* Employees, depending on the life cycle stage they are in, view reward differently. To obtain the most from your team, it is essential to remember the differences between each life cycle and to understand what employees' preferences are, not only in terms of work but also in terms of reward and recognition.

Governance

Good corporate governance rests solidly on sound and effective communication. It is essential to learn how to strike a balance between good governance and being too transparent.

The question being asked is: If we disclose all our remuneration data, schemes, and how they operate, are we giving away our competitive advantage? The debate continues as to whether non-executive directors should receive shares and bonuses in the organisation they serve. The general answer is: No.

In emerging markets, particular attention needs to be paid to linking pay to corporate performance and publishing exactly how they are linked.

Branding

Is there a link between corporate branding and reward? Is there a remuneration discount if one works for a well-branded organisation? What is that discount? Very little information is available about this poorly understood trend.

What is clear is that, in emerging markets, most people want to work for organisations that are well known brands. This issue offers numerous opportunities for further research.

Broad-banding/flatter structures

Broad-banding constitutes a pay structure that consolidates a large number of pay grades and salary ranges into fewer, broader bands, with relatively wide salary ranges (Economic Research Institute, 2004). A single band usually spans the pay opportunity formerly covered by several separate salary ranges. Most bands have a minimum and a maximum, but no midpoint (Braddick, Jones & Shafer, 1992). Broad bands generally fall into one of two categories, namely salary or career bands (Neubauer, 1995).

- *Salary bands* represent a collapse of the traditional structure into several overlapping bands. The purpose of salary bands may be to alleviate the 'topping out' of large numbers of employees who are at, or near, the maximum of their ranges (Braddick et al., 1992);

- *Career bands* are similar to salary bands, except that their purpose shifts from an attempt to simplify salary administration to one of management development. Career bands are used to facilitate lateral moves, thereby reinforcing the fact that career growth can be lateral as well as vertical.

Reasons for implementing broad-banding include the following (Kanin-Lovers & Cameron, 1994):

- *Reducing the administration burden.* Many organisations spend an excessive amount of time trying to manage restrictive minimum, maximum and midpoint policies;

- *Accommodating a variety of market situations.* Organisations can compare themselves to a wider variety of competitors. Broader ranges accommodate a greater variety of market differences, both functionally and geographically, for jobs that essentially have the same internal value.

Too few organisations have implemented broad-banding successfully in emerging markets. This is an untapped opportunity which needs to be pursued to alleviate the focus on miniscule changes to job descriptions which tie up job-grading committees for hours on end, with non-value-add work.

Pay for performance

Performance-based pay focuses on evaluating the performance contribution of an individual, a team or an organisational unit, and paying them accordingly. The emphasis here is on the value of the performance contribution, rather than on the value of the job (Torrington et al., 2009). Pay for performance increases (in addition to general increases) reward individuals for doing their job well.

Performance-related pay (PRP) has many theoretical attractions when seen from the perspective of managers (Torrington et al., 2009, p. 173):

- It serves to attract and retain good performers, creating incentives for the most talented and hard-working people to earn more than they would be able to, under a system which pays a flat rate irrespective of personal performance;

- Since it distributes rewards according to the efforts and skills that people contribute, it is regarded as a fair system;

- It motivates people by rewarding them for putting in additional effort to achieve specific objectives;

- It is a means whereby managers can exercise control over people's priorities without the need for close supervision;

- It reinforces the individual employment relationship and undermines the influence of trade unions;

- It forces managers and staff to communicate directly and regularly about roles, duties, expectations and development needs.

Market pricing

Another approach commonly used in emerging markets is market pricing, which relies almost exclusively on the rates paid in the external market, when determining pay structures. Organisations that follow this approach collect as much market data as possible, and match as many of their jobs with the market data.

Following market prices as an approach to compensating the process of balancing internal and external pressures, is a matter of judgement for the organisation.

Salary surveys are not well developed in all emerging markets, which makes obtaining market rates particularly challenging. Steady inroads are, however, being made and this challenge will be obviated in time to come. In the meantime, building pay scales from an internal equity point of view and from a number of benchmark jobs, will need to suffice. Flexibility and quick response time are needed in fast-moving markets, particularly when large multinationals move into a country and are willing to pay top dollar to establish themselves quickly. It throws the whole market out of sync and creates unrealistic pay levels, especially for scarce and technical jobs.

Team-based pay

Teams have emerged as a widely used design approach in large organisations, for a number of reasons – these include the changing nature of work, their match with employee involvement and total quality-management programmes, and the development of knowledge about how to design and manage teams (Vosloo, 2005). Teamwork is widely commended as a means of encouraging employees to assume responsibility for identifying and solving problems related to poor communication, inappropriate coordination, low motivation and slow response. Also, it is assumed that the self-interest of those with the highest skills levels will motivate them to train and assist team members with lower skills levels, with a view to increasing the latter's skills and efforts, thereby boosting team performance and bonuses (Vosloo, 2005). Team pay also enhances flexible working within teams (Armstrong & Baron, 2003).

Many of these trends have been on the radar screen for a few years now. However, the order of importance has changed, and some have become more important in specific industries. Well-informed remuneration committees know these trends and are applying their minds as to which are most appropriate for their organisation. Trends should never be applied blindly.

Conclusion

In this chapter the importance of rewarding leadership was examined, and components of the remuneration and total reward systems were explained. HRM's responsibility, how much to pay, total reward statements and the challenges facing the HRM department and the CHRO when it comes to rewards, were covered. All the above factors should be taken into account when designing a remuneration programme, to ensure fair, consistent and transparent remuneration for all employees, employers and expatriates.

References

21st Century Pay Solutions Group. (2009). *Salary structuring.* Rosebank: 21st Century Pay Solutions Group.

21st Century Pay Solutions Group. (2013). *Snap survey.* Rosebank: 21st Century Pay Solutions Group.

Armstrong, M. (2006). *A handbook of human resource management practice.* (10th ed.). UK: Cambridge University Press.

Armstrong, M. & Baron, A. (2003). *Performance management: The new realities.* London: Chartered Institute of Personnel and Development.

Armstrong, M. & Murlis, H. (1994). *Reward management: A handbook of remuneration strategy and practice.* (3rd ed.). London: Kogan Page.

Arnolds, C.A. & Venter, D.J.L. (2007). The strategic importance of motivational rewards for lower-level employees in the manufacturing and retailing industries. *SA Journal of Industrial Psychology, 33*(3), 15–23.

Baruch, Y., Steele, D.J. & Quantrill, G.A. (2002). Management of expatriation and repatriation for novice global player. *International Journal of Manpower, 23*(7), 659–671.

Braddick, C.A., Jones, M.B. & Shafer, P.M. (1992). A look at broadbanding in practice. *Journal of Compensation and Benefits, 27*, 28–32.

Brun, J-P. & Dugas, N. (2008). An analysis of employee recognition: Perspective on human resources practices. *The International Journal of Human Resource Management, 19*(4), 716–730.

Bussin, M. (2002). *Choosing the right incentive scheme – Guide 9.* The Nuts & Bolts Business Series – Remuneration Series. Johannesburg: Knowledge Resources.

Bussin, M. (2007). *Paterson course.* Rosebank: 21st Century Pay Solutions Group.

Coleman, N.K. (1999). Global pay and results. In H. Risher (Ed.), *Aligning pay and results: Compensation strategies that work from the boardroom to the shop floor.* New York: AMACOM Books, 259–273.

Corporate Leadership Council (CLC). (2008). *CLC quarterly report on HR news and trends.* Retrieved June 16, 2008 from www.clc.executiveboard.com

Dessler, G. (2009). *Fundamentals of human resource management.* London: Pearson Education.

Döös, M. & Wilhelmson, L. (2009). *Organising work for innovation and growth: Experiences and effort in ten companies.* Sweden: VINNOVA.

Entrepreneur Magazine South Africa. (2013, February). *The best ways to reward employees.* Retrieved March 5, 2013 from http://www.entrepreneur.com/article/75340.html

Gilman, N.P. (2009). *Methods of industrial remuneration.* Charleston, SC: BiblioLife LLC.

Gross, S.E. & Friedman, H.E. (2007). Creating an effective total rewards strategy: Holistic approach better supports business success. *Mercer Human Resources Consulting CD – Your guide to the age of talent.* United States: Mercer.

Guthrie, J. (2007). Remuneration pay effects and work. In P. Boxall, J. Purcell and P. Wright (Eds.), *The Oxford handbook of human resource management*. Oxford: Oxford University Press, 344–363.

Harris, S. & Clements, L. (2007). What's the perceived value of your incentives? *The Magazine of World at Work: Workspan, 2,* 21–25. Scottsdale, USA: WorldatWork Press.

Kanin-Lovers, J. & Cameron, M. (1994). Broadbanding: A step forward or a step backward? *Journal of Compensation and Benefits, 9,* 39–42.

Kaplan, R.S. & Norton, D.P. (2004). *Strategy maps.* Boston, MA: Harvard Business School.

Kingdon, G.G. & Knight, J. (2006). How flexible are wages in response to local unemployment in South Africa? *Industrial and Labour Relations Review, 59*(3), 471–495.

Luthans, F. (2005). *Organisational behaviour.* New York: McGraw Hill.

Manson, B. (2009). *Britain: Income inequality at record high.* Retrieved June 4, 2009 from World Socialist website. http://www.wsws.org/en/articles/2009/06/inco-j04.html

Marchington, M. & Wilkinson, A. (2008). *Human resource management at work: People management and development.* London: CIPD.

Mathis, R.L. & Jackson, J.H. (2003). *Human resource management.* (10th ed.). Ohio: Thomson Learning.

Matthews, C. (2013, February). Obama's proposal to boost the minimum wage: Will it help or hurt workers? *Time Magazine.* Retrieved March 4, 2013 from http://business.time.com/2013/02/14/obamas-proposal-to-boost-the-minimum-wage-will-it-help-or-hurt-workers/

Mello, J.A. (2011). *Strategic management of human resources.* (3rd ed.). Canada: South-Western Cengage Learning.

Milkovich, G. & Newman, J. (2009). *Compensation.* (9th ed.). Boston: Irwin McGraw Hill.

Nelson, B. & Spitzer, D.R. (2003). *The 1001 rewards & recognition fieldbook: The complete guide.* New York: Workman Publishing Company.

Neubauer, R.J. (1995). Broadbanding: Management fad or saviour? *Compensation and Benefits Management, 11,* 50–54.

Odendaal, A. (2009). Motivation: From concepts to applications. In S.P. Robbins, T.A. Judges, A. Odendaal and G. Roodt (Eds.), *Organisational behaviour: Global and South African perspectives.* Cape Town: Prentice Hall, 168–191.

Pearlstein, S. (2006). Solving inequality problem won't take class warfare. *The Washington Post.* Retrieved July 20, 2014 from http://www.washingtonpost.com/wp-dyn/content/article/2006/03/14/AR2006031401786.html

Peterson, S. & Luthans, F. (2006). The impact of financial and nonfinancial incentives on business unit outcomes over time. *Journal of Applied Psychology, 91*(1), 156–165.

Phillips, M. (2009). *Salary structuring.* Rosebank: 21st Century Pay Solutions Group.

Republic of South Africa. (2013, January 17). Basic Conditions of Employment Act (75/1997): Amendment of Sectoral Determination 9: Wholesale and Retail Sector, South Africa. *Government Gazette, 571,* no. 36076. Pretoria: Government Printers, 1–6.

Rubino, J. (2006). *Principles of powerful living.* Mumbai: Jaico Book House.

Silva, S. (1997). The changing focus of industrial relations and human resource management. International Labour Organisation (ILO) Workshop on Employer's Organizations, 5–13 May 1997, Turin, Italy.

Statistics South Africa (StatsSA). (2012). *Quarterly labour force survey, Quarter 4, P0211.* Retrieved March 5, 2013 from http://www.statssa.gov.za/publications/P0211/P02112ndQuarter2012.pdf

The World Factbook. (2009). *Distribution of family income – Gini index.* Retrieved March 1, 2013 from https://www.cia.gov/library/publications/the-world-factbook/fields/2172.html

Torrington, D., Hall, L., Taylor, S. & Atkinson, C. (2009). *Fundamentals of human resource management.* London: Pearson Education.

Vosloo, S.E. (2005). Compensation. In P.M. Muchinsky, H.J. Kriek and A.M.G. Schreuder (Eds.), *Personnel psychology.* Cape Town: Oxford University Press, 263–295.

Weiss, J.W. (2001). *Organisational behaviour and change: Managing diversity, cross-cultural dynamics and ethics.* Mason, OH: South-Western College Publishing.

WorldatWork. (2007). *The World at Work handbook of compensation, benefits and total rewards.* Hoboken, NJ: John Wiley & Sons, Inc.

Xpatulator website. (2013). Retrieved March 8, 2013 from http://www.xpatulator.com/

CHAPTER 11: Communicating with Employees – Social Media

Dave Duarte

Introduction

Social media have risen from obscurity to mainstream acceptance in the span of the first decade of the 21st century. In the coming decade we are likely to see the impact of social media technologies reshape the way we work together, raise funds, elect leaders, buy things, find work and find workers.

Organisations around the world are starting to take social media more seriously, especially in light of Generation Y and the Millennials (the so-called Digital Natives) entering the workplace with a new set of expectations about how the world should work.

With social media comes a flattening of hierarchies which, in turn, has consequences for the way we lead, retain and communicate with employees. The benefits are improved organisational memory, productivity and community among companies that adopt these media well. However, if the use of social media is repressed or left to chance, it can be a disruptive force.

We still have a great deal to learn about how to use social media effectively in business. Some issues that manifest are of a technical nature, such as which software to use or how to use it. Other issues are related to process, for instance, how to get people to buy into your company's social media, or how to ensure that such media are used effectively.

In this chapter the focus is on procedural rather than technical issues related to effective social media use. First, there is an introduction to exactly what social media are all about, and how they can be used in HR functions.

The focus also falls on certain common issues pertaining to social software, such as a lack of buy-in, concerns about productivity, cultural readiness and reputation risk.

What are social media?

'Social media' is a term used to describe various technologies that enable people to communicate publicly. Best known are public sites such as Facebook, but forums, intranets, mobile chat platforms like MXit, and comments on articles are all types of social media. The main requirement is the ease and low cost to the individual of publishing in an electronic format.

The first question, then, is whether social media which are published behind the company firewall count as such. The answer is, yes. Social media can be limited to a particular audience of company employees only. In this chapter the focus will be on both internal and public social media, since both have implications for HR practitioners.

Social media communication is important in the organisational context because it allows more people to share their perspectives with others, than can be handled by traditional forms of organisational communication such as meetings, emails and phone calls. There are two reasons for this:

- *Social media communication is asynchronous.* It can be accessed as and when people need it, it does not require immediate attention;

- *Social media communication is many-to-many.* Instead of one person addressing many people (e.g., when a policy is sent out, or when a leader issues a statement), or people communicating one-to-one (e.g., phone calls or face-to-face conversations), social media allow many-to-many communication (where many people share perspectives on an issue simultaneously and on record).

While email can be asynchronous and many-to-many it is not considered part of social media (even though some employees may use it to voice their perspectives), because it is not accessible beyond the inboxes of the people it has been sent to, whereas social media should be accessible to others as and when they want it.

Social media platforms tend to become enriched as they are used. Comments add value to articles. Forum questions and answers build knowledge bases. Wikis become enriched as people edit them and share their expertise.

In the case of social media platforms such as Kickstarter and IndieGogo, people can make a public appeal for funds that can then be collectively raised in small amounts by anyone who finds their idea appealing. This holds much promise for organisations which are interested in leveraging the latent knowledge and resources of their workforce. As more ideas are published and made accessible, so the organisation's shared knowledge base increases. Social media can also be useful in increasing levels of engagement or gaining insight into important issues.

Social media at work

Social media have changed the way people interact. Millions of people log onto Facebook every day for updates on what their friends, family and even their work colleagues are doing. Twitter helps spread news faster. LinkedIn has made our CVs publicly accessible online. And Google Hangouts has made it easier for groups of people to teleconference from anywhere in the world, using nothing more than smart phones or laptop computers.

There are thousands of popular social applications that help people connect with others in different ways. For example, GoodReads connects bibliophiles to help them find and rate books; TripAdvisor lets travellers share reviews and tips which potentially improve their holidays; Slideshare is a presentation-sharing network; IMDB is a social network hosting film reviews; amongst many more. Through these networks and many others like them, people are learning the value of asynchronous, many-to-many collaboration and communication, and are using these media to make smarter choices in their personal lives.

This not only presents new opportunities for business collaboration and communication, but also raises challenges in terms of productivity and security. People use social media throughout the day – somewhere in the world people are using personal social media tools during work hours, while others are using them after hours. However, a certain amount of professional social networking is likely to be taking place, even if that only means accepting a LinkedIn invitation to connect with a colleague, customer or competitor.

Since users are learning how social interfaces work in their personal capacities, expectations of workplace software may be higher, too. Regardless of whether or not IT mandates social media use, the rise in the number or people bringing their own smart phones to work means that those same people have access to social media during work hours, and many of them are connecting with their work colleagues on social media platforms. In response to this, a number of companies have created business software designed to meet the expectations and habits of social media-savvy workers. The four most used globally are Yammer, Chatter, Telligent Enterprise and Jive. A South African social software company that is worth investigating is WyseTalk. It may be useful to choose a locally owned social software company, due to the higher levels of direct support and customisation it offers.

Productivity

A common concern about social media in the workplace is that it may negatively impact productivity. Three recent studies have, however, provided compelling evidence to the contrary.

- *Leisure browsing improves productivity*. Researchers at the University of Melbourne found that people who were allowed to access the Internet freely at work were more productive than those whose access was blocked (Coker, 2009);

- *Cyberloafing refreshes attention*. Singapore University researchers found that students who took breaks from work to 'cyber loaf' (i.e., browse around online) were less mentally exhausted and bored, and more psychologically engaged (Chen & Lim, 2011);

- *Cute pictures enhance carefulness.* Researchers at Hiroshima University in Japan found that participants who looked at pictures or videos of cute animals (e.g., cat pictures commonly shared on social networks) performed better in tests of concentration, speed and accuracy (Nittono, 2012).

Furthermore, Joe Nandhakumar and a research team at Warwick Business School found that company policy which actively encouraged social media usage among employees led to increased customer interaction and, eventually, higher productivity. This was primarily due to the benefits of virtual collaboration. 'Ubiquitous digital connectivity should be seen not as an unwelcome interruption but as part of the changing nature of knowledge work itself that needs to become part of normal, everyday practices of contemporary organizations' (Nandhakumar, 2013).

A separate study performed by McKinsey (2010), entitled 'The rise of the networked enterprise', found that companies/departments that used social software experienced the following benefits:

- 77 per cent gained faster access to information;
- 60 per cent reduced communication costs;
- 52 per cent gained enhanced access to internal experts;
- 44 per cent cut their travel costs;
- 41 per cent experienced increased employee satisfaction.

With this evidence and more, it seems that far from making employees unproductive, social media use can be exceptionally beneficial to the productivity of both users and employers.

Social media and HR

The primary reasons for using social software internally are to boost innovation, alignment and engagement. However, according to a 2012 study by software company Silkroad, 75 per cent of HR managers surveyed felt their company lagged behind in using social media management software. Social media can, in fact, be used by HR during each phase of the employment cycle: from attraction to retention to separation. A more detailed explanation follows.

Attraction

- *Employer branding.* Brands on social media are more accessible than those that are not. Effective employer branding should be done in conjunction with a marketing team which can complement HR's insights with their production expertise, in areas such as copywriting and design. Probably the most effective tool for employer branding is a LinkedIn company profile page, as this enables you to establish direct contact with professionals in the industry in which you are looking to recruit. Employer branding can and should, however, extend to all the company's public profiles on social media: blogs, Twitter, Facebook, Instagram and Pinterest, most notably;

- *Talent communities.* Social media make it easy to organise people around topics of shared interest. It has been said that Facebook is for the people you went to school with, while Twitter is for the people you wish you went to school with. With this in mind, some brands use online platforms as a way to attract talent. For example, Cerebra (a Johannesburg-based Marketing Agency) has been using a site called 27dinner.com to draw Internet marketers together for a monthly dinner. Cerebra has benefitted from its heightened industry profile, while gaining access to talent – those people who self-select to attend this kind of event.

Recruitment

- *Identifying candidates.* In 2013, LinkedIn exceeded 200 million users, more than 50 per cent of whom had complete profiles on the site. This is an entire network of people who can be tagged, sorted and filtered based on recruiters' particular requirements for a position. LinkedIn also has tools for recruiters that help them organise talent into folders to which they can add keywords and reminders. This can ultimately lead to a drastically reduced 'cost per hire';

- *Peer-to-peer recruitment and referral schemes.* Sites such as HiringBounty.com incentivise people to refer suitable candidates for jobs. The idea is that employers post jobs directly onto this website, while those looking to make some money browse the jobs on offer. LinkedIn makes this even easier, as companies can use an 'apply with LinkedIn' button on online job advertisements. When a candidate applies, not only will their LinkedIn profile be submitted with their application (along with relevant filters for skills and education), but potential employers can see whether anyone in their organisation knows the candidate who is applying for the role (provided the candidate and the employee are already connected on LinkedIn). This represents another reference check, and perhaps one that is more convenient and accessible for the HR team responsible for recruiting;

- *Social scoring.* Depending on the industry, there are various ways in which candidates can showcase their skills to attract the attention of recruiters. For example, players of the massive multiplayer online game, World of Warcraft, have used their in-game status as guild leaders to gain employment in roles that require strategic as well as leadership skills (Seely-Brown & Douglas, 2004).

In the marketing field it is increasingly important to demonstrate your skills on social media by amassing an engaged following, for example, by having a Klout score above a certain number, because Klout.com has a widely accepted way of measuring online influence, and peers can endorse one another as regards their influence in various subjects. Companies who hire software programmers may use Stack Overflow scores for reference purposes: this is an online platform for asking and answering computer-programming questions, where users gain points and badges for answering questions correctly. The badges and points earned on a user's StackOverflow.com profile can help employers identify programmers with the appropriate level of knowledge and commitment to learning that they require for a particular job;

- *On-demand staffing.* As major organisations look to freelance networks and independent contractors to provide them with specialised skills, the trend to look out for is the algorithmically enhanced management of freelance networks, where more specialised roles are required.

Onboarding

- *Role-specific wiki pages.* Wikis are websites (like Wikipedia) that can be edited by users. It is a revolutionary form of collaborative publishing that allows for multiple perspectives on any particular topic. Wikis make provision for a document to be kept up to date through small changes and updates that users make on an ongoing basis. Thus, wikis can be extremely useful in the organisational context, as roles and job descriptions evolve. An ever-changing document in the form of a wiki page can be used to explain the different elements of a role. For example, the page for a marketing manager could hyperlink to a checklist for event organising. Also, if someone leaves their job or is promoted, s/he can bring the incumbent up to speed with their new role by providing them with access to the wiki that describes their new position;

- *Experience forums.* Online forums where users share their expertise in response to questions can be very compelling, as evidenced by sites like Quora.com, Yahoo Answers, and niche topic forums such as MyBroadband. In the organisational context a similar format can be used to build a shared base of organisational knowledge. Through the process of asking and answering questions on these in-house forums, problems can be solved and expertise showcased. One useful tip to encourage sustained, high-quality participation on these spaces, is to help people earn points and badges as a form of acknowledgement for sharing their expertise (Cheng & Vassileva, 2006)

Learning and development

- *Learning communities.* The promise of e-learning is to conveniently and inexpensively up-skill employees by delivering learning content straight to wherever they are, be it at home or at work. However, one of the downsides of e-learning is that participants often do not gain much from the peer interactions that many face-to-face courses provide. Social learning seeks to fulfil this need by enabling discussions about course content, thus providing some of the benefits of face-to-face learning while enabling more peer-to-peer collaboration and knowledge sharing. The Ogilvy Digital Marketing Academy (ODMA) used software called Ning to create an online network for learners. Having a social network to complement classroom-based learning made the courses much more interactive. Students helped one another by offering encouragement, and asking and answering questions. This helped to reduce the support strain on the course facilitators, as students assisted one another and learned from other people's challenges, rather than relying on the course facilitators to solve their problems individually through email or via one-on-one consultations by phone or in person;

- *Gamification of skills.* Using points and badges to reward different levels of skill or achievement in organisational learning initiatives can be highly motivational. At the ODMA, awarding badges for different levels of participation in digital courses not only increased levels of engagement in the courses, but also helped facilitators to more easily identify people who were particularly good at certain skills upon completion of the programmes. For example, if in a course module on Search Engine Optimisation a student achieved 100 per cent participation as well as at least 80 per cent on their assignment, they would earn the accompanying badge that would be displayed on their profile page on the ODMA social learning platform. The result was a marked increase in project quality, knowledge levels and interaction among the students who took the course.

Leadership and innovation

- *Leadership blogs.* Leaders who keep blogs or participate in company forums become accessible in an asynchronous way that allows them to more conveniently participate in company discussions, and to continually reinforce their messages in different ways, in response to the various challenges raised in company forums;

- *Participation in decisions.* Social software can allow employees to participate in leadership decision-making. Leaders can also poll employees for their perspectives, or solicit feedback and ideas.

Retention

- *Access and mobility*. The *2011 Cisco connected world technology report* found that Gen Ys are 'getting increasingly more demanding about their workplace flexibility when it comes to their choice of computing devices, work hours, and access to social media networks during the workday'. A full 40 per cent of university-educated under-30 respondents said they would take a lower-paying job that offered more in the way of device flexibility and social media access during work hours, and 56 per cent said if their job blocked access to social sites, they would not accept the offer or would join the company and look for ways to circumvent this policy;

- *Transparency*. It is said that people join companies, but leave bosses. Social software can provide a simple, anonymous way to get feedback about managers in the company, directly from their staff. Software solutions such as GetaGreatBoss.com can collect ratings and reviews on managers, for the benefit of HR managers as well as job seekers wanting to find out who exactly they will be working for and with. This is part of a broader trend towards greater individual and organisational transparency, driven by ease of publishing and access to published data;

- *Remote working and engagement*. Having a casual way to stay in touch with what is going on in the office helps connect remote workers to the company culture;

- *Building networks of shared interests*. Employers should, in my opinion, encourage social media use among employees, if for no other reason than to strengthen relationships in the company. Zappos, the e-commerce company, has hundreds of employees who use public social networks such as Twitter – this not only showcases the company's culture, but helps connect active employees with one another. Of course, this kind of public engagement should happen in the context of a clear company social media policy that sets guidelines for employees' social media interaction.

Separation

- *Alumni community*. Former employees can remain a very valuable resource for companies. Thanks to their experience of how the company works, and perhaps because they may have a greater emotional connection with the company, they could be used for occasional consulting, to refer business to the company, or perhaps even to be rehired at a later stage in their careers. This is especially true for companies such as Ogilvy, and Ernst and Young, who tend to hire very smart young people straight out of university, and who then go on to work for their clients. In the case of Ernst and Young, an alumni community has developed on LinkedIn that allows the company to easily stay in touch with former staff, and even to help them network with others.

Dealing with the challenges of social software adoption

Perhaps the primary challenge with social media use in organisations is that the software might be implemented, but then never actually used by the very employees it was intended to help. Certainly, with my own social software company, Huddlemind, I found this to be the case with our early clients. We would give them what we considered to be the best software for social learning and collaboration on the market – and which had proven effectiveness at other clients – but in many cases it would end up unused after an initial surge of participation. The main lesson learnt from all this, was that the software is not what makes people participate socially within a work context, but rather that there are people-driven enablers of social software adoption that have nothing to do with the technical aspects of the software, and everything to do with the human aspects of productivity, collaboration and motivation.

In my experience, the three determinants of social software adoption and use are:

- *Organisational readiness for the software.* Is the software being introduced at the right level? Are respected people in the organisation backing its use? Is training being done on how to use the software correctly? Have the benefits of the software been explained and accepted? Is there clear policy in place that describes acceptable and unacceptable ways of participating in social networks?

- *Incentives for participation.* Initially, we found that there needs to be a clear benefit for people to use social software – at least until the act of using it has been habitualised. We helped the marketing team of a multinational brewer to implement the software we introduced to them, by organising a charity drive using the network. The participants in the programme discovered that it was much easier and more enjoyable to organise and report on the project in a social manner, than through traditional emails and meetings. They thus began using the software for other projects they collaborated on. Incentives may be virtual, for example participation points and badges;

- *Community management.* Perhaps the most important aspect of social software adoption, in our view, was the need for moderation and community management. Community managers stimulate and encourage participation in social networks, for instance by welcoming new users, asking key people to answer questions on the network, or organising gatherings and special events via the network. Community managers should also moderate activities and apply the rules of participation, such as blocking conversations that become defamatory.

Social software use should not merely be viewed as yet another 'thing to do', but rather as another way of getting things done. However, not all people in a company are likely to take up and use a new software tool equally well. Training and following a gradual approach to introducing the technology are, therefore, vital.

A principle here is that new followers emulate other followers, not the leader. Therefore, it is imperative never to roll out new software to the whole company at the same time, but rather to start with a small group of employees who are most likely to use the new tools enthusiastically. Then, get feedback from these people on how to improve the software and align it better to the company's needs. From here you should roll out to successively enthusiastic groups of company employees. If access to the software is seen as a benefit, rather than a compliance requirement, you're really winning.

Besides learning about how people use the software, a side-benefit can be that users take greater ownership of it. 'People support what they help to build,' according to Gloria Burke, Director of Knowledge Strategy and Governance at Unisys. 'And, once it is built, they have a stake in its success' (Increase your company's productivity with social media, *Harvard Business Review*, 2011). Burke helped introduce Inside Unisys, a social network internal to the firm, which is now actively used by over 15 000 employees.

Social media policy

With entire organisations connecting to the outside world publicly, the potential for PR blunders, Wikileak-type scandals, and general impropriety is greatly enhanced. However, with the right guidelines in place, social media can and should be used safely and beneficially.

Research by Altimeter (2011) found that companies that experience social media-related crises – such as a damaging rumour being spread that affects the share price or product sales – lacked the following:

- Internal education;
- Professional staff;
- A triage plan;
- An employee policy;
- Influencer identification;
- Moderation; and
- Community guidelines.

According to Proskauer Rose's (2012) second annual *Social media in the workplace – around the world 2.0 report*, 68.9 per cent of employers said they had to create policies specifically to regulate social media use – a 13.8 per cent increase from the previous year.

Regardless of whether social software is introduced by IT, marketing or HR, it is important to have a simple policy that clearly outlines the terms of engagement. The simpler, the better, although it is important to ensure that governance issues are dealt with upfront. To quote Dee Hock, founder and former CEO of VISA: 'Simple, clear purpose and principles give rise to complex and intelligent behavior. Complex rules and regulations give rise to simple and stupid behavior'.

A financial services company that I consulted for in Johannesburg, blocked access to public social media completely for each employee, until they signed the basic three-page social media policy, which was written in plain language (as opposed to legalese or corporate-speak). This approach allowed employees who were interested in using social media at work to identify themselves, and it also ensured that they knew the terms of engagement.

A good social media policy should do the following:

- Introduce the top one or two purposes for which the company would use social media. For example, to improve knowledge exchange, collaboration or peer-to-peer networking;

- Ensure that employees know they are responsible for what they post and will be held accountable for it;

- Lay out basic terms of engagement, for example, that defamatory content is not permitted, or that client confidentiality is to be maintained at all times;

- Remind employees that everyone is responsible for the quality of the network, for example, by moderating one another's posts, or generally staying on-topic;

- Identify the person, people or team to be contacted in regard to suggestions or questions, or to whom employees can report related problems.

Implementing a social media policy is not only about imposing restrictions. It can and should also provide an enabling framework which allows creativity and collaboration to flourish.

Social media and company culture

In 2010 I was asked to visit Ogilvy Cape Town, to help them learn how to use digital media more effectively. At that stage the company was the country's largest advertising agency, creatively superb at doing traditional (print, radio, television, billboard) advertising, but losing clients who wanted a digital (online and mobile) aspect to their marketing. This posed a potential existential threat to the agency, and we needed to overcome complacency and help staff realise the urgent need to up-skill in digital media use.

The ODMA was launched with the stated mission of shifting Ogilvy Cape Town's culture to enable greater digital participation. Agency leaders, Rob Hill and

Gavin Levinsohn, led the charge from the front and demonstrated through their own bravery and communication that this change was important. The intervention turned out to be remarkably successful because of the focus on company culture, rather than simply looking at what technologies needed to be introduced. The result was that the agency gained new business and won more awards – especially in the digital categories – than any of its competitors.

Since technology changes the way in which people work together it is, in fact, a cultural issue, regardless of whether we acknowledge it as such. While it seems to be generally understood that culture is important, it is quite an ephemeral concept that may be difficult to work with. In order to be able to deal with it, I had to make it more tangible for myself. So, for the ODMA intervention, I broke down the concept of 'culture' into five elements that I could work with. Now, if you ask me what company culture is, I will tell you it consists of PARTS: people, art, rituals, tools and stories.

- *People*. Identify influencers in the company and get them onboard with proposed change, by giving them first access to the training and providing targeted assistance in coaching them to success. Such special care pays off as they, in turn, help others;

- *Artefacts*. What tangible signs of change can you offer to reward participation and change? In the case of the ODMA there were trophies made of Lego, gorgeous certificates, and prizes such as iPads for the best employee-driven digital projects;

- *Rituals*. We introduced weekly gatherings called 'How-to Fridays', where outside experts were invited to present their latest technology-related projects;

- *Tools*. Internet access should be enabled for participants, and cool tools such as iPads provided for key people to use in their work;

- *Stories*. Significant effort, time and money were invested in celebrating success stories, like campaigns featuring digital elements. These provide models for emulation and help change seem more readily achievable.

Approached at a systemic or cultural level like this, it is much more likely that the introduction of social media will be aligned with company values, used effectively, and provide the kinds of benefits described in this chapter.

Conclusion

Adopting and adapting to social media are clearly vital for any company which wishes to remain agile, relevant and engaged. For HR practitioners it is important to ensure that the use of social media is not simply driven as a marketing or IT issue, but rather as something that has people, learning and company culture at the heart of it.

References

Altimeter. (2011). *Social media crises on the rise: Be prepared by climbing the social business hierarchy of needs*. Retrieved July 28, 2014 from http://www.web-strategist.com/blog/2011/08/31/report-social-media-crises-on-rise-be-prepared-by-climbing-the-social-business-hierarchy-of-needs/

Brown J.S. & Thomas, D. (2004). *A new culture of learning: Cultivating the imagination for a world of constant change*. CreateSpace Independent Publishing Platform (Amazon self-published).

Cheng, C. & Vassileva, J. (2006). Design and evaluation of an adaptative mechanism for sustained educational online communities. *User Modeling and User-Adapted Interaction, 16*, 321–348.

Cisco connected world technology report. (2012). Retrieved July 28, 2014 from http://www.cisco.com/c/dam/en/us/solutions/enterprise/connected-world-technology-report/CCWTR-Chapter1-Report.pdf

Coker, B.L.S. (2011). Freedom to surf: The positive effects of workplace internet leisure browsing. *New Technology, Work and Employment, 26*(3), 238–247.

Lim, V.K.G. & Chen, D.J.Q. (2009). Cyberloafing at the workplace: Gain or drain on work? *Behaviour & Information Technology, First article*, 1–11. DOI: 10.1080/01449290903353054.

McKinsey. (2010). *The rise of the networked enterprise: Web 2.0 finds its payday.* Retrieved July 28, 2014 from http://www.mckinsey.com/insights/high_tech_telecoms_internet/the_rise_of_the_networked_enterprise_web_20_finds_its_payday

Meister, J.C. 2011. Increase your company's productivity with social media. *Harvard Business Review*. Retrieved July 28, 2014 from http://blogs.hbr.org/2011/09/increase-your-companys-productiv/

Nittono, H., Fukushima, M., Yano, A., & Moriya, H. (2012). The power of Kawaii: Viewing cute images promotes a careful behavior and narrows attentional focus. *PLoS ONE, 7*(9), e46362. DOI:10.1371/journal.pone.0046362.

Proskauer, R. 2012. Social Media in the Workplace Around the World 2.0 Survey. Retrieved July 28, 2014 from http://www.proskauer.com/files/uploads/Documents/2012_ILG_Social_Network_Survey_Results_Social_Media_2.0.pdf

Silkroad. 2012. *Social media & workplace collaboration.* Retrieved July 30, 2014 from http://pages.silkroad.com/Social-Media-and-Workplace-Collaboration.html?campaign=70160000000Xuuh

Subramaniam, N. Nandhakumar, J. and Baptista, J. (2013). Exploring social network interactions in enterprise systems: The role of virtual co-presence. *Information Systems Journal, 23*.

CHAPTER 12: Employment Relations in Emerging Markets

Barney Jordaan

Introduction

In his book, *Employment with a human face: Balancing efficiency, equity and voice*, John Budd (in Cornell, 2004) states that '[t]he starting point for analysis of the employment relationship should be the objectives of this relationship. ... These are efficiency, equity, and voice' (see also Purcell, 2012a).

His central thesis is that in democratic and ethical societies, efficiency, equity and voice are moral imperatives. The ideal employment relationship is one that results in the efficient production of goods or services, provides employees with equitable and fair conditions and circumstances of employment, and ensures that employees have both an individual and a collective voice in deciding on issues of concern to them.

The purpose of this chapter is to reflect on the state of employment relations in South Africa generally, and to flag potential lessons for emerging markets faced with similar global and other pressures in the workplace.

For present purposes, the term 'employment relationship' refers to the relationship between employer and employee at the individual level, whereas 'employment relations' (or 'industrial relations') refers to the relationship between the employer and employees collectively.

The global marketplace

Emerging economies have witnessed significant changes in the last decade or two as a result of two contradictory pressures: first, as global markets opened up, market competition has increased, neoliberal reforms have emerged, and privatisation has increased apace, all of which place strong downward pressures on labour standards. Increasingly, labour has become more informal and less secure, cost-cutting through outsourcing of labour has become more the norm and the enforcement of labour standards has become more difficult as a result.

At the same time, however, these pressures have been somewhat mitigated by the growing adoption of international labour standards, and the role played by international bodies such as the International Labour Organisation (ILO) with its 'decent work' agenda. Multinational corporations are also playing their part in this changing landscape: many have ruthlessly pursued agendas of cost-cutting and union bashing, often without regard for host country norms, while others have actively sought to apply best practices from their country of origin in their host countries. In the midst of all of this stands a trade union movement that often meets considerable resistance from employers and governments, yet has to defend workers' rights and interests against a context of declining employment security and labour conditions, raising questions about unions' adequacy and ability to do so.

As employment relations (ER) practitioners, we know that relationships in the workplace are affected not only by factors operating within the organisation (e.g., management style, physical environment, communication, health and safety, etc.), but also by the external economic, social, political and regulatory environment. In this contribution a key focus will be on the internal environment, but reference will be made to the impact of the external environment as well as the important question of whose responsibility it is to address particularly the socio-economic factors that impact on the internal environment.

The state of ER in South Africa

A selection of recent newspaper headlines bears testimony to the parlous state of ER in this country: 'Violent strikes get bosses to listen'; 'Anglo American counts the cost of violence and strikes'; 'How the good life took Cosatu's eye off the ball'; 'Bosses have "lost touch" with workers'; 'Looking back at how Cosatu trashed its high ideals'. The 2012–2103 *Global competitiveness report* of the World Economic Forum[1] ranks South Africa 144th out of 144 countries surveyed in terms of the level of cooperation in labour relations.[2] The Council for Mediation and Arbitration (CCMA), reputedly one of the busiest (if not the busiest) agencies of its type anywhere, reportedly dealt with over a million referrals in the first ten years of its existence, and currently deals with over 120 000 disputes per year.[3] This excludes thousands of disputes being dealt with by bargaining councils in the private and public sectors. Yet, despite the availability of these institutions (whose brief it is to help resolve disputes peacefully), violence – and sometimes extreme levels of it – continues to mar many workplace disputes. Recent events in the platinum sector bear stark testimony to this.

How is it possible that a country with a rich history of management–union collaboration between the late 1980s and mid-1990s, and with a world-class statutory framework that specifically promotes equity, voice and efficiency,[4] fares this poorly?

A number of factors contribute to the situation, some of which are difficult (if not possible) for management, labour or even government to control, such as a fluid and uncertain political and economic environment and the continuing effects of the country's pre-1994 political history. To what extent must the present labour relations regulatory framework take the blame for the current state of affairs?

The so-called 'rigidity' of the South African labour market

Few would argue against the proposition that unemployment, poverty and inequality in South Africa contribute substantially to the high levels of social and labour unrest experienced over the years and continuing into the present. However, opinions differ about the extent to which the regulatory framework is responsible for this. Those pursuing a free market or neoliberal agenda argue that labour laws distort the market. Our labour market, in particular, is reputed to be too rigid, particularly as far as wage flexibility and the ease of hiring and firing are concerned. Indeed, the 2012–2013 *Global competitiveness report* of the World Bank (2013)[5] rates South Africa a low 140th on the list for wage flexibility[6] and 143rd for the ease of hiring and firing.[7] This perceived rigidity is said to limit economic growth and job creation, thereby perpetuating inequality and high levels of unemployment. These, in turn, fuel social and labour unrest.

Taken to its logical conclusion, this argument suggests that increased flexibility should deliver economic and social stability through economic growth, higher levels of employment and the reduction of social inequalities. In other words, 'set the workers free' and allow market forces to rule.

However, according to the August 2011 International Monetary Fund (IMF) report on Macroeconomic policy and poverty reduction, there is no definite relationship between labour market deregulation and any genuine improvement in economic performance, such as higher growth, investment or employment rates.

The report states, in fact, that the sole focus on improving the business climate is not a sound basis for economic policy, which must balance other goals, including: political stability, social safety nets to protect the poor and vulnerable, and protecting worker rights.

For neoliberals, the main problem lies with the LRA itself, with bargaining councils being blamed as a key reason for wage inflexibility, and the Act's constitutionally sanctioned protection against unfair dismissal taking the blame for the perceived difficulties in firing workers.

Besides the fact that it would be difficult, both morally and constitutionally, to justify the selective application of protectionist measures,[8] I argue in this chapter that the policy underpinning the LRA is essentially sound, supporting as it does Budd's statement of the objectives of the employment relationship.[9]

I would also submit that while labour market policy has to support economic growth strategies, the empirical case for linking labour laws with negative employment and human development outcomes is weak for both developing and developed countries. In fact, the evidence tends to go the other way:

> While some labour law rules may not be well matched to emerging markets, the argument that labour laws in general hinder economic growth is not well grounded: labour laws can play a developmental role by, among other

things, providing insurance against labour market risks, assisting market access, and overcoming information asymmetries and collective action problems (see Deakin, 2013).[10]

There is also evidence that collective bargaining is correlated with reduced dispersion of earnings and that cooperative labour relations are correlated with higher productivity and profitability for firms (Deakin, 2013).

Further, while in the developed country context, laws on worker representation are also correlated with greater equality as measured by labour's share in national income, in the developing country context, worker representation laws are correlated with greater equality as measured by the Gini coefficient, and with personal wellbeing as measured by the Human Development Index (Deakin, 2013).

The policy considerations underlying the regulatory framework

I would submit that the regulatory policy framework is sound, in principle (see Benjamin, 2005; Bhorat et al., 2002). The *Basic Conditions of Employment Act* adopts a policy of so-called 'regulated flexibility': on the one hand, it provides a 'floor of rights' aimed at providing minimum levels of protection to workers i.r.o. working hours, rest and notice periods, leave, etc., by regulating and limiting the employer's ability to impose those terms of employment at will. At the same time, however, it allows for a measure of flexibility in that parties are able to agree on better terms and may also, through collective bargaining, 'contract out' of some of the Act's terms. Provision is also made for exemptions (called 'variations' in s49 of the Act) to be made by the Minister of Labour in certain circumstances. The Act does not prescribe wage levels but leaves the determination thereof to employers and workers to negotiate in person, or through collective bargaining between employer and trade union. In certain economic sectors where workers are particularly vulnerable, sectoral determinations also provide for minimum wage levels.

The philosophy of the LRA is very different. It serves as the conduit through which certain fundamental rights (e.g., to freedom of association, to strike and to fair labour practices) are given effect to, but it also promotes the principle of self-government between employers and workers through the process of collective bargaining. Apart from creating a framework for bargaining and the peaceful resolution of labour disputes, the Act does not interfere in the collective relationship, the manner in which the parties engage or the outcome of their deliberations: here, market forces reign.

The role of government

Government is a key role player in the creation of an environment (political and otherwise) in which the aims of our labour legislation can be achieved (Guthrie, 2002).

These goals, as stated earlier, include the promotion of economic growth, skills development, equity, employment justice and greater collaboration between capital and labour in the work environment.

Yet in 2012, government set an example that flew in the face of these laudable objectives: the Department of Labour embarked on road shows to explain proposed amendments to labour legislation before general consensus could be achieved between it and its social partners at the National Economic Development and Labour Council (NEDLAC) and, critically, before parliament had even had an opportunity to debate the draft amendments! Ironically, the versions of the Bills that the department focused on had been amended twice at least. At the time of writing (May 2014, two years later) the amendments have still not been implemented. And all of this occurred after the fiasco of the department's failed first attempt at ramming through earlier versions of the amendments in 2010–2011.

This type of unilateral action and disregard by government of its social partners and democratic institutions not only sets a bad example, but flies completely in the face of the spirit and provisions of the 1995 LRA. Unless and until we are able to appreciate and establish a real social compact between the social partners around the challenges facing the world of work and the policies we require to achieve development and growth, we are likely to continue to feature on the bottom rungs of reports by the IMF, World Bank and others.

The attitude of the economic actors: Outdated ideologies

Empty slogans and rhetoric might convince and move a gullible union membership, but until unions wake up to the realities of the global market and economic realities of our time, and replace rhetoric and platitudes with intellectual vigour and rational debate, it will be very difficult to find the kind of common ground needed for developing collaborative and consensus-based responses to those challenges.

Clinging to an outdated model of 'capital exploitation of labour' only perpetuates a sense of victimhood, and victims, they say, eventually turn into aggressors. Achieving a change in mindset that can move the role players from a culture of confrontation to increasing levels of cooperation will not be easy, of course.

A key challenge for management, however, is not only to convince union leadership of the value of collaboration despite underlying ideological differences, but also to convince union membership that while all negotiations involve a level of conflict and posturing, gains made through collaboration are far superior to those gained through 'struggle'.

This is why any attempt at increasing levels of collaboration needs to be accompanied by real gains for workers as well.

The attitude of the economic actors: Outdated corporate leadership models

An emphasis on leadership skills that deliver profits seems to continue to guide executive thinking and management behaviour. Instead of inclusive leadership styles that would allow decision-makers the chance to hear others' concerns, viewpoints and suggestions before making a decision that affects them (i.e., giving 'voice' to 'stakeholders'), many of our captains of industry and executive management continue to cling to an outdated idea of 'decisive' (i.e., exclusionary, power-based) leadership.

The focus is on profits and the interests of shareholders (and, very often, the executives themselves), rather than on other stakeholders as well, including workers, the environment and society at large. In their book, *Firms of endearment* (2007), Sisodia et al. provide ample proof of the fact that the former is an outdated (and in any event less effective) approach to leadership.

A more inclusive style of leadership is not only more effective and beneficial to shareholders, but also helps decision-makers make more informed, rational and sustainable decisions. It is also necessary in the modern era which is experiencing a 'historic social transformation' of capital (see Chan Kim & Mauborgne, 2003).

The attitude of the economic actors: How mindset affects the approach to workplace conflicts

The so-called people, problem and process (PPP) or content, process and relationship (CPR) structure widely used in conflict resolution and mediation offers a useful way of explaining where the root causes of the adversarial approach in ER stem from. Our assumption or mindset about who we are dealing with ('people' or 'relationship') affects the way in which we engage with them ('process') and either causes us to define the issues we negotiate about (i.e., the 'problem') in a narrow 'either/or' manner, or to focus on ways of integrating our different interests.

These assumptions determine our strategy or approach, i.e., whether we approach the people and the problem in an adversarial and positional manner, or engage them in a joint problem-solving and collaborative manner. Our strategy, in turn, guides the behaviours and tactics we use to achieve the results we foresaw at the start of our interaction, i.e., a victory over 'them', or a wise agreement between us that involves a sincere attempt at maximising gains for all parties. The former inevitably produces either a winner and a loser, or, more often than not, two losers[11] or a 'race to the bottom', as it has been called. However, an approach that focuses on collaboration rather than competition, supported by positive negotiation behaviours,[12] tends to produce mutual gains that, in turn, build relationships and feed into the manner in which we engage around similar problems in future.

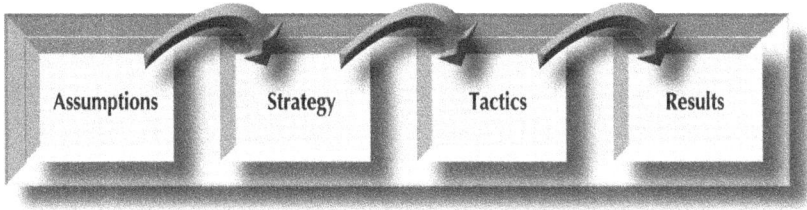

Figure 12.1: The influence of attitudes and assumptions on outcomes

The interesting thing is that parties have a choice in terms of the attitudes they bring to the negotiation table, that is, how they view each other;[13] how they frame the issues;[14] and how they approach them.

The key challenge

As long as management and workers approach their common problems with adversarial goals, mindsets, strategies and tactics, they will regard management's primary concern, 'efficiency', as diametrically opposed to the workers' key concerns of 'voice'[15] and 'equity'.[16] Yet these interests are clearly not mutually exclusive but are, in fact, complementary: efficiency is maximised in environments where employees are treated equitably and are engaged (Purcell, 2012b).[17] Yet the role players (employers and trade unions) tend to pose this as a mutually exclusive choice between, on the one hand, efficiency (driven largely by management diktat) and, on the other hand, engagement and equity (which must be 'fought for' instead of being accepted as a given and fundamental right). Framed in this manner, the discussion is most likely to involve a tug-of-war over whose interests should prevail, rather than a collaborative endeavour to see how they can be integrated and reconciled.

Factors that inhibit collaboration

I would submit that the two key factors that drive adversarialism and make a change in 'mindset' very difficult, are the socio-economic circumstances of a large portion of the workforce, and what has been referred to as a 'trust deficit' in workplaces.[18]

The elephant in the room

In emerging markets, the employment relations climate is often deeply entwined with the socio-political and economic issues facing workers. Achieving efficiency and equity in this environment requires greater engagement not only at the level of the enterprise, but also between the economic actors at macro-level:[19] the engagement agenda cannot but involve engagement on those issues as well. This is not a matter of corporate social responsibility, but a matter of enterprise risk management and survival (Ganson, 2011; Ganson & Wennmann, 2013). Yet one often hears employers say that this is not their problem; that housing, access to basic services and decent schooling, etc. belong in the realm of the political. Compare this attitude to the following statements by Vic van Vuuren, ILO representative in South Africa, as quoted in a recent interview in the *Sunday Times*:

> Management is divorced from the socio-economic challenges facing their employees, such as displacement from their homes, the long distances they have to travel and the slum-like conditions they live in. ... There has been a first world approach: 'Government, you take care of all of this'. But the government is not taking care of all this, for whatever reason. ...[I]t is not the responsibility of the private sector to fund houses and all that ... But in the mining sector, the levels of engagement with local government about the provision of services such as housing, education and transport must be much greater. Companies should even get their hands dirty and help local government officials who don't have the expertise to increase their service delivery. The better the service delivery, the more pressure it will relieve at the workplace.

In other words, there not only is a link between the socio-economic circumstances of workers and the workplace, but management may be able to, for its own sake, alleviate the former to improve the latter.

'Trust arrives on foot, but leaves on horseback'[20] – adversarial relations in spite of a new LRA model

At the heart of the malaise lies the fact that in both the public and private sectors, levels of trust between management and employees generally are low, and sometimes extremely so. The consequences of this 'trust deficit' are rather predictable: high levels of unnecessary or unresolved conflict; low productivity; absenteeism; low morale and sometimes high staff turnover. Where trust is already low, 'traumatic' but foreseeable events such as workplace change and restructuring, redundancies and the like inflict further and sometimes fatal blows to employment relations, largely because of the way these changes are perceived by the 'victims', or are carried out by management, or both.

It is both sad and ironic that after 18 years of the LRA's 'New Deal' for labour relations, adversarialism remains the dominant feature of labour–management relations in both private and public sector organisations. Often times, as an advisor to local corporate and multinational organisations I am surprised at the lack of progress made. In fact, in some instances I was left with a distinct impression of deterioration rather than progress.[21] While the factors mentioned in the preceding paragraph certainly play a role in this, there is no denying that at the workplace level a general lack of trust is a major contributor – probably the major contributor[22] – to the inability of managers and workers to collaborate in achieving common goals.

Perhaps because of the extent of regulation of the employment relationship in this country, high levels of 'formalism' exist in organisations: management by relationship is superseded by management by the rules.[23] The result is that workers and their representatives tend to become very 'rights' oriented, thereby further entrenching the current rights-based versus process-oriented workplace culture, while managers tend to become reactive: action (against, e.g., absenteeism, under-performance, internal conflict) only occurs when rules are broken. The same happens with engagement: it only happens when bad news, (e.g., of a pending redundancy), has to be transmitted. So engagement, which has been shown to lie at the heart of improved performance and workplace harmony,[24] tends to happen only in 'have to' situations, i.e., when the law compels management to. Not surprisingly, an emphasis on trust is replaced by a culture of compliance among employers for the sake of avoiding immediate risks, rather than compliance based on best practice and basic human values.

In terms of John Purcell's adapted model (Figure 12.2), most corporate organisations I have dealt with describe their workplace relationships as 'formalised' and 'compliant', but with low levels of trust (quadrant 3). Most public sector organisations, including parastatals, hover between level 2 (non-compliant, but formalised, low trust) and level 3 (high formalisation but low trust; a functioning organisation but with generally strained relationships). If we add to low trust levels outdated, unclear or unknown and inconsistently applied workplace rules, the organisation becomes a distressed or even dysfunctional one. Such an organisation is usually characterised by persistent conflict and disputes, hostility, non-collaboration, reduced productivity, high staff turnover levels and increased levels of absenteeism.

Levels of litigation tend to increase as well, because the protagonists are either unable or unwilling to utilise consensus-seeking processes to resolve their differences.

The ideal quadrant (level 4), is characterised by, among others, high levels of collaboration, employee involvement, information sharing and the effective management of conflict.

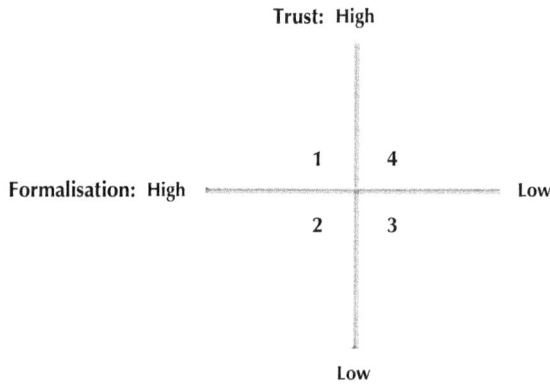

Figure 12.2: Purcell's model of IR patterns
Source: Purcell 1984, p. 61

Ingredients of trust[25]

The literature on the topic of workplace trust suggests that the following are its key ingredients:

- Effective communication (including information sharing);
- Credibility, i.e., intent, believability, etc.;
- Competence, also as far as the so-called 'soft skills' are concerned;
- Consistency, in the sense of 'visibility', 'predictability';
- Concern for employee wellbeing;
- Respect.

Of course, trust is a two-way street. In unionised environments, especially, the abovementioned elements (which really are leadership qualities) need to be present on the side of the union representatives as well, before higher levels of workplace cooperation and trust will develop.

In the face of increasing statutory regulation and hence formalisation of the workplace, the challenge for management and Human Resource (HR)/ER professionals is to actively work on improving, and then maintaining, levels of trust at all levels in their organisations.

A useful exercise for organisations is to require managers to reflect on the following:

- Where, on a scale from 0–10 (0 = low) would you plot your own level of trust in your employer?

- Where do you think your reports would plot their level of trust in the employer?

- Where do you think they would plot their level of trust in you as their manager?

- What explains the levels of trust in a–c (i.e., which of the elements of trust are either absent or present)?

- What can you do to improve the levels of trust between you and your own reports?

Dealing with workplace conflicts

The costs of workplace conflicts are well documented.[26] One by-product of high formalism and low trust in organisations (as per Purcell's model) is that workplace issues, including grievances and disputes, are often not dealt with at all by management,[27] or are dealt with inappropriately with recourse to formal procedures, instead of managers opting for early attempts at resolution through informal dialogue. Workers and their unions respond by challenging management decisions in equally formal ways by handing the resolution thereof to external adjudicative bodies. Thus management loses control over the costs of the dispute, the process for resolving it, and, critically, the outcome.

A big contributor here is the general fear of conflict that pervades many organisations and a lack of skill to prevent, defuse and resolve conflicts.[28] It is no wonder, then, that when we see conflict we either fail to deal with the issue or we resort to attack, using whatever forms of coercive power or legal remedies are available to us. Yet, as one of the early pioneers of conflict resolution, Mary Parker Follett (in Graham, 2003, p. 86, fn 1), once said: 'It is possible to conceive conflict as not necessarily a wasteful outbreak of incompatibilities, but a normal process by which socially valuable differences register themselves for the enrichment of all concerned.'

One challenge, therefore, is to begin to see conflict not only as inevitable, but also as a potential opportunity to resolve differences, find common ground and strengthen relationships. Within organisations this translates into becoming 'conflict wise', i.e., harnessing the power of conflict to promote understanding, cooperation and growth. In Jim Collins' best-selling book, *Good to great*, he recalls how the 11 'great' organisations (they had each delivered cumulative returns at least three times greater than the market over a 15-year period!) all displayed a similar approach to dealing with conflict:

> All the good-to-great companies had a penchant for intense dialogue. Phrases like 'loud debate', 'heated discussions' and 'healthy conflict' peppered the articles and interview transcripts from all the companies (Collins, 2001, p. 77).

A 2003 UK survey of top management teams found that the more productive ones treated conflicts as opportunities for collaboration, in order to achieve the best solution for the organisation as a whole. Conversely, when a separate research team studied a group of business failures arising from highly unsuccessful strategic decisions, they found a remarkably consistent pattern of stifled debate, with negative opinions or adverse information discounted as unhelpful (Finkelstein, 2003).

A way forward

If we are to give effect to the ambitions of the *Labour Relations Act* – of advancing economic growth, social justice, workplace participation and labour peace – organisations would need to invest both time and money in the following:

- Improving the ability of managers, employee representatives and employees, generally, to deal with differences more effectively. Making conflict resolution training a compulsory part of a workplace skills plan is a useful start. Testing for such skills when making key appointments is also a good idea. These skills, of course, are 'portable' and also useful outside of the work environment;

- We need to see the LRA's notion of *audi alteram partem* – hear the other side – as not being applicable only when managers have to deliver bad news to employees (e.g., of a pending redundancy or other dismissal), but to all levels of decision-making that might impact not only on employees' terms and conditions of employment, but also the quality of their working lives. The European Institute for Business Administration (now known as INSEAD) study (see Chan Kim & Mauborgne, 2003) provides ample proof of the benefit of this for improved loyalty, motivation and productivity in the workplace: 'When employees don't trust managers to make good decisions or to behave with integrity, their motivation is seriously compromised. Their distrust and its attendant lack of engagement is a huge, unrecognized problem in most organizations.' Their central finding is that employees will commit to a manager's decision – even one they disagree with – if they believe that the process the manager used to make the decision was inclusive and fair;

- Participation alone is not enough, however. As the INSEAD research shows, it needs to be accompanied by tangible benefits so that employees can experience the benefits of collaboration;

- We need to develop effective systems for problem solving and conflict resolution, based on the principle that a focus on persuasively reconciling the interests of those in dispute should come before recourse to the coercive use of legal rights and power to resolve differences. Workplace conflict is probably the most avoidable cost that organisations face. In addition, it is one of the most damaging in terms of relationships, under-performance and waste of valuable management time. We typically respond as follows in the face of conflict ('conflict' here broadly referring to differences in views, interests, beliefs, approaches, values, etc.): first we avoid dealing with the problem, then we use coercive power or our rights to deal with it, leaving the option of a collaborative search for solutions that could satisfy our respective interests as a last resort after all else has failed (Ury, Brett & Goldberg, 1988, pp. 3–19).

Power and rights-based responses carry far greater direct relationship and sometimes reputational costs than processes focused on achieving agreed solutions to differences. Yet we seem to be psychologically hard-wired to focus most of our energies on avoiding the problem until external circumstances, or the size of the problem, force us into power-based solutions (discipline, dismissal, strikes, etc.) or rights-based options (arbitration or adjudication). Joint problem-solving or collaborative approaches to dealing with the problem – potentially the best solution in terms of cost, time and control over process and outcome – seem to be the last resort.

A healthier, more cost-effective approach that is more in keeping with the LRA's original intent and is far more conducive to developing trust and sustainable solutions, would be not to avoid issues that are important to us or to others who need our cooperation and support, but to engage them collaboratively in order to find a solution that 'integrates' our different interests, leaving recourse to rights-based and power-based solutions as fall-back options if collaboration cannot produce an agreed way forward;

- To become more 'dispute wise' (see American Arbitration Association, 2006), a cultural shift is required within organisations. This shift would make it more natural for employees to engage in dialogue and problem solving than to fight potentially adverse managerial decisions. They would then see conflict as an opportunity for understanding, learning and collaboration. It is also necessary to develop a level of conflict 'literacy' in the organisation (i.e., understanding of what causes it, how it escalates and how it can be managed for best results). This will help build conflict management skills. Internal procedures need to be adapted to conform to a more effective system for dispute resolution and create opportunities for early resolution. Lastly, a conflict management culture needs to be 'embedded' in the organisation. It is not enough to simply develop protocols or systems and provide training. Conflict leadership (see Leathes, 2009) is required to ensure that open communication and effective conflict management become part and parcel of the culture of the organisation at all levels;

- Introduce values-based decision-making, not merely compliance and risk limitation. Management's actions and employment-related decisions impact on an organisation's values: Are their actions and decisions aligned with the organisation's values, or is there divergence between what the organisation professes to believe in and what its managers actually do? Are the organisation's employment relations practices aligned with its business practices? Take this all-too-common scenario: suppose that a senior employee is suspected of dishonesty. Given the potential consequences for the organisation's public or market reputation, and perhaps out of concern for the future of their colleague, senior management decide to give the wrongdoer an ultimatum: resign or face disciplinary action. Fortunately for both, he decides to resign rather than face the consequences. (Fortunately for him, because his reputation remains intact; fortunately for the company, because it is able to avoid the reputational fall-out of the senior's conduct.) A month or so later a more junior employee commits a similar transgression. This time, however, management decide to show their disapproval and 'zero tolerance' of this type of behaviour, and forthwith suspend the employee pending a hearing that eventually results in a dismissal. Upon receipt of a letter from the employee's lawyer or union complaining about inconsistent treatment of the employee (for by now news of the senior's lucky escape has become known), HR's advice is urgently sought. Typically, in this situation, management would ask two questions: Have we created some kind of precedent? If so, what is the worst-case scenario, legally speaking? Management are informed there is a risk of a finding at the CCMA or bargaining council, to the effect that they acted inconsistently, but that the risk can possibly be limited with an early settlement offer at conciliation. Management heave a sigh of relief at hearing that the risk can be mitigated. Here is another example: a manager insists that a particular employee, who is perceived to be an under-performer (but whose performance ratings are average, at worst) should form part of a group of staff targeted for retrenchment. Despite HR's protestations that the individual falls outside the ambit of the company's selection criteria, the manager is adamant that the employee must somehow be brought into the net. While this might make the manager's life easier, it poses legal risks for the company. Fortunately, with good advice, the risk could possibly be limited.

In both examples there is one question that management failed to ask, namely: How do we justify our actions in terms of the company's values? Is what we did (by letting the senior get off virtually scot-free) reconcilable with our values of 'transparency', 'integrity' and such like? The longer-term damage done by not adhering to the company's values far exceeds the price of a risk-limiting settlement at the CCMA.

- We must develop a collaborative mindset and new skills. Writing and research on the benefits of collaboration within organisations have exploded over the last few years, as a simple world-wide web search will reveal.[29] Collaboration is a much-misunderstood concept, however, as shown in Table 12.1.

Table 12.1: The meaning of collaboration

What collaboration is not	What it is
It is not all about cooperation	It is an inclusive process of productive enquiry
It does not require joint ownership	It entails managed participation
It is not the best way to avoid conflict	It actively surfaces conflict and induces a problem-solving capability to navigate it
It is not a bureaucratic process	It involves adapting techniques to fit the current issues
It is not only relevant when objectives are shared	It supports all decision-makers in all circumstances, especially where objectives are not shared
It does not rely on trust	It stems from clear and accepted accountabilities

- The increasing diversity of the workplace dictates the need for even more multidisciplinary approaches to resolving the issues facing the employment relationship. This would require those in ER, HR, leadership, conflict resolution and employment law to 'de-clutter' the field of jargon and to get back to basics, as well as for an integration ('de-siloing') of these disciplines. We need to help managers 'connect the dots' between what they learn, e.g., on leadership, labour law and business ethics courses, so that they see the whole and not merely its constituent parts.

A role for civil society

The growing inadequacy of traditional institutional actors (e.g., the state and unions), in defending workers' rights and resolving new issues emerging in workplaces, has created both the space and the need for 'new' actors to fill the gap. Examples of such actors include non-governmental organisations (NGOs), employment agencies, HR consultancy firms, coaches, employment mediators and arbitrators, grassroots activists and social movements, and so forth. Some of the actors are not necessarily new, but are playing a stronger/new role in (re)shaping ER at the workplace level. In some contexts, these actors interact and permeate one another's sites and spatial boundaries in acknowledgement of, and to complement, one another's resource/capacity constraints. While operating largely outside the workplaces or beyond cross-organisational boundaries, these actors and their interactions play an important role in shaping ER at the workplace level. The emerging role of these new actors, in their individual and/or institutional capacity, has been documented in a number of studies.[30]

However, these studies have focused primarily on developed countries. By contrast, studies on employment relations in emerging economies continue to focus largely on conventional actors and often at the macro level. Little attention has been paid to new issues which emerged and the impact of new actors, for example, the role of HIV/AIDS peer educators in South Africa.

Conclusion

The employment relationship cannot be separated from the socio-economic environment in which organisations and people operate. As is frequently evident in South Africa, what happens within organisations is often influenced by what happens outside the workplace. This is even more so if the problems workers face on the outside spring from a lack of satisfaction of their basic human needs. This problem, although it also occurs in developed economies, is most prevalent in developing countries. While management cannot be expected to provide for all the needs that government, for instance, neglects or fails to provide, they need to be at least conscious of the connection between employee commitment and productivity on the one hand, and their socio-economic circumstances on the other, so as to be alert to any opportunities for improving the circumstances of the workforce,[31] in return for increased 'social capital'.[32] Engagement with other social actors such as NGOs could be crucial.

In such environments in particular, investing in improving levels of trust within the workplace is critical to improving organisational performance (efficiency) and economic growth. To do so, managers need to realise that giving workers a real 'voice', along with ensuring that they receive equitable treatment and are subjected to reasonable conditions of work, is essential to building trust. Without trust, managers and workers will continue to approach their differences in adversarial, unproductive and damaging ways. However, with greater trust it is possible to adopt new mental frameworks that see the 'other' side as partners in problem-solving, the issues for negotiation as being joint problems, and a collaborative approach as a superior first option.

At a practical level, this change in attitude and approach must be supported by conflict leadership in organisations. This means that conflict must be seen as a strategic issue which, if managed properly, can have a multitude of benefits for the organisation. This, however, hinges on developing conflict resolution skills and using best practice approaches to prevent conflict escalation and ensure that conflicts – if they do arise – are productively managed. It also means that party representatives who engage in collective bargaining should reinvent their approach if they want to build greater trust, inculcate respect for one another, and establish improved communication.[33]

Endnotes

1   Retrieved May 15, 2014, from http://www3.weforum.org/docs/CSI/2012-13/GCR_Pillar7_2012-13.pdf.

2   The country is also rated a low 134th as far as pay and productivity are concerned, but a high of 33rd as far as the cost of redundancy is concerned. This appears to be at odds with the low ranking of 143 for hiring and firing practices.

3   See http://www.ccma.org.za/Display.asp?L1=36&L2=21.

4   The key objectives of the *Labour Relations Act* (LRA) (see s 1) are to advance 'economic development' (i.e., efficiency), 'social justice' (i.e., equity), labour peace and 'the democratisation of the workplace' (i.e., voice).

5   'The World Bank's views on the objectives of economic growth and development, and the best way to attain these objectives, are continuously evolving. For example, in its World Development Report 2013, the Bank puts forward a nuanced view on labour regulations, suggesting that governments should strive for a balanced combination of labour regulation and management practice that is unique to their country's stage of development. This message differs markedly from the perspective associated with the report in its earlier years' (Manuel Commission, EU, June 2013). The commission also remarked: 'It is important to remember that the report is intended to be a pure knowledge project. As such, its role is to inform policy, not to prescribe it or outline a normative position, which the rankings to some extent do.'

6   Despite the fact that in the majority of cases wages are set by agreement, whether individual or collective.

7   Yet, ironically, as high as 33rd for the (low) cost of redundancies. This stands in stark contrast to the perception that dismissal is unduly difficult. The fact that the CCMA deals with more than 120 000 cases per year, the vast majority of which concern dismissals, also casts doubt over the veracity of the claim that dismissals are difficult to execute. See also Paul Benjamin, A review of labour markets in South Africa. Labour market regulation: International and South African perspectives, October 2005. Retrieved May 16, 2014 from www.hsrc.ac.za/en/research-outputs/ktree-doc/1312

8   For instance, protecting consumers, but not equally (or perhaps more) vulnerable categories like employees. The same debate is raging in the United Kingdom. See 'Reframing resolution - managing conflict and resolving individual employment disputes in the contemporary workplace', Advisory, Conciliation and Arbitration Service (Acas) Policy Discussion Papers, March 2014, at 6–8. Retrieved 26 May, 2014 from http://www.acas.org.uk/media/pdf/6/9/reframing_policy_paper_FINAL.pdf

9   While also giving effect to our international obligations as a member of the ILO as well as the constitutional imperative of the right to freedom of association and fair labour practices.

10   See also Deakin, et al.

11   Even if we 'win' the negotiation, the way in which we did so and the lack of gains for the other side usually cause harm to the very relationships we need to nurture and grow. And, as stated earlier, in this scenario the victim inevitably becomes the future aggressor.

12   See 'The behaviour of successful negotiators'. Retrieved 25 May, 2014) https://system.netsuite.com/core/media/media.nl?id=9041&c=1035604&h=47e32ba37e2a3295bec0&_xt=.pdf

13   As opponents with their own, often hidden agendas, or as parties who, like us, try to maximise value for themselves.

14   A choice between farming the problem as a narrow 'either/or' dilemma that can be re-
      solved only through power play and recourse to our rights, i.e., coercively; or as a joint
      problem, i.e., How can we work together to satisfy our respective interests in a mutually
      beneficial way?

15   Purcell (2012a) differentiates between organisational engagement and engagement with
      the job, both of which he regards as critical for productivity.

16   Or 'employment justice' as Purcell (2012a) calls it. He distinguishes between informa-
      tional, procedural and substantive justice. The latter refers to the manner in which em-
      ployees are treated.

17   See Purcell (2012b). This search for 'voice', he says, 'is not just to meet the needs of
      employees, important though that is. We know that the experience of involvement is
      closely associated with positive employee evaluations of management responsiveness.
      This feeds through into productivity. The more extensive the range of voice systems used
      in organisations the more likely it was that managers reported benefits from increased
      output to declining absenteeism. Voice systems which combine 'embedded' direct forms
      of involvement with indirect voice via representative bodies are strongly associated with
      higher levels of organisational commitment.' He also refers to a European Company
      Survey which found that firms where managers and employee representatives made
      'sincere efforts to solve common problems' had higher than average productivity and
      experienced increases in productivity. These firms also had, unsurprisingly, a good work
      climate.

18   Trust 'is the belief that someone or something is reliable, good, honest, effective' (*Merri-
      am-Webster dictionary*); or the 'firm belief in the reliability, truth, or ability of someone
      or something' (*Oxford dictionary*). See the paragraph below, titled 'Trust arrives on foot
      but leaves on horseback'.

19   Such as we had in the mid-1990s with the establishment of NEDLAC. In fact, the 1995
      LRA was one of its crowning achievements, with the economic actors, business, labour
      and government achieving consensus on the philosophy and provisions of the Act.

20   The origin of the quotation is uncertain.

21   In one memorable case the author was involved in a mining company that had been
      rated as a 'high trust' organisation by union officials and shop stewards during a skills
      training course, but was rated 2/10 by the same union two years later. The key change
      factor? Fresh, 'decisive' company leadership.

22   'No other factor had the same power. Trust, like engagement, is a risk since it requires
      hope for the future and expectations of others, especially leaders, that they have the
      ability to do the right or best thing, are guided by some principles of benevolence or well-
      meaning, especially in treating people with respect, that they have integrity and honesty
      and are predicable (Purcell, (2012a).

23   See Acas, March 2014 at 4: informal processes are dependent on the existence of
      high trust relationships between employee representatives and managers - where such
      relationships are absent, workplace dispute resolution can become adversarial and
      tends to revert to the formal application of procedures, as organisations seek to protect
      themselves against litigation.

24   'When employees don't trust managers to make good decisions or to behave with
      integrity, their motivation is seriously compromised. Their distrust and its attendant lack
      of engagement is a huge, unrecognised problem in most organisations' (Chan Kim &
      Mauborgne, 2003, p. 123). The authors also found that '[e]mployees will commit to a
      manager's decision – even one they disagree with – if they believe that the process the
      manager used to make the decision was fair.'

25 For an in-depth analysis of the phenomenon of trust, see Covey (2006). See also Purcell (2012a and b).

26 See Bertel (2013), see also http://www.conflictatwork.com/conflict/cost_e.cfm and http://www.entrepreneur.com/article/207196

27 See Acas Policy Discussion Papers March 2014 at 12: the avoidance of conflict can have a negative effect on the generation of 'social capital' which is fundamental to collaboration, cooperation between staff and effective organisational performance.

28 See Acas Policy Discussion Papers March 2014 at 5: 'It is clear that many more problems could be prevented from escalating into disputes if line managers were better able to manage conflict. .... One consequence of this is that a general preference among managers for pragmatic approaches to conflict resolution has increasingly been replaced with a rigid adherence to process and procedure. While a lack of skill may be part of this problem, there is often a lack of support from senior management, who may not see conflict management as a priority.

29 See, e.g., http://communitydoor.org.au/collaboration/what-is-collaboration-and-collaborative-practice on the benefits of, and need for, collaboration.

30 See, e.g., http://www.abbott.com/static/cms_workspace/content/document/Citizenship/Reports/2006_gcr.pdf

31 One should not underestimate the value of symbolic gestures, e.g., an executive pay cut or the foregoing of executive bonuses. See the interview with Ketso Gordhan, CEO of Pretoria Portland Cement Co Ltd, *Sunday Times*, March 23, 2014, where he discusses how his organisation benefited from taking salary cuts and foregoing bonuses in order to alleviate some of the problems faced by the workforce.

32 The benefits that flow from trust, reciprocity, information and cooperation.

33 Such an approach would have the following elements: joint training in new bargaining models and skills; commitment to a bargaining protocol and timetable; flexible mandates; no log of claims, rather solutions must be developed during the bargaining process, not stated as positions in advance; there should be a focus on separate and joint needs; brainstorming and option-generation should be part of the process, along with joint problem-solving; the right to industrial action in the final instance is recognised; and while hard bargaining is not excluded, the parties must adopt constructive behaviours and tactics to move the process forward or break a deadlock.

References

Advisory, Conciliation and Arbitration Service (Acas). (2014, March). *Reframing resolution – Managing conflict and resolving individual employment disputes in the contemporary workplace*. Acas Policy Discussion Papers. Retrieved May 26, 2014 from http://www.acas.org.uk/media/pdf/6/9/reframing_policy_paper_FINAL.pdf

American Arbitration Association. (2006). *Dispute-wise business management: Improving economic and non-economic outcomes in managing business conflicts*. Retrieved May 23, 2014 from https://www.adr.org/aaa/ShowPDF?doc=ADRSTG_004327

Benjamin, P. (2005). *A review of labour markets in South Africa. Labour market regulation: International and South African perspectives*. Retrieved May 16, 2014 from www.hsrc.ac.za/en/research-outputs/ktree-doc/1312

Bertel, D.G. (2013). *Costing conflict: A multiple case study approach to quantifying conflict in the mining industry of South Africa*. Unpublished Master's thesis, Stellenbosch University, Stellenbosch, South Africa.

Bhorat, H. Lundall, P. & Rospabe, S (2002). *The South African labour market in a globalizing world: Economic and legislative considerations.* Retrieved May 26, 2014 from http://www. ilo.int/wcmsp5/groups/public/---ed_emp/documents/publication/wcms_142363.pdf

Chan Kim, W. & Mauborgne, R. (2003). Fair process – Managing in the knowledge economy. *Harvard Business Review,* January, 123–132. Also available at http://www.unmc.edu/ media/gpphli/interregional/fair_process__managing_the_knowledge_economy.pdf

Collins, J. (2001). *Good to great: Why some companies make the leap and others don't.* New York: Harper Collins Publishers, Inc.

Covey, S.M.R. & Merrill, R. (2006). *The speed of trust: The one thing that changes everything.* New York: Free Press. Retrieved May 15, 2014 from http://power-train.net/uploads/ speed_of_trust_summary.pdf

Deakin, S. (2013). *Labour law and inclusive development: The effects of industrial relations laws in low- and middle-income countries.* Paper presented at 26th Annual Labour Law Conference, Johannesburg, July–August.

Deakin, S., Malmberg, J. & Sarkar, P. (2013). *Do labour laws increase equality at the expense of higher unemployment? The experience of six OECD countries, 1970–2010.* Centre for Business Research, University of Cambridge Working Paper No. 442. Retrieved May 20, 2014 from http://www.cbr.cam.ac.uk/pdf/WPfourfourtwo.pdf

Finkelstein, F. (2003). *Why smart executives fail.* London: Portfolio (Penguin Putnam).

Ganson, B. (2011). *Business and conflict prevention: Towards a framework for action.* Paper delivered at Geneva Peace-building Platform No. 2, 2011. Retrieved from http://www. gpplatform.ch/sites/default/files/PP%2002%20-%20Business%20and%20Conflict%20 Prevention%20-%20Ganson%20-%2028%20November%202011_0.pdf

Ganson, B. & Wennmann, A. (2012). Confronting risk, mobilizing action: A framework for conflict prevention in the context of large-scale business investments. *FES International Policy Analysis Series.* Berlin: Friedrich Ebert Stiftung. Retrieved May 20, 2014 from http://library.fes.de/pdf-files/iez/global/09577.pdf

Graham, P. (Ed.). (2003). *Mary Parker Follett: Prophet of management.* Washington, DC: Beard Books.

Guthrie, D. (2002). The transformation of labor relations in China's emerging market economy. *Research in Social Stratification and Mobility, 19,* 139–170.

Leathes, M. (2009). *Conflict leadership.* Retrieved May 23, 2014 from https://imimediation. org/conflict-leadership

Purcell, J. (1984). *Good IR: Theory and practice.* London: McMillan Press Ltd.

Purcell, J. (2012, March). *Acas future of workplace relations.* Discussion paper series. Retrieved May 26, 2014 from http://www.acas.org.uk/media/pdf/g/7/Voice_and_Participation_in_ the_Modern_Workplace_challenges_and_prospects.pdf

Purcell, J. (2012, April). The limits and possibilities of employee engagement. *Warwick Papers on Industrial Relations* no. 96. Coventry: Warwick Business School.

Sisodia, R.S., Wolfe, D.B. & Sheth, J. (2007). *Firms of endearment: How world class companies benefit from passion and purpose.* New Jersey: Wharton School Publishing.

Ury, W. Brett, J.M. & Goldberg, S.B. (1988). *Getting disputes resolved.* New York: Jossey-Bass Inc.

Van Vuuren, V. (2014, May 11). Interview, *Sunday Times.*

CHAPTER 13: The Management of Health and Wellness in Emerging Markets

Tony Davidson

Introduction

Companies in emerging economies often find themselves having more onerous responsibilities towards their employees than those in established economies, as emerging economies face a greater burden of disease than poor or wealthy ones (World Health Organisation, 2012). During the transitional process, many emerging countries have to deal with problems facing poor economies, including infectious diseases such as HIV/AIDS, tuberculosis (TB), cholera etc., while established workers and the middle class tend to be afflicted with lifestyle or non-communicable diseases (NCDs) such as high blood pressure, cancer, diabetes and heart disease. This is referred to as the 'double burden' of health issues in emerging economies.

As far as NCDs are concerned, significant risk factors specifically linked to urbanisation and modernisation include physical inactivity, unhealthy diets (including refined products, excessive salt, fat and sugar intake), obesity, tobacco use, excessive alcohol consumption, and exposure to environmental pollution. Becoming upwardly mobile grants people access to disposable income, which sees them buying more private motor vehicles, as well as larger quantities of drugs and alcohol. The result is often an increased number of motor vehicle accidents, homicides and antisocial behaviour, which can also have a significant impact on the workplace.

The complexity and cost of managing illnesses and injuries in emerging markets greatly outweigh the increased budgets which the state can provide to protect, diagnose, cure and heal its citizens. Private companies also need to recognise that their decisions can impact on the health of their employees and the communities in which they operate. It is equally important to bear in mind that sophisticated consumers believe companies have an obligation to manage the impact of their operations and to take reasonable responsibility for the people in the surrounding communities.

In most emerging economies, private healthcare is generally unaffordable for the average employee, and the state's provision and delivery of healthcare, as well as a social net, tend to be patchy, slow, and of poor quality. Companies which wish to have a productive and stable workforce need to decide whether it is worth their while to provide some access to healthcare and offer assistance in terms of social issues, in the absence of reliable and good-quality services.

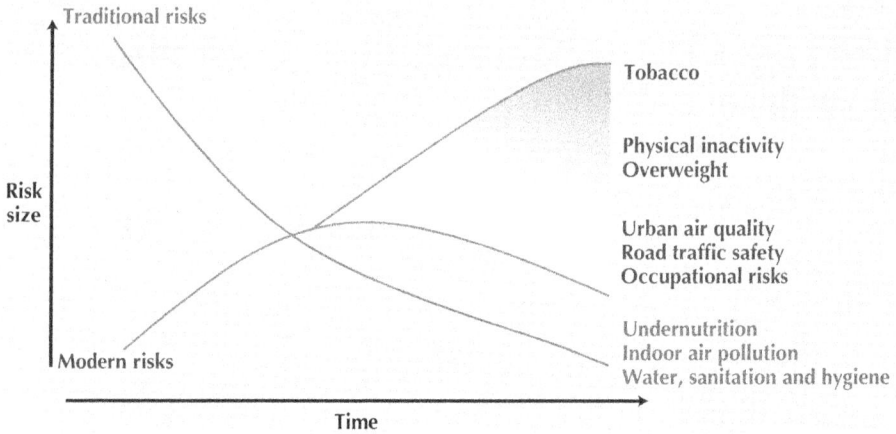

Figure 13.1: The risk transition

(Over time, major risks to health shift from traditional risks (e.g. inadequate nutrition or unsafe water and sanitation) to modern risks (e.g. overweight and obesity). Modern risks may take different trajectories in different countries, depending on the risk and the context.)

Source: WHO 2009 (http://www.who.int/healthinfo/global_burden_disease/global_health_risks/en/)

Through corporate social investment and occupational health programmes, the health of employees and community members can be managed cost-effectively. As healthcare and social services fall outside the usual skillset of managers, introducing and managing programmes can be bewildering, complex and time consuming, and it is easy to feel that they do not provide any value. However, numerous recent studies have suggested that companies working to address workplace health experience a variety of direct and indirect financial benefits through taking measures to prevent and treat disease.[1] These benefits include the following:

- Lower rates of employee turnover and absenteeism;
- Lower rates of presenteeism (underperforming due to feeling unwell at work);
- Reduced employer liability;
- Improved profitability due to increased productivity and decreased healthcare costs;
- A workforce diversity reflecting a range of age groups, sexes, talents and skills;
- Improved employee morale;
- Access to international markets where brand equity is important;
- Access to international financial markets where human and employee rights are important; and
- Company reputation and a secured social licence to operate.

While dealing with diseases in the workplace provides key business benefits, there are also strong arguments for widening the net of healthcare to include those communities and families whose members are employed by the company. Benefits include reducing the source of numerous infections and social ills which impact the workplace, enhancing the company's reputation as a responsible organisation in the eyes of community members, and reducing the likelihood of social unrest.

How does a manager who wants to be a responsible social citizen with a productive workforce deliver appropriate, cost-effective health services?

The South African Board for People Practices (SABPP) is developing national HR standards, in a similar fashion to ISO 14001, for environmental standards (http://www.sabpp.co.za/). The approach looks at the broad HR offerings including talent management, HR risk management, workforce planning, learning and development, performance management and rewards, employment relations, organisational development, HR service delivery, HR technology and measurement in HR. Of note, there is a chapter which focuses on wellness in the workplace. The wellness chapter stresses the integration of wellness interventions into HR services to ensure the management of risk and the optimisation of performance.

In common with many of the fields mentioned above, the field of organisational health and wellness is quite specialised and focused, as the issues it deals with are complex. Amongst the disciplines involved are medicine, psychology, industrial hygiene, human resources and labour law, to name a few. The main focus will therefore be on two areas where much time is spent, namely absenteeism and wellness. Other areas will be mentioned, but only in brief.

The organisational health and wellness model

An organisational health approach is reliant on a set of tools which allows companies to take a holistic, integrative approach to health management. Integrating the different disciplines of the organisational health model makes dealing with complex issues such as HIV/AIDS, stress, wellness programmes and substance abuse approaches more practical. Many companies have health and wellness programmes, but unless 'health' and 'wellness' are clearly defined by the programme organisers, the outcomes tend to be non-specific and difficult to measure.

Broad interventions beyond traditional health interventions (e.g., safe transport and debt counselling) are often placed under the banner of employee wellness. These interventions are important, but how they are structured within the organisation needs to be clearly defined. Managers need to consider where such programmes should be housed. The programmes may indirectly improve health and wellness, but are their effects best measured in terms of health outcomes, or would improved productivity be a more appropriate effect? The World Economic Forum (WEF) (2007) addressed this issue and provided more focused definitions. In summary, health is about outcomes, whereas wellness is about process.

- *Health* is defined as 'a state of complete physical, mental and social well-being where people have met their potential and are at their most productive'. Health is not the absence of disease or infirmity;

- *Wellness* is defined as 'an intentional choice of a lifestyle characterised by personal responsibility, moderation and optimal personal enhancement of physical, mental, emotional and spiritual health'.

Note that the actual components of lifestyle choice are not included in the definition.

The WEF monograph suggests that incorporating more scientifically proven components provides some measure of effectiveness. The further one moves away from traditional health measures, the more difficult it is to identify cause-and-effect relationships.

The organisational health approach is specific and introduces programmes with measureable outcomes. The tighter the definitions, the more robust the outcomes report!

Organisational health practitioners use components from many disciplines in the business and health sciences, to provide an integrated solution for dealing with health-related problems in the workplace.

The disease–wellness continuum (see Figure 13.1) shows that those who strive to be on the right of the neutral point are high-performing or 'engaged' individuals. In some cases, people with infirmities may be on the left of the neutral point, but they, too, can work to arrive as close to their potential as possible.

Managers are generally happy in instances where employees are free from overt illnesses and are performing satisfactorily at the neutral point. This fits the old definition which views health as the absence of disease. Huge opportunities are missed when employees are not performing optimally, i.e., where they can be more resilient, energetic and productive.

The irony is that most of our time and money is spent attempting to return unwell or ill employees to the neutral point.

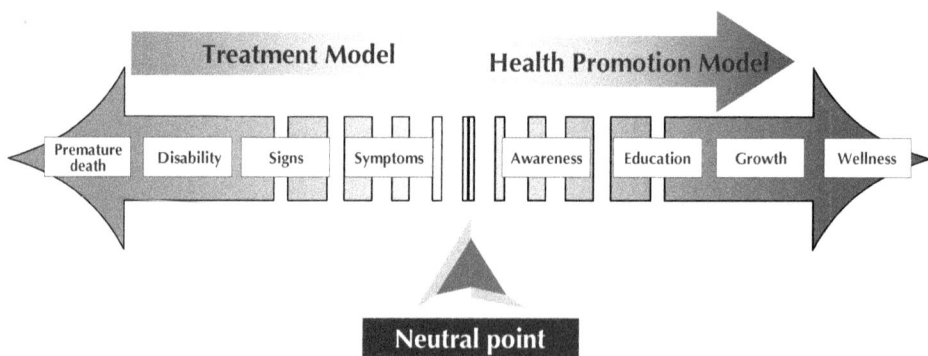

Figure 13.2: The disease–wellness continuum

The organisational health model consists of five components:

- *Primary healthcare* – this provides for screening, prevention and the promotion of health by using wellness techniques: healthy and well individuals are more energetic, creative and productive!

- *Occupational health* assesses the risk to all employees' health and provides the tools to prevent or minimise the impact of those risks (caused by accidents or exposure to particular hazards);

- *Employee assistance programmes* (EAPs) provide psychosocial support to employees, while educating and enabling line managers to handle individuals with underlying problems that are impacting their productivity;

- *Health benefits management* – this component provides support to HR in reducing absenteeism, ensuring the proper use of workmen's compensation, through the *Compensation for Occupational Injuries and Diseases Act* (COIDA), and through the fair and effective management of employees whose work performance is impaired due to ill health/injury;

- *Curative care/medical aid* – this component is more relevant for companies with in-house schemes. However, this is a complex field and having a consultant who is not dependent on commissions on your side, will help you understand the key issues and the clinical rules of medical aid benefits.

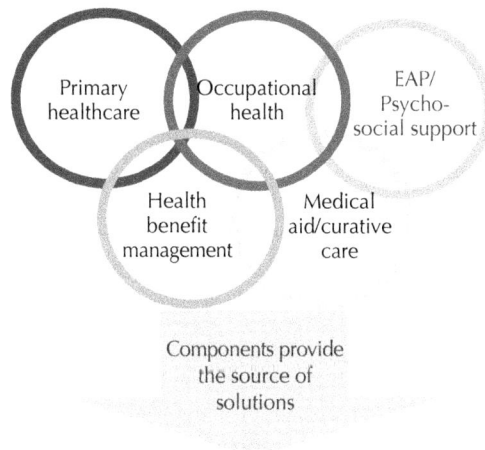

Introduction of integrated solutions for issues such as

- HIV/AIDS;
- Wellness screening and chronic disease management;
- Substance abuse;
- Absenteeism and incapacity.

Figure 13.3: An organisation health model

In many companies, these services are absent or are offered in a haphazard fashion. By introducing and integrating these components, companies can make quicker and more holistic decisions about health-related matters. Health is no longer a soft issue; medical insurance costs alone can consume in excess of ten per cent of an organisation's wage bill.

Implementation of health programmes

There is no single management plan or process that can be systematically applied across the diverse range of socio-economic environments in which companies operate. A well-considered process is presented in Table 13.1. The various steps outlined here can help to determine the type and level of intervention required, which can then be applied in a particular setting. These key steps, which form part of a health impact assessment, should be worked through or engaged with before investing time and resources in introducing health services into the organisation. They can also be incorporated into other impact assessments being performed to assess the viability of a business.

The components of the organisational health model can be merged with this implementation checklist – an example will be given in the section dealing with the development of an absenteeism programme.

Table 13.1: Key steps and associated objectives in developing an organisational health model

No.	Step	Objective
1	Screening	To decide whether or not specific issues or diseases need to be addressed/managed.
2	Scoping	To obtain a better understanding of the nature and extent of the disease(s) and associated risks, and in doing so, defining the way forward for the development of a management plan.
3	Situation analysis	To develop a health baseline.
4	Stakeholder analysis	To gain an understanding of stakeholders and to identify potential partners.
5	Policy, priority, goal and objective setting	To define policy, set priorities based on steps 3 and 4, and identify available resources, before defining achievable and practical goals and management plan objectives.
6	Option appraisal	To select the most appropriate disease management intervention.

→

No.	Step	Objective
7	Programme design, budgeting and resourcing	To define the programme budget and resources, and set the key performance indicators and targets with associated timelines.
8	Programme implementation	To implement the programme and manage it against key performance indicators and targets.
9	Monitoring and evaluation	To assess programme success against the baseline, objectives, targets and key performance indicators (KPIs), and to make the necessary changes, where appropriate.

Source: Starke (2008)

A critical factor in the success of any health-related management programme is the recognition that it is a key business issue that cuts across multiple staff and line functions. It is vital that senior management take a prominent leadership role in articulating corporate objectives and translating these into performance expectations. Senior management should provide the resources (financial and technical) needed to implement the programmes and should hold all levels of management accountable for performance.

Wellness

The scope of wellness

As mentioned in the introduction to this section, the WEF proposes using a scientific focus with clear measures of effectiveness. The scope can range from a purely medical model aimed at minimising chronic lifestyle diseases or NCDs such as hypertension, obesity, high cholesterol, diabetes and ischaemic disease, to a broad model which includes nine dimensions of wellness, as proposed by Ohio State University. A more pragmatic seven-dimension model, developed by Rhodes University[2] includes the traditional physical health model, along with the following wellness dimensions:

- Emotional
- Intellectual
- Financial
- Occupational
- Spiritual
- Social.

An individual's wellbeing in all these dimensions is important for a fulfilling life. Most dimensions have some effect on other dimensions and therefore need consideration, but defining outcomes in the workplace for all these dimensions, where the needs of both the employee(s) and the organisation are met, will certainly be challenging, regardless of the gross domestic product (GDP) of the country in which the organisation operates.

In emerging economies with poor state resources as well as inadequate housing, water and sanitation infrastructure and transport, organisations face a particularly taxing undertaking. There is the challenge of meeting the needs of the organisation, which would want fit and healthy employees who are more productive, versus the needs of the average employee, who would much rather resolve current issues (e.g., safe and reliable transport to and from work) than have access to medical screening or worry about a potential heart attack a few decades down the line. Without doubt, having broader societal issues sorted out, raises the general threshold of productivity.

A focus on NCDs remains important in this context, as they pose a clear threat not only to human health, but also to development and economic growth. NCDs are responsible for 63 per cent of all deaths globally; they are currently the main killer world-wide. Eighty per cent of related deaths occur in low- and middle-income countries. Half of those who die of chronic NCDs are in the prime of their productive years, therefore the disabilities and deaths caused by these illnesses also negatively impact industry competitiveness across borders (Bloom, Cafiero and Jané-Lopis et al., 2011).

The NCD challenge in middle-income countries is fast rivalling that of high-income countries, and is rising rapidly in low-income countries. Although high-income countries currently bear the biggest economic burden of NCDs, the developing world – especially middle-income countries – is expected to carry an ever larger share of this burden as their economies and populations grow. In absolute terms, deaths from NCDs in middle- and low-income countries are projected to rise by over 50 per cent, from an estimated 28 million in 2008 to 43 million by 2030. The change will be particularly substantial in sub-Saharan Africa, where NCDs will account for 46 per cent of all deaths by 2030, up from 28 per cent in 2008, and in South Asia, which will see its share of NCD deaths increase from 51 per cent to 72 per cent over the same time frame. Morbidity data, while less systematically available, paint a similar picture. By 2030, cancer incidence is projected to increase by 70 per cent in middle-income countries, 82 per cent in low-income countries, and 40 per cent in high-income countries (WHO, 2011a).

Cardiovascular disease and mental health conditions are the main contributors to the global economic burden of NCDs. Although research on the global economic effects of NCDs is still in an emerging stage, economists are increasingly concerned that NCDs will have long-term macroeconomic impacts on labour supply, capital accumulation and GDP worldwide, with the consequences being most severe in developing countries.

Considerations when implementing wellness programmes

When comparing two individuals with equal motivation but different lifestyle habits, the person who is fit, has a reasonable body weight, does not smoke and drinks moderately, is much more productive. To ensure sustainability, the cost-effectiveness of wellness interventions is very important. Outcomes take a few years to emerge, therefore managers need to have a three-year horizon in order to judge the success or failure of any programme. Numerous studies have highlighted the success of wellness interventions:

- Fit people are 30 per cent less likely to be admitted to hospital than healthy people. The older the age group, the greater the gap between fit and unfit people (Discovery Health, 2007);

- For each dollar invested in a limited prevention package (focused on exercise and diet advice) for individuals at high risk from developing diabetes, a minimum average return of US$2 in low-income countries and more than US$3 in middle-income countries could be expected in saved treatment costs (Stanciole, 2011);

- American data (Burton et al., 1998) show that in the workplace, for every one-point increase in the body mass index (BMI – a relationship between height and body weight),
  - healthcare costs increase by 4–7%
  - the likelihood of diabetes claims increase by 11.6%
  - the likelihood of heart disease increases by 5.2%

- One American company's (Berry LL, 2011) wellness programme succeeded in moving ten per cent of its employees from high to medium risk, and its return on investment is $6 saved for $1 invested;

- As far as HIV is concerned, research in Zambia shows that it costs approximately $9 000 to replace a worker, but only a few dollars per worker per year to sensitise him/her about HIV/AIDS. Companies spent on average US$371 treating undiagnosed workers in 2006, but only US$55 administering medical treatment to an HIV-positive employee (Kelly & Allison, 2009).

It must be emphasised that the workplace in emerging economies faces the double burden of both infectious and chronic diseases. Where companies in developed economies can concentrate on preventing and managing chronic disease, those in emerging economies need to manage diseases such as HIV/AIDS, TB and malaria.

This implies that wellness programmes need a broader focus in emerging economies. In the first phases of development there is often a difference in terms of demographics, with workers suffering from infectious diseases while managers (who are from a different social and often ethnic group) have to deal with chronic diseases.

The challenges become greater when a one-size-fits-all marketing approach fails. Over time, the disease profile tends to generalise across the organisation.

Although different diseases and approaches manifest within organisations, common themes can be identified. In almost all cases of disease there is some element of prevention, i.e., the disease can either be prevented or the risk reduced. In terms of infectious diseases, the HIV risk can be reduced by using condoms and other safe sex techniques, incidences of malaria can be reduced by using mosquito nets and insecticides. TB presents more of a challenge, but two key messages need to be communicated and practised: if you feel unwell and are coughing, go to the clinic for screening, boost your immunity with good nutrition, and reduce your alcohol and drug consumption (a tough ask!!).

Once a diagnosis is made, individual behaviour plays a key role in the outcome of any disease. With both groups of diseases, good nutrition, exercise, sleep and stress management will have a powerful impact on the prognosis. A major difference between the two types is the public health issue related to the spread of infection, and health staff tend to prioritise these conditions over NCDs. The challenge is to work towards managing all diseases proactively, for example, if a key member of staff (a skilled technician or director) has a heart attack or stroke, replacing that person and dealing with the loss of skills can be quite serious.

Organisations cannot battle diseases alone – the state and non-governmental organisations (NGOs) need to assist. In this regard, the WHO (2011b) has produced an excellent monograph, entitled 'Best buys', which organisations can use to lobby governments. Based on a set of criteria which include outcome-effectiveness, cost-effectiveness and feasibility of scale-up, it is proposed that organisations introduce five overarching priority prevention interventions. These include four population-wide methods to curb key risk factors – accelerated tobacco control, salt reduction, the promotion of healthy diets and physical activity, and a reduction in the harmful use of alcohol. The fifth priority intervention focuses on cardiovascular disease risk reduction through access to essential drugs and technologies (Beaglehole et al., 2011).

If managers wait for macro interventions, the delay in acting locally may be costly. The key areas of wellness to prioritise are empowerment and risk reduction. Creativity is an essential element of the delivery model. Key to the success of any programme is ensuring that workers are part of the solution, as is multi-stakeholder involvement in developing commitment.

Although the workplace may be the site of interaction, the behaviours being targeted or influenced take place off-site. Depending on the workers' culture, involving community, religious and traditional leaders may be required. In many third-world countries, HIV/AIDS programmes suffered and their success was greatly delayed because of the clash of cultures that ensued when all-knowing, first-world-orientated doctors spoke out against local customs. Only when these issues were addressed (even in the face of rising death rates), was resistance to changing sexual behaviour removed.

'Wellness' was defined in the introduction, and Berry, Mirabito and Baun (2010) expand on this definition by adding that it is 'an organized, employer sponsored program that is designed to support employees (and, sometimes, their families) as they adopt and sustain behaviours that reduce health risks, improve quality of life, enhance personal effectiveness, and benefit the organization's bottom line'.

Multiple outcomes are possible, with the employer in all likelihood using benevolent self-interest as the reason to drive wellness. The role of business leaders in taking ownership of wellness interventions cannot be overemphasised. Small-budget programmes which are delegated to the wellness coordinator are doomed to fail. Business leaders themselves need to lead the fight against diseases impacting on the workplace. The WEF (2007) monograph had the following summary to offer managers:

- *Take the pulse.* First assess the health of your employees. The metrics will provide a baseline for measuring progress, and will help to prioritise which areas of lifestyle/infectious diseases to address. Furthermore, understanding barriers to health through focus groups and surveys is essential. Ongoing monitoring and evaluation require resources to ensure the success of the programme;

- *Embed a culture of health.* Align and build wellness into the mission, business objectives and policies of the organisation. Health programmes might need to be seen as a strategic imperative, based on the information taken from the pulse (see above). Engaging with the programme at all levels of the organisation is important. Wellness champions for each department could operate as change leaders;

- *Manage the change*

  - Commit the appropriate resources to improve the health of employees. Remember: minimal investment in health programmes constitutes a waste of money. Significant resources are required to cross the threshold to gain employees' attention and get them to consider changing their behaviour. Sending out the odd email or doing an annual screening test will not change behaviour, nor will it improve productivity or save you money. Only once a sound programme is implemented, will behaviour change and improved health impacts be evident.

  - Engage with employees to develop wellness programmes that will produce long-term results and are consistent with the culture and goals of the organisation. Managing change has numerous challenges and an approach using wellness champions has been proven to be successful (Patterson & Grenny et al., 2008).

- – Design a programme that is broad in scope and high in relevance and quality. A one-size-fits-all approach will not work.

- – Accessibility needs to be considered. People with very long commutes will need time to exercise at work. How can the company facilitate this? Can cost barriers be reduced through company subsidies?

- – Communication with exciting branding and relevant messages is essential to maintain interest in the programme.

- *Collaborate and consolidate*

  - – Communicate with employees and work with outside bodies, where appropriate. Collaboration is very powerful in the wellness space.

  - – Integrate with other workplace programmes, such as EAP. Depression complicates lifestyle change and vice versa, therefore internal referral of employees is an important component of both programmes.

- *Lead by example*

  - – Executives – starting with the CEO – can encourage and inspire employees and communities by showing that they are dedicated to living well.

Wellness is an important facet of successful businesses, but it needs serious commitment over a number of years before there is enough traction to see significant impacts. Programmes will provide good returns as long as there is evidence of professional planning and implementation.

Managing absenteeism due to sickness

Doctors who consult in organisational health spend much of their time helping to manage sick absenteeism and incapacity. The information below is based on the observations of numerous occupational medicine professionals who have worked in industry for many years. The South African Society of Occupational Medicine (SASOM, 2003) produced guidelines and determined the thresholds used in this chapter, based on empirical observation over many years, rather than relying on peer-reviewed research.

Causes of excessive absenteeism

Being so ill or injured that they cannot work is only one reason why people take sick leave. When absence rates are high, many employers believe absence is only due to employees having a bad attitude towards work. This may be a contributing factor, but other issues need to be considered, as absenteeism is usually due to a combination of factors, with four determinants interacting.

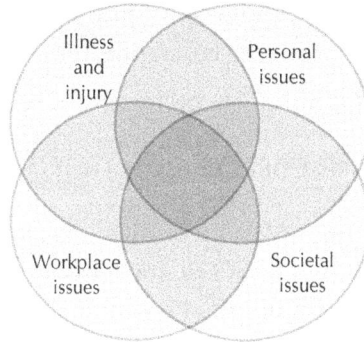

Figure 13.4: The complex interactions of sick absenteeism

Illness and injury. A key issue is why different people with identical symptoms deem themselves fit or unfit to come to work. Genetics, lifestyle, social and psychological factors all contribute to individuals becoming ill and making decisions about productivity.

- *Individual issues.* Unique characteristics such as gender, age, social status, self-esteem and a good, supportive personal network, influence proneness and attitudes towards illness and work.

- *Workplace management and culture*

  - The saying that 'you get the absenteeism you deserve', is based on companies not putting the appropriate preventive techniques in place.

  - The collection, collation, analysis and utilisation of absence measures are critical for monitoring all forms of leave. Sick absence will be taken if employees believe it is their right to use their sick leave, because they can play the system. If systems are in place to confront individuals when they cross thresholds, absence can be controlled.

  - Managers are often reluctant to confront employees, they feel disempowered by labour laws, and many do not have the skills to manage employees' poor productivity.

  - Employees who feel disengaged, who lack a sense of ownership or commitment to the business, are more likely to abuse their sick leave.

  - A poor work culture and low employee morale all drive up absenteeism rates.

- *Societal issues*

  - Bear in mind that societal issues impact on absence – poor transport systems, crises in shanty towns and no/very poor childcare support are examples of factors which impact on employees getting to work. Of note, when strikes are called, and where 'no-work-no-pay' rules are adhered to, some employees go to the doctor to collect sick certificates, so that they can get paid during the strike.

The costs of absenteeism

Absenteeism is costly in terms of lost productivity. Remember: for each R1 lost in direct costs of absenteeism, the company could be losing another R3 in indirect costs! South African data show that in 2013, 3.96 million workers were absent due to sickness – up from 0.7 million in 2000: an increase of 466 per cent. In 2013 alone, the loss of output due to absenteeism totalled R4.29 billion in direct costs. Cumulatively since 2000, the economy has lost R55.2 billion in real terms due to absenteeism.[4]

To ensure that productivity remains at an acceptable level it is necessary to manage absenteeism proactively. By monitoring employees closely, management will be alerted to any trends or changes in absenteeism and can use this information as a means of detecting problems in their area of responsibility – appropriate intervention at an early stage, handled with care and counselling, can serve to improve morale and productivity.

Management's role

If management fail to focus on absence, some employees will start taking advantage of their lax approach. There is an ethos amongst certain employees that sick leave is a right, and they manipulate the system to ensure that they take as much sick leave as possible. Tools are available to assist in monitoring and evaluating absenteeism. Using these tools provides powerful ammunition to line managers who have to bring absence under control.

Importantly, absenteeism requires a carrot-and-stick approach to reduce instances of abuse. In organisations with low trust, high hostility and non-engagement, it is difficult to secure appropriate cooperation when it comes to increasing productivity and reducing absence. Employees who come to work because they require a paycheque are not open to positive reinforcement. In higher trust organisations, motivation and positive reinforcement work very well. Discipline is only required for a few outliers.

These tools rely on the careful recording of absenteeism. Fundamentally, if there is no focus on data collection, absence management becomes very difficult. Tracking can be a simple process: a line manager in a small business can use an A4, single-page, 12-month calendar for each employee. When an employee is absent, the manager can highlight the affected days and jot down the diagnosis, if provided. The single-page view of absence provides a quick picture of an individual's quantum and patterns of sick leave.

In larger organisations, sophisticated systems are provided by all the major HR transactional information technology (IT) systems. These systems allow management to track losses in terms of days and wages spent on sick leave (direct costs), to make comparisons across departments and to highlight problem individuals/departments. In many organisations, the collection of absenteeism data is patchy – this leads to incomplete and inaccurate reports, which in turn renders the HR absenteeism system obsolete.

Following data collection it is important to analyse the information, before investigating instances of sick leave. The first phase is to collate the information into meaningful rates.

Collating absence data

Absence data are dependent on the accurate noting of the number of sick leave days taken. The data will reveal the number of days lost, as well as the number of absence incidences. Three key parameters drive absence management:

- Time (number of days) lost, i.e., the sick absence rate (SAR);

- Frequency with which individuals take sick leave (number of events taken), i.e., the absence frequency rate (AFR); and

- Time taken per event, on average, i.e., the absence severity rate (ASR).

Other information may also be valuable. Record whether sick certificates were issued, and by which doctor(s). If diagnoses are recorded on the sick certificate, record them as well. Many countries frown on doctors providing diagnoses as this infringes on the employee's/patient's right to privacy, therefore managers cannot depend on them to reveal this.

In general, diagnoses are not necessary unless absence rates become problematic, or the workplace environment is causing/aggravating the illness or injury, thus resulting in absence. In cases where a diagnosis is potentially embarrassing for a patient, doctors use euphemisms to protect the dignity of the patient – this confirms that written diagnoses should not carry too much weight (for example, a venereal disease may be described as a skin ulcer or as abdominal pain).

Absence rates can be used flexibly to meet the needs of those individuals drawing up absence reports. Time frames could span a month, a quarter, a year or a three-year cycle, for instance. Rates can be used for individuals, departments or for the organisation as a whole. Calculations need to be adjusted according to the needs of the individuals drawing up the reports. The most effective use of these rates is for quarterly reports which provide information about employees who have crossed the so-called action thresholds (see later).

Absence rates are an instrument for highlighting potential problems. Discussions with employees will help to ascertain whether their absence is due to abuse or genuine illness, and whether the absence is problematic or not.

The sick absenteeism rate (SAR)

NB: This should not be confused with the gross absenteeism rate (GAR), which considers all forms of leave.

The SAR is defined as the number of days lost over a particular period of time. The desirable rate is two per cent or less. An action level or the threshold of acceptable absence is four per cent.

$$SAR = \frac{\text{Number of sick absence days} \times 100}{\text{Potential working days}}$$

Example

There are 15 people in the department, and 22 working days this month. Five people were sick for one day each. One person was sick for two days, while one person was sick for three days.

Sick days lost	= 10
Potential working days	= 22 x 15 = 330
SAR	= 10/330 x100
	= 3%

Conclusion: **The absence rate is above the ideal. The situation is not yet critical, but it is vital to track incidences to ensure that this rate does not show an upward trend.**

The absence frequency rate (AFR)

The absence frequency rate reflects the number of events lost during a particular period of time. It is important to note that abuse is more likely to be identified when employees take short-term absence (two or fewer days) frequently, rather than long term-absence rarely.

$$AFR = \frac{\text{Number of incidents of sick leave over a period}}{\text{Average number of employees for that period}}$$

The 'ideal' employee takes two or fewer events of absence per year. However, unfortunate people can be struck with more bouts of genuine illness or injury. To accommodate this, make allowances for another two events, before taking any action of note.

When calculating an individual's AFR, the denominator is obviously 1. When performing a departmental review, the average number of employees who worked during that period will constitute the denominator.

Monthly or quarterly reviews within departmental reviews can be confusing, arithmetically speaking. The 'ideal' AFR is two or fewer incidents per employee, per year.

Based on this principle, the management rule is to allow for four events per year, per individual, before becoming concerned.

When reviewing monthly or quarterly data by department, the results need to be annualised, i.e., one month's total needs to be multiplied by 12, and the quarterly total by 4. Where does genuine sick leave end and abuse begin? This is always difficult to peg down, but an AFR of greater than 4.0 is worth investigating.

Example

There are 15 people in the department and 22 working days this month. Five people were sick for one day each. One person was sick for two days, while one person was sick for three days.

No of incidents of sick leave in period	= 7
Ave no of employees	= 15
AFR	= 7/15 x 12
	= 5.6

Conclusion: **This is the short-term sick leave taken in the department during the month. The five single days of absenteeism need to be looked at. One month's data is not enough to conclude that there is a problem. Tracking over time is necessary.**

The absence severity rate (ASR)

The absence severity rate looks at the average length of absence of a group of events, over a particular period of time, expressed as a number.

$$ASR = \frac{\text{Total number of days sick leave taken}}{\text{Total number of incidents of sick leave}}$$

Three days or fewer is defined as short-term sick absence – this is where abuse will most likely manifest. A grey area exists between four and six days. Seven or more days suggests genuine illness. With this duration of absence there has usually been a hospital admission, a significant injury or a medical investigation which implies that ancillary evidence of the absence is available.

Example

There are 15 people in the department and 22 working days this month. Five people were sick for one day each. One person was sick for two days, while one person was sick for three days.

Total number of days sick leave taken	= 10
Total number of incidents	= 7
ASR	= 10/7
	= 1.43

Conclusion: **Short-term absence has been confirmed, and possible abusive patterns have been found. Again, one month's data is not enough to take action, but line managers now know they need to keep a close watch on absence patterns.**

Managing individual absenteeism

Controlling excessive sick leave is a line management function. HR and medical personnel can support managers in dealing with absence. The ideal would be to discuss each sick leave event with an individual when s/he returns to work. The meeting should be held within a supportive framework, where emphasis is placed on the fact that the absence had an impact on a department in which the employee's presence is valued. This interaction informs employees that they are being observed and, should they have genuine problems, the line manager can be approached to discuss these issues. If, in a rolling 12-month period, an individual takes more than ten days or four events, a more formal meeting should be held. In such cases it is important to inform the employee that a threshold of concern has been breached, and their absence therefore requires discussion. The meeting needs to cover topics such as possible underlying issues (work- or home-related). Employees need to understand the impacts and costs associated with their absence. At this stage, a request can be made for a medical report detailing the reasons why so much time has been lost. The personal consequences of absence also need to be discussed – if the absence becomes excessive, an incapacity process can begin. If appropriate, the employee may then be referred to a doctor who has a relationship with the company. His/her subsequent report can be used to decide on the best path to take in managing the individual – if underlying illness is found, encourage good medical care to control symptoms and reduce absence. In emerging economies where private healthcare is difficult to access, managers need to consider whether it is worth their while to subsidise or pay for a medical referral.

The time saved in arriving at a decision is often worth the cost of the consultation. If no underlying issues are found, appropriate counselling or discipline should be applied.

Managers often find a relationship with a doctor most useful. Although line managers can call doctors in their practices or at clinics to access information, doctors prefer not to discuss patients with their employers. A consulting doctor can act as a bridge, since doctor-to-doctor conversations tend to provide more useful information. This will help to establish whether the sick leave is warranted, or whether other action is required.

Line management must make the final decision about whether or not to grant sick leave. (Information obtained from the company doctor is given in an advisory capacity, and only takes into account medical information.)

Where an individual makes frequent use of sick leave and valid sick certificates are produced but productivity drops to an unacceptable level, performance procedures may be instituted. Action should focus on productivity losses due to absence from work, rather than on the illness.

Absenteeism is best controlled where there is leadership commitment to bring absenteeism under control. Some companies go so far as to include absenteeism processes and outcomes under line managers' KPAs. Line managers need to be trained to understand the issues associated with absenteeism, and to develop the confidence to confront those individuals who take excessive leave of absence.

Who can sign sick certificates?

First-world-orientated managers feel that the bio-psychosocial model of health is the only valid approach with which to describe illness and absenteeism. As a result, they are very sceptical about sick notes written by alternative practitioners and traditional healers. In a recent case which went to the South African Supreme Court of Appeal, the five judges ruled that employers need to consider cultural issues before taking action.[5] Of note: the judges did not consider the *Basic Conditions of Employment Act*, where clause 23(2) states that the "Medical certificate must be issued by a medical practitioner or any other person who is certified to diagnose and treat patients who is registered with a professional council established by an Act of Parliament". Since traditional healers have no professional council, sick leave based on traditional health principles may lead to problems with absence, which in effect means employers will need to consult with a traditional health practitioner in order to manage absence!

South African legislation makes provision for an *Allied Health Professions Act*, therefore many allied health practitioners (such as acupuncturists, therapeutic massagers, reflexologists and others) can sign sick certificates. An essential part of the legislation is that the practitioners can only give a person time off work as a result of a diagnosis directly associated with their scope of practice. It is on this basis that managers can limit the sick leave proposed/allowed by alternative healers. Clearly, legislation in other economies will greatly influence absence management in this regard.

Implementing an absence management system

The 'standard' approach to implementing an absence management system is for HR to introduce this via a silo approach, which shows little consideration for underlying issues. In using the organisational health approach a more integrated system emerges, which improves the integration of the programme. Five key components of the organisational health system can help to deliver the goods.

- *Health benefit management/HR component.* This is where the traditional absenteeism management system is in place. Reports which are collated and generated through HR reporting systems form the nuts and bolts of a good absenteeism programme. The relationship between line managers and HR is critical in ensuring that when HR reports that individuals are exceeding thresholds, line managers or supervisors take action.

  Having a healthcare professional to assist HR in deciding what to do about excessive absence is worthwhile. Deciding to call an employee's doctor for more information or helping line managers to delineate whether any absence constitutes abuse or genuine illness, can save a great deal of time.

  As mentioned earlier, illness is only one cause of ill health – many people use their sick leave because they are unhappy or demotivated at work. Taking one or two midweek days off work does not require a sick certificate, and is one way of abusing sick leave allowances.

  The most important predictor of absence is the sense of ownership and engagement an employee has with the workplace (Eriksen, Bruusgaard & Knardahl, 2003). HR practices in an organisation which foster a close, warm and loyal relationship amongst employees will not usually manifest problems with absenteeism.

  Other components of the organisational health model are also useful for managing absence.

- *Primary care disciplines.* The role of screening is discussed above. Clearly, identifying and controlling risk factors can help to reduce absenteeism. Promoting healthy lifestyles, with wellness programmes to encourage behaviour change is another important component of absenteeism management. Research shows that when senior leadership buy into a healthy lifestyle, and implement and overtly support programmes such as eating healthy lunches or exercising during lunchtime, employees tend to follow suit.

  On-site clinics with contracted medical staff can have a huge impact on absence: 1) the proximity of the clinic to the workplace improves efficiency in delivering healthcare; 2) contracted staff will put the patient's interests first, but will also consider the employer's concerns in respect of productivity. Sick certificates issued at the worksite clinic tend to allow for fewer days off work. Employees should point out that healthcare staff need to take an ethical approach in managing employees on-site, in order to develop and maintain trust. They cannot act as agents for management by breaching confidentiality or manipulating patients in order to increase productivity.

- *Psychosocial support programmes.* These are commonly called employee assistance or employee wellness programmes (EAP/EWP).

  Stress is defined as the body's psychological and physical response to changing conditions, be they real or perceived. Low levels of stress are desirable, beneficial, and even healthy. Positive stress helps improve performance, and is a factor in motivation, adaptation and reaction to the environment. Excessive levels of stress, however, may lead to many physical problems which could be harmful and may ultimately lead to absence from work. Absenteeism is a common outcome when employees do not cope. The early identification and appropriate referral of individuals for counselling and support can have a very positive impact on absenteeism.

Example

The impact of an integrated organisational health approach to absenteeism

An experienced warehouse worker with a poor absenteeism record strained his back at work. The injury was relatively minor, but each time he returned to work, he would complain of back pain and take another few days off. Within a year he had exhausted the absence allowance of his three-year cycle.

The warehouse manager decided to have the employee boarded. As part of the process, the employee needed to see the occupational health nurse, who had counselling skills.

On interviewing the employee, she found out that the underlying issues included alcohol addiction and serious debt problems.

The employee was encouraged to enter a rehab programme. He completed the programme successfully, returned to work with a positive attitude, his back fully recovered, and there were no further absenteeism problems.

- *Occupational health.* Identifying and managing workplace health hazards helps reduce incidences of absence. If substances in the workplace emit noxious fumes, respiratory illnesses such as asthma may develop. Introducing personal protective equipment or engineering solutions to reduce exposure to dangerous fumes will prevent employee absence related to those causes. Poor ergonomic design can cause muscle strain and back pain, while poor adherence to safety precautions leads to higher incidences of time-off injuries. On-site medical staff can identify these risk factors and provide solutions to prevent mental breakdown and employee absence.

- *Curative care/use of insured medical benefits.* Due to the generally inefficient delivery of healthcare offered by emerging economy governments, thousands of hours of work are lost while employees wait in queues. In many cases, a shortage of prescription drugs can lead to inadequate control of symptoms and chronic diseases. In government hospitals, the waiting time for common yet important operations such as coronary artery bypass surgery for stable angina can exceed six months. Without this operation, patients tend to become anxious and stop working at the first sign of discomfort. The private sector, which is much more efficient, has the capacity to work with very short waiting times. Although the costs are high, it is really worthwhile running a cost-benefit exercise which considers costs against productivity gains and employee loyalty. It is most frustrating to identify an experienced employee whose performance has slowed and who takes many days off work to deal with an ailment which is amenable to treatment, yet the treatment is not accessible. Losing experienced employees in an emerging market economy where skills are in short supply can have serious consequences for a firm's operational capacity.

Based on the organisational health model, a broad and integrated approach can effectively control absenteeism.

Conclusion

Organisations in emerging economies are faced with a double burden of disease, an inadequate social net, and employees with high aspirations to improve their lot in life. There is a certain expectation that the workplace will help those employees (and, perhaps, even their families and communities).

The decision to provide health-related interventions should not be taken lightly. A carefully planned systemic approach, which considers many factors (such as the prevalence and impact of a disease now and in the future) is required. Limited resources need to be used carefully, programmes should be integrated and there should be collaboration with external NGOs and state facilities, if possible. For best results, involving senior managers who lead by example, is essential. Good monitoring and evaluation systems will also help drive the programme and will assist with effectiveness over time.

Health issues tend to be complex and can drain valuable resources away from organisations in emerging economies. Under these circumstances, health and wellness should be seen as another of the strategic issues which HR directors need to grasp and manage.

Endnotes

1   See http://welcoa.org/worksite_benefits.html
2   Rhodes University. Health & Wellness. Retrieved January 20, 2014 from www.ru.ac.za/
    wellness
3   Adapted from World Economic Forum. (2007). Working towards wellness. Monograph
    produced by PriceWaterhouseCooper. Retrieved January 10, 2014 from http://www.
    weforum.org/pdf/Wellness/report.pdf
4   Retrieved January 10, 2014 from http://www.adcorp.co.za/Documents/Adcorp%20
    Employment%20Index%20201309.pdf
5   *Kiewitz Kroon Country Estate v. Mmoledi* (29/11/13). ZASCA 189

References

Beaglehole, et al. (2011, April 23). Priority actions for the non-communicable disease crisis. *Lancet, 377*(9775): 1438–1447. DOI: 10.1016/S0140-6736(11)60393-0.

Berry, L.L., Mirabito, A.M. & Baun, W.B. (2010). What's the hard return on employee wellness programs? *Harvard Business Review, 88*(12) (December), 105–112.

Bloom, D.E., Cafiero, E.T., Jané-Llopis, Abrahams, E., Gessel, S., Bloom, L.R., Fathima, S., Feigl, A.B., Gaziano, T., Mowafi, M., Pandya, A., Prettner, K., Rosenberg, L., Seligman, B., Stein, A. & Weinstein, C. (2011). *The global economic burden of non-communicable diseases.* Geneva: World Economic Forum.

Eriksen, W., Bruusgaard, D. & Knardahl, S. (2003). Work factors as predictors of sickness absence. *Occup Environ Med, 60,* 271–278.

Kelly V. & Allison, D. (2009). *The costs and benefits of HIV workplace programmes in Zambia – A technical approach paper.* London: The HLSP Institute.

NLM classification: WA 105, Geneva. (n.d.). Retrieved January 10, 2014 from http://www.who.int/healthinfo/global_burden_disease/global_health_risks/en/

Patel, D.N., Nossel, C., Alexander, E. & Yach, D. (2013). Innovative business approaches for incenting health promotion in sub-Saharan Africa: Progress and persisting challenges. *Progress in Cardiovascular Diseases, 56*(3), November–December, 356–362.

Patterson K., Grenny J., Maxfield, D., McMillan, R. & Switzer, A. (2008). *Influencer: The power to change anything.* New York: McGraw Hill.

South African Board of People's Practice. (n.d.). Retrieved May 25, 2014 from http://www.sabpp.co.za/category/hr-standards/

South African Society of Occupational Medicine (SASOM). (2003). *Approach to absenteeism.* Retrieved January 10, 2014 from www.sasom.org

Starke, L. (Ed.). (2008). *Good practice guidelines on HIV/AIDS, TB and malaria.* ICMM. Retrieved January 10, 2014 from www.icmm.com

World Economic Forum (WEF). (2007). *Working towards wellness.* Monograph produced by PriceWaterhouseCoopers. Retrieved January 10, 2014 from http://www.weforum.org/pdf/Wellness/report.pdf

World Health Organisation (WHO). (2009). Global health risks: Mortality and burden of disease attributable to selected major risks. ISBN 978 92 4 156387 1.

WHO. (2011a). *Scaling up action against noncommunicable diseases: How much will it cost?* Geneva: WHO.

WHO. (2011b). *Preventing chronic diseases: A vital investment – A WHO global report.* Geneva: WHO.

WHO. (2011c). *From burden to 'best buys': The global economic burden of non-communicable diseases.* Prepared by the World Economic Forum and the Harvard School of Public Health. Retrieved January 10, 2014 from http://www.weforum.org/EconomicsOfNCD

WHO. (2012). *World health statistics 2012.* Retrieved August 25, 2014 from http://www.ahp.org.za/files/2566/EN_WHS2012_Full.pdf

.

PART IV: Learning from Practice

CHAPTER 14: Developing a Personal Vision

Lele Mehlomakulu

Introduction

> Start with the end in mind … To begin with the end in mind means to start with a clear understanding of your destination. It means to know where you're going so that you better understand where you are now and so that the steps you take are always in the right direction.
>
> – Stephen Covey

Any contractor will tell you that you cannot put up a building without a plan or a blueprint. Yet most of us try to build our lives without any real blueprint, and are surprised when we end up with unfulfilled and unhappy lives. Everyone needs to have a specific plan to keep them focused on purposeful living. If you don't know where you are going, anywhere is good … but it might not be where you ultimately want to be. When people ask me if I have a personal vision or vision statement, I am always confounded by what they actually mean, and have learned that 'personal vision' means different things to different people. For one group of people it is about a snapshot of the future, while for another it is about both the snapshot and the journey to get there. For some it is about only one area of their lives, while for others it is about two or more areas, such as their family, career, health, spirituality, relationships or society at large.

When I was doing research on this topic, I was reminded of a day many years ago when I was still at school. As it was my birthday, I went to one of my teachers – a nun – and happily informed her that it was my birthday, hoping she would give me a gift. I was not so lucky. To my dismay she told me that my birthday would never be as important as the day I died. I cannot recall how I reacted at the time, but the traumatic impact of her statement was long lived, as I mulled over her response for many years to come.

Then one day, out of the blue, it dawned on me that her response had not been about dying, but about living a purposeful and meaningful life. It had taken a few years, but the realisation led to me search for and find a way to clarify my purpose in life. Up to that point I had been living my life according to a routine set by parents, teachers and lecturers, according to their expectations. I was afraid to get involved with bigger things and anxious about what the consequences of my decisions would be, were I to venture out of my carefully 'sculpted-by-other-people' life. I had neither a vision nor a destination, and it was easier living a life for which I could blame other people if anything went wrong. With that realisation I set about trying to understand what I wanted in life, what I was good at, and how I could go about realising my dreams, and doing things I enjoyed and was good at. I was surprised that the outcome was not a bizarre revelation of some unknown 'avatar' of myself, but of my true self which had been there all the time, waiting to be unravelled and released. So while in a sense I was back where I had begun, I was there under different terms. The exercise led me to a completely new way of thinking and behaving.

> We shall never cease from exploration
> And the end of all our exploring
> Will be to arrive where we started
> And know the place for the first time.
>
> – T. S. Eliot

This new clarity led me to resign from an unfulfilling job, to join an organisation that gelled well with my plans. By then I had learned that I could not practise my profession at just any organisation that offered me a job, unless it fitted in with my personal vision and goals. I had learned the importance of value alignment, and since then my decisions about where I go and which job I take have been guided by my personal vision. And because of this alignment, my personal vision has not differed vastly from the visions of those organisations I have since worked for. Visionary leaders do not separate their personal vision from their organisational vision, and through self-reflection are able to form a significant personal vision to which they can commit fully (Yoeli & Berkovich, 2010).

You have most likely read about alignment at length in the preceding chapters, and by now you must realise that if your agenda is not the same as that of the people you support, your strategies will not succeed. This is not to suggest that you will (or should) surrender your identity to the organisation you work for: it simply means that who you are and what you value should not contradict the make-up of the organisation you work for, and vice versa. Ideally, your vision should align with the values and culture of your organisation.

People sometimes get stuck in situations which they should not be in, because they keep trying to 'fit in'. They join companies for the wrong reasons, stay in toxic relationships and settle for second best because they lack direction and do not know what they want for themselves. They are presumably waiting for Lady Luck to visit, and to steer them towards a life of bliss.

Why must you create a vision statement?

In the preceding chapters you learned more about the role of the Chief Human Resources (HR) Officer, and discovered various ways of leading an HR function that is aligned to the organisation. However, you cannot be a leader unless you have a compelling vision to help ground and guide you. Here are a few points to think about:

- A vision provides you with clarity in respect of alignment, and keeps you focused on those efforts which will lead you towards what you really want. That will also enable you to prioritise better;

- A vision can help you succeed far beyond where you would be without one (Bennis, 2009). Peter Senge (1990, p. 7) adds that one of the goals we need to achieve in the process of gaining personal mastery, is the 'discipline of continually clarifying and deepening our personal vision, of focusing our energies, of developing patience and of seeing reality objectively';

- When you have clarity about where you want to go, your life choices are more directed and you are more confident about making decisions. Think of it as a bridge between where you are now, and your future;

- A vision statement provides you with a standard according to which you can measure your progress. It shows that you are not just tagging along and hoping to strike it lucky somewhere;

- You cannot lead others if you don't know where you are going.

What is a vision?

A vision is a statement which captures everything you would like to be and do – in effect, your sense of having a calling, a purpose and a life of meaning. It is also about the career path you want to follow and what you want to accomplish. A vision statement is your idea of 'the good life'. As a professional, your vision should reflect what you do, what you are good at and what you want to achieve, and it must clearly state who it is you want to impact. The last aspect is very important. You cannot be everything to everyone, nor is it possible for your value proposition to benefit every organisation which exists, or each and every person you interact with. If your vision cannot impact the important people or aspects in your life, it will not energise you. Alternatively, if your vision is far removed from what people or events in your life can offer you, you need to be honest with yourself and ask if they are a good match for you.

How do you create your own vision statement?

Creating a vision or vision statement can be a daunting task at the best of times, but it does bring clarity and keeps you focused on what you really want. Your vision should provide a clear sense of purpose and must inspire you.

The most difficult part is knowing where to begin. Your vision might be about yourself and/or about your organisation. Whichever it is, it provides a guideline for how you behave and what decisions you make.

> Owning our story can be hard but not nearly as difficult as spending our lives running from it …. Only when we are brave enough to explore the darkness will we discover the infinite power of our light.
>
> – Brené Brown

When you write down your personal vision, it helps to consider all the aspects which make up your life, because while certain aspects may be more important than others, they all deserve some consideration in the crafting of your personal vision statement. Use the following guidelines to think through the questions you need answered in order to do this (the guidelines have been adapted from various sources, and should help to get you moving). Use the worksheet at the end of this chapter. Once you have thoughtfully answered all the questions, you will be well on your way to crafting your personal vision statement. Let's take this journey with a guy I call Jim, who has also decided to craft a vision statement for himself.

Step 1: Eliminate distractions

Sit down somewhere by yourself. You do not need to set aside whole hours to do this, but take enough uninterrupted time to think, without any distractions. Take time off work, book yourself into a hotel for a day, send the family away for the afternoon, or go to the office over the weekend. You need to do this work on your own. While you might later require the input of other people, it is important that your vision statement is not influenced by what others want for you. This process can take more than one sitting, so plan for it thoughtfully.

Step 2: Find your true self

This stage, which helps you determine your reason for being, is probably the most important. Ask yourself what you want to do with your life, what inspires you, and what you would do even if you were not paid to do it. It is important not to limit yourself to what other people think of you, or to make assumptions about yourself which are not supported by evidence. This is a time to identify those things you are good at and which keep you energised, so be sure to silence your demons.

There is no right or wrong way of finding your true self. The Internet, bookshops and libraries are filled with various texts suggesting what you must do to find your true self. Various psychological tests have been developed to offer an even more comprehensive assessment of who you are, what your preferences are, and the areas in which you are likely to be most successful. At the end of the day you want to get to a point where you are clear about who you are, what you want, and who you want it for. The template at the end of this chapter will help you answer the following questions:

- What do you love?

    This is about the things that energise you, that get you out of bed in the morning and make you feel alive. It could very well be ice-cream, but you want to focus on the things that really matter, like solving problems, being creative, taking care of people, teaching, exercising, championing causes or making a difference at work. It is not about what other people want for you; it is about that which you would climb mountains to attain because you are so motivated by it. It helps to think about the people whose lives you want to impact in a positive way, the things you believe in and the values you embrace. It is also about the areas in your life where you showcase the best of yourself. Do not waste time thinking about the things that will please other people, regardless of their good intentions in this regard.

    Jim loves his family, and will do anything for the welfare of his wife and children. He is very ambitious and wants to leave a lasting legacy after he is gone. Jim also believes in the principle that honesty is the best policy, and hates it when people take short-cuts. He wants to make a difference.

- What have been your greatest achievements in life and what are you good at?

    These are the moments you look back on with pride – moments when you felt you succeeded at something. These instances say a great deal about what you are willing to commit to, what you are strong at, and they remind you of the behaviours, actions and strategies which led to those successes. It could be that moment when you managed to finalise a difficult project, when you saved the company some money, or when you helped a neighbour secure funding for his studies. Also think about your strengths and weaknesses, as difficult as this may be. We become modest about our achievements and abilities, or too ashamed to look at our weaknesses. Also incorporate any future achievements you aspire to, with respect to your skills, qualifications, likes and experiences.

    Jim ponders this and recalls a time when he was promoted. He remembers how hard he worked during that particular year, and how his boss remarked on his dedication to his job. Jim usually puts everything into his work, is always organised, is good at problem solving and manages his time well. That is why he can also take the time to be with his children in the evenings and help them with their homework or discuss important family matters. He also ensures that he is there for his kids' weekend rugby and netball matches. He often takes them to the local orphanage, where they help by playing with and educating some of the children. On Fathers' Day this year, Jim's children presented him with a 'Father of the Year' award.

- If nothing in the world mattered, what would you live for?

    The temptation to do things to please others is always there. Every day we are presented with images and messages from the media telling us who, what and how we should be, which makes us believe that if we look perfect and lead perfect lives, we won't feel inadequate (Brown, 2010). We tend to live our lives to please others, while inwardly fearing failure and judgement, as well as the 'shame' that comes with it (Brown, 2010). The question is: If it did not matter what people thought or said about you, what would you do? If it did not matter how much you earned, what would you focus your energies on? The answer to this question requires us to think about ourselves authentically, and this connects us to the purpose of our lives and our personal values.

    This is an easy one for Jim. He knows that if nothing mattered, he would spend his time helping people be the best they can be – especially those who are helpless. He would also spend as much time as possible with his family.

- If you could do anything, and had all the resources you needed, what would you do? How would you like to feel?

    This question helps you to think beyond life's limits, and to open up to what you are really meant to be and do. It is about the things that make you feel good and proud of yourself, and the things that will lead you to a fulfilled life.

This second step provides clarity about who you really are, what is important in your life and when you are at your best. You might not be able to arrive at the answers immediately, but with sufficient reiteration and authentic introspection you will ultimately get there. Without those answers you cannot align your decisions and behaviours with your true purpose.

Jim's wife once asked him what he would do if he won the lottery, and his answer was simple: 'I'd make the world a better place. Nobody would go hungry and everybody would get free education and healthcare. The streets would be clean and crime free.'

Step 3: Find your true motivation and identify your values and philosophy

Visions are seldom selfish statements about what we plan to take from the world. Vision statements are meant to improve not only our lives, but also to build and inspire the lives of our families, the people within our work environments, and our societies. Ask yourself what the motivation for your vision is, why you want to do what you want to do, who you want to benefit and how. The most important thinking here is about those dimensions of your life which you are not willing to compromise on, in the process of attaining your vision. It is your principles and your values which guide you in business, at work, at home, in relating to other people and in relating to life. These principles and values become the standards you live by. 'If we are clear about the values that guide us in our efforts to show up and be seen, we will always see the light' (Brown, 2013). Do not merely jot down the whole list of words you learned at the company's induction session, but choose five or six values which encapsulate those attributes that are not negotiable and that guide your behaviour and thinking.

The following are Jim's values: honesty, accountability, responsibility, hard work, family first and community service. Jim cares about disadvantaged children and feels that giving his all for his family and his organisation is important – even challenging. Jim will capture all these answers on his worksheet, to reflect back on and refine once he has completed the exercise.

Step 4: Refine and document

> If you have a goal, write it down. If you don't write it down, you do not have a goal, you have a wish.
>
> – Steve Maraboli

You are now ready to draft your vision statement. You might have to go through the questions a few times to ensure that you have answered them as honestly and authentically as possible. Use the answers to help focus your vision statement. Identify recurring themes within your answers, then select the most important words and use your creativity.

It is important to relax and allow a vision to form in your mind as you picture your life in the future. Envision the future as a reflection of your strengths and the things you love, your values, and see how that vision attracts the people you want in your life. Envisage the relationships you would have with those people, causes and organisations which allow the best in you to manifest. Allow your mind to come up with a compelling vision which excites and energises you. Your statement should not be too lengthy, and must reflect those things that are important to you and that will lead you to take action.

Your personal vision statement is, of course, adaptable – you should not write it once and then shelve it. However, if it keeps changing you may need to spend more time finding your true self, before you compose your vision statement. How often you revisit your vision statement and amend it depends on events or changes in your life which necessitate a different course of action. Your vision about a life partner might change briefly (or permanently in the event of the death of a spouse, for instance), or a sudden illness might cause you to rethink your career, job and goals. While it rarely changes, as you grow, so should your vision statement.

Jim's vision statement reflects the people and things he loves and values.

> My personal vision is to be honest at any time and place; achieving all my life's ambitions; to be successful in my job; for my family to know that I am there for them in any situation and that I value them. I want to make a difference in the world and to die knowing that I changed at least one person's life in my lifetime.
>
> – Jim Mofokeng, August 2013

Step 5: Commit to your goal

You will never fulfil your vision if you are not committed to it. This could exist in the form of a contract with yourself, you could tell people about your vision so that you remain committed and loyal to it, or, better still, you could give it life in the form of a plan of action. Most people follow their vision statement with a mission statement. A mission statement differs from a vision statement in that the latter only encapsulates what you want to do or be in the future, while the former describes what you want to do *now* in order to achieve your long-term aspirations. A mission is therefore a statement that produces goals and a plan of action.

Your mission is directed by your vision. You cannot have goals without direction, yet some people blindly craft goals and plans related to their careers and lives, in the hope of getting lucky. If you do not know where you are going, you have no basis for saying how you will get there successfully. Unfortunately, unlike a car, we cannot just park our lives in the garage until we are ready to go somewhere. Life happens, and unless you have direction, 'anywhere' becomes a destination. Unfortunately, very few people end up at the right destination by accident. You will always come back to your goals and plans, like you do your vision, and you might even refine those if and when your vision changes, or if you discover or learn better ways of achieving it.

Conclusion

A personal vision is a helpful tool which encourages you to reflect on your character, skills and attributes, as well as the things you focus your energy on. Although at times you may wander off course, become unsure or doubt yourself, you can always return to your vision. Such is the nature of purposeful journeys. Think of your vision as the GPS of your life: punch in the coordinates and it will take you to the right place. But, given our ever-changing environment, the route might change. The coordinates will remain the same, but along the way new roads will have been built, new buildings will have materialised, and some of the old roads may have been closed. Things happen which upset our carefully crafted plans. As Mike Tyson once said: 'Everyone has a plan until they get punched in the mouth.' If your GPS system is not up to date and current, if it has not kept abreast of changes, you might find yourself taking forever to reach your destination – if you get there at all. When your GPS system is up to date, all you need to do is enter the correct coordinates, get into the vehicle and follow the instructions. Life is the same. If you know where you are heading and you have the right skills and resources to get you there, you should not have a rough time. The road might be bumpy here and there, but you will most likely be prepared for any surprises, you will learn along the way, and will be better prepared for another journey further down the road.

I am not encouraging you to ignore significant others' birthdays, like my teacher suggested, but rather I am urging you to live a life beyond just dreams and wishes. I am encouraging you to remember that successful people do not rely on luck – they become lucky because they have a vision and work hard to achieve it. The first step to getting there is knowing where 'there' is. Here is a quote I rather like:

> To laugh often and much; to win the respect of intelligent people and the affection of children, to earn the appreciation of honest critics and endure the betrayal of false friends; to appreciate beauty, to find the best in others, to leave the world a bit better whether by a healthy child, a garden patch, or a redeemed social condition; to know even one life has breathed easier because you lived. This is to have succeeded.
>
> – Ralph Waldo Emerson

Table 14.1: Vision worksheet/template

Preparing for your personal vision statement
Name: Jim Mofokeng
Date: August 2013
What do I love/enjoy doing? Working hard My family Making a difference in the world Living honestly
What are the greatest achievements/the best moments of my life? My recent promotion The award from my children Planning and solving problems Spending time with my family
If I had all the best resources, and money was not a problem, I would do the following… Spend time with family Make the world a better place Help those in need
My most important values are… Accountability, responsibility, hard work, family first and community service.
I care about… My family The fate of society Making a difference
My personal vision statement is: My personal vision is to be honest at any time and place; achieve all my life's ambitions; be successful at my job; for my family to know that I am there for them in any situation and that I value them. I want to make a difference in the world and to die knowing that I changed at least one person's life in my lifetime.

References

Bennis, W. (2009). *On becoming a leader*. New York: Basic Books.

Brown, B. (2010). *The gifts of imperfection: Let go of who you think you're supposed to be and embrace who you are*. Center City, MN: Hazelden.

Brown, B. (2013). *The daring way™*. Unpublished course material.

Covey, S. (2004). *Seven habits of highly effective people: Powerful lessons in personal change*. New York: Free Press.

Eliot, T.S. (1959). *Four quartets*. London: Faber & Faber.

Senge, P. (1990). *The fifth discipline: The art and practice of the learning organization*. New York: Doubleday.

Yoeli, R. & Berkovich, I. (2010). From personal ethos to organizational vision: Narratives of visionary educational leaders. *Journal of Educational Administration, 48*(2), 451–467.

CHAPTER 15: Assessing the Situation and the First 100 Days

Shirley Zinn

Introduction

The objective of this chapter is to provide practical guidance to transitioning executives as they enter new positions.

The first 100 days in an executive role: Why having a plan is important

Thousands of executives transition into new roles every day, without receiving much guidance. Every transition is unique, hence there are no quick and easy recipes. Transitioning into a new role is never as simple as it seems. Even before the excitement of having been appointed in a new role has dissipated, the reality of what now faces you, as an executive, starts to sink in. This time is fraught with emotional, social, cultural and professional re-adjustments and alignments, all of which is very demanding and risky for any new incumbent, as well as for those s/he has to engage with. If you are a new appointee, the very strengths that led to your appointment could become liabilities not only for you, but also for those around you, if you do not have a plan.

Whether a new role comes via an internal promotion and whether you come from outside the organisation, a plan, detailing how best to navigate your way into and through the organisation, how to integrate swiftly and be effective as you step out of the starting blocks and grasp the organisational context, is key to your success. It is important to note that those executives entering from outside have a very different set of realities from those who are promoted from within. The situation becomes even more complex for executives working outside of their home country. But more about this later.

Having a 100-day plan is critical to ensuring the success of any newly appointed executive. It lays the foundation for understanding the organisation and its people, processes, systems, clients, key stakeholders, history and track record, as well as its desired future state. It also enables an executive to own the new role and understand what needs to be done, and to take charge. Essentially, an executive's efforts, along with those of his new company, need to be focused on the cycle of coming in, acclimatising, diagnosing, providing solutions, executing, and building off solid foundations.

The consequences of not having a 100-day plan

Almost 40 per cent of new leaders fail within the first 18 months. Executives transitioning into new roles are particularly vulnerable during this period, because they lack detailed knowledge of the challenges facing them in their new environment, and do not always know what needs to be done in order to succeed. Many have not yet developed the networks and key stakeholder relationships required to sustain themselves in their new position. Building credibility and trust with a new boss and team, requires that an executive understand where the low-hanging fruit are to be found right from the outset, as that will help a leader to achieve possible quick wins.

Practical steps in drawing up your 100-day plan

Take active steps to successfully integrate into your new role by adding value from Day One. It is vital to take into account what happens in the days leading up to Day One. Taking mental and physical 'time out' while you are between roles is very important. Often, putting your old job behind you is not that easy to do. The anxiety of taking on a new role, despite knowing that you were successful in your previous role, comes from having no guarantees that you will be equally successful going forward. Harbouring such doubts could be a debilitating factor.

According to Watkins, author of *The first 90 days* (2003), the transition period necessitates a very quick understanding of the strategy of a new business, an understanding of how best to work with your new boss, build a team, align with the organisational strategy, and also an understanding of the skills, systems and structure prevailing in the organisation. Watkins also refers to the possible organisational dispositions a new executive might encounter and may have to deliver on. These include

- turning the business around;

- starting a new business;

- positioning him/herself with a larger scope than the previous role necessitated; and

- taking on a large, high-profile special project.

From the day that your appointment in the new organisation is announced, following your departure from your previous firm, you need to start preparing to transition by accelerating your learning and beginning conversations with key stakeholders. Be conscious of any assumptions you make when meeting people, because some may become derailers in your attempts to build mutual trust and encourage collaboration.

Don't depend too heavily on the on-boarding process in your new organisation. Design your plan proactively, but remember that it is subject to change

Executive on-boarding plans are, admittedly (and, possibly, notoriously) not well implemented in most organisations, despite the best of intentions. Most executives find themselves tossed in at the deep end, where they either sink or swim. As a new incumbent – should you decide to stay – you rapidly need to determine how to stay afloat (i.e., swim, not sink). In many instances that much-needed support and enabling framework are not yet in place, and the on-boarding process is not much help. The failure rate in terms of outsiders coming in is much higher than amongst internal appointees. As the saying goes: you only get one chance to make a first impression. Negative perceptions at the start are very difficult to reverse. The challenge here is for you, as a new executive, to avoid thinking that your appointment was a flawed decision or even a mistake, otherwise retention risk could begin to creep in very soon after your start date. Many executives already know during their first week in a new company whether or not accepting their new role was a good move.

Underperformance, poor or low productivity, and even possible derailment could have severe consequences for any appointee, as well as for the team and the business.

Insight 1:
Get to know your team and your peers

Getting to know your team is a priority. People want to be respected at a fundamental level and they often harbour fears and anxieties about a new leader. They worry about what might happen to them, what will change, and whether this means they have to start from scratch. Connect with them, understand their strengths and how you might leverage those strengths and validate their efforts. Understand the cynics and naysayers, and try to proactively win them over. Give them purpose and meaning, and take into account their interests before you try to initiate any novel interventions.

Insight 2:
Align your plan with the reality on the ground

Before you rush into action, do the necessary due diligence study and diagnostics. Find out as much as you can about the strategy, history, dynamics, folklore and who's who of the firm. Yes, this could lead to information overload, but it will be well worth the effort. Also identify the best sources of information and start engaging with them. Be discerning and listen carefully without jumping to unfounded conclusions. Get to know your team, key allies, suppliers, the boss, analysts and top management, inter alia. Learn more about the evolution of the organisation's vision, mission, culture and values.

When the situation calls for immediate action in a direction you may not have anticipated during the lead-in discussions, reflect carefully on the goals you are committed to and be honest about whether they are attainable. Do not start out as a hero who later fails to deliver. You may have to revisit your coming-in strategy: I certainly had to do that during my time as an executive. The challenge is that you may not have the luxury of time, and without the benefit of insight or hindsight, this may result in mistakes. Small mistakes made in the early days can have a disproportionately huge impact on yourself, your team and the business.

Identify your key transition milestones, bearing in mind that everything is not always what it seems and that you may have to refine these.

Insight 3:
Engage key stakeholders

Engaging with key stakeholders means that you also have to navigate attitudes and emotions, and people's responses to you. This could be daunting, and your own EQ needs to kick in here. You might be that outsider who has to engage with the insider who did not get the job. Choose your words and actions carefully, so as not to further alienate potential supporters. Win them over instead. Take note of your own energy levels as you navigate your way through the organisation. Be prepared to encounter scepticism and cynicism, and prepare to be tested or even dismissed, as people adapt to the change which your presence brings. Always manage the impulse to become defensive, resentful or judgemental.

This does not mean you should accept abuse, but rather look for that balance that will ensure that you are eventually invited in and welcomed into the fold. Practising the art of not taking things personally and not over-reacting will stand you in good stead over the long term. This often requires courage in the extreme. Try not to conjure up conspiracy theories and do not accept the internal criticism that 'people are out to get you'. Fact is, you *will* be tested and provoked. Beware of this and avoid the trip-wires.

The challenge is to be conscious of others' scrutiny and to focus your efforts on building credibility and winning people over. Be professionally accessible, but guard against being overly familiar with anyone – this is a principle that should hold true throughout your career.

Where to start and what to do? Show people that you are willing to make tough calls, while remaining humane. Trying too hard to prove a point can be counter-productive. The trick is to know when to listen, when to remain silent, and when to speak out. These basic principles should also set the tone for your efforts to build a cohesive team.

Waves of change – a study by Jack Gabarro, of new general managers in various company settings – found that they typically plan and implement change in distinct waves (Watkins, p. 83): stage one (the first six months) focuses on their acclimatisation and transition, while stage two (six–12 months) is characterised by immersion; stage three (12–18 months) focuses on reshaping, and stage four (18–36 months) is about consolidation and deepening the executives' knowledge of the organisation.

Insight 4:
Avoid surprising people

Avoid surprising anyone – especially your boss. Even if you come up with a great idea, try to work with your team to ensure that it is a collective value-add, rather than a surprise aimed at adding 'brownie points' to your personal score-sheet. Conversely, do not only wave the 'we-have-a-problem' flag to the boss and your team, but try to work on and suggest solutions as a group. Also, never disparage the previous incumbent, in the hope of garnering praise for yourself. Denigrating past efforts or failures and those who played a role in them is not a helpful way to start off a new role. Rather do the diagnostic and try to resolve any existing issues by bringing workable solutions to the table. Clarify mutual expectations with everyone and deliver on goals. Make sure your performance deliverables are clear to you and your boss, even if you are the one who has to initiate clarifying discussions. Arrange your one-on-ones with the boss and make sure you are prepared for meetings. Negotiate your deadlines and the resources required before simply accepting the unachievable and failing because of that.

Every organisation has its politics, intangibles and topics which are not up for discussion. Ensure that you have a good grasp of this, so that you do not inadvertently step into something you are not too sure how to handle.

What usually happens on Day One? Like most new executives you will find yourself meeting with your line manager and filling in forms related to your choice of benefits, signing for office supplies, setting up your workstation and finding out about your allocated parking space. You may even, eventually, meet your team. You will most probably be handed reading material to bring you up to speed. Most organisations strive to provide more assistance than this, but few succeed – unfortunately. However, even while you are performing these seemingly mundane tasks, remember that you are being scrutinised and that people are watching you. As you settle in, find out who the people with influence are, who has the expertise, knowledge, status and control in the organisation, and who you need to connect with.

Insight 5:
DOs and DON'Ts

DOs:

- Build effective relationships with key stakeholders from Day One;

- Do your homework: glean and develop insights from your board, other executives, the community, analysts, regulators, your competition, customers, colleagues and employees across the business;

- Get to grips with the culture in the organisation and how the business is organised to work;

- Adjust to the new culture, and influence it as you mature in the organisation;

- Conduct your diagnostics before trying to put forward solutions. First identify and then prioritise where the biggest challenges and opportunities lie;

- Listen to dialogues and conversations within the organisation. Ask questions and gather intelligence;

- Identify the barriers to growth and performance facing you and your team, and put the requisite solutions in place as soon as possible. Hire people who will support your vision;

- Carefully plan milestones and quick wins (short, medium and long-term plans), and revise these as time passes and new information emerges;

- Build credibility and trust, and encourage people to join you on this journey;

- Avoid unchecked assumptions, over-zealousness and snap judgements;

- Build on the foundations of your strategy by turning great ideas into results;

- Share your plan with others and speak to your priorities;

- Manage your time and find a work-life balance that works for you;

- Be bold and courageous;

- Be values-led and vision-driven.

DON'Ts

- Avoid compiling never-ending bucket lists. The clock is ticking from Day One. That is the pressure you have to feel;

- Try not to get side-tracked: there are many issues that can distract you. Focus and stay on course;

- Do not let yourself be overwhelmed by critics, cynics and sceptics – listen, but move forward;

- Stop trying to fix things that do not require fixing. Prioritise, so that you maximise your impact.

My own story

During my career, especially in the previous role I held as Human Resources Director for the largest bank in Africa, I listened carefully to the strategic discussions that took place between the executives and the CEO during the recruitment process, and put together a plan that I thought would be responsive to their stated needs.

The final version of my 100-day plan was completed and ready a week before my start date at the bank. I was pleased about the fact that I was so organised, only to become dismayed when I found out that I was required to do something significantly different from what I had planned – something which had not been on my list at all.

My 100-day plan, entitled 'Ready to make a difference', read as follows:

Page 1: 'Hit the ground running'. Here, I drew up reminders for myself:

- Build relationships
- Understand your role and mandate ... listen more, talk less
- Take charge of your own on-boarding
- Engage key stakeholders and assess the management team
- Review governance and financial information
- Get a head start before the first day
- Get results – make an impact
- Think 'team'
- Get buy-in for one burning imperative
- Invest in early wins to inspire confidence
- Establish an aspirational destination
- Assess the facts of the current scenario and identify growth opportunities.

Page 2 was headed 'People Strategy', and bullet points included the following:

- Develop and execute a people strategy which is integral to the overall business strategy

- Business strategies define market, product and financial priorities. People strategies focus on the right combination and type of people, and the level of performance required to succeed. Consider

- skill sets to invest in

- transformation

- the performance levels required

- the number of employees needed to achieve the required productivity and service levels

- the total reward strategy that defines the employee value proposition

- the cost base associated with different segments of employees

- how to improve the return on human capital

- creating opportunities to dominate the market.

Page 3 outlined the following actions:

- Get a multi-dimensional view of the business. Look at the business from as many different perspectives as possible: that of board members, the executive team, industry gurus, colleagues, customers, the competition, front-line people.

- Ask: What are the biggest opportunities and challenges? What are the biggest strengths and weaknesses, challenges and opportunities facing the organisation as a whole? Gain a comprehensive understanding of these.

- Set goals that represent making a tangible difference. An example would be: 'We are going to set a goal of improving productivity and performance by doing more with less.'

- Determine what you need to do to deliver on your day job. You may have been hired because they thought you were great, but what are the basic nuts-and-bolts deliverables everyone expects from your department?

- Never waste a lunch. You will not be able to achieve your goals unless you establish a network of commitment, communication and support. Take lunch in the company canteen, rather than in your office, in order to maximise your ability to build relationships at all levels.

- Find out as much as you can about the c-suite. Who is the CEO, CFO, CIO, and the rest of the executive team? What are their credentials and track-records? What are their business philosophies and leadership styles? Understand who they are and how they work, so that you might build effective relationships with the key-decision makers on an informed basis.

The reality was that the bank had made a business decision, just prior to my arrival, that was to impact significantly on my envisaged plan. On Day One I was asked to put together a process which would see staff being retrenched. I will admit that this had not been on my radar at all, and it compelled me to weigh up whether I should stay or leave. I decided to stay and assist in driving the process with as much dignity as I could, given the scenario. The moral of the story is that a significant challenge might present itself and that you need to be ready for it, right from Day One.

Conclusion

Organisations hire people and want (or even expect) them to be successful. Your first few weeks are critical to your future in the organisation. You want to make an impression as swiftly as you can, before that window of opportunity closes. Generally, organisations do not plan to throw people in at the deep end and then watch them sink. Change creates fear and anxiety in most people, and this could lead to poor decision-making or serious mistakes. Change brings many more positives than negatives, but it really depends on the way in which you approach your new role, the team, the boss and the business environment in general. Research shows that most executives know within the first few weeks whether they have made a good or bad decision in terms of their career move. How you behave, and what you do during your first 100 days, can make or break your career. There are many ways to avoid failing during the first 12 months. It might be useful to employ a coach to assist you as you work through this period, because the journey can be quite lonely and solitary.

Your positive impact needs to be felt as soon as possible upon entry. Your words and actions during the first few days are critical, as wrong messages, misperceptions and mistaken impressions are near impossible to reverse once they have been created. 'Don't blow your new job' and do not be afraid to be bold and courageous at the same time. Ensure that you deliver sustainable results, because in the end that is what matters, and that is what will move you forward in the organisation.

CHAPTER 16: Leading and Aligning the HR Function

Seshni Samuel

Establishing the right structure and culture for organisational success

Have a concrete understanding of your organisation's core purpose

At the heart of every great and enduring organisation is a core vision, an ideal or a purpose that influences and guides the ethos, culture, spirit and direction of that organisation. It is vitally important that this core purpose or reason for existence be authentic, embracing and inclusive – after all, this purpose must enable and empower individuals and teams within the company to align their own sense of purpose and ambition with that of the organisation.

An aligned sense of purpose is a critical foundational step in promoting employee engagement. One could argue that to succeed and thrive in growing, innovative and rapidly changing emerging economies, engaged employees are even more important. Engaged employees expend discretionary effort and show greater loyalty, going above and beyond in delivering on goals, meeting client expectations, and being brand ambassadors and advocates for the organisation.

As an HR executive establishing the right structure and culture for organisational success starts with having an in-depth and honest understanding of your organisation. With an authentic understanding, you can then define those cultural attributes that are required (within your employee population and by external stakeholders) to feed and underpin success, allowing you to attract, develop and retain the right calibre and quality of talent in your market to compete effectively. Further to effectively drive success, this understanding of core purpose and the culture it influences must not only be vested in management, but in all employees, as well as clients and other stakeholders that the organisation works with.

Aligning the HR function with the organisation requires HR to have an authentic understanding of an organisation's core purpose and the culture required to underpin its success, it further requires HR to work with other functions across the business to ensure that this purpose and culture are embraced both internally and externally in all organisational processes to create resonance.

Allow employees, clients and communities to align with this compelling core purpose

When employees find personal alignment and a sense of identification between the broader purpose of the organisation and their personal goals, there is a better chance that these individuals will be engaged and motivated to help the organisation succeed.

The essential questions are *Why?* and *What?* Your employees are constantly asking themselves, Why does this matter to me? Why should I do this? What is my company trying to achieve? What am I achieving?

When employees can deeply connect to a compelling *Why?* and *What?*, they will be able to work out the *How?* by themselves, and will do so in innovative ways that help the company adapt and grow. The more transcendent this core purpose is, the greater the latitude it allows for directional creativity, the greater the level of employee and client identification it will achieve.

Consider an organisation such as Virgin, which has managed to embrace the concepts of 'fun', 'breaking the boundaries' and 'making life easier' across a variety of sectors, from healthcare to telecoms to airlines, which resonate with both clients and employees who seek those values. Virgin's larger-than-life CEO, Richard Branson, actively reinforces this culture and ethos even in his personal life, intrinsically reinforcing this culture internally and externally.

Organisations achieve organisational shift and market-leading growth when employees feel they can identify with the organisational purpose, its culture and values, and believe that within the organisation there is space for them to perform at their full potential. Imagine how powerful your organisation would be if it created an environment that allowed everyone within it to operate at their full potential. This power is amplified when external society, your clients and communities, identify as strongly with your organisational ambitions as your employees do. This power is diluted when your external and your internal identity do not align. It is possible to be successful for a period of time without a core purpose, but it is not sustainable and you will not be capitalising on your full growth potential either.

Jim Stengel, in his book *Grow* (2011), explores how organisations that have successfully identified their core purpose, vision or ideal, use this to power and fuel their growth and sustainability. Stengel compared the performance of companies, over a 50 year period, that communicate and live their purpose with those that are inconsistent and unclear on this issue, and found that companies with clear purpose outperform those without, by a factor of 400 per cent.

Knowing why the organisation exists, what it stands for and aspires to achieve, helps employees, clients and society to easily identify and align with the organisation's ambitions. Similarly, a lack of clarity creates dysfunction and disempowerment. A core purpose that resonates and is lived both internally and externally, guiding all decisions and activities, builds trust, credibility and sustainability, and empowers the desired 'right' activities.

Core purpose builds trust, which is critical in emerging markets

This organisational identity is even more important in emerging markets, where an organisation may not have full brand awareness or where it is trying to establish a corporate identity or brand.

In many emerging markets, the public and the private sector have been uneasy bedfellows, thanks to seeds of distrust being sown over long periods of time, and watered on both sides by histories of colonialism, corruption and exploitation.

Emerging markets are faced with many investment opportunities, while striving to establish their own identities and achieve their ambitions. Emerging markets are confronted with the challenge of capitalising on this important period in their economic history – a time of great opportunity that could leave a long-term legacy which benefits their people and society, if leveraged correctly.

Those organisations that different countries, companies and communities within emerging markets choose to work with, and whom they come to rely on, are those they can trust the most. Trust is built when organisations understand their core purpose and act in accordance with it.

Always act in accordance with the core purpose to build brand, credibility and resonance

EY (previously Ernst & Young) is one of the world's largest professional services organisations providing audit, tax, advisory and transaction services. I currently serve as EY's Talent leader for Europe, Middle East, India and Africa. At EY we are united through our global purpose, 'To build a better working world for our people, our clients and our communities.' We believe that as a leading professional services firm the insights and quality services we deliver help build trust and confidence in capital markets and in economies the world over. We develop outstanding leaders who team to deliver on our promises to all our stakeholders. In doing so we play a critical role in building a better working world for our people, our clients and our communities. Simply put, we strive to make business work better, with the conviction that when it does so the world works better.

This need for better business and confidence in capital markets is even more important in emerging markets. Our purpose guides our activity. We want our activity to resonate with our people, our clients, our communities, governments and regulators, wherever in the world we operate. All these parties can expect from us the highest standards of corporate conduct as we work towards a common good.

Our global organisational purpose, 'building a better working world', steers every individual in our organisation and underpins our values and behaviours. In acting out this purpose we are involved in a number of initiatives that allow us to align our goals as an organisation with those of our clients, our people and our communities. An example is our commitment to entrepreneurship. As part of delivering on our purpose, we focus time, energy and resources in working with and supporting aspiring entrepreneurs, helping them to make a success of, and grow, their businesses. Our employees are motivated by the work they do in helping entrepreneurs and it, in turn, helps many of them with their personal ambitions to make a difference and have an impact by creating jobs and driving economic activity. We further work alongside and align with other organisations that support entrepreneurship globally, such as Kiva, a non-profit micro-financing organisation, NFTE-Network for Teaching Entrepreneurship, Endeavour, a network focused on developing high-impact entrepreneurs. We also work with schools that support entrepreneurship, such as the African Leadership Academy. We host the World Entrepreneur of the Year function that brings together the exceptional entrepreneurs we work with in each country where we operate, providing a global platform to celebrate and acknowledge entrepreneurial achievements. When we do this we reinforce our commitment to help build a better working world, and also create alignment internally and externally that further supports our core purpose. There are many other examples of activities that we drive to reinforce this core purpose, both internally and externally on a continuous basis.

Many organisations sell themselves short by creating a purpose which is linked to being Number 1, achieving a growth rate of X, or a turnover of Y. While these may be worthy ambitions or milestones in tracking their progress, they should not be confused with an overall purpose, ideal or vision.

Having a transcendent purpose, vision or ideal helps companies to win the hearts and minds of their employees and clients. Sometimes this needs to be clearly articulated, as we have done at EY, but even if this is not done, the question to ask is: Are we living our purpose, and what are people's perceptions in this regard?

Even in emerging market countries, where Google does not do campus recruitment, the company can frequently be found topping graduate employee brand surveys. Google has become a beloved employee brand, representing its anti-establishment stance and philosophy through statements like: 'You can make money without being evil', 'You can be serious without a suit', and 'Work should be challenging and the challenge should be fun'. Google's cultural philosophy statements reinforce the casual, fun environment they want to establish, which, in turn, stimulates creativity and innovation – elements that are critical to their organisational success. Further, their famous Googleplex work environment reinforces this through multiple recreation facilities and free nutritious snacks and meals being made available to staff. To motivate employees, Google famously used a concept referred to as 'Innovation Time Off': software engineers were encouraged to spend 20 per cent of their work-time on projects that interest them. Time Off has increased revenue by inspiring some of Google's most successful projects, including products like Gmail, Google News and AdSense. Google has an intuitive understanding of the impact its culture has on the company's organisational success. This aspect is so important that the company created the role of chief culture officer (CCO), which is undertaken by their HR director. From both the EY and the Google examples it is clear that if the organisation's purpose does not translate into action, it will not truly help the brand or its growth.

Consider what it will take to make your brand a beloved brand, within emerging markets. It has to be authentic to who you are as an organisation, for example at EY we have opened business centres in emerging nations that promote business, opportunity and economic activity in these markets, helping both new and existing investors navigate the landscape and set themselves up for success. (For an example of our Africa Attractiveness thought leadership see http://www.ey.com/ZA/en/Issues/Business-environment/EY-africa-attractiveness-survey-2014 or google 'Africa Attractiveness'. Similar thought leadership can be found for other emerging markets.)

A clear core purpose enables an organisation to attract, retain and develop the right people

Intuitively, we all know that attitude influences success. Individuals who embrace the right attitude in life see opportunities where others see unsolvable dilemmas, they act on these opportunities and convert them to success stories. They believe in themselves and their ability to influence and impact their destiny. For most individuals, these attitudes and perceptions are formed very early in life. Some psychologists estimate that by the time a child turns seven, all of his/her core values have already been formed. Many organisations spend a great deal of time focusing on instilling organisational values in employees, but we can only appeal to values which already exist in the people we bring into our organisations. We can reinforce these values and appeal to them, but very rarely can we create them. We can 'water' these values and behaviours and help them flourish, but we do not plant the seeds. We cannot appeal to attitudes and values whose seeds have not been planted. Establishing the right culture for your organisations starts with the people you allow into the organisation, and vice versa: the people you allow into your organisation will influence your culture. If an organisation is clear on its purpose and value, it will attract people who also prize those attributes which help to reinforce culture and engagement.

Having the right culture and purpose allow you to win the war for talent in emerging markets

There is an exacerbated war for talent in emerging markets. Infrastructure and development backlogs mean that most public education systems do not deliver on the skills and needs of a growing market. Most countries have laws requiring skills transfer and the adequate representation of locals vs. expatriates. While mature markets offer valuable skill sets, expatriates are far more expensive than locals and provide lower levels of sustainability.

Universum, a global company that surveys students, highlights that emerging market companies without a valued employee brand may need to pay up to twice as much, to attract the same calibre of talent. More often than not they fail to attract any top talent, which creates a cycle of mediocrity. Many global organisations battle to understand why they are extremely successful in mature economies, but less so in emerging markets. Executives must bear in mind that the quality of talent that a brand attracts in a mature market may not be the same in an emerging market, especially if the employee brand and core brand are not being reinforced and lived to the same extent in those emerging markets. Conversely, there are some organisations whose brand is stronger and more powerful in emerging markets and can be a powerful lever for growth and attracting talent and resources to supplement other parts of the organisation.

This battle will only be intensified into the future as mature markets fail to produce enough people of employable age. Both mature and emerging markets will compete for skilled talent from emerging markets. According to a 2012 World Economic Forum report, by 2030 the United States must add 26 million workers to its talent pool in order to sustain the average 1-4 per cent GDP growth seen over the last 20 years, while Western Europe will require 46 million additional employees. As globalisation makes it easier for talent to move across borders we might see a brain drain from emerging markets to mature markets, unless emerging markets also find ways to create more attractive, stable environments. We are already seeing salaries in emerging markets grow at higher levels than mature markets as we begin to compensate for this effect.

Bring the right people into your organisation who will reinforce and build on the desired organisational culture

Organisations, which represent the collective consciousness of the individuals within them, also need a system of beliefs, behaviours and attitudes that will enable them to succeed and grasp opportunities in the market. This collective consciousness manifests as the organisational culture, which is influenced by all within the company, but is heightened by the behaviours, beliefs and attitudes of those in leadership and in positions of authority. *It is critically important that the leaders of organisations live, lead, understand and support the organisational culture.* Ensuring that organisations have the right leaders in emerging markets, who can carry and uphold the company culture, is critical.

In his book *Good to great* (2001), management guru, Jim Collins, reflects on how the culture of an organisation often trumps strategy. When culture aligns and underpins the organisational strategy we have the makings of a successful organisation. Collins further highlights the value of bringing the right people into the organisation, stressing that having the right people 'on the bus' is more important than having the bus facing in the right direction. If you have the right people on the bus, they will steer the bus accordingly.

Organisational culture influences success

In my previous role as partner within our Enterprise Resourcing Planning (ERP) business unit, I had the opportunity to implement systems in both emerging and mature markets, and to advise boards and steering committees on managing ERP implementation risk. After spending a few weeks in an organisation, you can, with a high degree of success, predict whether their ERP implementations will fail or succeed. Having a technically successful implementation is easy and linear – depending on the technical abilities and management of the ERP project team, of course. But, whether the business actually attains the intended benefits of the system implementation, supports the use of the system and is prepared to change the way it works by using the system to its competitive advantage and as a platform to enhance growth and agility, depend largely on the culture and leadership of that organisation.

Why do some organisations successfully implement systems such as SAP and use them as a platform for excellence while others fail, despite using the same implementation partner? A large part of the answer lies in the organisational culture. It is these experiences that have underscored to me the importance of leadership, culture and organisational development in creating a platform for organisational success.

Make diversity and inclusiveness part of your DNA

For any organisation to be successful, it must be able to represent the market within which it operates. This in turn will support access to and understanding of local markets.

A diverse team, led by an inclusive leader who encourages teaming and collaboration, can bring out the best in every member of the team, by capitalising on every individual contributing to their full potential. The financial benefits of diverse teams have been well established through several studies.

The diversity agenda is critical in emerging markets because many governments are realising that to be globally competitive they need to create opportunities for all their people and they therefore use legislation to promote companies to follow through.

The talent pool in emerging markets is diverse and a failure, for example, to be able to attract women to an organisation, will not allow you to capitalise on the full talent pool available. Diversity supports innovation and innovation is critical to success in rapidly evolving emerging markets. For example, the technology innovations in mobile banking in East Africa created entirely new markets for previously unbanked populations and redefined the need for a 'bricks and mortar' bank.

A diverse and inclusive culture where employees feel free to be themselves, and believe that opportunities to achieve success are equally available to all who work hard and distinguish themselves, improves employee engagement and motivation.

Key cultural components of success in emerging markets are adaptability to change and organisational readiness for change

Emerging markets offer many opportunities. It is estimated that in Africa, by 2020, the population of working-age people will be greater than that of India and of China. Africa's rate of urbanisation is one of the fastest the world has ever seen. A booming population could help Africa capitalise on opportunities – much like the baby boomer generation did for America – but this will only happen if those employees are skilled and equipped to meet the challenges of the future. Alternatively, it could be one of the greatest risk factors Africa will face, should its population's basic needs not be adequately met.

Organisations that quickly recognise and act on those opportunities soon gain an advantage. Circumstances and market conditions may also change rapidly – again, those firms that are more adaptable and flexible will benefit. It is an environment in which new players can quickly establish themselves (e.g., Capitec and Equity Bank in the financial sector) by embracing new mindsets within existing industries.

Case study: Culture change journey in EY Africa

EY is a leading professional services organisation, employing more than 152 000 people in over 140 countries. *Forbes* magazine voted EY the 'Best accounting firm to work for' (2012 and 2013) and the company has placed in the *Fortune* 'Top 100 companies to work for', for 14 consecutive years. EY is considered amongst the best companies to work for in almost every country we operate in. In 2013, the Universum global student survey positioned us as the second most attractive employer to work for in the world after Google. This is a considerable achievement for an organisation that is not consumer facing.

I joined EY in 2005 as a senior manager and became a partner in 2007. In 2011, I was appointed to the Africa executive team in the role of talent leader, EY's internal equivalent of HR director. In 2013, I was appointed to the EMEIA (Europe, Middle East, India and Africa) executive leadership team as the EMEIA Talent leader. In addition I sit in EY's Global Emerging Markets Committee.

EY is considered by many to be a leader in emerging markets. The company holds market-leading positions in India, China and the Middle East, and has the largest integrated professional services footprint across Africa, operating in 33 countries across the continent. EY believes in developing and emerging markets – the firm has invested more than $1 billion over the past five years in emerging markets, in particular Brazil, China, Africa and India.

One of the projects that has been the most meaningful to me during my career, is the Africa culture change journey that the African executive leadership team managed in 2011, under the guidance of EY Africa's CEO, Ajen Sita. This case study explores this project.

EY Africa used to operate as 33 separate and independent country units, but these have since come together in a single integrated professional services firm, to act as a cohesive force with the ambition to powerfully and seamlessly fulfil client needs across the continent.

For us, a critical part of the 'integrated Africa' solution lay in creating and supporting an organisational culture that would allow the company to meet its strategic objectives in an authentic and empowering way; a culture that would allow us to be one firm across Africa, meeting the needs of our clients for seamless, consistent, exceptional service across Africa, while still being flexible, agile and responsive to local market conditions and needs, and respecting the diversity of the continent that we were trying to bring together.

As we undertook this culture change journey there was the realisation that the Africa integration solution transcended processes, legal entities and systems. So began the search for a unique organisational culture that would define and unite the different offices. We called this journey 'Our FY', in recognition of the fact that a shared aspirational organisational culture belongs to all those who create it and keep it alive.

Annually, at EY we participate in a global people survey, which allows us to understand and compare the level of employee engagement in Africa with our global organisational and industry norms. The survey revealed how our people felt at a specific point in time, measurable on a scale of 1 to 5 across a range of important questions, but as a leadership team we needed more. We did not know why employees felt engaged to the extent that they did, or what else could be done about improving levels of engagement. As a result I became very interested in the

Bluprints process, which seemed ideal to help us define and further live a culture that could drive our growth.

In August 2010 we launched the process, based on the Bluprints concept. We began the journey by asking all 5 400 of our employees across the continent, the same simple question: 'What should we be doing more of, and less of, in order to become the professional services firm that builds a better working world across Africa for our people, our clients and our communities?'

The thought was that this simple question would allow all our people to contribute to building a shared and celebrated organisational culture, since the process gave our employees a platform and an opportunity to share their views.

The online process required feedback on EY Africa's business enablers (i.e., what we should do more of) and its business disablers (i.e., what we should do less of) as highlighted below:

- *Top line* (business enablers – what we should do more of). These are our non-negotiable factors, behaviours, practices and principles that
    - are good for EY Africa;
    - we *have to have;*
    - must be maximised.

- *Bottom line* (business disablers – what we should do less of). These are our non-negotiable factors, behaviours, practices and principles that
    - are bad for EY Africa;
    - we cannot *afford to have;*
    - must be minimised.

In an empowering and consultative process, 84 per cent of EY Africa's employees across the Africa sub-area gave input into what to do more of and what to do less of. A total of over 11 000 inputs were received from employees in the form of free feedback, i.e., respondents were free to express themselves. The feedback was then analysed and categorised into 74 distinct themes (top and bottom line).

Next, employees were asked to vote on the most important top- and bottom-line themes respectively. It appeared that employees valued the sense of empowerment gained from participating in this process. An important part of the process is trusting that your employees intuitively know and understand what the right behaviours are that will support organisational success. The harder part is living this and bringing it to life, just as most of us know what is required to lead fit and healthy lives, but few of us have the discipline to follow through.

Once the top ten enabling and disabling themes had been identified, employees were asked to submit creative ideas to represent the concept of the theme as a visual icon. The use of iconography and symbols was instrumental in creating and reinforcing company culture, by using a right-brain language to create associations.

More than 1 300 creative ideas were submitted as part of an exciting competition. The executive had very interesting debates on which icons would best reflect our culture, and this made an interesting change from the spreadsheets and presentations which we were far more comfortable with. Dealing with pictures and icons forces people to use different ways of thinking and creates new visual maps and associations. Think about something that exerts a powerful cultural influence. Religion, for instance: much of this is established through ritual and symbolism. So, too, an organisational culture needs to be reinforced through rituals, symbolism and rites of passage.

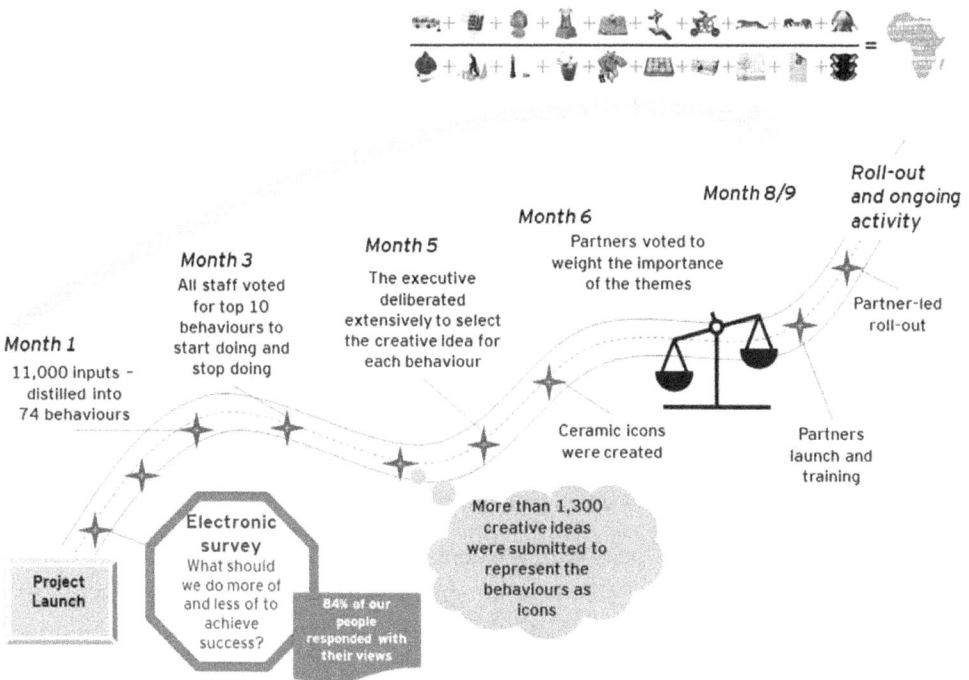

Figure 16.1: Implementation process – defining and implementing behaviours for success

The result: EY Africa's own winning formula as an organisation, defined by its people across the Africa sub-area. 'Our EY' reinforces EY Africa's purpose and creates an EY Africa identity, giving employees a unique EY culture and sense of belonging. It provides a mechanism for cultural integration across all the countries EY operates in, which is vital for underpinning much of the financial, process and system integrations the business has already undertaken. 'Our EY' represents a platform for ongoing employee engagement and ownership of a co-created 'leading people' culture that reaches across geographies, languages and cultural barriers.

Why was this exercise so important to us and what did we hope to achieve?

- It helped to underpin the cultural integration of multiple offices and partnerships across Africa, through a unified, cultural identity. The process united us as an organisation through a common culture (set of behaviours) that we want to drive across Africa, thus helping us to achieve trust and collaboration internally, and to provide consistent, exceptional client service externally. It further enabled us to capitalise on our Africa integration and to define how we collaborate and share EY culture across Africa;

- In the process we gave voice to and created a platform for all our people across Africa, to share and express their views on the common culture we want to develop for our combined success. This helped to establish a sense of participation, ownership, involvement and excitement, i.e., engagement;

- We could engage all our people on the topic of what they believe we need to start doing and stop doing, by allowing them to contribute to defining the EY we want and need, going forward. They did this not only for themselves, but also for our clients and our communities, thus helping to define our unique formula as an organisation aimed at achieving even greater success in the future. This, in turn, helped us understand the organisation-wide perspective on those unique cultural attributes that would lead us to succeed. Every individual and country had a unique role to play in helping to define the 'Our EY' Africa culture;

- The 'Our EY' formula helped us solidify our purpose, hone our identity and expand our sense of belonging to a larger EY Africa family, which has facilitated our integration into our EMEIA and into the global organisation as a whole;

- Every six months we measure the extent to which we are living our formula. This is followed up by POD (people organised to deliver) sessions, where the findings are discussed. We identify solutions and interventions which help us drive sustainability and ownership of a common culture;

- New employees join the organisation on a daily basis and at every level, through 'Our EY', and even if people do not consciously feel they are executing the strategy, they understand what behaviours are required in order to contribute to the success of our organisation in everything they do every day;

- 'Our EY' has helped unite us across Africa by creating a shared EY culture across our sub-area, in support of our values, our performance, our work environment and how we add value for our clients;

- Going forward, 'Our EY' continues to help us achieve and live our purpose, by reinforcing our unique identity and sense of belonging, and giving us all a voice, We can therefore celebrate and perpetuate a shared culture across Africa, as defined by the way we live our values.

Figure 16.2: Example of "icon gallery" displayed in EY offices

A dictionary was created to facilitate a common understanding of those behaviours that support our desired EY culture.

Table 16.1: Our dictionary

Winning with our people	<ul><li>Inspired, motivated and empowered people</li><li>A great place to work</li><li>A leading people culture</li><li>We are in this together</li></ul>
Teaming and integration	<ul><li>Work as one firm</li><li>Team players who can depend on each other</li><li>An environment of trust and support</li></ul>
Attract and retain the best talent	<ul><li>Recruit, reward, recognise and retain outstanding talent</li><li>Provide opportunities and experiences for excellence</li><li>Invest in future leaders</li><li>Continuous learning and development</li><li>A lifelong relationship</li></ul>
Performance and results driven	<ul><li>Deliver high performance and impact</li><li>Make a difference to our people, client and communities</li><li>Achieve our goals and targets</li></ul>
Adaptable to change	<ul><li>Have a 'can do - make it happen' attitude</li><li>Be agile, flexible and creative</li><li>Use new ideas to continuously improve</li><li>Grow with our clients</li></ul>
Quality in everything we do	<ul><li>Live and act professionally</li><li>Demonstrate quality with exceptional client service</li><li>Set ourselves the highest standards</li><li>Strive for excellence in all we do</li><li>Take ownership and accountability</li></ul>

Effective leadership	• Motivate, inspire and empower others
	• Always do the right thing
	• Act boldly, courageously and decisively
	• Believe in our ability to achieve great things
	• EY ambassadors and advocates
Growing our business	• Obsessed with market growth and leadership
	• Execute with passion, energy and enthusiasm
	• Drive a performance sales culture
	• Be focused and disciplined in achieving our goals
	• Build our competitiveness
Living diversity and inclusiveness	• Diversity strengthens us and we celebrate it
	• Respect and appreciate each other
	• Achieving full potential for all our people
	• Leverage diversity to achieve more
	• All our people belong and have a place
Positive impact on our clients	• Exceptional client service
	• Truly connect with our clients and understand their needs
	• Bring strategic and innovative solutions to the table
	• Build strong relationships
Arrogance	• Assuming we know best
	• Lacking humility
	• Resting on our laurels
Poor communication	• Lack of timely feedback
	• Unclear outcomes
	• Too much, too little, too late
Destructive behaviours	• Silo mentality
	• Backstabbing and favouritism
	• Empire building, gossip and cliques
	• Failing to share knowledge and information

Negativity	• Dwelling on the negative • Discouraging colleagues • Pessimism and cynicism
Being reactive	• Not attentive to client expectations • Ill-discipline, poor planning and knee-jerk responses • Missing deadlines and dropping the ball
Accepting mediocrity	• Permitting non-performance • Accepting sub-standard work • Allowing second best • Letting our standard drop
Unrecognised performance	• Failure to recognise and reward • Taking others for granted • Unappreciative • Overlooking talent
Bureaucracy	• Unnecessary administration • Inefficient processes • Prolonged decision making
Neglecting our clients	• Taking clients for granted • Losing focus on clients and markets • Lack of preparation and understanding of clients' needs
Lack of clarity	• Unclear goals and direction • Blind to the bigger picture • Lack of purpose or meaning

Strengthen the global, empower the local

Africa's social systems, beliefs and cultures are as diverse as its peoples and as disparate as its climates. While 'Our EY' gave us the opportunity and the platform to unite our people across the continent with a common set of behaviours, the success of this initiative lies in its ability to be understood and adopted. A key component of the firm's vision and strategy is what we refer to as 'Strengthen global, empower local'. The challenge: to successfully launch one impactful Africa-wide formula, with buy-in from the Africa-wide executive leadership, while continuing to empower local partners in their country units.

The formula was introduced to employees by local partners in each business/country unit through POD sessions. With each such session limited to 20 employees, over 250 POD sessions were conducted across 28 African countries. Although only one formula (co-created by all employees) was discussed, the issues which were uncovered and the questions probed during the sessions, remained pertinent to each local office.

Every six months, employees have a chance to voice their opinion on how successfully the formula is celebrated. 'Our EY' voting is conducted via an electronic survey, and is open to all employees simultaneously, so that they in effect rate the same behaviours. The results, however, are sliced, diced and segmented into business- or country-specific categories so as to give meaningful feedback to management, raise discussions and drive appropriate interventions which are locally relevant.

Live it and breathe it

Sustaining a culture and embedding it within the organisation is as important as defining it. To embed the behaviours in the organisational culture and daily work interactions, the formula is integrated into the company's language. Internal communications continue to reinforce the 'Our EY' message: when a major pursuit is successful it is celebrated, with recognition given to the pursuit team for demonstrating a 'positive impact on our clients'.

On a larger scale, the firm launched an Africa-wide recognition programme, 'Make a difference'. The aim is to more frequently give recognition to staff, for instance when values-driven behaviours are displayed, to promote the feeling of being a valued employee, and to get into the habit of saying 'thank you'. The programme consists of awarding beautifully made coins ('Make a difference' coins) to employees who demonstrate good 'Our EY' behaviours. At the start of the programme, the coins were awarded to management and leadership, with the proviso that the person who receives the coin can pass it on to any other staff member, at any level, in any country. In the process, the coins function as self-sustaining currency that helps to drive 'Our EY' behaviours. In addition, the programme saw the launch of the 'Our EY' internal website, where individuals can pay tribute to the person to whom they award the coin.

The programme helps employees connect with one another, and across business units and countries. It is also innovative as it empowers each employee who is recognised, to recognise somebody else in return. There are no guidelines on which behaviours are important, nor is there merit recognition: the sole requirement is that they simply need to be 'Our EY' behaviours. Individuals can therefore use the programme in a way that is meaningful to them. Since the website has been launched across Africa, it offers employees insight into the personal side of colleagues in other countries.

Figure 16.3: Example of recognition coins that are awarded to those who live the behaviours according to colleagues

When designing 'Make a difference', the coins were intended to form the heart of the programme: they not only represent a self-sustaining currency that helps employees live the 'Our EY' behaviours, but are valuable in monetary terms. The silver-coated coins feature the wording: 'Thank you for living "Our EY" and making a difference', along with a compass to indicate that the business is moving in the right direction, every time colleagues give recognition to one another. Being in possession of a coin means an individual has to walk over to someone else to hand it over. This encourages employee interaction – something which is a challenge for employees in consulting environments, as they frequently have to travel to client sites. 'Our EY' is an Africa-wide programme with a personal touch.

Africa is sometimes considered and spoken of as one country/region, yet it is home to over 2000 languages and cultures. 'Our EY' has found expression in the universal language of art, to represent the behaviours created by its own people and to unite the manifold cultures of Africa into a single EY Africa culture. The organisation continues to innovate in respect of ways to further sustain and embed 'Our EY' in everything we do. 'Our EY', in turn, continues to connect EY Africa's employees across the continent and empower them to bring the formula to life.

Tips for a successful organisational cultural journey

- Understand the business needs – what works for one business may not work for another. It is vital to know what you are trying to achieve and why it is critical for success;

- Commitment is imperative – ensure that you receive ongoing executive and partner support and involvement;

- Create an empowering platform which allows everyone to contribute and to have a voice;

- Foster innovation and creativity by capturing the imagination and spirit of the organisation;

- Launch meaningful initiatives by delivering messages that are relevant to the local context;

- Work towards sustainability by embedding the organisation's culture in existing processes and systems.

In conclusion, leading and aligning the HR function to achieve organisational objectives requires a robust and authentic understanding of the organisation, the strategy and objectives, and the culture required for success. This understanding will allow the HR director to drive organisational success through core purpose and culture, rather than projects. Culture creates a viral, social, longer-lasting fabric for success. Culture is unique, harder to copy and offers a sustainable competitive advantage in rapidly changing emerging markets.

References

Collins, J. (2001). *Good to great*. New York: Harper Collins.
Stengel, J. (2011). *Grow: How ideals power growth and profit at the world's greatest companies*. New York: Crown Business.

CHAPTER 17: Designing the HR Function

Theo Veldsman

Introduction

It is widely recognised that the way organisations are designed has a profound effect not only on an organisation's ability to execute its strategy successfully, but also on optimal resource deployment and utilisation; the efficiency of its mode of working; the optimal flow of people energy; the level of engagement by people; the healthiness of an organisation's culture and dynamics; consequently on the overall performance of an organisation and ultimately on an organisation's continued sustainability.

It is indeed possible to compete by design (Galbraith, Downey & Kates, 2005; Nadler & Tushman, 1997; Smith, Zimmerman & Willet, 2003; Veldsman, 2002). This is even truer in the emerging world order (Kelliher & Richardson, 2012; Tofaya, 2010).

Organisational design (OD) equates to the operating model of the organisation. Formally defined, OD (or organisational architecture) pertains to the logic required by an organisation (or part of the organisation – in this case, the HR function) to define, unlock and deliver ongoing value for stakeholders.

In short, OD equates to an organisation's delivery logic. It entails architecting (or configuring)

1. the grouping of the organisational work, to be found in its core work and support processes, into work domains (or units) (the *horizontal design*);

2. awarding the requisite level of work to work units and their work roles (the *vertical design*); and

3. building the necessary integrating, coordinating mechanisms and governance needed to ensure that all of the forementioned work together synergistically and accountably (the *lateral design*) (cf. Galbraith, 1995; 1997; 2006; 2008; Galbraith, Downey & Kates, 2005; Kesler & Kates, 2011; Nadler & Tushman, 1997; Stanford, 2007; Veldsman, 2002).

As posited in preceding chapters, in a knowledge society people have moved centre stage in securing the future, sustainable success of organisations (Ulrich, Brockbank, Younger & Ulrich, 2012, 2013; Wright, Boudreau, Pace, Sartain, McKinnon & Antoine, 2011). The architecting of an effective and efficient OD for the HR function is thus mission critical for the organisation, since the function provides the people expertise to the organisation which is essential in enabling the organisation to make people central to its success. Hence, one of the building blocks of the People Effectiveness Landscape, is the People Operating and Governance Architecture (POGA); i.e., the design of the HR function. POGA refers to how the HR professional community of the organisation architects the people management value chain (i.e., its people work) to ensure that the organisation's people are value unlockers and wealth creators, in this way capacitating the organisation to compete successfully and sustainably (Sparrow, Hird, Hesketh & Cooper, 2010).

The metaphor of a house best represents OD as the architecting of the organisation's delivery logic. The *overall house plan* represents the overall design of the organisation (its *strategic design*, as contained in the basic delivery shape, e.g., a functional, process or divisional design); the respective *rooms* which make up the house (its *tactical design*, as found in the design of its respective work units); and the *furniture* within each room (its *operational design*, made up of the constituent elements of a work unit, namely work portfolios, roles and teams).

The purpose of the chapter is to address the most effective design of the HR function. Put differently, to explicate the best, fit-for-purpose delivery logic for the function.

The chapter follows the contours of a high-level, strategic design process. (Thus, discussions about the tactical and operational designs of the HR function are excluded, given space constraints.)

The topics covered include

1. establishing the necessary preconditions for a successful OD intervention;

2. bringing the essential OD building materials on-site;

3. deciding on a basic delivery logic for HR;

4. building consequentially, the strategic horizontal (the house with its rooms); vertical (the requisite ownership and owners of rooms) and lateral HR ODs (living together in the house);

5. putting it all together into an integrated strategic HR OD (the overall house plan);

6. doing the strategic organisational design alignment (fitting the house into the townhouse complex); and, finally,

7. facing up to the design challenge of being a global organisation.

The chapter draws heavily on the following sources (that will not be quoted throughout, in order to enhance the readability of the chapter): Anand and Daft (2007); Brickley, Smith and Zimmerman (2003); Galbraith (1995, 1997); Galbraith, Downey and Kates (2005); Kesler and Kates (2011); Nadler and Tushman (1997); Roberts (2004); Stanford (2007); Veldsman (2002).

A high-level, strategic design process

Preparing the building site: Establishing the necessary preconditions for a successful OD intervention

The essential preconditions, which in fact prepare the organisation for a successful OD intervention, are the following:

- It is important to eradicate, upfront, any prevailing *myths regarding OD*, i.e., adopting the right frame of reference (or mindset) with respect to OD. Some of the more important myths to eradicate are:

    1. OD is *common sense or a dark art* of dubious reputation for which no (or, at most, a restricted) unproven body of knowledge exists. *Reality:* An extensive body of knowledge regarding OD exists;

    2. OD can be done on *the back of a cigarette box or a serviette*, preferably over a good bottle of wine, at the speed of lightning. *Reality:* A proper, well-considered and complete OD requires an integrated, systematic design process addressing all of the building blocks making up a fit-for-purpose OD;

    3. OD only involves rearranging boxes, titles, reporting lines, i.e., redrawing *organograms*. *Reality:* OD as the operating model of the organisation deals with an in-depth architecting of the delivery logic of an organisation. The drafting of the organogram is but one of the last steps in the OD process;

    4. It is possible to *build one's design around people and their expertise*, or to eliminate destructive interpersonal and team dynamics, however illogical the new design may be. *Reality:* OD as the operating model exists apart from the people who must staff up the design;

    5. *Imitating what others are doing*, frees you from asking tough questions about your own organisational design. *Reality:* You can learn from other designs, but in the end you have to go through the discipline imposed by the OD process, to arrive at your own fit-for-purpose design;

    6. OD does not require the shifting of *mindsets, frames of reference, attitudes and behaviour*. Going through the motions of rehashing the existing is good enough. *Reality:* The emerging world order, and the consequential reformulated, strategic positioning and strategy of your organisation require a fundamental rethink of your OD, i.e., how to set up and conduct your business effectively;

    7. OD equates to *business re-engineering*. *Reality:* OD is aimed at doing the right things in the right place with the required autonomy and governance, i.e., OD deals with the effectiveness of the organisation, and with doing the

right things. Re-engineering presupposes the design, and aims to enhance the efficiency of doing things right in the organisation: doing them quicker, better and simpler.

Only by dispelling the myths regarding OD upfront, and by embracing the true nature of OD as a critical organisational discipline and key leadership task, will an organisation be able to compete through design.

- Favourable readiness factors, critical to a successful organisational design intervention, are in place:

    1. *Sponsorship* for the intended OD intervention must be at the right organisational level relative to the organisational entity to be designed – at least at the top organisational level of the entity or one level up;

    2. A well-articulated *business case* must have been formulated for the OD intervention;

    3. The expected *benefits* of the new design must outweigh the *costs* of the OD intervention, including both the hard and soft benefits and costs. The assumption is that the impact of the new design will be measured;

    4. A shared agreement must exist on the *strategic intent* of the organisation – this forms the departure point for a fit-for-purpose design;

    5. A well-functioning *leadership community/team* with healthy dynamics exists. An effective design process and robust design need fierce, zero-based conversations in which there is no room for holy cows. Only if the former is in place, can the latter occur;

    6. An integrated, comprehensive and systematic *design process*, informed by leading OD practices, will be used. This process needs to be enabled through sound project management and change navigation. OD triggers widespread insecurities, challenges empires, disrupts relationships, upsets career paths, invokes destructive organisational politics and raises the spectre of retrenchments;

    7. There must be a willingness to allocate the necessary *resources* (time, people, money) to the OD intervention. A proper design process is resource intensive. A strategic design typically takes eight to 12 weeks; a tactical design for a work unit about six weeks, times the number of work units to be designed; a full-blown operational design covering all of the work units can take up to a year;

    8. The necessary *OD expertise*, at the requisite level of complexity, must be available, as determined by the OD need.

If the above preconditions are not in place, the likelihood of a successful OD intervention is slim. The OD intervention will cause more harm than good; lead to more organisational agony than organisational reinvention; and create more confusion and chaos than clarity and focus.

Bringing the essential OD building materials on-site

The assumption is that the organisation has been readied for the OD intervention; conditions are favourable for a successful intervention, or have been made favourable.

As the first formal step in the OD process, critical building materials must brought on-site, as they represent essential inputs into the building of a robust design.

The quality of the building material will significantly affect the robustness of the final design, and determine whether it is fit for purpose. The minimum requisite OD building materials are:

- A well-defined *need for a new/reconceived OD*, e.g. the HR OD, and the *expected benefits* the new design must bring about. Some of those OD needs could be a new strategic intent for the organisation or HR; a changed stakeholder relationship management model (e.g., a new shareholder); a shift in a key design given (e.g., deregulation, geographical expansion, technological innovation). It could also be a changed design criterion (e.g., greater client focus; enhanced capacity to act); and/or an immediate or envisaged change in an organisational success factor (e.g., speed of responsiveness; cost effectiveness). Another reason could be a newly appointed leader(ship) wishing to review the appropriateness of the existing OD. A major weakness may be present in the existing design, and this may impact negatively on organisational performance (e.g., poor organisational coordination; excessive, ongoing conflict between areas/units; unclear roles, responsibilities and accountabilities; duplication of activities which result in poor economies of scale; poor responsiveness to client needs; and/or inflexibility). Further reasons for OD include organisational growth/ expansion or a merger/acquisition;

- A sound diagnosis of the major *strengths and weaknesses of an existing design* – if a design is already in place. For instance, in the case of HR, OD strengths such as strong professional/technical expertise, and high professionalism, but weaknesses such as poor responsiveness, low client-centricity and poor migration of innovations across the organisation may be present;

- An in-depth understanding of the *organisational context* in which the organisation has to function. Examples include matching the design to the characteristics of the operating context of the organisation (e.g., hyper-turbulence; industry regulation) with its associated contextual complexity; the strategic intent of the organisation (e.g., innovation); the types, stakes and interests of stakeholders; and the availability of critical resources in the operating arena of the organisation.

The contextual complexity of the organisation needs further elucidation: Within the chosen/desired operating arena, an organisation – through its strategic choices – has to deal with a certain degree of contextual complexity (i.e., the league the organisation wants to play in). This degree of contextual complexity affects the nature and dynamics of the inner organisation context (i.e., the level at which the organisation wants to play the game, within its selected league). In turn, contextual complexity sets the complexity of the OD requirements imposed on the organisation by its operating arena.

The contextual complexity of an organisation is a function of five variables, namely the *space* and the *time boundaries* within which the organisation has to or wishes to operate; the *scope of the organisation* in terms of markets, customers and products/services; the *variety within the organisation* with respect to aspects such as strategic intent, policies and standards, work processes, design and culture; and the *degree and rate of change the organisation is exposed to.*

The contextual complexity which an organisation faces grows exponentially as the chosen *space boundary* of the organisation moves from a local to a global operating arena; the chosen thinking *time boundary* expands from short term (less than a year) to long term (longer than ten years); the *scope* of the organisation expands from a single product/service, one type of customer/client and one market to multiple, related (and even unrelated) products/services, customer/client and markets; the *variety* within the organisation to lead and manage the organisation effectively increases from a single to multiple strategic intents, policies and standards, sets of business processes, functionalities and success metrics; and the *degree and rate of change* shift from incremental to revolutionary.

- Identifying the *organisational givens* which impose constraints on the organisation's design, e.g., geography, technology, legislation and the contextual complexity of the organisation (see above). These givens need to be incorporated into the design. In the case of the given of a geographically dispersed organisation, for example, a regionalised design may have to be adopted;

- A complete map of the *core work and support processes, with their interdependencies,* which the organisation requires in order to get its work done. Figure 17.1 gives an example of such a high-level process map for HR, detailing its people value chain. The process map provides an overview of the work that needs to be done within the organisational space demarcated for (re) design. Critically important is considering a complete portfolio of processes along with complete processes in terms of the latest thinking about the area; correctly mapping the logical process flow of the work; and showing all interdependencies between process activities and between processes;

- A clear specification of the conditions that the organisation's design must facilitate, enable, encourage and provide for, i.e., its *design criteria* (usually between three and five prioritised criteria). The design must facilitate, enable, encourage and provide for a capacity to act; build focused competencies; enhance customer-centricity; promote teaming; result in the minimisation of duplication; and offer a one-stop service. The design criteria serve as ultimate reference point when debating and deciding which, among several different design options, is the best fit for purpose. In the case of the HR function, its design criteria need to be congruent with the design criteria applied to the overall organisation. Short descriptions (= definitions) need to be given of each criterion to clarify exactly what is meant by the criterion. This will make uniform the understanding of criteria, e.g., what is meant by client-centricity.

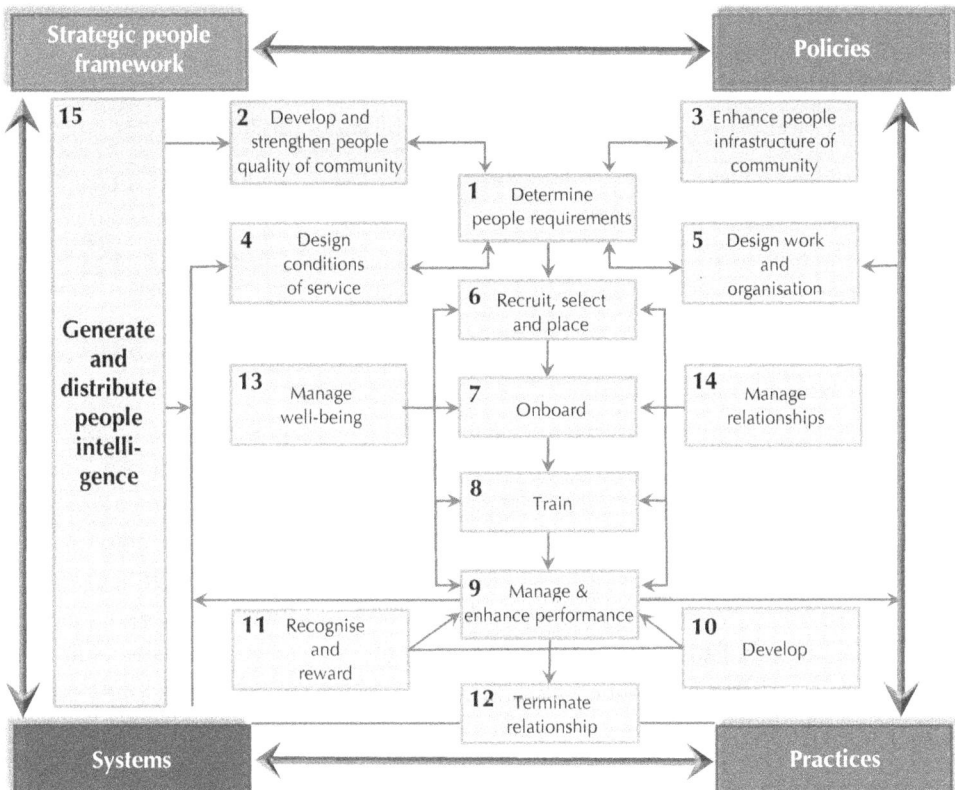

Figure 17.1: The work of HR – the people value chain

Currently, the widely accepted departure point (dominant design criterion) for HR is that of people professionals *partnering (= client-centricity)* with their clients (Ulrich, 1997; Ulrich & Brockbank, 2005). This implies taking co-responsibility with clients to bring about and maintain enabling and empowering conditions under which the organisation's people can contribute fully to its sustainable success, by ensuring that the right people are in the right numbers at the right time in the right place; able, willing, wanting and being allowed to perform with a sense of purpose; thereby giving the organisation a sustainable competitive edge in its chosen markets.

Given partnering as design criterion, there have been general shifts in the *overall engagement mode* people professionals employ when engaging with clients. The mindshift that has occurred is from being a technical specialist in a support and service role, for instance, to being a genuine business partner. Such mindshifts are given in Table 17.1.

Table 17.1: Mindshifts in the engagement mode of future-fit people professionals

From	To
• Product-centric	• Client-centric
• Technical solutions	• Business solutions
• Risk avoidance, reactive	• Risk-seeking, proactive
• Transactional contributions	• Transformational contributions
• Activity focus	• Output, value focus

• The crafting of a *design vision* ('A day in the life of … '), describing in narrative form how the organisation will look when it operates in accordance with its design criteria. The design vision greatly assists in conceptualising in real, concrete terms how the organisation will work when the design vision has become a daily reality. What is most helpful in this case, is to choose a metaphor to visualise more concretely, the new mode of working. A *sports* metaphor would be apt here: we want to work like a team of athletes (independent specialists making independent contributions); a relay team (the sequential handover of work, requiring cumulative efforts to achieve a shared goal); a soccer/rugby team (an interdependent team, performing together in real time to produce a joint result); or a volleyball team (an in-time multi-skilled, multi-tasking team tackling a piece of work as it arises). Or, a *music* metaphor: a symphony orchestra (outstanding specialists, working to the same 'score sheet' under the baton of a single, overall leader) vs. a jazz band (specialists working together creatively around a shared intention and outcome, taking clues from one another as the work unfolds).

Deciding on a basic delivery logic for HR

In the first formal step of design, the essential design building materials were brought on-site, for use in building a robust design. In the next design step, a fundamental choice must be debated, namely the *basic delivery logic* which must inform the design of the HR function, as aligned to the organisation's strategic intent and overall organisational design.

Figure 17.2 depicts the design axes in terms of which a basic logic delivery can be plotted. The emerging new world order is moving away, as per the design axes from either/or choices (e.g., a product/service *or* market/customer design logic). In this order, 'and' design logic choices need to be considered. In fact, nowadays they have become essential (e.g., a product/service *and* market/customer delivery logic).

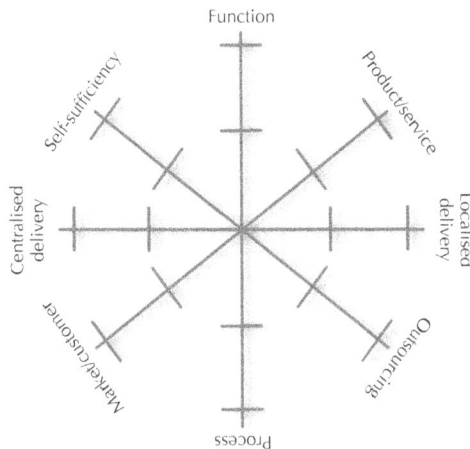

Figure 17.2: The organisational design logic axes to decide on a basic design delivery logic

In applying the design axes, as per Figure 17.2, to the basic design logic of the HR function, the following choices are possible, where the final choice must be a function of the design departure point (design criterion) for the HR function of *partnering* (= client-centricity) with clients, and any other design criteria decided on:

- *Function* (e.g., the HR functional areas, such as talent sourcing, employment relations, rewards, training and development) and/or *Process* (e.g., the people value chain);

- *Market/Customer* (i.e., those divisions/work units of the organisation to be serviced by the HR function) and/or the *Products/Services* delivered by the HR function (e.g., reward packages, assessments, union collective agreements, leadership development programmes);

- *Centralised delivery* (i.e., a centralised HR department) and/and *Localised delivery* (i.e., a HR partner per department/division/work unit of the organisation);

- *Self-sufficiency* (i.e., delivering all the HR services from own, internal resources) and/or *Outsourcing* (i.e., making use of external HR service providers, where appropriate).

Building the strategic horizontal HR organisational design: The house with its rooms

In the preceding step of the design process, a basic delivery logic was chosen, aligned to (and in support of) the organisation's strategic intent. Next, the delivery logic must be translated into a strategic horizontal HR organisational design (i.e., the house with its rooms). It is about architecting the flow of the people management value chain by creating areas of focused competencies and specialisation (rooms) in a such a way as to enable the organisation to make people its competitive edge, by turning them into value unlockers and wealth creators. The strategic horizontal design in essence is about the best division of labour.

A leading practices operating model for the HR POGA is given in Figure 17.3, with the typical design criteria shown in italics next to each of the 'rooms in the house'. This operating model can be entitled a *customer-centric, expert base business, enabling design*. The essence of the delivery logic is a design centring around HR client communities to be serviced in a 'one-stop' seamless manner, optimally matching people needs to people solutions. The design metaphor that best informs the proposed HR POGA given in Figure 17.3 is that of a soccer/rugby team.

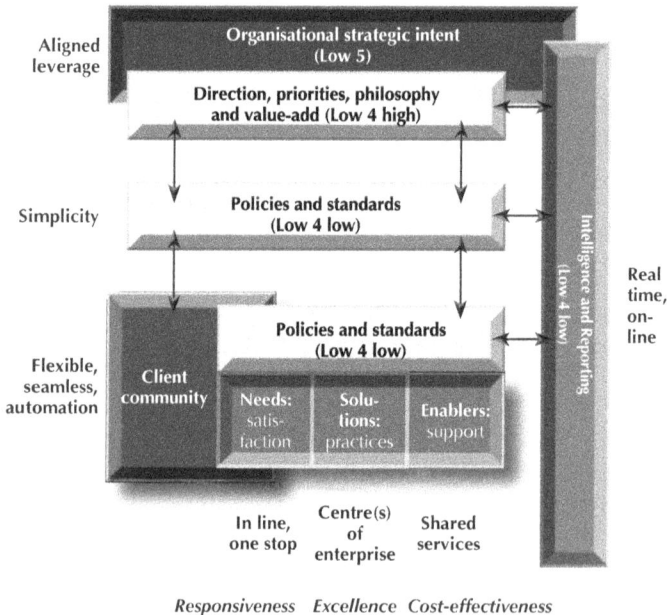

Figure 17.3: A leading practices strategic horizontal HR organisational design
*Note: LOW = Requisite Level of Work (see the strategic vertical HR organisational design)

Below, the elements making up the proposed HR POGA (see Figure 17.3) are elucidated: Primary work domains, roles, and basic modes of client engagement.

Primary work domains

As shown in Figure 17.3, the strategic horizontal HR organisational design consists of four primary work domains:

- Domain 1: People direction, priorities, philosophy and value add (or returns);
- Domain 2: People policies and standards;
- Domain 3: People workflow (the people value chain discussed above), subdivided into needs, solutions and enablers;
- Domain 4: People intelligence and reporting.

Domains 1 to 3 are the typical, conventional primary HR work domains, and are readily apparent. Domain 4, however, requires further discussion because it is out of the ordinary. If people are moving centre stage in securing the future sustainable success of organisations, then real-time people intelligence and reporting become mission critical (e.g., a people balanced scorecard or dashboard, and employee climate surveys). The analogy here is that of financial reporting, with its commensurate intelligence needed to make informed financial decisions at the executive and board levels.

Roles

Client partnering, as architected into the proposed HR POGA, contains five core people professional roles, as depicted in Figure 17.4. These roles are an adaptation and expansion of those which Dave Ulrich (Ulrich, 1997; Ulrich & Brockband, 2005) proposed for HR (see Chapter 19 for a more detailed discussion).

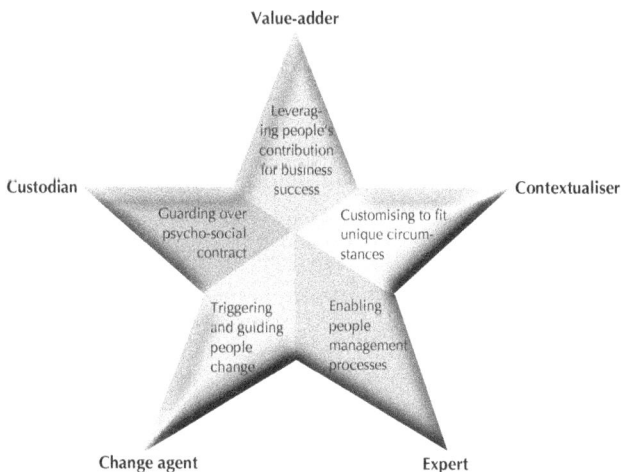

Figure 17.4: The core client-partnering roles of the people professional

Given the core client-partnering roles of the people professional, the HR POGA (see Figure 17.3) requires at least the following generic people professional roles by work domain, all informed by the underlying core partnering roles:

- *People leadership,* providing the overall people direction/philosophy and guidance to people leadership and management within the organisation, and being part of the executive and senior management teams of the organisation (Domains 1: People direction, priorities, philosophy and value add (or returns) and 2: People policies and standards).

- *People generalists* or client executives, positioned as close as possible to clients, providing a one-stop service to clients in defining their people needs; sourcing the appropriate people solutions to satisfy those needs; overseeing the successful embedding of solutions; and ensuring that line management is competent in using those solutions with their accompanying practices, with confidence (Domain 3: Needs).

- *People specialists,* located in centralised centre(s) of expertise (or excellence), crafting and/or insourcing and implementing the required people solutions and practices, and rendering specialised daily people services to the organisation through the people generalists (Domain 3: Solutions).

- *Transactional processors,* situated in a centralised people shared service centre, dealing with the transactional, administrative processing underlying the people solutions and services; the handing of people queries; and the keeping of people records (Domain 3: Enablers).

- *People intelligence and reporting,* collecting management information and generating management reports regarding the state of people management in the organisation and people's contribution to the success of the organisation. Also, ensuring the timeous preparation and submission of statutory people management reports, as required by legislation (Domain 4: People intelligence and reporting).

Modes of client engagement

Three distinct but interdependent modes of engagement between people professionals and clients, delivered through the roles discussed above, can be distinguished. They inform the customer-centric, expert base business, enabling design (see Figure 17.5). For the sake of simplicity, only the client-facing HR roles, as crafted above, are given in the figure. Note the contextual embeddedness of the modes of engagement. These modes have to be designed based on, and lived with, high contextual intelligence, to ensure a best contextual fit.

The three modes of client engagement entail the following:

- *Mode 1:* crafting and rolling out the organisation's strategic people framework, in alignment with its organisational strategic intent, to make the organisation future-fit;

- *Mode 2:* enabling the day-to-day delivery of standardised, formalised people services associated with the people value chain;

- *Mode 3:* solving ad hoc, out-of-the-ordinary and unexpected people issues/ problems (e.g., interpersonal conflict, decreasing morale, increasing people turnover).

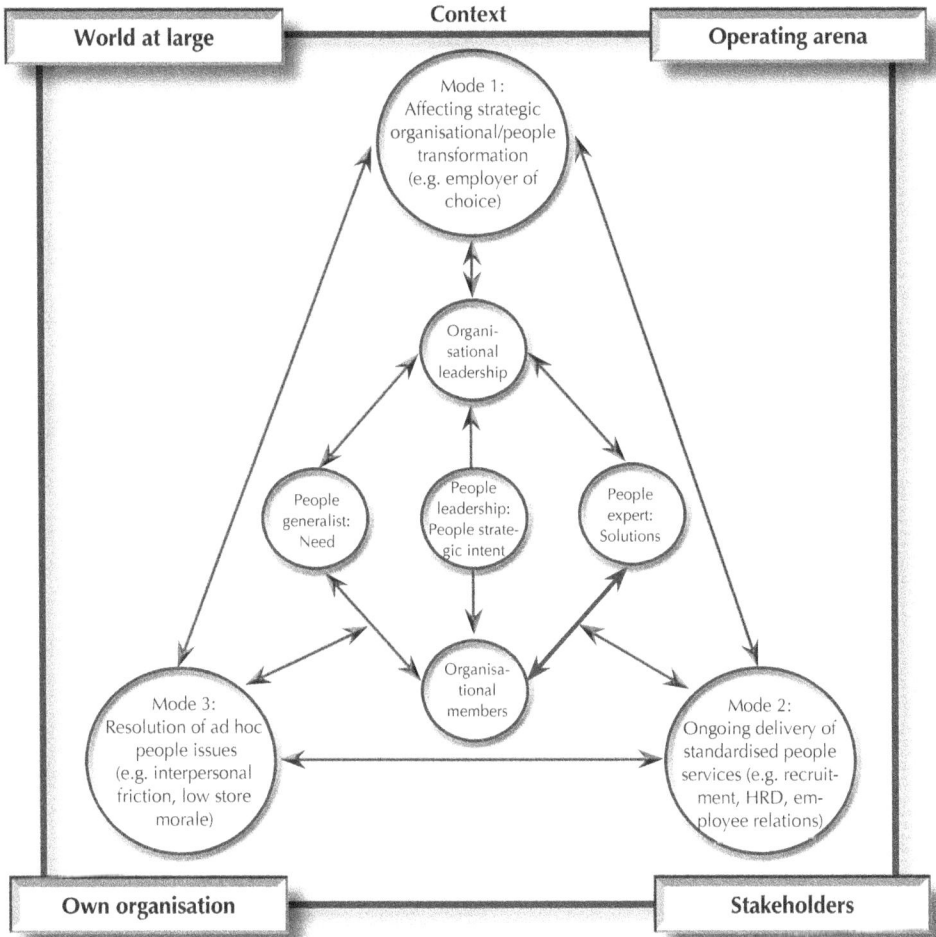

Figure 17.5: Modes of engagement

It is beyond the scope of this chapter to map the processes associated with each mode of engagement. For interest's sake, and to illustrate such a map, a Mode 1: Strategic organisational/people transformation process map is depicted in Figure 17.6. Where two or more roles are involved, the role taking the lead is given first.

Each mode of client engagement has its own unique critical success factors. For example, in the case of Mode 1: Strategic organisational/people transformation, typical success factors are: strategic focus and synergy, and rolling out the strategic people framework within the window of opportunity (see Figure 17.6). In the case of

Mode 2: Standardised people service delivery, the critical success factors include a clear mapping of processes, overall value chain integration, well-constructed service level agreements (SLAs) and delivery predictability. For Mode 3: Resolving ad hoc people issues/problems, the critical success factors are the proper scoping of the issue/problem; responsiveness in terms of the perceived urgency of the need, and a well-constructed, pragmatic plan of action.

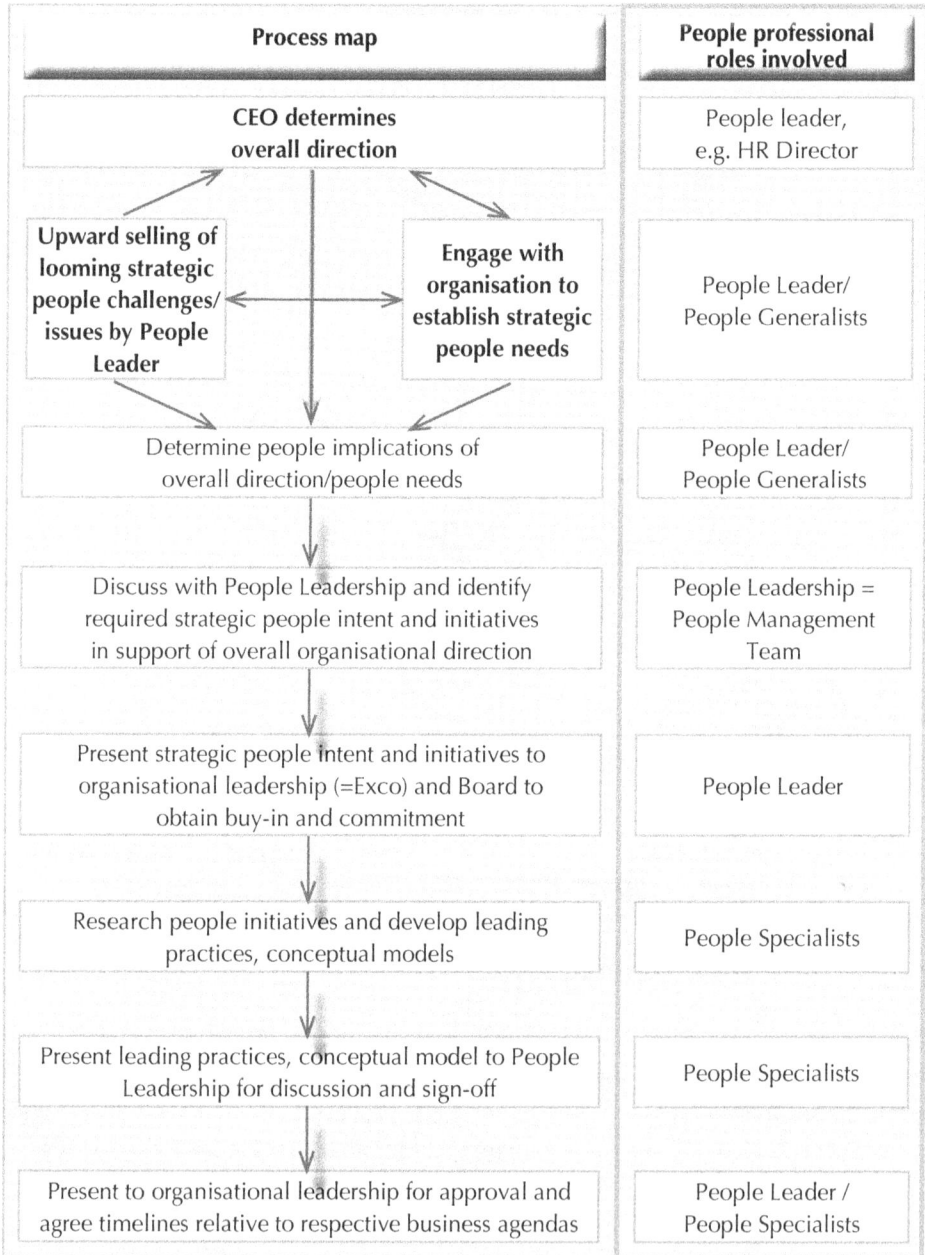

Process map	People professional roles involved
CEO determines overall direction	People leader, e.g. HR Director
Upward selling of looming strategic people challenges/ issues by People Leader / **Engage with organisation to establish strategic people needs**	People Leader/ People Generalists
Determine people implications of overall direction/people needs	People Leader/ People Generalists
Discuss with People Leadership and identify required strategic people intent and initiatives in support of overall organisational direction	People Leadership = People Management Team
Present strategic people intent and initiatives to organisational leadership (=Exco) and Board to obtain buy-in and commitment	People Leader
Research people initiatives and develop leading practices, conceptual models	People Specialists
Present leading practices, conceptual model to People Leadership for discussion and sign-off	People Specialists
Present to organisational leadership for approval and agree timelines relative to respective business agendas	People Leader / People Specialists

Process map	People professional roles involved
Operationalise leading practices, conceptual model, and if necessary customise for different organisational units	People Specialists / People Generalists
Develop integrated strategic project plan (including change navigation) in partnership with stakeholders	People Specialists / People Generalists
Execute flawlessly	People Generalists / People Specialists
Measure value-add	People Generalists / People Specialists
Once implemented, incorporate into ongoing standardised people delivery process	People Specialists

Key rules for success
- Focused set of strategic people initiatives: Less is more.
- Involvement of / consultation with stakeholders throughout respective processes.
- Proper organisational implementation contracting (to fit into business agendas).
- Delivery within strategic window of opportunity.

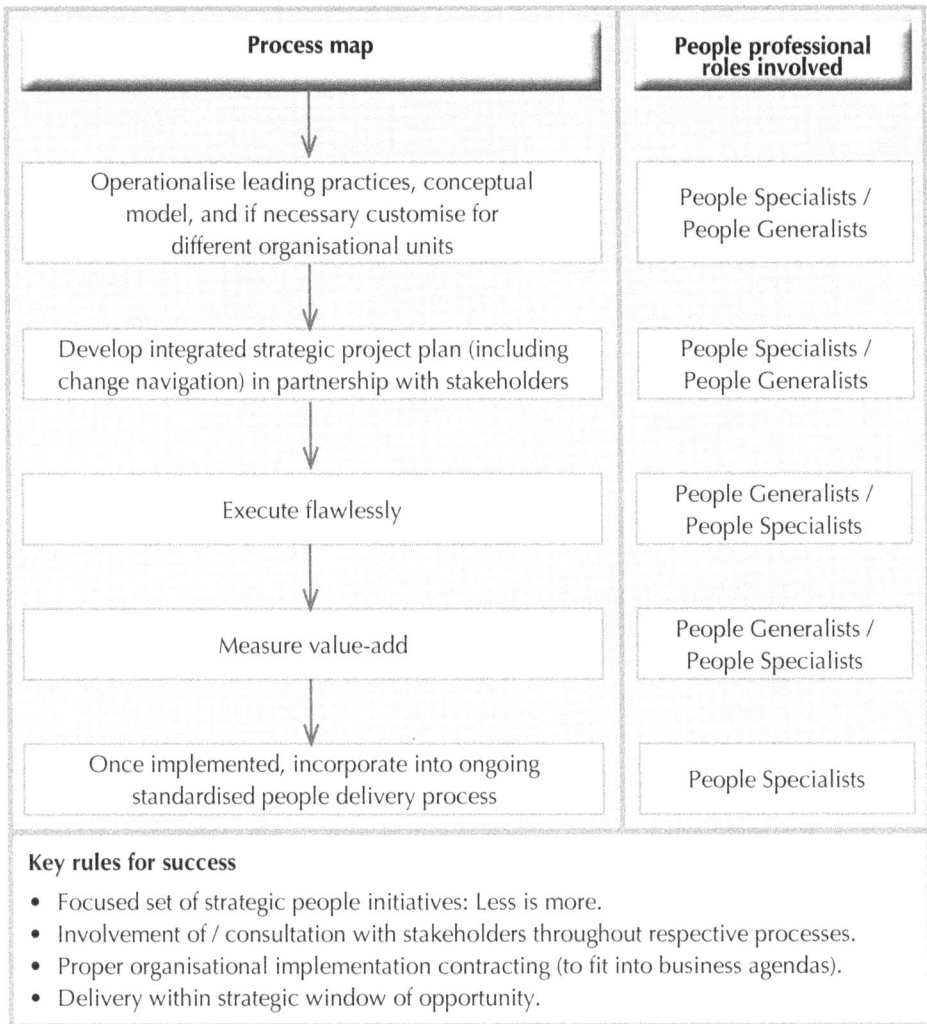

Figure 17.6: Process map of Mode 1: Strategic organisational/people transformation engagement

Building the strategic vertical HR organisational design: The requisite ownership of the HR rooms

The preceding design step created an HR house with rooms, i.e., focused competencies and specialisations, as expressed in work domains, roles and modes of engagement. This constitutes the effective division of labour. The vertical HR organisational design aims to establish the requisite ownership of each room in terms of required work and profiling the roles of the owners. This means considering the vertical dimension of the organisation, i.e., organisational levels. A handy way of conceptualising the requisite ownership of work of each room, is to employ Stratified Systems Theory (Jaques, 2006; Jaques & Clement, 1994; Shephard, Gray, Hunt & McArthur, 2007).

This theory offers a useful way of establishing the requisite complexity demanded by different levels of work (LoWs) (see Figure 17.7).

X	Requisite level of work			
	Level of work	**Work elements**	**Typical decision time horizon**	**Typical work roles**
Contextual complexity — Space/time boundaries, scope, variety, change	**6: Business protection/ enhancement**	• Context shaping • Corporate governance	10 years plus	Board director
	5: Strategic direction	• Returns / yields • Direction, objectives, philosophy	5-10 years	Enterprise / BU executives
	4: Strategic translation / implementation	• Policies and standards • Organisational systems	3-5 years	Functional executives
	3: Operational execution	• Resourcing • Delivery work process	1-3 years	Process leader
	2: Operational practices	• Delivery practices	3-12 months	Front line leader (=supervisor)
	1: Operational delivery	• Daily delivery	Up to 3 months	Operator / practitioner

Figure 17.7: An overview of LoWs: Requisite LoWs x contextual complexity

An important extension of the original conceptualisation of LoWs is the inclusion of contextual complexity (see section on OD building materials). Thus, the *total complexity* faced by a people professional is equal to his/her LoW complexity multiplied by the contextual complexity of his/her organisation. For example, two people leaders who are both at LoW 4 will face significantly different total complexities if one is a leader in a context of low complexity, and the other is embedded in a context of high complexity.

- The former may be in a context where his/her organisation is local; requires a two- to three-year strategic time thinking framework; has a single market with a certain type of customer and product/service; leads the organisation with a single strategic people intent, set of people policies and standards, people work processes and practices, and people outputs delivered; and faces slow, incremental change;

- The latter may be in a context where s/he needs to give people leadership to a global organisation which requires a ten-year plus strategic time thinking framework; has dissimilar markets and types of customer and products/services; is the typical diversified corporation; s/he has to lead the organisation with a portfolio of diverse strategic people intents, sets of people policies and standards, different people work processes and practices, and diverse people outputs to be delivered; and has to deal with revolutionary, recreative change.

The critical design decision with respect to the strategic vertical design is the identification of the highest requisite LoW required by the respective HR work domains, with their associated roles. Figure 17.7 depicts the suggested highest requisite (highest) LoWs for the various HR work domains. According to this figure the requisite ownership of each room, in terms of LoWs and the respective HR work domains, is:

- Domain 1: People direction, philosophy and value add (or returns): LoW 4 – High;

- Domain 2: People policies and standards: LoW 4 – Low;

- Domain 3: People workflow (the people value chain), subdivided into need satisfaction, solutions and enablers: LoWs 4 – Low and 3;

- Domain 4: People intelligence and reporting: LoW 4 – Low.

An excellent way to anchor the strategic horizontal and vertical ODs, and to ensure the total coverage and alignment of the work that needs to be done, is to generate a portfolio of role profiles/descriptions for the respective generic roles identified in the horizontal design, i.e., profiling the owners of the rooms at their respective requisite LoWs, e.g., people leadership; people generalists. The role profile is a concise one-page to one-and-a-half-page document, structured in terms of the core purpose of the role (a three-to-four-liner); major task/key performance areas (no more than five task areas); and critical outcomes (no more than five outcomes). (Of course, the next logical step, but not part of the strategic OD, is to translate the role profiles into the required competencies needed by the role incumbents.)

Building the lateral HR organisational design: Living together in the house

At this point in the strategic design process, the work domains with roles and modes of engagement (the *horizontal design*) and the requisite levels of work and work roles by work unit (the *vertical design*) have been architected. This is the *differentiation process* of organisation design. Critical in the OD process is the *integration* of the differentiated dimensions of the organisation, i.e., identifying the interdependency between work domains and work roles, and then designing the integrating, coordinating mechanisms and governance necessary to ensure that all of the aforementioned work together synergistically and accountably. Put differently, the strategic lateral HR OD, involves putting together the differentiated design pieces. Frequently, the strategic lateral design is ignored in the OD process, at the expense of the consequential emergence of functional/process silos and a significant loss of overall organisational synergy. It can be hypothesised that those organisations that can get their strategic lateral design right, will be able to compete most effectively with their design, since the organisation will be infused by high levels of spontaneous synergy.

Two aspects of the strategic lateral design are important here, namely 1) crafting integrating, coordinating mechanisms; and 2) designing the overall governance of the organisation.

1. *Crafting integrating, coordinating mechanisms.* To design fit-for-purpose, effectively integrating coordinating mechanisms, it is vital to understand the *interdependencies* between the elements of the horizontal and the vertical designs. A simple yet powerful way of mapping the interdependencies between work domains and work roles is to build an interdependency matrix (see Table 17.2). The same type of matrix can be generated for the HR work domains. Important here are the interdependencies in both directions: from role A to role B, and vice versa. The nature of the dependency may differ, given the specific relationship direction.

    Three types of interdependencies have to be considered in the relationships depicted in such an interdependency matrix:

    -   *Pooled:* Independent roles – no interdependency, the outputs of the respective roles are summated;

    -   *Sequential:* Interdependent roles – the output of one role forms the input of another;

    -   *Reciprocal:* Interdependent roles – the output of one role becomes the input of another role which, in turn, becomes the input of the first role.

Table 17.2: An interdependency matrix for the crafted people professional roles

	Client 1 2 3	People leadership	People generalist	People specialist	Transactional processor	People intelligence and reporting
Client	-					
People leadership		-				
People generalist			-			
People specialist				-		
Transactional processor					-	
People intelligence and reporting						-

For each interdependency identified, an integrating, coordinating mechanism has to be architected. These mechanisms specify the how and where of engagement across the organisation, so as to create overall organisational synergies. Typical mechanisms are the hierarchy established through reporting relationships; a matrix design; organisational integrator roles; cross-functional teams; lateral integration processes (user forums, joint planning centres); SLAs; communities of practice; informal networks; and/or normative integration through organisational culture. It is beyond the scope of this chapter to discuss these mechanisms in-depth.

2. *Designing the overall governance of the organisation.* Governance pertains to the allocation of authority, accountabilities, responsibilities and autonomy to work roles – and, by implication, work units. Also, the desired decision-making style needs to be determined. Put differently, it pertains to the allocation and exercise of decision-making rights. Critical here is architecting governance in

congruence with the design vision (with its corresponding mode of work), For example, governance, when it comes to an athletic team, will look different from that of a soccer or rugby team. Consider the significant governance difference in command-and-control vs. high-performance/high engagement/high flexibility ODs. Table 17.3 profiles the governances of these two designs in terms of a governance design matrix.

Table 17.3: Contrasting governances of a command-and-control vs. a high-performance/high engagement/high flexibility organisational design

Action domain		Accountable party: Role	Responsible parties: Roles	Decision-making styles				
				Tell	Consult	Co-determine	Self - manage ('upward consult')	Self-govern ('upward tell')
				(0%)	(25%)	(50%; 50%)	(100%)	(100%)
L O W 5	*Results/ yields*	As high as possible in the organisation, as close as possible to the top	No/little autonomy to responsible parties					
	Direction, initiative, philosophy							
L O W 4	*Policies and standards*							
	Organisational systems and resourcing							

→

Action domain		Account-able party: Role	Respon-sible parties: Roles	Decision-making styles				
L O W 3	Opera-tional delivery processes							
L O W 2	Opera-tional delivery practices							
L O W 1	Daily op-erational delivery	As low as possible in the or-ganisa-tion, re-lative to where the action has to be taken	As much autonomy as possi-ble to re-sponsible parties					

Note: * Percentage autonomy awarded by accountable party to responsible parties

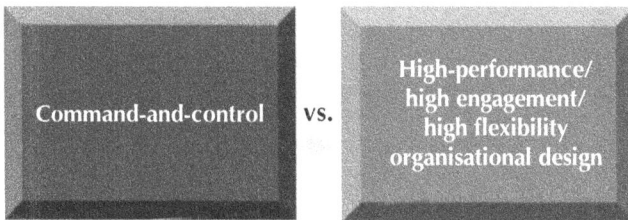

Command-and-control vs. High-performance/ high engagement/ high flexibility organisational design

With the emerging new order typifying the context in which organisations currently operate, the shift is, generally speaking, towards high-performance/high engagement/ high flexibility governance. Using LoW 5 as the reference point from which autonomy is awarded, the emerging decision-making styles would be the following, as reflected in Table 17.3:

- Returns/yields; direction, philosophy, initiatives; policies & standards; organisational systems and resourcing: *Consult to co-determine*;

- Operational delivery processes and practices: *Co-determine to self-manage*;

- Daily operational delivery: *Self-manage to self-govern*.

It against this backdrop of these OD leading practices that the governance model for the HR function has to be architected.

Putting it all together into an integrated strategic HR design: The house plan

The outcomes of the horizontal, vertical and lateral designs now have be integrated into an overall HR design in the form of a visual, strategic organisational map. Put differently, the overall house plan now has to be drafted. This is the climax of the design process. Similar to a house plan, the placement of the rooms relative to one another must occur in accordance with the basic delivery logic chosen. Where interdependencies exist, the map must show 'room overlaps'. The design must also show what external support services must be provided, and at what LoW, to enable the OD to function. The organisational map forms the basis of the tactical OD, i.e., the design of each of the rooms making up the organisational map (= house plan).

Figure 17.8 gives an example of such an HR organisational map, based on a front/back organisational design, using a partnering delivery logic:

- On the client-facing side of the organisation, groupings (rooms) are done in terms of clients and/or markets ('front' of the organisation);

- On the product/service side of the organisation, groupings are done in terms of products/services ('back' of the organisation), with the support services.

A single comment regarding the proposed HR organisational map is relevant here. The room called 'people solutions' is made up of a portfolio of conventional functional HR areas. To further enhance client-centricity, a more radical approach to this room would be to architect it in terms of the three modes of engagement:

- Mode 1: Strategic organisational/people transformation;

- Mode 2: Standardised people service delivery; and

- Mode 3: Resolving ad hoc people issues/problems.

The respective functional HR areas would be incorporated into the three engagement modes or 'sub-rooms'.

Levels of work		Lateral
Level 6: Business oversight	**Governance and oversight: Board**	HR Board committee
Level 5: Strategy generation	**Organisational strategic intent: CEO**	Exco
Level 4: Strategy translation/ implementation	**People strategic intent: Direction, priorities, philosophy and value-add CHRO**	
	People policies and standards	HR mancom

	People needs	People solutions	People intelligence & reporting	People delivery support	
Level 3: Operational execution (dept. managers)					HR mancom
Level 2: Operational supervision (unit heads)	In line; people client part- ners per organisa- tional area; identifying and satisfy- ing client needs	Design/ sourc- ing and delivery of people needs: talent, manage- ment, organi- sational design, develop- ment and change, employee relations, employee well-being, conditions of service	Employee climate surveys; HR audits; HR bal- anced scorecard: statutory reporting; manage- ment reports; bench- marking	Solution adminis- tration; employee records; help desk; payroll; HR IT systems	User forums
Level 1: Operational delivery (team leaders with teams)					User forums

Business partners: Supporting units
- Marketing (low 3)   - Finance (low 3)   - IT (low 2)

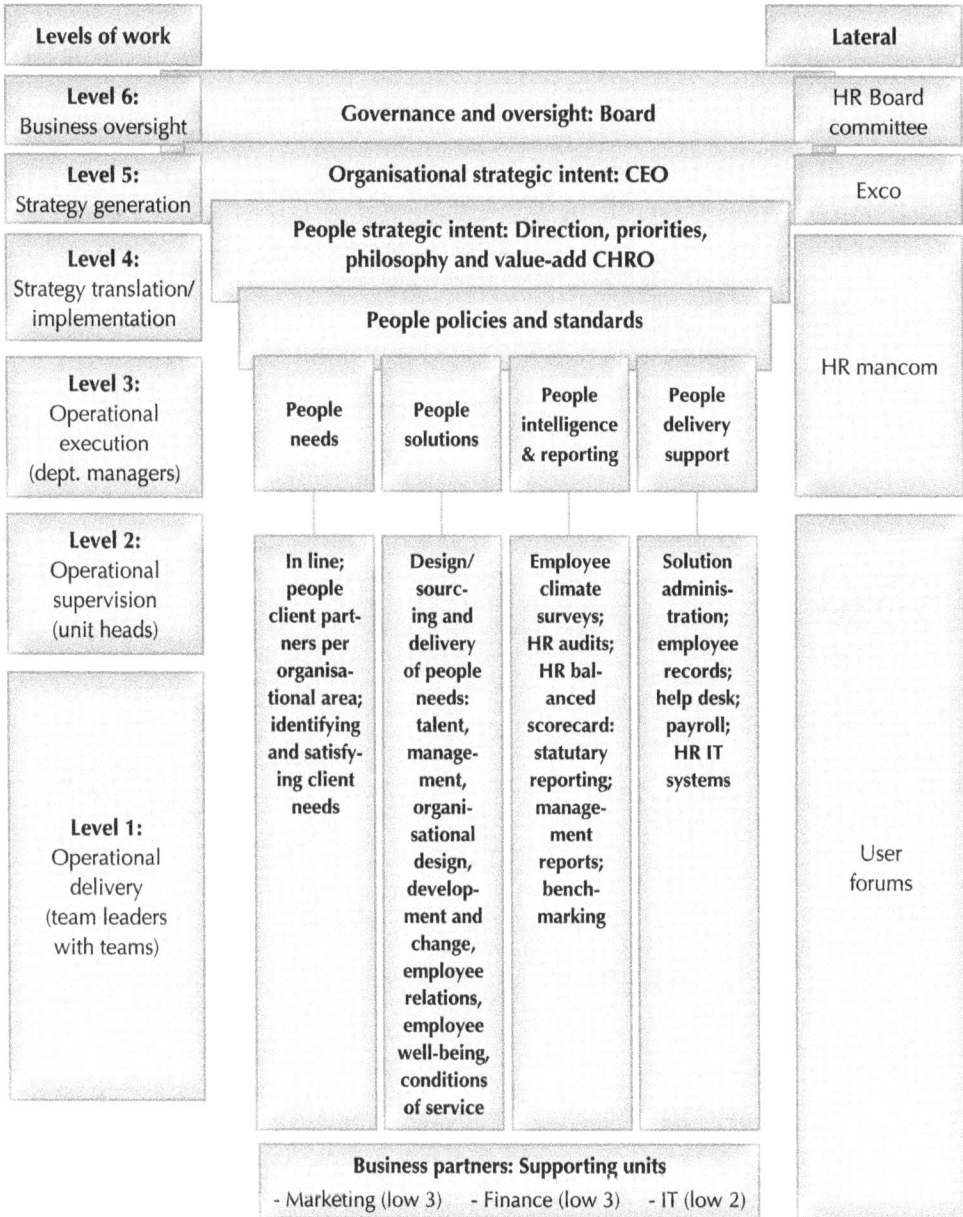

Figure 17.8 An integrated, strategic HR design: The HR perspective

Figure 17.9 provides the same HR organisational map but from a business perspective.

335

Levels of work						Lateral
Level 6: Business oversight	**Governance and oversight: Board**					HR Board committee
Level 5: Strategy generation	**Organisational strategic intent: CEO**					Exco
Level 4: Strategy translation/ implementation	**People strategic intent: Direction, priorities, philosophy and value-add CHRO**					
Level 3: Operational execution (dept. managers)	**Centers of excellence** (people policies, standards, method-ologies	**Business Unit A**	**Business Unit B**	**Business Unit C**	**People delivery support**	HR mancom
Level 2: Operational supervision (unit heads)	**Resourc-ing** / **Talent manage-ment**	Head of people manage-ment (dotted or solid reporting line to CHRO	Head of people manage-ment (dotted or solid reporting line to CHRO	Head of people manage-ment (dotted or solid reporting line to CHRO	**Solution adminis-tration; employee records; help desk; payroll; HR IT systems**	
Level 1: Operational delivery (team leaders with teams)	**Devel-opment** / **Well-being** / **Employee relations** / **Intelli-gence & reporting**	People client part-ner(s) People delivery general-ists/spe-cialists	People client part-ner(s) People delivery general-ists/spe-cialists	People client part-ner(s) People delivery general-ists/spe-cialists		User forums / Communities of practice

Business partners: Supporting units
- Marketing (low 3)   - Finance (low 3)   - IT (low 2)

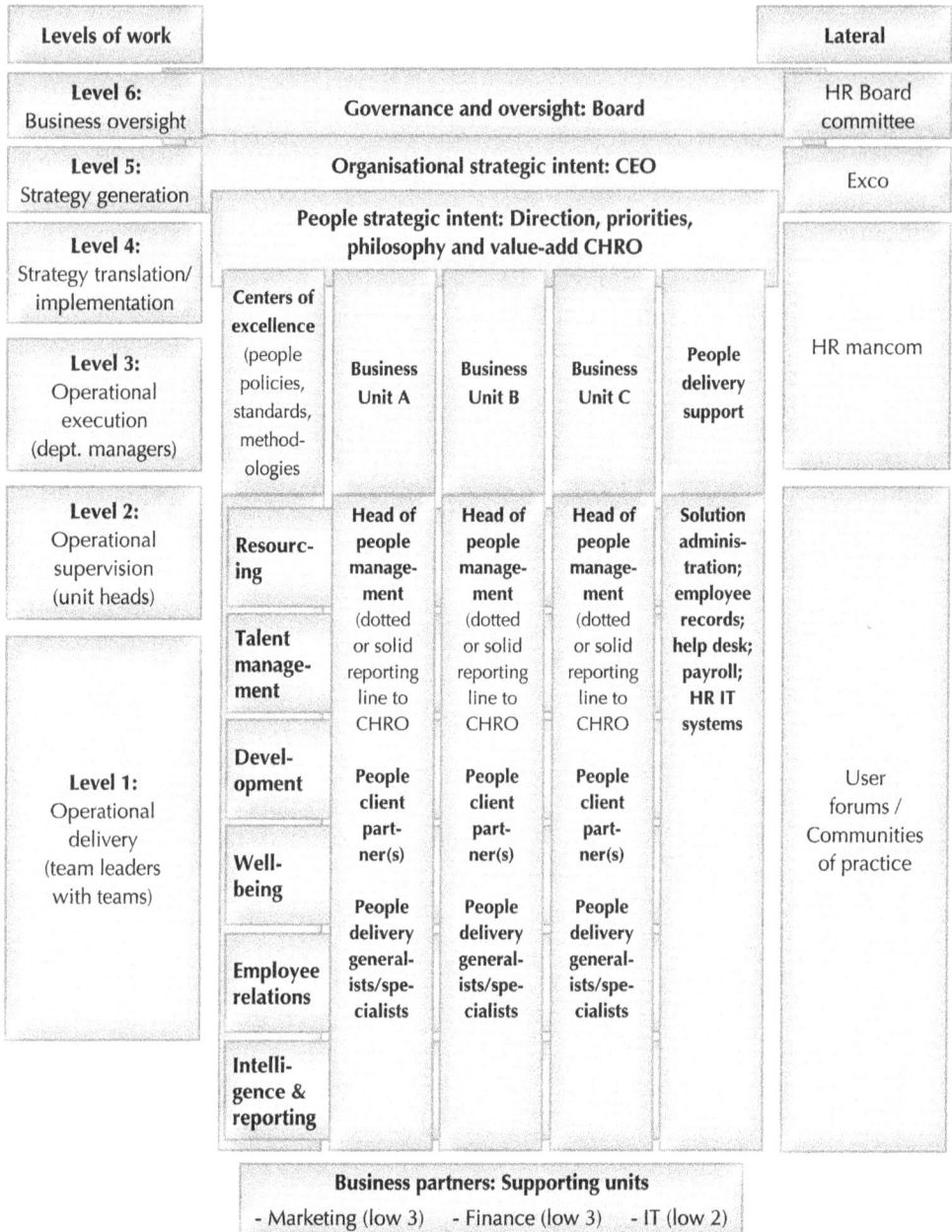

Figure 17.9: An integrated, strategic HR design: The business perspective

Only now can an HR organogram be drawn, based on the HR organisational map. The organogram needs to reflect the delivery logic informing the organisational map. Without such an organisational map as a basis, architected around a well-thought-out delivery logic and compiled from the strategic, vertical and lateral designs, drawing an organogram becomes an illogical, emotionally charged, whimsical exercise in futility, which is at the mercy of the wax and wane of political and personal dynamics within the organisation.

Doing the strategic organisational design alignment: Fitting the house into the townhouse complex

The strategic OD of the HR function is now complete. The design solution is on the table. Now it is vital to put the design 'back' into the organisational landscape, i.e., to 'fit the house into the townhouse complex'. This is critically important as it will show where misalignments exist between the design and the other organisational building blocks making up the landscape. These misalignments represent risks which could sabotage and even sink the design, because the other building blocks would not reinforce but rather would undermine the design. The closing of misalignments uncovered in this way has to be addressed in the design implementation plan.

Figure 17.10 depicts an organisational landscape, constructed by Veldsman and Geldenhuys. The landscape is based on a chaos/complexity world view (Gharajedaghi, 2011; Nedopil, Steger & Amann, 2011). Here, the organisation is seen as a dynamically interconnected, systemic whole.

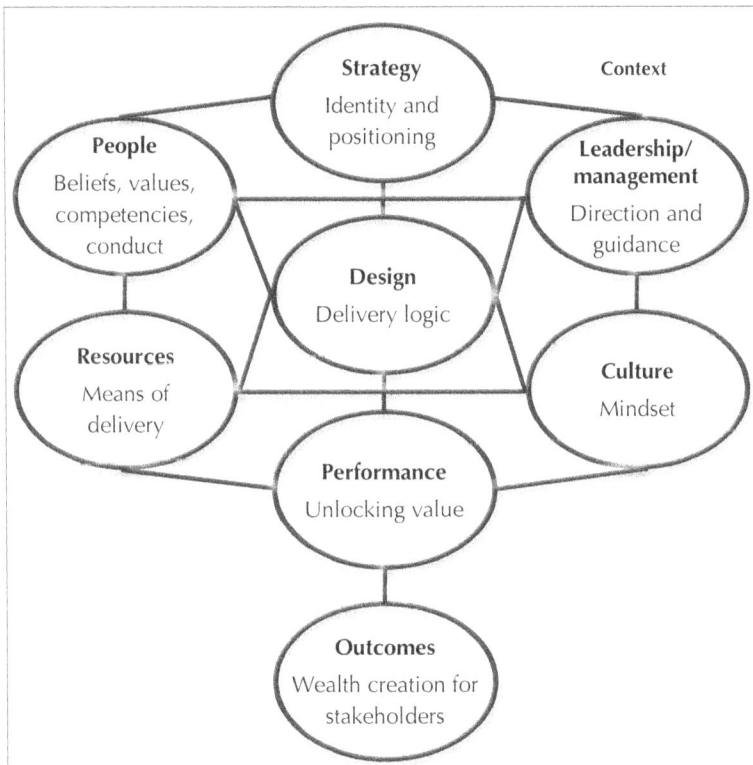

Figure 17.10: The organisational landscape: A chaos/complexity view

According to Figure 17.10, the necessary organisational alignment required to support/reinforce the proposed design would be effected by people; culture; leadership/management; resources (including technology and systems) and performance alignment. Strategic alignment – the departure point for the design process – has to be taken into account throughout the OD process as a whole. Due to space constraints, the respective alignments cannot be further discussed in any detail here. The major insight to take away at this point is the criticality of the overall organisational landscape alignment.

Facing up to the design challenge of being a global organisation – playing in the global village

Being a global organisation, or intending to become a global player, has become common among organisations operating within an emerging world order characterised by increasing interconnectedness (Galbraith, 2000). The typical evolutionary path of organisations which are globalising, is made up of four stages (see Figure 17.11). Different organisational designs are associated with each of the four evolutionary stages, therefore depending on the HR function and its OD, each globalising, evolutionary stage will be different.

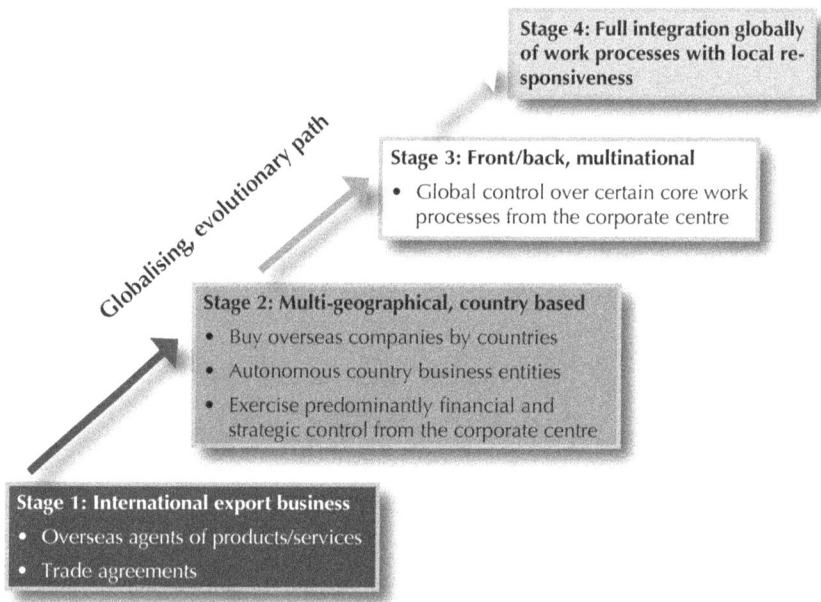

Figure 17.11: The typical evolutionary path of globalising organisations

At each evolutionary stage, the major challenge to globalising organisations is to find the right balance between a *reach need*, i.e., the local and/or global integration of work; and an *acting need*, i.e., the local and/or global responsiveness on the ground in those locations where the organisation has an operational presence (Galbraith, 2000). Figure 17.12 presents the different permutations of these two needs.

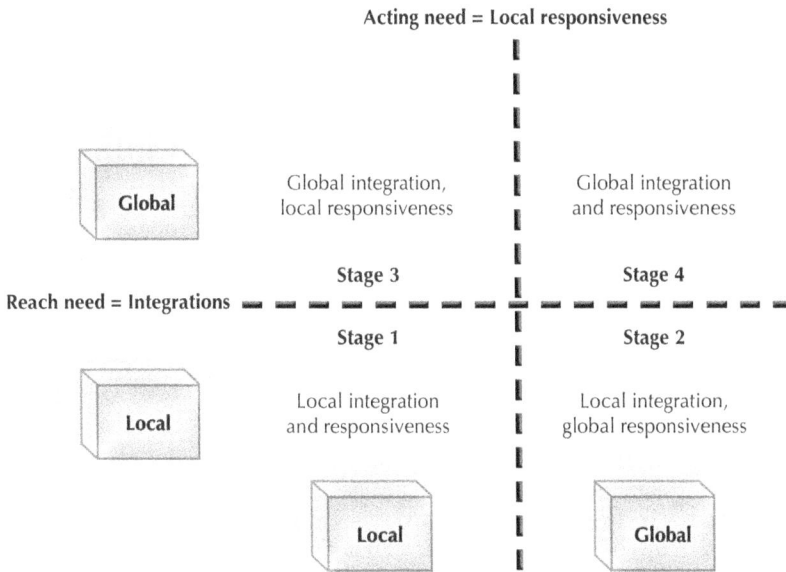

Figure 17.12: Finding the right balance between reach and acting needs

Table 17.4 depicts different typical HR ODs for the various permutations of reach and acting needs, relative to the stages of the globalising evolutionary path.

Table 17.4: Typical HR ODs relative to the globalising evolutionary path stages

HR WORK DOMAINS	BALANCING RESEARCH AND ACTING NEEDS RELATIVE TO THE GLOBALISING EVOLUTIONARY PATH STAGES			
	Stage 1 Local integration and responsiveness	*Stage 2* Local Integration, global responsiveness	*Stage 3* Global integration, local responsiveness	*Stage 4* Global integration and responsiveness
1: People direction, philosophy and value add/ returns				
2: People policies and standards				
3A: People workflow: Need satisfaction				

→

339

HR WORK DOMAINS	BALANCING RESEARCH AND ACTING NEEDS RELATIVE TO THE GLOBALISING EVOLUTIONARY PATH STAGES			
	Stage 1 Local integration and responsiveness	*Stage 2* Local integration, global responsiveness	*Stage 3* Global integration, local responsiveness	*Stage 4* Global integration and responsiveness
3B: People workflow: Solutions				
3C: People workflow: Enablers				
4: People intelligence and reporting				
HR OD	Completely separate, autonomous HR functions by country. All work domains are country based: 1 to 4	Local HR functions handle work domains 1, 2, 3A. Work domains 3B and 3C are regionalised to cater for regional differences, e.g. different tax regimes for the payroll. Work domain 4 is globalised	Work domains 1, 2, 3B, 4 are globally integrated. Work domain 3A is localised for in-country responsiveness. Some of work domains 3B and 3C may be regionalised to cater for regional differences but also to achieve regional economies of scale	Client-facing work domain is localised: 3A. All other work domains are globally integrated: 1, 2, 3B; 3C; 4, though some in-country autonomy may be given to localise work domains 2 and 3B to attain a better in-country fit

Local	Regional	Global

Conclusion

Organisations can indeed be competitive in terms of their organisational design. This particularly applies to their HR function, if it is accepted that people have moved centre stage, in terms of their contribution to sustainable organisational success, given their role as value unlockers and wealth creators in the knowledge economy. Organisational design is, after all, the organisation's delivery logic aimed at defining and creating value.

This can only be true, however, if the design is directly aligned to the organisation's strategic intent; if an integrated, comprehensive and systematic design process is followed uncompromisingly, informed by leading OD practices, covering all levels (strategic, tactical and operational)[1] and all dimensions of design (horizontal, vertical and lateral); if the overall goal is to architect an integrated design (the house plan) and not to draw an organogram; if the overall organisational design fits into the total organisational landscape; if a well-thought-out implementation plan is crafted and excellently executed, enabled by strong change navigation; if the expected benefits of the new design are clearly articulated, monitored and tracked; and if the new design is religiously committed to (for at least three to five years), until a significant key design parameter changes, e.g., the organisation's strategic intent.

In the end, when all is said and done, all organisations are perfectly designed to get the results they get, according to A. Jones (source unknown). This equally applies to the HR function.

Endnote

1 Tactical and operational design were not covered in this chapter.

References

Anand, N. & Daft, R.L. (2007). What is the right organisational design? *Organisational Dynamics, 36*, 329–344.

Brickley, J.A., Smith, C.W. & Zimmerman, J.L. (2003). *Designing organisations to create value.* New York: McGraw Hill.

Galbraith, J.R. (1995). *Designing organisations.* San Francisco: Jossey-Bass.

Galbraith, J.R. (1997). *Organisational design.* Reading, Mass.: Addison-Wesley.

Galbraith, J.R. (2000). *Designing the global organisation.* San Francisco: Jossey-Bass.

Galbraith, J.R. (2006). Matching strategy and structure. In J.V. Gallos (Ed.). *Organisation development.* San Francisco: Jossey-Bass, 565–582.

Galbraith, J.R. (2008). Organisation design. In T.G. Cummings (Ed.). *Handbook of organisation development.* Los Angeles: Sage, 325 352.

Galbraith, J.R., Downey, D. & Kates, A. (2005). *Designing dynamic organisations.* New York: Amacon.

Gharajedaghi, J. (2011). *Systems thinking: Managing chaos and complexity – A platform for designing business architecture.* Amsterdam: Elsevier.

Jaques, E. (2006). *Requisite organisation: A total system for effective managerial organisation and managerial leadership for the 21st century.* Baltimore: Cason Hall & Co.

Jaques E. & Clement, S.D. (1994). *Executive leadership: A practical guide to managing complexity.* Cambridge, MA: Carson-Hall & Co.

Kelliher, C. & Richardson, J. (Eds.). (2011). *New ways of organising work.* New York: Routledge.

Kesler, G. & Kates, A. (2011). *Leading organisation design.* San Francisco: Jossey-Bass.

Nadler, D.A. & Tushman, M.L. (1997). *Competing by design.* Oxford: Oxford University Press.

Nedopil, C., Steger, U. & Amann, W. (2011). *Managing complexity in organisations.* Houndsmills: Palgrave Macmillan.

Roberts, J. (2004). *The modern firm.* Oxford: Oxford University Press.

Shephard, K., Gray, J.L., Hunt, J.G. & McArthur, S. (2007). *Organisation design, levels of work and human capability.* Ontario: Global Design Society.

Sparrow, P., Hird, M., Hesketh, A. & Cooper, C. (2010). *Leading HR.* Houndsmills: Palgrave Macmillan.

Stanford, N. (2007). *Guide to organisational design.* London: The *Economist,* in association with Profile Books.

Tafoya, D.W. (2010). *The effective organisation.* New York: Routledge.

Ulrich, D. (1997). *Human resource champions.* Boston: Harvard Business School Press.

Ulrich, D. & Brockbank, W. (2005). *The HR value proposition.* Boston: Harvard Publishing Company.

Ulrich, D., Brockbank, W., Younger, J. & Ulrich, M. (2012). *HR from the outside in: Six competencies for the future for human resources.* New York: McGraw Hill.

Ulrich, D., Brockbank, W., Younger, J. & Ulrich, M. (2013). *Global HR competencies.* New York: McGraw Hill.

Veldsman, T.H. (2002). *Into the people effectiveness arena: Navigating between chaos and order.* Johannesburg: Knowledge Resources.

Wright, P.M., Boudreau, J.W., Pace, D.A., Sartain, E.L., McKinnon, P. & Antoine, R.L. (Eds.). (2011). *The Chief HR Officer: Defining the new role of human resource leaders.* San Francisco: Jossey-Bass.

CHAPTER 18: Two Sides of the Same Coin: Aligning Marketing Principles to the Application of Strategic Human Resources

Linda Fine

The changing world of work

Look around you – the world of work is evolving at an unprecedented rate. Technology continues to have a fundamental impact on the changing landscape of work, paradoxically allowing people to become more connected to each other than ever before, while at the same time creating an alarming disconnectedness in true human interactions.

Twenty years ago it would have been unlikely for a manager not to physically see one of his/her employees for most of the week, month or even year. It was even more unlikely that a manager would have been able to give performance appraisal feedback without directly facing and talking to the employee, or that an employee could access the skills, work experience and endorsements of thousands of colleagues in his/her professional network in real time, or that people around the world would 'bid' for a piece of work, deliver the project and then receive payment without ever having met the person who contracted the job. These are just a few examples of new business models and efficiencies in the workplace that rely on limited human interaction.

However, one fundamental thing has not changed. 'Human organisations are more organism than mechanism' (*Personnel Today*, 2009, p. 2). As workers and consumers, they respond and behave as unique human beings rather than homogenous cogs in a machine. This is an important consideration for marketers and human resource (HR) professionals alike. In this chapter, I explore how applying marketing principles to the management of human capital can unlock the potential of HR to deliver strategic value to the business, and build on its reputation and credibility within the organisation.

Client vs. employee – what's the link?

There is much literature arguing the case of the client vs. the employee as the key focus for companies – in terms of where the company should place its emphasis to ensure maximum return. Some say 'the customer is king', as employees would not have gainful employment if there were no customers to sell to or to service.

The other argument is that employees are king, because if companies spend their time and effort building a great place to work, ensuring employee engagement and expanding the capability of their workforce, the client/customer would ultimately win. The latter view is well illustrated in the success of HCL Technologies, one of the largest IT outsourcing companies in the world, as reflected in the book, *Employees first, clients second*, the premise being that an internal focus on employees as a first priority directly impacts improved value for clients.

Essentially, both arguments have something in common: both illustrate the co-existence of customers and employees who are inextricably linked, irrespective of where a company claims to place its emphasis. One pays salaries, the other is paid a salary, yet they exist for and because of each other.

Thanks to rapid advances in technology, people have easy access to information that enables them to be more discerning when making decisions. This holds true for customers, who can research products and services extensively before making a decision to purchase and can use social networks for vetting or affirming their choices. The same is true for employees, who can research companies online to assess different companies or institutions to work for, again using social networks to affirm whether they would be a good cultural fit when joining that organisation.

Marketing is a business discipline which follows a structured business approach to dealing with consumer behaviour. The discipline uses as its point of departure an exceptional understanding of customers, and segments them so that they can be better addressed and served. Marketers have been quick to leverage technological advances as part of their marketing strategy, as evidenced by company websites, e-commerce for the convenience of online purchasing, contact centres to deal with consumer queries, and social media to like and recommend products and services. Marketers know they need to balance the needs of their customers while optimising the objectives of the business. HR can learn from this: their clients are managers and employees who are frequently more knowledgeable and discerning than external clients, and often have more intimate knowledge of the inner workings of the organisation and its people. Although HR is well versed in human behaviour – practitioners mainly spend their time ensuring that employees and/or managers are happy and satisfied – they devote less time to balancing the needs of the employee, the manager and the company.

The HR function – time for a shift

HR professionals' backgrounds are generally strongly steeped in human behaviour, psychology and behavioural sciences – disciplines and skills which help them understand what motivates people and how this translates into employee behaviour and performance in the complex world of work. This educational background and expertise give HR professionals a good understanding of people and how they function as individual contributors, of the importance of personal mastery as the fundamental starting point for growth and career success, of how people function in teams, as well as the general interconnectedness of people within a complex system. These skills are exceptionally powerful, especially in light of the 'organisms-rather-than-mechanisms' view of Sir Ken Robinson (2009).

With Generation Y starting to make up a large proportion (almost more than half) of the workforce, employees have become more discerning in terms of what they want from a job, the work environment, a career, a manager, and, more importantly, how they are prepared to spend their discretionary time and effort at work.

The complexity of business today means that advanced people and organisational skills, in the absence of strong business acumen, a thorough understanding of the business at hand, employee needs and aspirations, the competitive landscape, the available technology, and the external market environment, can seriously hamper HR's ability to embed a truly integrated and value-adding people strategy. It also impacts on the ability to articulate and position the people strategy in business terms, not only in respect of the employee experience and employee satisfaction. In the past, this resulted in widespread business criticism of the HR function as not being strategic in nature, since practitioners are unable to adequately balance the needs of the people with those of the business.

In the controversial article 'Why we hate HR' (Fast Company, 2005), a rather harsh argument is raised that proposes why HR does not add strategic value for businesses. Despite the controversy, a few truthful facts emerge: as custodians of a company's talent, HR has to understand how people meet the objectives of the company. Instead, business acumen is the single biggest factor that HR professionals lack today; HR often spends more time worrying about the execution of the activity than the value it will ultimately add to the business. They pursue standardisation and uniformity in the face of a workforce that is heterogeneous and complex – so although compliance is necessary, HR should still be spending a lot of time on exceptions to cater for individuality and business circumstances.

HR practitioners often wait for managers to knock on their door, when in fact they should anticipate what the business issues are and provide flexible solutions.

HR management has a reputation for being soft and fluffy. The reality is almost always 'hard', as the interests of the organisation invariably prevail over those of the individual. The best of both worlds is that 'the reality should be some combination of hard and soft' (Fast Company, 2005, p. 10). Finding HR professionals who can balance the hard and the soft to benefit both the employee and the employer, is key.

The role of the HR function – evolution from personnel to human capital

Understanding why HR is perceived as not adding strategic value often lies in the evolution of this function, which has changed quite considerably from its historical role of custodian of the routine functions of hiring new employees and maintaining employee records. Personnel Management (as it was known prior to and until the 80s) was a reactive maintenance function aimed at improving the efficiencies of people and administering employees during their life cycle with the company.

Today the role of HR is not only more varied in terms of practitioners being custodians of various business outcomes (e.g., effective HR processes and data, enabling managers to manage employees, creating a great place to work and enabling business to achieve its business objectives), but it is also more complex (in terms of generational differences, mobility aspirations, low-cost resourcing, remote workforce and social media, to name a few).

No accolades for keeping the 'pool blue'

What does it take to keep a swimming pool blue the whole year round? Chemicals/salt, a filter, a chlorinator, a pump, cleaning tools and some test equipment, and perhaps the occasional shock treatment. In summary, it requires quite a bit of time and effort. However, swimmers expect the pool to be blue whenever they want to swim. No one ever raves about a blue pool. However, when the pool is green, you generally have very unhappy swimmers who might choose not to swim that day. HR is very similar: HR practitioners often only hear from managers and/or employees when things go wrong. There is an expectation that certain hygiene factors will naturally be in place and will always be working perfectly.

The effective administration of employee data and processes throughout the employee life cycle (albeit often time consuming, complex, resource intensive and requiring extreme accuracy) is purely a 'ticket to the game'. An HR team is rarely praised for keeping correct employee records, complying with labour legislation, or ensuring that employees are paid correctly and on time. However, if the vital lifeblood of HR seeps away, the discipline is almost always severely tainted. This does not mean that setting up an HR practice which runs smoothly during all phases of the employee life cycle, complies with legislation, has the right governance and approvals in place, offers the right level of information and service to managers, and provides an environment that fosters happy employees, is an easy task. In fact, quite the contrary. However, if this is all the HR team can deliver on, they will never be viewed as strategic. Ongoing and effective people operations are needed to keep the employee wheel of the organisation turning – that much is a given.

Importantly, HR professionals will never be trusted to play the strategic HR partnership role they so desperately want, unless the foundation of HR (i.e., the policies, processes, workflows, compliance and data management) is firmly in place and running smoothly at least 90 per cent of the time.

Build it and they will come – not an effective approach

Some organisations have very effective HR teams that develop world-class programmes and benefits, but few employees know that these programmes exist, or understand the benefits and/or value thereof. Having all the right HR policies and practices in place can only be effective when existing and potential employees know that these HR programmes exists, when they understand the offering, and, importantly, perceive value in it. That is why HR professionals need to wear a marketing hat as well as an HR one – a role which is sometimes underestimated, simply ignored, or, in most cases, lacking due to a shortage of skills.

As Peter Drucker (Forbes, 2006, p. 1) so simply put it, 'the purpose of business is to create and keep a customer'. HR is no different – its purpose is to attract and retain key talent.

Let's take a look at some of the critical success factors marketing practitioners use, and see how this thinking can be applied to effective HR practices.

Critical success factors

A client-focused mindset

Marketing as a discipline generally focuses on the client by placing him/her at the centre of everything it does. Terms such as 'client-centricity' and 'consumer sovereignty' are key elements in the design of marketing programmes: living these approaches makes customers feel special, and ensures that their needs and wants are addressed.

HR should approach their people strategy with a similar mindset. In the present information age, clients have access to vast amounts of information and are therefore very aware of the choices they have. They are discerning in terms of their needs and wants, as are employees and managers – they, too, want to feel special and hope to benefit from programmes designed with their needs in mind.

HR is often perceived to be a function that enforces the needs of the organisation through a carrot or stick approach, essentially helping managers execute, through people, what the organisation wants and expects to be done. However, effective HR professionals spend more time grappling with the key business drivers, and the needs of employees and managers, and then only developing the necessary HR frameworks and programmes to help the organisation attract and retain talent. This entails getting an in-depth understanding of the needs of current as well as prospective employees and managers, as talent will naturally be more engaged and motivated when working in an environment that caters to their needs.

Segmenting the audience and targeting marketing

Having a client-centric mindset is not enough, as it is impossible to treat all customers the same – especially when there are hundreds, thousands or even millions of them.

Marketing professionals generally start with market *segmentation*, which involves subdividing a large, homogenous market into clearly identifiable segments with similar needs, wants or demand characteristics. They then select their *target market(s)*, which represent a group of customers at which they wish to aim their marketing efforts and, ultimately, their products/services. This process makes it easier to design a marketing programme with the exact target segment in mind. The four basic segmentation principles used for differentiation are: demographic, psychographic, geographical and behavioural differences (Kotler & Armstrong, 2000). HR professionals can benefit from understanding this important exercise. A workforce is often very diverse, geographically dispersed and requires a targeted approach when implementing programmes and interventions. This requires an understanding of the demographic breakdown of the workforce (in terms of age, race, gender, education and income), which often has a bearing on whether employees have an interest in or a need for a specific initiative. For example, with a younger workforce, work/life balance, remote access, working conditions, room for career growth and promotion, and employee wellness are key deciding factors when an employee considers either joining and/or staying with an organisation. Even within programmes, segmentation is needed to understand how best to design and position the initiative effectively for the audience. For example, when designing retirement programmes, the focus will differ for each age bracket: for younger employees the emphasis will be on the need to save and on the time value of money, which will help ensure that they are in a comfortable position at retirement. However, when addressing employees who are on the verge of retirement, the education process will more likely focus on how to preserve one's life savings during retirement, or on preparing for retirement (psychologically and financially).

A geographic breakdown is key, as certain locations may be at different stages of maturity, therefore not all programmes and initiatives will be appropriate. Furthermore, when some employees are located on-site at a client, they may not have the same access to programmes as employees who are located at the employer site.

Employees are becoming increasingly discerning, therefore recognising where employees are the same and where they differ, remains paramount.

Understanding the competition

All good marketing organisations constantly scan the market and engage in market research to ensure that they understand who their competition is, what products/services they offer, their pricing models and where they are generally strong and weak. This allows organisations to strategically find a niche and/or a means of differentiating themselves from their competitors.

Effective HR professionals spend time analysing their competitors in terms of those companies they could potentially lose talent to. Some may be in competing industries, but in many cases competition stretches far wider. What do these companies provide for their employees in terms of the work environment, pay, benefits, training and career development opportunities? Those factors form the basis on which organisations compete for talent.

Active participation in 'best employer' surveys can help HR organisations assess their standing in the job market and benchmark themselves against the employer market in general, and/or against specific companies/industries. HR practices are evolving at a rapid rate, and knowing how you fare against the competition is a vital part of any good HR strategy.

Talent is exceptionally mobile, and with free access to information about career opportunities and the working environment at competing workplaces, it is important for HR to remain one step ahead, by scanning the external environment at all times.

The brand and value proposition

Almost all products and services have a very clear value proposition which focuses on the customer and addresses why s/he should buy/use a certain product and/or brand. The value proposition represents the set of benefits or values the company promises to deliver in order to satisfy the needs of customers. This encompasses not only the specifications of the product/service and/or brand, but importantly the benefits and value associated with buying or using it. It serves as a means to acquire new customers and retain existing customers, and/or to ensure repeat purchases. Marketers also refer to the unique selling proposition (USP), i.e., the elements which make the product/service different/better than that of a competitor.

In recent times, HR professionals have realised the need to clearly articulate the company's employee value proposition (EVP), which aims to convince current as well as prospective employees of why the company is a great place to work for, and highlights the unique factors that differentiate the company from other employers of choice. This is an absolute necessity when building the employer brand and ensuring that it resonates with both existing and prospective employees. In addition to the EVP, other factors which impact the employer brand are the image, reputation, perceptions of the company as an employer, the culture, the way employees are treated and, importantly, the commercial brand. The stronger the employer brand, the greater the likelihood that the company will be able to attract and retain the best talent. However, it is also good for commercial business, as consumers and organisations make decisions about who to do business with, based on a company's reputation as an employer.

The interwoven nature of the commercial/customer brand and the employer brand highlights an ideal opportunity for HR and marketing practitioners to work together so that the customer brand and the employer brand are in sync, both internally and externally.

Good corporate citizenship

In the same way customers want to buy from businesses that are good corporate citizens, so employees want to work for companies that do what is right with respect to the environment, the community and society in general.

In light of building both the commercial and the employer brands, these areas need to be considered and addressed in the brand strategy, as they can positively or detrimentally impact the target audience's perception of the brand, and can seriously impact their decision whether or not to engage with the organisation.

When embarking on graduate programmes, HR needs to ensure that the value proposition addresses these key elements, because Generation Y employees consider good corporate standing essential in their decision to join an organisation.

The marketing mix

This represents the actions or tactics companies use to promote their brand or product. Traditionally, the marketing mix is comprised of four key elements: product/service, price, promotion and place/distribution. As consumers, we are familiar with how companies use these elements to effectively market their products or services. HR practitioners should address their HR strategy with the same considerations in mind. For example, one key area may be the onboarding or inducting of new employees and what the organisation does to assimilate and orient them into the organisation. The *service* offering to the business is essentially getting new employees up and running in their roles and aligned to the organisation's culture as soon as possible. The *price* might be the fact that it takes them out of the workplace for two full days, which has cost/benefit implications. It could also involve the actual cost of running an induction programme. All of these factors must be taken into consideration when determining the potential value the initiative will have for internal customers (new employees and managers). The *distribution (place)* is where this occurs (physical company training centre), but remember that e-learning/web-based applications can overcome most physical/logistical challenges. Other considerations, such as *promotion*, are important: How will new employees know about this – via a welcome email from the CEO, or an invitation as they accept a job with the company? What additional opportunities for promotion exist to build a relationship with the employee target market at this early point in their career with the company?

HR initiatives that are planned with each of these elements in mind are likely to be more appropriate and relevant to the respective target audience(s).

Promoting, communicating and positioning the offering

Having a great product is all good and well, but if no one knows about it chances are it will not sell very well. Some of today's leading brands have built their reputations on the perceptions and aspirations they established through promotion. Hence, the proliferation of advertising and promotional activities in today's market ensures that consumers are aware of the products that are available, what makes them unique, their benefits, what they cost, where they can be purchased, and so forth.

Promotional capability or raising awareness of HR initiatives is probably one of the weakest areas amongst HR professionals. So much time is spent building the right 'product' (writing the policy, designing the benefit programme or building the training intervention), that not enough time is spent ensuring that the right people (target audience) are aware of the programme/initiative and/or are enticed to use it, participate in it or take advantage of it and understand the value of it. In HR terms, promotional activities may include easily accessible online self-service portals, the running of competitions or viral social media campaigns, the use of bathroom posters, electronic pop-up messages, emails, teaser campaigns and desk drops, to name a few, and will depend largely on the initiative at hand.

Much as customers are being bombarded with marketing messages in the external environment, so too is there 'noise' in the workplace. Employees are constantly being exposed to messages, information and communication. When implementing HR initiatives, HR practitioners need to consider how best to position those initiatives in the minds of employees in a way that is simple, relevant and memorable.

Marketers spend a great deal of time ensuring that they position their products/ services correctly in the minds of their customers. A well-cited example is the positioning of the soft drink 7-up, which competes against the colas. The company cleverly positioned its product as the 'Un-cola' to highlight it as an alternative to cola (Ries & Trout, 1981), thus positioning 7-up away from the colas, rather than trying to compete head-on.

Similarly, HR needs to ensure that its offerings are well positioned and communicated to employees to ensure buy-in, adherence, participation and/or cooperation. This normally entails explaining why something is being done, how, when, the benefits, etc. Without such clear positioning and communication many HR initiatives fail, since employees do not understand why there is a need for or a benefit to be derived from the initiative/programme.

A classic example is performance reviews (appraisals), often positioned by HR as a mandatory process, where the 'stick' approach is employed to arrive at completion. Alternative positionings could include: 'How have you contributed to the organisation's success?', 'Do you know what you need to do to earn your bonus?', 'How have you progressed against goals set?' Positioned in this way, it is more about the individual and his/her contribution than the company's need to know everyone's performance rating.

Leveraging systems and data

We have established the importance of segmentation and target marketing to the success of both marketing and HR. An important enabler is having access to accurate and robust data and systems to provide input on who to target with campaigns/ initiatives.

Over the years, marketers have invested heavily in Customer Relationship Management (CRM) systems in order to understand their customers better, build relationships with them, and use their purchasing history to inform the company of other products/services customers may be interested in, in the future.

A more recent understanding on the part of business is that having a robust Human Resource Information System (HRIS) is also essential to start truly comprehending employees, thanks to the ability to mine data based on demographics, geographics, talent or any other dimension.

On the one hand, this is dependent on the HR function having a strong administrative component, with a culture of discipline and rigour in terms of data capturing employee information, so as to ensure its integrity. On the other hand, it also requires a skilled analyst to ensure optimal workflow and processes around information and the point at which information is captured, updated and checked, in accordance with current policies.

Using data analytics to indicate trends

Having access to accurate data is one thing, knowing how to use the information for better planning, progress monitoring and identifying key trends, is another.

Marketers have traditionally used data on consumer buying and spending habits to better target future campaigns, or to analyse data to assess the success or return on investment (ROI) of a campaign/activity. For instance, the rate at which discount vouchers attached to a print advertisement are redeemed, can help measure the conversion to seeing the advertisement and the actual purchasing behaviour.

Marketers are currently faced with a significant opportunity to understand consumer buying behaviour and predict future buying patterns thanks to Big Data, a 'collection of data from traditional and digital sources inside and outside the company that represents a source for ongoing discovery and analysis' (Forbes, 2013, p. 2). It allows marketers to pull levers that can create opportunities in areas such as cross-selling, location-based marketing and in-store behaviour analysis. In retail, it can also be extremely powerful in optimising merchandise in terms of assortment, pricing and placement.

Although Big Data may not currently be a priority for many HR professionals, the opportunities opening up as a result of its use is creating great interest and has numerous benefits. For example, imagine the power of recruitment consultants being able to access and mine consumer buying information in order to identify, source and access select talent groups. Already, solution providers are offering new Big Data tools to help recruiters find unique candidates in specialised markets (Bersin, 2014).

However, as a starting point, current best practice refers to the importance of having some level of analytical skills in the HR team, to be able to better mine current demographic and talent data. This is helpful not only in identifying trends, and monitoring progress and improvement against people targets, but also in making better people decisions going forward. Analytics such as employee attrition (or, conversely, retention), headcount growth, payroll costs, training investment and workplace diversity are all key metrics that need to be understood by the HR team and managed in line with the targets and objectives of the organisation.

Collaboration with customers

Technological advances have driven a sudden convergence of the digital, mobile and social spheres, resulting in a new dynamic in stakeholder relationships by connecting customers, employees and partners in new ways, both to organisations and to one another (Competing in tumultuous times, 2014).

Marketers successfully use the Internet and social media as a means of proactively connecting with their customers and affording them the chance to voice complaints, make enquiries, recommend a product/service and interact with the company more directly.

In the workplace, such connectivity fundamentally changes the way people engage and the manner in which talent is managed. HR can now harness this skill thanks to the opening up of multiple opportunities for innovation, learning and knowledge sharing.

HR needs to be the custodian of creating a more open and collaborative culture, as this can be successfully harnessed to help organisations grow more effectively and efficiently.

Young employees entering the workplace have high expectations for online collaboration, knowledge sharing and general transparency from top to bottom.

Recruitment, learning and development can be vastly improved within organisations by engaging social media and fostering collaboration. 'LinkedIn', for example, allows recruitment consultants and the workforce to find and recommend potential candidates for vacant roles, often referring passive candidates who are not even in the job market.

Learning and development platforms allow employees to learn collaboratively online, while exposing what learning they enjoyed and sharing this with colleagues.

HR needs to work closely with the business to endorse, drive, implement and support the use of collaborative platforms. Opening up channels for external as well as internal collaboration usually requires more administration, some control, and a level of risk/exposure. However, this is a small price to pay for the potential rewards which such sharing reaps for an organisation.

Feedback loop for continual improvement

Marketers know the importance of going directly to customers for feedback about their product/service. This is done by conducting ongoing customer satisfaction surveys and ensuring that any feedback is used to make changes or improve the offering in the future.

Similarly, it is important that HR professionals conduct employee satisfaction surveys on a regular basis, to ascertain the level of employee engagement and satisfaction. This allows the HR department to monitor progress and assess their value-add in certain key areas, as well as to identify areas requiring focus and/or continual improvement. It also helps to affirm whether the EVP is still relevant. Importantly, when the outputs of employee surveys are taken seriously by companies, and employees realise that their voices are being heard and their ideas executed/ issues addressed, this leads to a more robust HR strategy that is aligned to meeting the needs of the target audience. It also further invites more active participation in future surveys.

Measuring ROI or value

The success of any marketing campaign is generally based on measurable outcomes – mostly linked to brand building, market share and/or sales.

HR is often required to drive cyclical processes, which results in the success of a campaign being measured or assessed based on the completion of the activity itself, rather than the outcome/value it was meant to achieve. So, for example, ensuring that all employees have completed their performance contracts on time is frequently a cyclical and onerous process that HR is responsible for driving to completion. However, the success of this exercise should not be measured on the metric of getting all employees to sign off on their performance contract, but rather on the quality of the deliverables (key performance indicators [KPIs] and key performance areas [KPAs]), and whether this adequately cascades the strategy down the organisation, in an aligned way.

HR practitioners need to become much more proficient at predefining what business value their activities impact. Thereafter, they need to measure the positive impact on the business, rather than viewing success as the completion of an activity itself.

Conclusion

All employees are consumers in some shape or form. Their behaviour in the workplace, as employees, is influenced by their behaviour and expectations as consumers. This interrelationship is due to their inherent behaviour as human beings, their increasing access to information, and the growing social need to collaborate. This strengthens the case for a similar business approach to meet the needs of both internal and external clients.

For HR professionals to be valued business partners, a shift is required to better balance the behavioural science elements of HR management with a thorough understanding of key business drivers and principles.

By applying proven marketing principles with the customer (employees and managers) at the centre, the HR function will be better equipped to manage talent and implement initiatives and programmes that are relevant and visible to its target market. Importantly, it will be perceived as delivering the expected value to all business stakeholders.

Finally, the success of any business strategy involves a well-aligned and well-managed people strategy. It is ultimately the employees of an organisation who are the key and critical resources which determine whether a strategy will be executed. This requires a Chief Human Resource Officer (CHRO) who is perceived as a strategic business partner, who is integral to the executive team, and is key in helping to shape and build the people strategy. It further requires the necessary support to build an HR team with the capabilities to execute on this.

What an exciting time for HR to be integral to shaping and defining the new world of work. The time is now!

References

Bersin, J. (2013). *Predictions for 2014: Building a strong talent pipeline for the global economic recovery – Time for innovative and integrated talent and HR strategies.* US: Bersin by Deloitte. Retrieved August 28, 2014 from http://www.cdmn.ca/wp-content/uploads/2014/02/C-inetpub-wwwroot-Prod-uploadedFiles-122013PSGP.pdf

Craig, T. (2009). Sir Ken Robinson: The creative thinker. *Personnel Today*, June. Retrieved August 28, 2014 from http://www.personneltoday.com/hr/sir-ken-robinson-the-creative-thinker/

Deloitte. (2014). *How to compete in tumultuous times and operate in complexity.* Retrieved August 28, 2014 fromhttp://deloitteblog.co.za/2014/03/24/how-to-compete-in-tumultuous-times-and-operate-in-complexity/#sthash.rkVbDr8F.dpuf

Fast Company. (2005). *Why we hate HR – Counterpoint.* Retrieved August 28, 2014 from http://www.fastcompany.com/675596/why-we-hate-hr-counterpoint

Forbes Magazine. (2013, August). *What is big data?* Retrieved August 28, 2014 from http://www.forbes.com/sites/lisaarthur/2013/08/15/what-is-big-data/

Kotler, P. & Armstrong, G. (2000). *Principles of marketing*, 9th edition. New Jersey: Prentice Hall.

Nayar, V. (2010). *Employees first, customers second.* Boston: Harvard Business Press Books.

Ries, A. & Trout, J. (2000). *Positioning – The battle for your mind.* New York: McGraw Hill.

Trout, J. (2006). *Peter Drucker on marketing.* Retrieved August 28, 2014 from http://www.forbes.com/2006/06/30/jack-trout-on-marketing-cx_jt_0703drucker.html

CHAPTER 19: Leading HR

Theo Veldsman

Introduction

Leadership, inter alia leading HR, is about conceiving possible futures and realising a chosen, desired future – in the case of leading HR, the desired people future of the organisation. The future forms the crux of leadership and leading. Leadership who pro-actively take charge of their organisation's future through pursuing a chosen, desired future, will be architects of their future, not victims.

Why the criticality of leadership in future actualisation? Leadership serve as the *beacon* for direction and guidance; radiate mobilising *energy* around which (sometimes widely diverse) people rally; *envision* people to visualise and explore previously unseen challenges and test apparently impossible boundaries; *enable and empower* people to rise above their circumstances, frequently during the darkest of times; and *model* the desired ways of acting, to be adopted by others. Leadership thus is a verb, not a noun; it is an action, not a state.

Given the criticality of leadership in general, why the critical importance of leading HR excellently? Within a knowledge society only 15 per cent of the resources of an organisation are tangible; 85 per cent are intangible (Lev, 2001). Tangible resources refer to, for example, facilities, technology and finance, while intangible resources embrace, for example, an organisation's reputation, brand, patent rights, capabilities and people (Greco, Cricelli & Grimaldi, 2013). At least 70 per cent of intangible resources are resident in the organisation's people, in the form of expertise, knowledge and skills. Without doubt, in a knowledge society people have moved centre stage in ensuring the future sustainable success of organisations (Ulrich, Brockbank, Younger & Ulrich, 2012 and 2013; Wright, Boudreau, Pace, Sartain, McKinnon & Antoine, 2011).

So, the challenge facing HR as the people experts of the organisation is to become leaders in the fullest sense of the word, from an organisational (or business) perspective (Weiss, 2013).

In facing up to and engaging with the future in the new, emerging world order (Ernst & Young, 2009; Hatum, 2013; Oxford Martin Commission, 2013; Ulrich, Brockbank, Younger & Ulrich, 2012 and 2013; Veldsman, 2013) it can further be contended that the need is for different *and* better leadership. Hence also different *and* better HR leadership. 'Different', because the newly emerging world order imposes different demands and sets different challenges. 'Better', because of the less forgiving nature of the challenges, issues and problems today's leadership face.

The purpose of this chapter is to explore what it means to lead HR as a genuine leader from an organisational perspective in the new, emerging world order. The chapter unfolds around four interdependent, interacting themes, to form a tapestry: 1) What are the constituents of a *desired people future* (the 'why' and 'whereto'); 2) What does the process of leading HR entail, the *required acts of leadership* (the 'how'); 3) What *roles* must HR leadership play with respect to leadership acts (the 'who'); and 4) What *qualities* must infuse leadership acts and roles, to bring about leadership excellence in leading HR (the 'what') in the new, emerging world order?

A desired people future

The centrepiece of leading HR is the realisation of a desired people future for the organisation. This concept relates to the people effectiveness of the organisation, and its resulting contribution to the performance and success of the organisation (cf. Paawe, Guest & Wright, 2013). The desired people future of an organisation, expressed in terms of people effectiveness, finds concrete expression in the following equation:

People effectiveness = f *(people competencies x people energy x people legitimacy x people autonomy x people fulfilment)*

Important to note with respect to the equation is the multiplicative relationship between the constituent elements: an increase/decrease in the value of an element will significantly enhance/detract from the overall people effectiveness of an organisation. A value of zero on one or more elements will reduce the overall people effectiveness of the organisation to nought.

The constituent elements of the above equation can be defined as follows:

- *People competencies ('can do')*. The abilities, both hard (i.e., skills, knowledge, expertise) and soft (i.e., personal attributes, attitudes, values, conduct), required by people to deliver on the mission of the organisation (i.e., the business of the business);

- *People energy ('will do')*. The people motivational power needed to realise the organisation's mission and vision (i.e., the dream of the organisation);

- *People legitimacy ('should do')*. The rightfulness and legitimacy people have to experience regarding what the organisation stands for, how it conducts its business, and how it lives its espoused values (i.e., the ideology of the organisation);

- *People autonomy ('allowed to do')*. The accountability, authority and freedom people need to be given to act, relative to the organisational aspirations and goals they want to pursue;

- *People fulfilment ('want to do')*. The need fulfilment people aspire to, wish for and will receive as a consequence of their conduct, effort and performance, relative to the organisational outcomes achieved.

Converting the above people effectiveness equation into a fully blown organisational effectiveness equation, results in the expanded equation given below. This equation unequivocally demonstrates the intimate and synergic relationship and interdependency between the people and organisational elements of the organisation (Weiss, 2013). In fully taking up a genuine leadership role, HR leadership must take full accountability for the organisational effectiveness equation:

Organisational effectiveness = f (people competencies/mission x people energy/vision x people legitimacy/ideology x people autonomy/goals x people fulfilment/outcomes)

In leading HR, the *mission critical leadership challenge* with respect to the desired people future, as expressed in terms of organisational/people effectiveness, requires

1. attaining a high *alignment* between the five pairs of the people and organisational elements (e.g., people competencies/mission); *and*

2. realising the desired *organisational effectiveness* through optimising the multiplicative relationship between *all* the constituent pairs.

However, the organisational effectiveness aspired to, in order to realise a desired people future, must be referenced at all times against the lasting, worthy legacy which the achievement thereof must leave behind (i.e., the difference the legacy makes).

Without such a reference point, the desired people future will become self-serving and subservient to parochial organisational interests. In leading HR, the pursuit of this legacy needs to be a consequence of all of the organisation's intentions, aspirations and actions.

What is the make-up of the lasting, worthy legacy that HR leadership must ensure their organisations leave behind? This legacy can be described as a 'high performance/high authentic/high responsibility organisation' (i.e., three interdependent dimensions).

The three dimensions represent the 'triple bottom line' of the HR leadership's aspirational, lasting and worthy legacy, which is depicted in the form of a triangle in Figure 19.1, where each dimension serves as an anchor point. The outcome specific to a legacy dimension is also given.

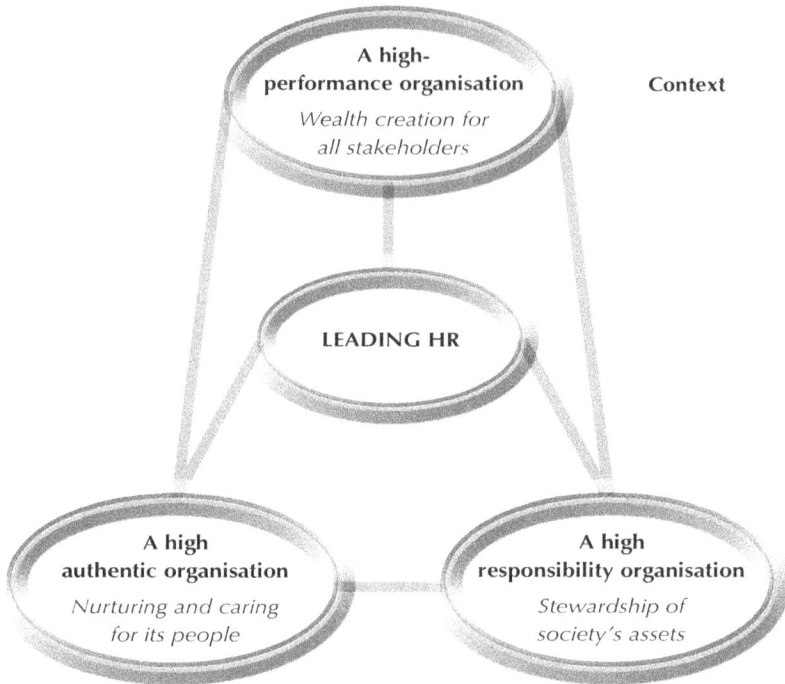

Figure 19.1: Leading HR in ensuring a lasting, worthy legacy

In leading HR, the *mission critical leadership challenge* regarding the desired people future is establishing a direct line of sight between organisational/people effectiveness and a lasting, worthy legacy: the triple bottom line of high performance/ high authentic/high responsibility organisation.

The acts of leading HR

The discovery, choice and realisation of a desired people future demand five acts in terms of leading HR (see Figure 19.2). In their totality these acts form the basis of intense, ongoing people discourse (or fierce conversation) (Scott, 2002) about the organisation and its people that HR leadership must invoke, cultivate, facilitate, nurture and entrench across the organisation. This discourse must not only involve the HR function itself, but also (more importantly) the whole leadership community of the organisation. In other words, the discourse is an organisational (not an HR exclusive) conversation.

The five acts forming the people discourse, as given in Figure 19.2, can metaphorically be seen as the five intertwined strands of a rope, all occurring concurrently in an interdependent fashion in real time. (A rope carries the symbolism of a means to ascend jointly to greater heights.) The strength of each stand determines the overall strength of the rope. Albeit that the five acts occur in a recursive, iterative fashion, and are active at all times, each has to be introduced as the focal point of conversation at the right time, as the discourse unfolds. Below, the respective acts are discussed in the approximate logical sequence of being invoked as the focal point. The order of the discussion is, however, based on the understanding that the other acts concurrently serve as the backdrop to the act being discussed. A rope is a rope by virtue of all of its strands.

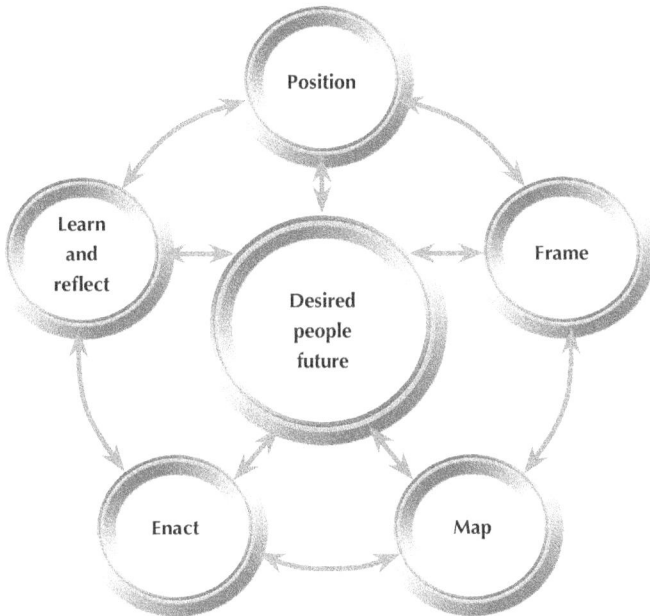

Figure 19.2: The acts of leading HR, making up the people discourse of the organisation

Act 1: Position

Leadership is embedded in a certain context with which a leader must engage constructively, in order to be effective and to make the organisation sustainably successful (e.g., Ulrich, Brockbank, Younger & Ulrich, 2013). Act 1, the position of leading HR, is all about the correct demarcation, and understanding by the organisational leadership, of their location in the world and in their organisation, with the consequential associated leadership people demands and requirements. The aim of this act in the people discourse is to ensure that the organisation's leadership deal with the right matters at the right time, in the right way and with the right parties, in the context within which they have to engage and lead the people of their organisation. This act necessitates the establishment of a high level of contextual intelligence amongst leadership, in order to bring about a 'best fit' between the leadership and their context.

At least two interrelated, critical questions regarding position have to be considered and answered through the discourse, to bring about a best fit between leadership and their context:

1. What is the *operating arena* (with its commensurate contextual complexity) of the organisation, now and going into the future? Every organisation is embedded in a certain operating arena, chosen deliberately or arrived at by default. The operating arena demarcates the location of the organisation, i.e., the playing field on and the league in which the organisation plays/desires to play, with the accompanying players, game plan and rules, e.g., developed countries and/or developing countries/emerging economies. Depending on the operating arena of an organisation, its leadership will have to deal with a certain degree of contextual complexity.

   Contextual complexity affects the 'pitch' of the leadership demands and requirements imposed on the organisation by its operating arena. Contextual complexity is a function of several complexity variables, namely

   - the *space* and *time boundaries* within which the organisation must/wishes to operate, i.e., narrow to wide;

   - the *scope of the organisation* in terms of markets, customers and products/services, i.e., uniform to diverse;

   - the *variety within the organisation* in terms of variables such as strategic intent, policies and standards, work processes, design, culture and outcomes, i.e., single to multiple; and

   - the *degree and rate of change the organisation is exposed to*, i.e., incremental to revolutionary.

The organisation's operating arena, with its commensurate contextual complexity, determines the external leadership and people demands as well as the requirements imposed on the organisation. For example, emerging countries are increasingly becoming the chosen operating arena for many global (or globalising) organisations as they look to the future, given the predicted growing dominance and influence of these countries in coming years in the globalising world (Guillén & García-Canal, 2013). Typically, emerging economies are countries which (Veldsman, 2013)

- are in a state of rapid transition and fundamental transformation;

- are undergoing high economic growth;

- are experiencing a tighter integration of their localised, closed economies and societies into the global village;

- are benefiting from a significant influx of high levels of foreign investment;

- are experiencing societal systems/infrastructure disconnects and imbalances;

- have a young population; and

- are experiencing a widening gap between the haves and have-nots.

In terms of contextual complexity, for example, a shift in the space boundary from local to global sets the leadership competency requirements of a 'global mindset' and 'intercultural sensitivity'. An expansion in scope and variety imposes the competency requirement of 'systemic thinking'. A shift from incremental to revolutionary change makes 'large-scale organisational change' an essential leadership competency.

2. What is the *requisite complexity of the leadership roles* that need to be performed by the leadership community for the organisation to be successful? Each leader fulfils a certain organisational role. A good fit must exist between the leader and his/her role. A role refers to the expected integrated set of actions a leader has to take in order to get things done in the organisation. Stratified Systems Theory (Jaques, 2006; Jaques & Clement, 1994; Shephard, Gray, Hunt & McArthur, 2007) provides a handy way of conceptualising the requisite complexity imposed by different levels of work associated with different leadership roles, and by implication the leadership demands and requirements made by these levels. Seven levels of work are distinguished: Level 7: Corporate prescience (i.e., global systems) through to Level 1: Quality (i.e., daily operational delivery). Space constraints prevent a detailed discussion of the leadership role behaviours required by each level of work. The important point here is the match between the leader and his/her role, and him/her acting in accordance with the requisite complexity of their particular level of work.

For the best contextual fit, level of work role behaviours furthermore have to match the leadership people demands and requirements imposed by the operating arena of the organisation, with its commensurate contextual complexity. In leading HR, the discourse invoked by this act of leading must center around leadership role execution at the requisite level of work and contextual complexity.

In leading HR, the *key leadership discourse theme* with respect to Act 1: Position, is the imperative of bringing about a contextual best fit, expressed in 1) the appropriate, shared demarcation, and understanding by the leadership, of the organisation's operating arena with its commensurate contextual complexity and the requisite complexity of their respective leadership roles; and 2) matching leaders to fit the context, both externally and Internally, in which they have to lead, and equipping them to lead effectively in that context. Jim Collins (2001), in *From good to great*, speaks about getting the right people on the bus, and the wrong people off it.

Act 2: Frame

Leadership find their rightful place in the world and in the organisation through the intense discourse regarding Act 1: Position. Strand one of the rope is now in place.

In leading HR, next an in-depth discourse has to be conducted about the leadership community's *mode of engagement* with their agreed-upon, demarcated context. This discourse is captured in Act 2: Frame, which deals with the tripartite of *world views*, *decision-making frameworks* and *value orientations*.

Leadership engage with their context through a certain set of lenses: an explicitly expressed or implicitly adopted *world view*. (Typical equivalent terms for 'world view' are mental models, paradigms, schemata or archetypes) (e.g., Sparrow, Hird, Hesketh & Cooper, 2010). A world view frames leadership's thinking about, interpretation of and engagement with, the reality of their context. On the one hand, a world view 'liberates' leadership's thinking about and understanding of their context by opening up new potential perspectives regarding the context. Concurrently, however, on the other hand a world view 'imprisons' leadership by creating blind spots about, and/ or by setting constraints on, their thinking about and their understanding of their context. Three examples of possible world views are:

- *Mechanistic*. Reality works like a machine in terms of given, fixed rules. It is made up of independent, replaceable parts which fit together like the gears of a machine;

- *Systems*. Reality consists of various systems which take inputs from their environment, and convert (the throughput process) these inputs into outputs which, in turn, enable the acquisition of inputs for the next cycle of conversion through a feedback loop related to the acceptability of the outputs to the environment;

- *Complexity/chaos*. Reality consists of a holistic set of reciprocally influencing and interdependent variables which, as a collectivity, continuously go through unpredictable states of order and chaos as their interdependencies change. Order is expressed in the form of emerging, self-designing patterns, governed by a few underlying rules.

From many quarters it is argued that at present a complexity/chaos world view provides the best engagement mode to make sense of and give sense to the new, emerging world order (Gharajedaghi, 2011; Kurtz & Snowden, 2003; Stacey, Griffin & Shaw, 2000; Wheatley, 2010).

Based on its chosen world view, leadership next need to have an intense discourse about what which *decision-making framework* to select, in order to enable them to engage constructively with the reality, as framed by their adopted world view. In other words, this framework needs to be congruent with their adopted world view of the leadership. Given the appropriateness of a complexity/chaos world view, the Cynefin decision-making framework (Snowden & Boone, 2007) provides a useful way for leadership to recognise, understand and engage constructively with the qualitatively different contexts they face in a chaotic/complex world. This decision-making framework is depicted in Figure 19.3 (note that space constraints prevent a more detailed discussion).

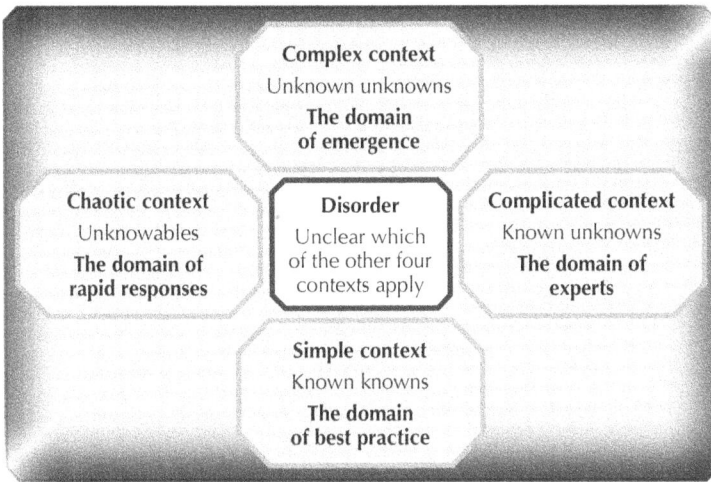

Figure 19.3: Different contexts with which leadership has to engage, based on a complexity/ chaos world view

Source: Snowden and Boone (2007)

Finally, the discourse regarding Act 2: Frame, has to address the *value orientation* leadership need to apply in making value judgements when engaging with their context.

Value orientation is a fundamental, value-based engagement with the world. It should not be confused with the more visible and concrete values of an organisation (i.e., integrity, client centricity, professionalism), although a value orientation can form the basis of such organisational values.

The value orientation allows leadership, when using their preferred decision-making framework, to award relative worth to the entities, events and outcomes they encounter. Relative worth relates to the value criteria of importance, rightfulness and desirability. Spiral dynamics is an example of a comprehensive value orientation framework, based on a bio-psychosocial theory of evolving human development, conceptualised by Clare Graves (1970), and converted into a value orientation framework by Don Beck and Chris Cowan (Beck & Cowan, 1996). Spiral dynamics is made up of eight different human niches, which are representative of different value systems that are colour-coded. Again, space constraints prevent a detailed discussion of this value orientation framework.

In leading HR, the *key leadership discourse theme* with respect to Act 2: Frame, is to engender the adoption by the leadership community of a shared, appropriate engagement mode as composed of a world view, i.e., the right lenses to look at the world; a decision-making framework, i.e., recognising and understanding contexts for what they are in order to make the right type of decisions about them and a fundamental value orientation, i.e., awarding relative worth to entities, events and outcomes.

Act 3: Map

Enabled by the discourse around Act 2: Frame, leadership can now, through the appropriate mode, constructively engage with their context, as demarcated in Act 1: Position. Strands one and two of the rope are now in place. The objective of Act 3 is to co-map the HR territory with the organisational leadership – the basic building blocks making up the HR territory, with their interrelationships and dynamics. This map can be called the people effectiveness landscape. Such a map is imperative if the leadership of the organisation want to ensure that people management contribute in a significant manner to the future sustainability of their organisations, and realise their desired people future.

Put slightly differently, Act 3: Map, leading HR requires the conceptualising of the HR territory, by providing the essential vocabulary (or thinking tools) for the people conversation conducted amongst the organisational leadership. The map enables an ongoing discourse not only on what the building blocks of the people effectiveness landscape are, their interrelationships and dynamics, but also what the leading best people thinking and practices are with respect to each building block. In this way HR leadership cement their role as people thought leaders in the organisation (e.g., Ulrich, Brockbank, Younger & Ulrich, 2013; Veldsman, 2008a and b; Weiss, 2013; Wright, Boudreau, Pace, Sartain, McKinnon & Antoine, 2011). The people effectiveness landscape, with its associated leading best people thinking and practices, thus serves as a conversational tool to direct and guide the discourse around the 'as is' and 'to be' people states in the organisation.

Figure 19.4 depicts a proposed people effectiveness landscape, with its building blocks and interrelationships, as framed by a complexity/chaos world view. Important to note is the systemic interplay of the building blocks making up the landscape which coalesces into self-reinforcing interaction patterns over time. A pattern can be either virtuous or vicious, i.e., the crystallised pattern in force can either enhance people effectiveness in an upward spiral of ever-improving people performance within the organisation and hence realise the desired people future. Or the pattern can detract from, or even destroy, people effectiveness and hence the desired people future. The degree of positive coherence attained across these building blocks in the landscape, i.e., through a virtuous cycle, will ultimately determine the (potential) degree of people effectiveness attainable/attained by an organisation, and the consequential ability to realise its desired people future.

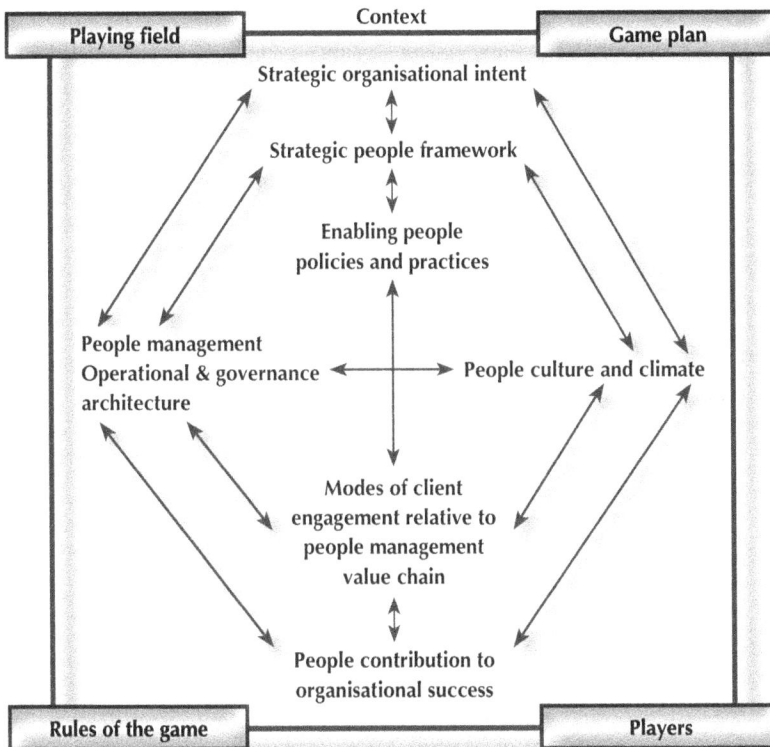

Figure 19.4: The people effectiveness landscape

In leading HR, the *key leadership discourse theme* with respect to Act 3: Map, is to embed and institutionalise a shared conversational map of the people territory, here called the people effectiveness landscape, in order to place the leadership in its people discourse about its people at the cutting edge, and even beyond.

Act 4: Enact

Leading HR through Act 3: Map provided the essential vocabulary (or thinking tools) for the people conversation amongst organisational leadership, allowing them to diagnose the people state of their organisation (current and future) in terms of leading best people thinking and practices. Act 4: Enact is about taking the discourse to the coal face where the action has to happen. It is the discourse about the what, how, who, when and where of the action the leadership have to take to realise the desired people future, using the people effectiveness landscape map to direct and guide their thinking and action. It is about converting the people effectiveness landscape into an actionable people strategic intent. This intent can be metaphorically seen as a future-directed arrow the leadership must put into their quiver to hit the desired people future as the 'target', as expressed in organisational/people effectiveness.

Organisations with a formalised people strategic intent perform 35 per cent better than their peers (PriceWaterhouseCoopers, 2002).

Figure 19.5 depicts a typical, comprehensive people strategic intent (also called a strategic agenda) (see Ulrich, Brockbank, Younger & Ulrich, 2013) as the future-directed arrow to realise the desired people future.

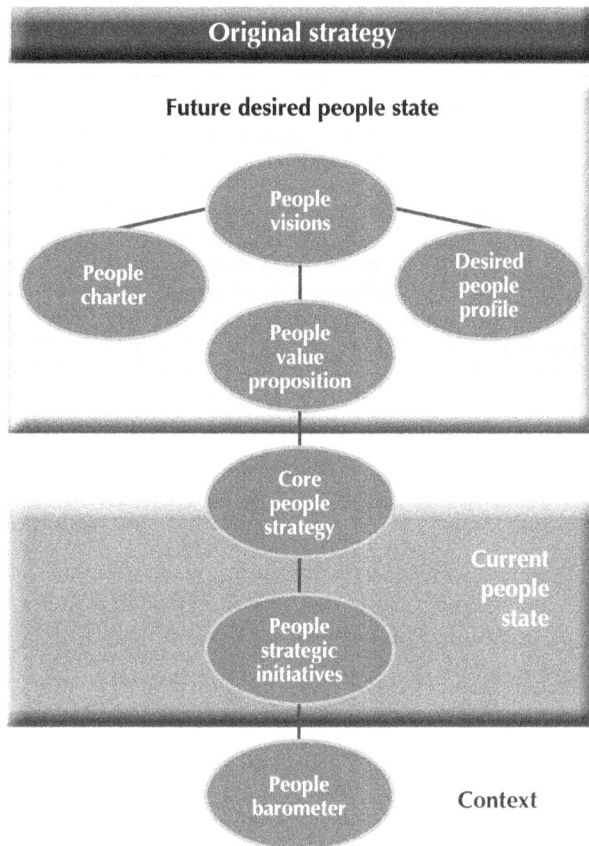

Figure 19.5: The interdependent action domains of a comprehensive people strategic intent

Based on Figure 19.5, a typical, comprehensive people strategic intent as a future-directed arrow consists of the following interdependent action domains:

- *Context.* The expected future trends that will affect the organisation and its people within its operating arena. Hence the importance of the discourse focusing on Act 1: Position, to correctly demarcate the organisation's operating arena;

- *Organisational strategy.* This is made up of a portfolio of six executive leadership tasks, the outcomes of which are models in terms of which the organisation wishes to function (e.g., Sparrow, Hird, Hesketh & Cooper, 2010). Figure 19.6 depicts a portfolio of executive leadership tasks with their resultant models. The portfolio of executive leadership tasks has to be viewed in a holistic, integrated and interconnected way. In other words, the tasks have to synergistically support one another at all times if the organisation is to be effective (i.e., doing the right things) and efficient (i.e., doing things right).

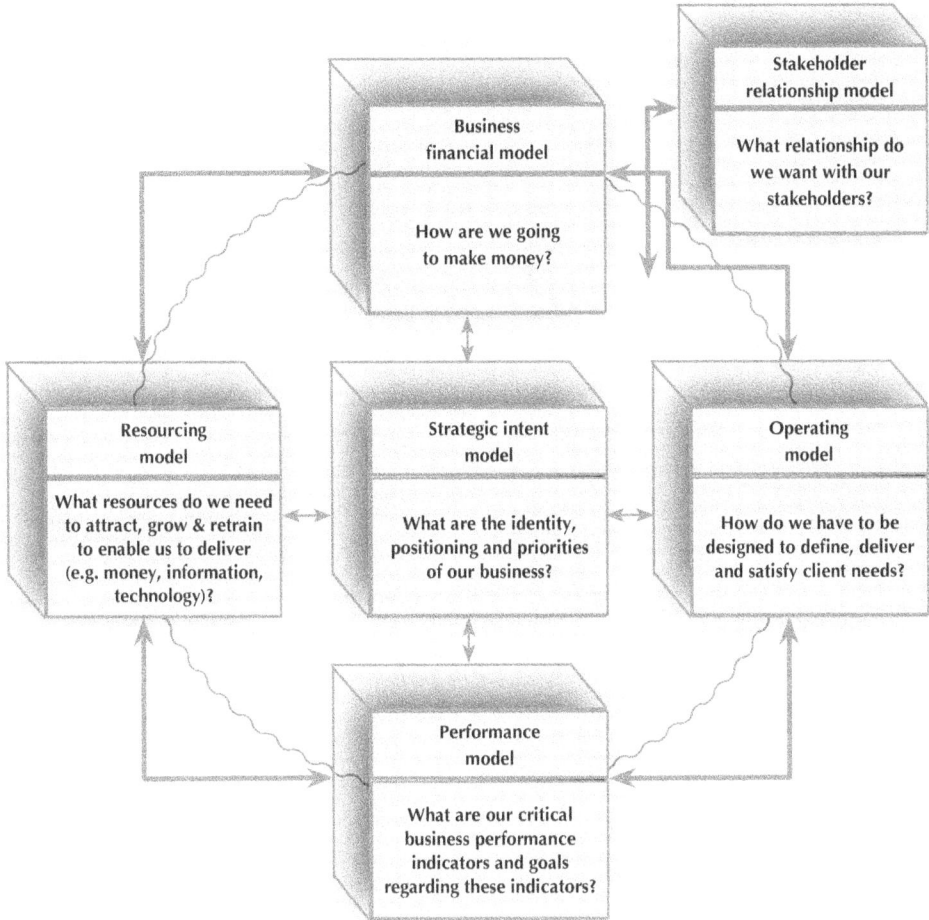

Figure 19.6: The portfolio of leadership tasks with their resultant models

Critically important here, is that leadership make a clear strategic choice regarding the expected role people must and should play in the organisational strategy, and its execution, i.e., the intended strategic role of people in making and keeping the organisation successful. People's role in and their contribution to each of the models in Figure 19.6 have to be thought through and clearly spelt out. For instance, Sparrow, Hird, Hesketh and Cooper (2010) place people at the centre of building new business models, in order to give a true, sustainable and competitive edge to organisations in the emerging, new world order. At least three strategic people choices can be discerned: 1) people as a cost to the organisation; 2) people as an asset (or the most important asset) of an organisation; or 3) people as value unlockers and wealth creators. The last choice appears to be the most appropriate to the emerging, new order.

- *Future desired people state*. This forms the *people strategic framework* of the organisation, the point of the future-directed arrow (see Figure 19.5). The framework consists of the following strategic elements:

    – *People vision*, i.e., the organisation's dream for its people;

    – *People charter (or people philosophy)*, i.e., the organisation's basic beliefs regarding its people and how an organisation and its people wish to set up and manage the basic relationship between them. The people charter not only gives concrete expression to the strategic people choice made by the organisation, but also expresses the nature of the psychosocial contract the organisation and its people desire to establish and maintain between them. The psychosocial contract refers to the reciprocal expectations that the organisation and its people have regarding their respective contributions and outcomes in terms of their basic relationship. From the organisation's side it includes performance, recognition and rewards; from the people's side, opportunities, needs, values and meaning. In a sense the people charter forms the 'Ten Commandments' of people management in the organisation;

    – *People value proposition*, i.e., the compelling reasons why people must join and stay with the organisation, e.g., it is a reputable organisation, offering challenging and meaningful work, with credible leadership, provides ongoing learning and development, and is diversity friendly. The people value proposition also gives concrete expression to the strategic people choice made by the organisation, and aims to maximise people's engagement in the organisation in terms of body, heart, mind and spirit;

    – *Desired people profile*, i.e., a high-level profile of the ideal type(s) of person the organisation wishes to employ. This profile is expressed comprehensively in terms of desirable attributes, knowledge, expertise and experience, attitudes, values and conduct.

- *Current people state*. This is where the organisation is at present with its people;

- *Core people strategy*. The broad thrust (or intent) of the strategic journey to be undertaken by the organisation to realise its *desired future people state* by converting the *current people state* into the future desired state, the shaft of the future-directed arrow (see Figure 19.5);

- *Strategic people initiatives*. The actions required in terms of the *core people strategy* to realise the *desired people state*, the shaft of the future-directed arrow (see Figure 19.5). The strategic people initiatives entail transforming the people effectiveness equation elements, e.g., people competencies ('can do') and people autonomy ('allowed to do'), which serve as the key imperatives to organisational success, from a people perspective;

- *People dashboard.* The measurement model (with metrics) to track and monitor the people state of the organisation, and its contribution to organisational performance and success, i.e., the tail of the arrow (see Figure 19.5). The dashboard indicates whether the arrow is on the right track, and whether leadership will need to make adjustments to the head or the shaft of the arrow, as the organisation journeys into the future.

In leading HR, the *key leadership discourse theme* with respect to Act 4: Enact, is to craft and roll out a people strategic intent, enabling the organisation to realise its desired people future and leave the lasting, worthy legacy of a 'high-performance/ high authentic/high responsibility organisation'. It is about hitting the future as a target.

Act 5: Learn and reflect

The final strand of the rope making up the people discourse is Act 5: Learn and reflect. In particular, this act has to be present throughout all of the other acts. This act encompasses the rate at which leadership, stakeholders and the organisation are innovating continuously, individually and severally – with respect to all of the prior acts of framing, thinking and actioning. Organisational learning/teaching becomes a core ingredient of an organisation's competitive edge in a world of ongoing change requiring relentless innovation and continuous improvement. Renewing one's thinking and doing as regards the people side of the organisation, relative to all of the above acts, is central for any organisation wishing to remain at the forefront (Ulrich, Brockbank, Younger & Ulrich, 2013).

Unless the organisation and its members, inter alia its leadership, learn/teach (L) faster than the velocity of change (C), then the organisation will not be sustainable in the future, given the hyper-turbulent conditions of the emerging new world order, i.e., $L \geq C$. Leading HR demands acting as a catalyst in transforming the organisation into a learning/teaching organisation, which is able to translate experiences into information, information into knowledge, and knowledge into wisdom, and to do this at an increasingly rapid rate, if the organisation is to remain a thriving, sustainable entity.

Transforming the organisation into a learning/teaching organisation requires that the following types of learning and teaching be entrenched at the individual, team, functional and organisational levels:

- *Learning the ropes,* i.e., the ability to grasp how things work and interrelate;
- *Learning how to perform,* i.e., the ability to be streetwise on how to produce results in a given setting;

- *Learning through redesigning*, i.e., the ability to change models, processes and resources in order to reach desired outcomes more efficiently ('doing things right');

- *Learning through reframing*, i.e., the ability to reflect on and change values, beliefs, assumptions and norms, in order to create new frames of reference (or paradigms) ('doing the right things');

- *Learning about learning*, i.e., the ability to gain deeper insight into how individuals and organisations learn, and to how to enhance learning processes.

In leading HR, the *key leadership discourse theme* with respect to Act 5: Learn and reflect, is to transform the organisation into a learning/teaching entity which is capable of consistently learning faster than the rate of change.

In summary, leading HR implies the process of initiating, stimulating and sustaining an intense, ongoing organisational discourse, in real time, around the organisation's desired people future.

This discourse is made up of five intertwined acts, like the strands of a rope: position, frame, map, enact, and learn and reflect. This discourse needs to involve the whole leadership community of the organisation. In the final instance, the ultimate outcome of this conversational process is a coherent story which leadership would be able to tell about their people and their critical role in the success of the organisation, now and going into the future. All leaders therefore need to become true storytellers, conveying a coherent people picture that makes sense, provides meaning and purpose to those they lead, and enables and empowers them to act in an inspired and committed way (Christie, 2004; Denning, 2011; Veldsman & May, 2013). Then, and only then, will the likelihood be high that the desired people future of the organisation will be realised because the discourse about people has been elevated to an organisational discourse in which the total leadership of the organisation participate, not only HR.

The roles HR leadership play with respect to leadership acts

In leading HR through the above intense, ongoing organisational discourse, in real time, centring around the organisation's desired people future, HR leadership as co-storytellers have to play certain *task* roles, apart from their process roles (e.g., facilitator, catalyst) with regard to the five acts making up the discourse as depicted in Figure 19.7. In this figure the respective roles are placed relative to the acts in the discourse to which they have to contribute. The roles are an adaptation and an expansion of those proposed by Dave Ulrich for HR (Ulrich, 1997; Ulrich & Brockband, 2005).[1]

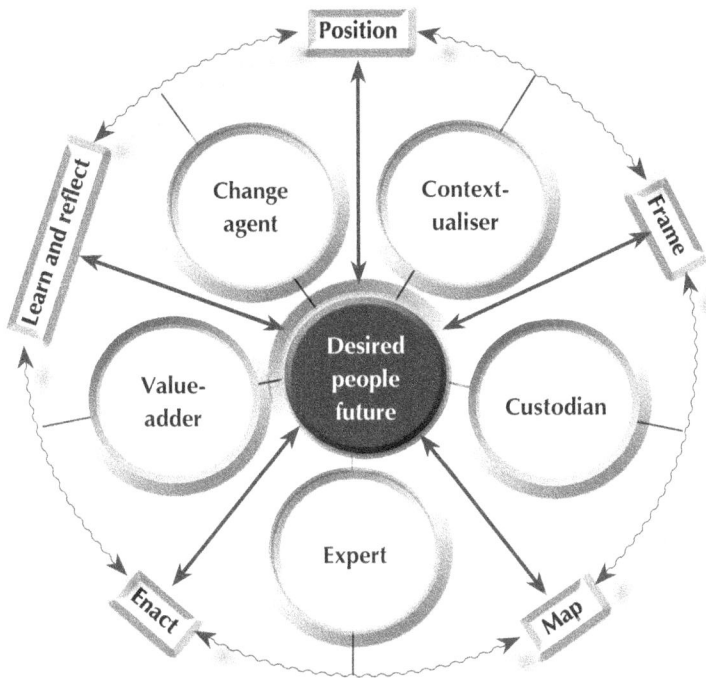

Figure 19.7: The roles to be played in leading HR

According to Figure 19.7, in leading HR, HR has to play the following five roles if the organisation's leadership is to arrive at a meaningful, coherent, enabling and empowering story about the desired people future of the organisation, and the intended journey to get there:

- *Contextualiser* (relative to Position and Frame): ensuring a contextual best fit between the selected context on the one hand and leadership's thinking, values, decisions, actions and competencies on the other hand;

- *Custodian* (relative to Frame and Map): institutionalising and guarding over the organisation's 1) people charter, which is expressive of the psychosocial contract between the organisation and its people (see above); 2) its people value proposition; and 3) its desired people future;

- *Expert* (relative to Map and Enact): enabling and ensuring leading-edge people thinking, practices and actions in the organisation;

- *Value-adder* (relative to Enact, and Learn and reflect): leveraging people's contribution to sustainable organisational success through crafting and rolling out a fit-for-purpose people strategic intent for the organisation;

- *Change agent* (relative to Learn and reflect, and Position): triggering and guiding organisational change and transformation.

In leading HR, the *mission critical leadership challenge* with respect to the roles HR has to play, is to ensure that the complete repertoire of the discussed roles is present and that the roles are well executed at the opportune time during the ongoing people discourse in the leadership community.

The leadership qualities needed to infuse HR leadership to bring about leadership excellence

In the final instance, as the discourse about the people of the organisation unfolds, leading HR is about those leadership qualities that must infuse the discussed leadership acts and roles – to bring about leadership excellence in the new, emerging world order. At issue here is the need for future-fit leadership to be demonstrated by the leadership community of the organisation, and modelled by the HR leadership. It can be argued that a better and different leadership, which is fit for the emerging new order, will be made up of ten interdependent qualities (see Figure 19.8) (Veldsman, 2012) (see also Chowdhury, 2000; Kets de Vries, 2004; Mackey & Sisodia, 2013). The term 'leadership' is used as an acronym to unpack these qualities, starting at 12 o'clock, and moving clockwise in the figure.

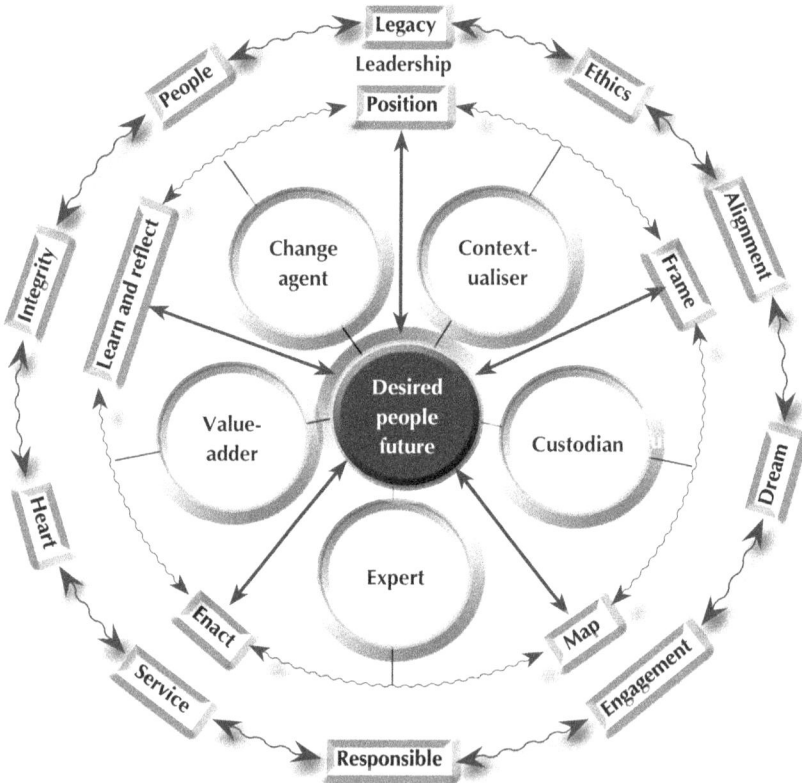

Figure 19.8: The qualities of future-fit leadership, demanded in leading HR

Future-fit leadership

- aspire passionately to leave behind a *legacy* of lasting value and worth for current and upcoming generations. Their relentless drive is to leave the world a better place (the people legacy of a desired people future was discussed above);

- behave *ethically* by doing the right (=the good) things for the right reasons in the right way at the right time. These leaders have a moral compass and demonstrate moral courage. They translate their value orientation into morally justifiable action;

- build *alignment* amongst diverse stakeholders by moulding them into a cohesive, vibrant community of trusted partners around a shared destiny: 'we are in the boat together';

- craft an inspiring, shared *dream*, by envisioning what the shared, desirable people future will look like, once the intended legacy becomes a reality;

- are *engaged* visibly at the coal face, **where the daily moments of truth are created in the organisation, by** showing through their personal example the way towards the shared, desired future;

- act *responsibly* by courageously being fully accountable for their decisions, actions and outcomes, and of those of travelling with them in the journey towards realising the envisioned legacy. They do not shirk their responsibility, shift blame or look for scapegoats;

- set out to *serve* by being humbly in the service of others and a greater, common cause and good which supercedes them, and is more enduring than themselves. They have moved beyond themselves and their precious egos;

- live authentically, straight from their *heart*, their passionately and genuinely held personal beliefs and values which colour all of their thinking, decisions and actions;

- lead with *integrity* by consistently, openly and honestly acting in terms of their ethically based convictions, in this way being trustworthy;

- treasure at all times the *people* they have to lead by treating them **with dignity, respect and care, honouring the trust the people bestow on them as their leaders.**

In leading HR the ultimate *mission critical leadership challenge* is to nurture and grow future-fit leadership, which is able to talk and live leadership excellence in terms of the ten leadership qualities, outlined above, as represented in the acronym 'LEADERSHIP'. The sum total of all ten suggested qualities is necessary in order to bring about mega-competence at leadership excellence level in the organisation, in its endeavour to actualise the desired people future with its consequential lasting, worthy legacy.

Conclusion

In leading HR from an organisational perspective in the emerging new world order, the critical operative term is to be found in the word 'leading', i.e., in jointly crafting with the organisation's leadership community a shared, desired people future which will leave behind a lasting, worthy legacy; in cultivating across that community an intense, ongoing people discourse made up of the acts of Position, Frame, Map, Enact, and Learn and reflect, in order to arrive at a coherent, meaningful story about the organisation's people; in fulfilling a portfolio of key roles during this unfolding discourse to make the discourse rich and worthwhile; and in ensuring that the essential qualities of future-fit leadership infuse all of the above.

Given the centrality of people in the sustainable success of organisations in the knowledge economy, leading HR from an organisational perspective is not an option, but an imperative. HR leadership have to walk the talk. Then, and only then, will they earn and deserve their place on the executive team and in the boardroom, and build their most critical competency: personal credibility (Ulrich, Brockbank, Younger & Ulrich, 2013). Then they will become true architects of the people future they desire for their organisations, not victims of a future overwhelming them.

Endnote

1. Ulrich and his co-workers presented a different portfolio of roles in their 2013 reported research, although with a high degree of overlap with the roles presented here. The revised portfolio appears closer to the HR content roles that do not fit the purpose of this chapter (Ulrich, Brockbank, Younger & Ulrich, 2012 and 2013). In Wright, Boudreau, Pace, Sartain, McKinnon and Antoine (2011) another portfolio of roles is presented, with some correspondence with Ulrich's 2013 study.

References

Beck, D. & Cowan, C.C. (1996). *Spiral dynamics: Mastering values, leadership and change*. Malden: Blackwell.

Chowdhury, S. (Ed.). (2000). *Management 21C*. London: Prentice-Hall.

Christie, P. (2004). *Every leader a storyteller*. Johannesburg: Knowledge Resources.

Collins, J. (2001). *Good to great: Why some companies make the leap ... and others don't*. New York: Harper Collins.

Denning, S. (2011). *The leaders' guide to storytelling*. San Francisco: Jossey-Bass.

Ernst & Young. (2009). *Global trends, 2009*. Cleveland: EYGM Ltd.

Fitzgerald, L.A. (2001). Chaos: The lens that transcends. *Journal of Organisational Change Management, 15*(4), 339–358.

Gaves, C.W. (1970). Levels of existence: An open system theory of values. *The Journal of Humanistic Psychology, 10*(2), 131–154.

Gharajedaghi, J. (2011). *Systems thinking: Managing chaos and complexity*. Burlington: Morgan Kaufman, Elsevier.

Greco, M., Cricelli, L. and Grimaldi, M. (2013). A strategic management framework of tangible and intangible assets. *European Management Journal, 31*, 55–66.

Guillén, M. & García-Canal, E. (2013). *Emerging markets rule: Growth strategies of the new global giants*. New York: McGraw Hill.

Hatum, A. (2013). *The new workforce challenge: How today's leading companies are adapting to the future*. Houndsmills: Palgrave MacMillan.

Jaques, E. (2006). *Requisite organisation: A total system for effective managerial organisation and managerial leadership for the 21st century*. Baltimore: Cason Hall & Co.

Jaques, E. & Clement, S.D. (1994). *Executive leadership: A practical guide to managing complexity*. Cambridge, MA: Carson Hall & Co.

Kets de Vries, M. (2004). What makes a leader great? *Strategic Direction, 20*(8), 4–9.

Kurtz, C. & Snowden, D.J. (2003). The new dynamics of strategy: Sense-making in a complex and complicated world. *IBM Systems Journal, 42*, 462–483.

Lev, B. (2001). *Intangible assets: Values, measures and risks*. Oxford: Oxford University Press.

Mackey, J. & Sisodia, R. (2013). *Conscious capitalism*. Boston: Harvard Business Press.

Oxford Martin Commission. (2013). *Now for the long term*. The report of the Oxford Martin Commission for Future Generations. Oxford: Oxford Martin School, University of Oxford.

Paawe, J., Guest, D.E. & Wright, P.M. (Eds.). (2013). *HRM & performance: Achievements and challenges*. Chichester: Wiley.

PriceWaterhouseCoopers. (2002). *Global human capital survey, 2002/3*. Executive briefing: Effective people management and profitability. London: Global Centre of Excellence, PriceWaterhouseCoopers.

Scott, S. (2002). *Fierce conversations: Achieving success at work and in life, one conversation at a time*. New York: Viking.

Shephard, K., Gray, J.L., Hunt, J.G. & McArthur, S. (2007). *Organisation design, levels of work and human capability*. Ontario: Global Design Society.

Snowden, D.J. & Boone, M.E. (2007). A leaders' framework for decision making. *Harvard Business Review, November*, 1–8.

Sparrow, P., Hird, M., Hesketh, A. & Cooper, C. (2010). *Leading HR*. Houndsmills: Palgrave MacMillan.

Stacey, R.D., Griffin, D. & Shaw, P. (2000). *Complexity and management: Fad or radical challenge to systems thinking?* London: Routledge.

Ulrich, D. (1997). *Human resource champions*. Boston: Harvard Business School Press.

Ulrich, D. & Brockbank, W. (2005). *The HR value proposition*. Boston: Harvard Publishing Company.

Ulrich, D., Brockbank, W., Younger, J. & Ulrich, M. (2012). *HR from the outside in: Six competencies for the future for human resources*. New York: McGraw Hill.

Ulrich, D., Brockbank, W., Younger, J. & Ulrich, M. (2013). *Global HR competencies*. New York: McGraw Hill.

Veldsman, D. & May, M. (2013). *Leadership stories: The search for meaning during change*. Saarbrücken: LAP Lambert Academic Publishing.

Veldsman, T.H. (2008a). People management in the new order: In pursuit of leading world-class practices (Part 1). *Management Today, 24*(8), 56–60.

Veldsman, T.H. (2008b). People management in the new order: In pursuit of leading world-class practices (Part 2). *Management Today, 24*(9), 60–64.

Veldsman, T.H. (2012). Requisite leadership for the emerging new order: The qualities of future-fit leadership. The imperative for leadership excellence going into the future. *Human Capital Review,* September.

Veldsman, T.H. (2013). People professionals fit for emerging countries. In S. Bluen (Ed.). *Talent management in emerging markets*. Johannesburg: Knowres, 179–202.

Weiss, D.S. (2013). *Leadership-driven HR*. San Francisco: Jossey-Bass.

Wheatley, M.J. (2010). *Leadership and the new science*. San Francisco: Berrett-Koehler.

Wright, P.M., Boudreau, J.W., Pace, D.A., Sartain, E.L., McKinnon, P. & Antoine, R.L. (Eds.). (2011). *The chief HR officer: Defining the new role of human resource leaders*. San Francisco: Jossey-Bass.

CHAPTER 20: Developing an HR Strategy which Supports the Organisation Strategy: A Practical Example/Sase Study

Peter Warrener

Introduction

This case study focuses on the potential pitfalls in developing or reviewing a human resources (HR) strategy in terms of the starting point, the content, the implementation thereof, as well as its potential sustainability, by ensuring that the strategy actually delivers on the crucial objective of supporting the organisation's strategy or strategic objectives.

It also deals with the direct and indirect benefits for both the HR function and the business, when the HR strategy is appropriately contextualised within the business.

The story points out what nearly went wrong in the process of developing an integral part of our HR strategy, how it was 'rescued', and how, looking back at several milestones within the overall unintended journey, one might be able to recognise potential warning signs which could prevent HR practitioners from falling into the same or similar pitfalls when preparing to initiate a review of, or develop, an HR strategy.

The case study identifies four cornerstones that offer a retrospective guideline to ensuring that the HR strategy which is eventually developed, deliberately and effectively supports that of the organisation. These cornerstones are founded on the following premises:

- Having an understanding of the support nature of the HR function;
- Selecting the correct starting point for the strategy review or development;
- Ensuring extensive engagement with internal stakeholders; and
- Ensuring line management accountability around the implementation of the strategy.

Being aware of the above has the potential to enable HR practitioners to be more likely to remain on course to deliver an HR strategy that is embraced, effective and value adding to the business – three requisite components for making any HR strategy meaningful and sustainable.

The aim is to highlight mistakes that were made during the process of reviewing a component of the prevailing HR strategy, and to expand on the abovementioned cornerstones, in an attempt to flesh out the detail of activities within what should be a useful framework for the introduction and practical implementation of an HR strategy.

By the end of the case study it should be clear that it is a fundamental and absolute requirement for the HR strategy to be both dependent on and subservient to the group strategy, in order to be relevant.

Industry context

It may be helpful to give a very brief overview of the environment and the context in which the case study unfolded. At Netcare we have the privilege of operating within the healthcare services sector, where we have the opportunity to make a tangible and positive difference in the lives of our patients and their families, through our everyday activities.

This privilege also carries with it an enormous responsibility towards these same 'customers', since the manner in which we conduct ourselves (our behaviour, actions and the way we interact within our business units) directly impacts on people's perceptions of the quality of our service and the standard of care we provide.

Patients who have been admitted to hospital, or who are being treated in a primary care facility or (possibly worse) by our emergency services, are very likely to be in a state of uncertainty and vulnerability – this has the potential to increase the pressure on our initial interaction with the patient/family member/friend, which in turn places greater demands on the behavioural skills and attitudes of our staff.

The quality of the interpersonal interactions which occur in a clinical setting will have either a positive or a negative effect on a patient's perceptions and views regarding an episode which most people would categorise as a classic 'grudge purchase'.

This factor presents an additional and slightly different challenge/responsibility in terms of the people aspect of our business, than what other sectors/industries are faced with. In the healthcare environment we deal with the frailties, complexities and uncertainties of people who are, quite often, in distress.

Integral to this is the fact that we also have to take cognisance of the changing profile of staff members. In the past, working as a healthcare provider was perceived as something of a 'calling', whereas now it is more often than not seen as a career or a job, much like any other.

Further, the increased medical knowledge that patients or their families may have and their justifiably high expectations of treatment and service in the private healthcare industry at their time of need are further challenges which demand that we dispense outstanding care and provide excellent service.

So, within this somewhat complex context, it is clear that getting any staff-related intervention (which should emanate from the HR strategy) absolutely right for our people is of paramount importance. If our staff do not feel cared for by their employer they are far less likely to be brimming with care for their colleagues, or, more importantly, the people they interact with: our patients and their families.

Pitfalls in reviewing or developing the HR strategy

Identifying our cornerstones

Cornerstone 1:
Having an understanding of the support nature of the HR function

The successful development of any support services strategy in a business is dependent, to varying degrees, on the actual positioning of that function and of the individuals leading that team. A fundamental understanding and genuine acceptance of the purpose and essence of the HR function are core to the successful development of an HR strategy.

The development of any support services strategy has to be based on the belief that the function should contribute to the overall strategy, rather than demonstrate the ability to strategise in isolation. Many HR practitioners have become so caught up in a functional (or sometimes even a personal) need to be perceived as the ideal *strategic business partner* to operations – how many times have we come across that? – that they completely forget that the HR function should be steeped in an all-encompassing *service to the business* philosophy.

To distort an old phrase: it is not about what HR can do for and to the business, but about what the business needs HR to do for it, and how HR translates this need into delivery. This concept should be at the core of the HR strategy.

Any HR-related strategic initiative that is not born out of the express need to achieve a component of the broader organisational strategy is most likely destined to fall somewhere on the spectrum between being relegated to a great Power-Point presentation after some fun-filled team-building activities, or ending up making a serious dent in the credibility of the function itself. This could be accompanied by a concomitant loss of morale within the HR team, which will probably be deflated by the lack of strategy implementation and the rest of the business may potentially be left with a negative impression of the function.

Appreciating the importance and reality of HR as a support service function designed to serve the business, provides the first cornerstone.

Cornerstone 2:
Having the correct starting point from which to develop the strategy

Who decided that the strategy needed reviewing or developing? What was wrong with it to begin with? Where and how was the strategy review or the development exercise conceived?

Many of us can recall an instance where some activity or strategic process was initiated without much of an understanding of why it started, what the exercise was intended to achieve, and who it was meant to benefit.

Without making it sound simplistic, understanding the process that underpins the decision to start any activity is of fundamental importance to the entire journey, and, obviously, to the destination.

How did we nearly get it so wrong?

Some time ago, during the Education Division's HR annual budget presentation process, a discussion evolved around the need to evaluate its activities. As is understandable, given the context of the budget process, the initial discussions and analysis were greatly limited to the costs being incurred and the benefits of the clinical training being done. The initial discussions and the questions they raised focused on quite broad (and ultimately anecdotal) 'information' on whether we should continue to 'train for the nation', rather than focus purely on the needs of the company. A strategic discussion was spawned within an hour, based primarily on financial data, without any input from the primary recipient or beneficiary of the product – the Hospital Division operational teams.

Fortunately, the monetary value involved in our training initiatives ran into tens of millions of Rand; I say 'fortunately' because that tended to slow down the potential decision-making process of what was threatening to become a one-dimensional evaluation of a very complex part of our business.

Without going into more detail than would be appropriate here, suffice to say that we face national challenges regarding the shortage of skilled nursing staff. Nursing students are an important resource for us, and will continue to be so in the future.

The discussion concluded that there should be a review of the education strategy; this was largely based on the premise that we needed to determine whether we should be spending as much as we were on training, and whether it added value to the business.

Simple enough so far? As the starting point of the review process an external education specialist was engaged to evaluate our operations and strategy at that time, to highlight areas of good practice (or concerns) and to benchmark any areas where we appeared to fall short in terms of best practice.

During an early information-sharing session facilitated by the external consultant, it became apparent that there were too few players in the forum to provide the levels of information needed to evaluate our activities. It was also obvious that at almost every junction there were questions or issues that related to, or impacted on, other areas of the business – particularly on the vital broader issues of staff development and motivation.

We knew that staff development and career progression opportunities, as two of the benefits of being a member of the Netcare family, were highly valued by staff. In recently conducted engagement surveys these were highlighted as key areas, thanks to positive feedback from respondents.

The reality dawned on the participants that this exercise could not be meaningfully or sensibly carried out in what was effectively an enclosed silo, disconnected from (or, at best, ignorant of) the absolute needs of the business. Thankfully, the process was halted. So often an initiative can generate its own energy and proceed at pace, involving more and more people without the starting point being fully validated or without the context for the energy and/or the intervention being properly thought through.

All too often in business, once an initiative is started it is forced through to its illogical conclusion. As long as it meets the due dates and is reported on regularly, it can drift through and be concluded prior to potentially spending its 'implementation life' on the shelf or in a folder ...

So what nearly happened?

If the process had not been halted, it is highly likely that senior HR and Education Division players would have headed off on a two-day workshop to review the education strategy. At the end of the workshop, the team (after working so diligently to produce the new strategy) would have been keen to get back to the office in order to begin organising a road show; the purpose of which would have been to proudly demonstrate to the rest of the business where the HR function was headed.

This is the point: the team (of a support services function) would have been telling the (core operational) business where they were going, without having even an inkling of where their function could (and, indeed, should) actually be playing a supportive role in getting the business to where it wants to go.

How did we ensure that the pressure to evaluate the education strategy took place under the auspices of the broader organisational strategy?

The first aspect that counted in our favour was the normal hurly burly pressures of the financial and calendar year end. There simply was not enough time to give the matter the attention it deserved, and the HR and education teams fully appreciated that the exercise could not be carried out in isolation, without consulting stakeholders within the business.

The second (and far more important) influencing factor was almost coincidental and certainly quite fortuitous. During this period we had been spending very useful time as an executive team on a scenario-planning process which was starting to shape an evaluation of the continued relevance of some aspects of our corporate strategy. This involved a detailed and analytical review of our six strategic pillars, which are:

- Organisational growth;

- Operational excellence;

- Physician partnerships;

- Best and safest patient care;

- Growing with passionate people; and

- Accelerating transformation (for more details on these and the priorities linked to the strategic pillars, see *Netcare Ltd annual integrated report,* 2012).

Subsequent to the abovementioned process, we had embarked on an in-depth team effectiveness analysis during which we reviewed aspects of our business model and the synergies between divisions, and evaluated the broader corporate route ahead. In summary, the process ultimately crystallised a great deal of thinking which underpinned and initiated a review and subsequent repositioning of key aspects of our organisational strategy.

Once it became clear that we were starting to evaluate the Netcare strategy, it naturally became straightforward to reignite the process of evaluating the HR and education strategies, and the logical decision was taken to continue the exercise within the broader process of the main strategic review.

It is important to note at this junction that once the overarching strategy was being revisited and the executive team members were clear on what needed to be done to get there, the unfolding of the HR and education strategy could evolve in tandem with (and under the auspices of) the requirements to develop and deliver the broader strategy.

Also noteworthy was the fact that these senior executives assumed a strategic evaluation mindset, and that we as a committee had a clear view that certain aspects of *how* we did things, needed to be slightly different.

A key word that surfaced during all our discussions was the drive to view ourselves as '*unique*', and this central concept underpinned what could be called sub-strategy revisions. Doing things 'the Netcare Way' became the 'call to arms' for a variety of new methodologies or activities across all areas of the group, as we strived to ensure that we gained some traction in our journey to uniqueness.

So it was that the education strategic review process evolved into the broader evaluation of the HR strategy as a whole, and the exercise was subsequently appropriately contextualised within a review of (and ultimately the requirements emanating from) the organisational strategy.

The HR strategy review process was now conceived in a legitimate and appropriate manner, and this provided us with the second cornerstone.

Cornerstone 3:
Ensuring extensive engagement with internal stakeholders –
engage, engage, engage

This cornerstone is not about consulting; consulting in an organisational context is often diluted and becomes more about lobbying or trying to get colleagues to agree to what you have already decided to do; quite often this starts shortly before or even after a new intervention or initiative has commenced.

What is meant by 'engage' in the context of developing strategy is asking colleagues what they believe they want or need from the HR function, which will help them to achieve their own strategic objectives. Proper engagement also means that members of the HR team must be fully prepared to potentially alter their preconceived notions of what they think/believe the business needs. Engaging is about being seen to be prepared to do things slightly differently, if that is what the business requires to fulfil its role in delivering on the group strategy. This is often easier said than done within the egotistical corporate arena. Naturally, guidance should come from the support functions, but decisions about priorities, timing and even the labelling of initiatives, must be developed with line managers' input.

Meaningful engagement can only occur where there is a sense of 'teamness' or common purpose. Without this positive dynamic, there will always be the risk of side shows and agendas creeping into the conversations and sidelining the primary objective of the support services functions. It may even prevent them from finding out what needs to be done to ensure that the overall aims of the operational function are achieved.

Embarking on the process of real engagement was a deliberate and structured process. All operational stakeholders were involved and were given equal opportunity to provide input, notwithstanding the fact that one of our three divisions was much bigger than the other two. It was crucial that all three executive teams felt engaged to the same degree in the process.

Ultimately, there was much more drilling down into the regional teams of the main division than the smaller divisions, but generally speaking the process was extensive and broad-based. The process was also conducted in a very open-ended manner, and thus while it may have been exhaustive, it provided the third cornerstone for delivering on something that would be acceptable, appropriate and sustainable for the business.

The various components of the divisional operational strategy objectives were studied in some detail, and the various HR practices and policies were evaluated against these. Was what the HR function was doing in line with what that division required it to do? What was missing and what needed to be reinforced or enhanced? What was a priority and what was not?

There were many central overarching HR themes across the three divisions, but the areas of interaction were highlighted as being more of a business need than others within the respective divisions. Thus slightly unique variations on the HR strategy began to evolve from within the divisions. These were then reworked and workshopped again within the divisions, with further in-depth validating and testing at an operational level.

Underpinning this thorough process was the knowledge that this offered a great opportunity for the support function to check for any disconnect between what the executives within the division thought was needed from the HR teams, and what the actual operators within the business thought was required. Not surprisingly, further important modifications were made at this stage. These modifications provided a very useful by-product in that they ensured alignment between the various management levels within the operating divisions.

During the HR strategy review, it was continually emphasised that the connectivity or purpose of the content of HR strategy is to service the needs of the operational strategies. It was during one of the latter validating sessions that someone asked: 'Why is it called the HR strategy, when it is about the staff of our division?' Thus the term 'Our People Strategy' was born.

The output of Cornerstone 3 was that a label for the strategy was born from within the business, and this was very obviously aligned to the staff within the business and was not linked to a function or the title of an individual.

Cornerstone 4:
Ensuring line management accountability during implementation – sharing the responsibility

Labelling the output as 'Our People Strategy' meant that it belonged to the business as a whole; it was not a functionally owned strategy to be driven to implementation through the ego of an individual, or because it contained a great deal of content based on global best practice, as communicated and informed by self-appointed experts in the field.

'Our People Strategy' belongs to everyone within the business. The nuance that there are slight differences based on the specific inputs of participants in the various divisions is important, because these nuances impact directly on the perceptions of ownership which, in turn, impact directly on the successful implementation of interventions within the strategy.

Most people-related interventions in a business depend greatly on the attitudes and goodwill of those line managers responsible for their implementation, yet the input of these individuals is seldom sought or embedded in the various programmes.

Following this process has meant that the strategy has a very good chance of staying 'alive', because the business will always be evaluating what is required in terms of *its* people strategy.

The aim is not to revisit in detail the components of the end product, the 'Our People Strategy', but rest assured that it contains all of the 'usual suspects' of an HR strategy which focuses on the following key components of the staff life cycle:

- Attraction of resources;
- Placement of resources;
- Employee engagement;
- Measurement;
- Recognition;
- Development; and
- Retention.

Importantly, the content of each of the above steps in the cycle is based on ensuring that the output is directly related to achieving key aspects of the divisional strategies. While there are slightly different priorities across divisions, there is very little variance in terms of the objectives or any of the fundamental principles.

Ensuring the effectiveness and sustainability of strategy into something that 'sticks'

The sustainability of 'Our People Strategy' is widely dependent on determining that the HR function is not solely responsible for ensuring that the various aspects of the strategy are implemented.

To structure this concept, we attempted to ensure that those prioritised activities within the HR strategy (which have been identified as meaningful to the success of the operational objectives) are physically incorporated into line managers' balanced scorecards for the year. What? Line managers responsible for implementing HR interventions? Not entirely ... but now everyone is at least taking responsibility for effecting the interventions that 'we all' agreed we wanted to put in place as part of 'Our People Strategy', because they are seen as the right thing to do for the business.

The suggestion is not that this final cornerstone is completely cemented and in place – that will no doubt take time – but it has been positioned as a very important and logical part of a process which requires broad-based accountability, in order to translate the strategy into activity.

Over the past few months we have further reviewed aspects of the strategy (with line management engagement), and we are currently putting in place interventions/programmes that will change how we address the following people issues:

- Interviewing for managers;
- Orientation and on-boarding;
- Employee performance and development;

- Talent identification and development;
- Employee engagement activity; and
- Staff behaviour and the link to a positive patient experience.

These interventions have been developed in conjunction with line managers, to ensure that the HR function maintains its support service objective by facilitating increasingly effective relationships between line managers and staff.

The aim is to position the interventions as an important aspect of uniquely dealing with people in *the Netcare Way*; many of the topics have been identified from within the business as priority areas, and as such we increasingly rely on line managers to be involved in the planning and implementation thereof.

Conclusion

What have we ended up with? A strategy that is focused on people-related interventions, and activities that are *owned by* the business, not paraded/touted through the business by the functional head as its sole proprietor and architect. Our strategy can be revisited by the business without the HR function being 'precious' about suggested amendments or changes. We have ended up with a living 'document' that has the underlying objective of serving and being of service to the needs of the business. Thus, if the needs of the business change, it follows quite logically (and hopefully painlessly) that there will be ongoing modifications to aspects of the strategy.

While the development of 'Our People Strategy' was clearly not masterminded, by any means, to be successful from the outset (in fact, it very nearly went very wrong), the simple steps of first building the cornerstones can be followed by many other organisations. We have attempted to ensure that similar processes are followed when reviewing other support service strategies.

Not everything in the case study can easily be implemented from the outset, but it is relatively straightforward to aim to lay the following cornerstones:

- Have a full appreciation of the support services role of the HR function; it is there to facilitate the achievement of operational objectives, rather than aiming to meet its own objectives in isolation;

- Ensure that the correct context and starting point exist for reviewing the HR strategy. These aspects have to be guided fully by, and must be subservient to, the strategy of the organisation;

- Work towards in-depth engagement with all stakeholders and be prepared to make as many amendments as make sense; and

- Include line management in the delivery and implementation of the key components of the strategy.

We were fortunate in that the scenario planning exercise and executive team activities made the overall strategic review process much clearer and more logical to proceed with. We were also lucky that the group was revisiting the overall strategy, and that the executives and heads of division were in 'strategic evaluation mode', as this made the consultation process much easier and a hundredfold times more meaningful, realistic and tangible. This may not be that easy to replicate in other organisations. Lastly, we were fortunate in that the HR leads fully appreciate that support services' functions (and, by implication, their strategies) should aim to do exactly that, i.e., 'support and serve', rather than attempting to direct the business.

Reference

Netcare Ltd Annual integrated report. (2012). Retrieved July 18, 2014 from http://www. netcareinvestor.co.za/pdf/jse_sri/environmental/E15_CC1_CC3_CC5_CC8_CC12_ CC14_Netcare-annual-integrated-report-2012-full.pdf

CHAPTER 21: From Strategy to Execution: Key Success Factors in Making Human Resource Strategy Happen (Précis of a conversation with the editor)[1]

Nolitha Fakude

Introduction

Committed to excellence in all it does, Sasol is an international integrated energy and chemical company that leverages the talent and expertise of more than 34 000 people working in 37 countries.

Sasol develops and commercialises technologies, and builds and operates world-scale facilities to produce a range of product streams, including liquid fuels, high-value chemicals and low-carbon electricity.

While remaining committed to its home base of South Africa, Sasol is expanding internationally based on a unique value proposition.

By combining the talent of its people and its technological advantage, Sasol has been a pioneer in innovation for over six decades. As market needs and stakeholder expectations have changed, so too have Sasol's methods, facilities and products, driving progress to deliver long-term shareholder value sustainably.

Sasol recognises the growing need for countries to secure the supply of energy and chemicals. For many countries – specifically those with abundant hydrocarbons – the in-country conversion of these resources into liquid fuels and chemicals goes a long way toward boosting national economies.

Established in South Africa in 1950, Sasol remains one of the country's largest investors in capital projects, skills development, and technological research and development. The company is listed on the Johannesburg Stock Exchange in South Africa, and on the New York Stock Exchange in the United States.

Sasol is one of the world's largest producers of synthetic fuels. The company mines coal in South Africa and produces natural gas and condensate in Mozambique, oil in Gabon and shale gas in Canada. Sasol continues to advance its upstream oil and gas activities in West and southern Africa, the Asia-Pacific region and Canada. In South Africa, Sasol refines imported crude oil and retail liquid fuels through its network of some 400 service stations, while supplying gas to industrial customers and fuels to other licenced wholesalers in the region.

The company has six shared values:

- *Safety:* We are committed to zero harm and all that we do, we do safely;

- *People:* We create a caring, engaged and enabled work environment that recognises both individual and team contributions in pursuit of high performance;

- *Integrity:* We act consistently on a set of values, ethical standards and principles;

- *Accountability:* We take ownership of our behaviour and responsibility to perform both individually and in teams;

- *Stakeholder focus:* We serve our stakeholders through quality products, service solutions and value creation;

- *Excellence in all we do:* We deliver what we promise and add value beyond expectations.

Key success factors in making HR strategy happen

Understand the key HR components of the business strategy

In 2006, a process of questioning and review by the newly appointed Executive Director: Strategy and Human Resources (HR) commenced in Sasol, focused on understanding the key HR components of the company's business strategy.

Several interviews with executives were held throughout the group, interrogating business priorities and determining where HR could play a role; what the group risks were, and where HR could make a contribution towards mitigating these risks; how other executives saw the role HR could play, and where HR could support the executives in realising group strategy.

In addition to understanding the key HR components of the business strategy, this rigorous and comprehensive questioning process served to introduce the new Executive Director to the business, enabled an in-depth understanding of the business and its leadership, while identifying the key HR 'hooks' in the business plans and activities.

Ensure that the 'current reality' of the HR function is understood

To provide a platform for commencing the HR strategy formulation process, two key tasks were undertaken:

- The core HR executive team was reviewed in order to secure members' commitment to and alignment with the HR strategy formulation process; and

- The HR function participated in a business-wide benchmarking exercise which provided a clear understanding of the current reality of the HR function in Sasol.

These two events provided a clear understanding of the issues that needed to be addressed in the HR function to ensure that best practice was achieved, while serving to ensure the alignment of the newly appointed HR executive team. The process of developing the HR strategy subsequently commenced with the aim of embarking on a journey towards transforming the HR function.

Establish a clear time horizon: Strategy formulation and execution is a marathon, not a sprint

This journey was determined as having a medium-term horizon of five years and a long-term horizon of seven years. These time frames, which were situated within the company horizon of ten to 20 years, also aligned with the period required to produce a qualified engineer, as this had emerged as a critical strategic issue within Sasol (four years of study, one to two years for the internship, followed by one to two years of work experience).

Clearly locate HR strategic imperatives within business imperatives

At the time, Sasol had identified four group business imperatives:

- Operational excellence;
- Capital excellence;
- Business excellence;
- Values-driven leadership.

These imperatives were underpinned by three foundational elements, two of which required the HR function to play a critical role. These foundations were:

- Developing and empowering high-performing values-driven people;
- Continuously improving and growing the existing asset base;
- Delivering on the South African transformational agenda.

The first and third foundational elements became the key drivers of the Sasol HR strategy.

Define, as clearly as possible, what the strategic drivers mean

In Sasol's case, at that time the first driver (developing and empowering high-performing, values-driven people) was explained and understood as the need to focus on values-driven leadership, and the belief that values-driven leaders inspire people to face the future with confidence and with a long-term horizon in mind. Sasol embraced the need for an organisational DNA that reflected its uniqueness as an organisation; the concept of the renewed organisation being uniquely 'you'; and the acknowledgement of universal values which are espoused and practised in all markets in which the business operates.

The HR strategy encapsulated these concepts, termed 'renewed values', which needed to anchor the core generic leadership competencies and behaviours eventually contained in the Sasol leadership development programme.

The second driver of HR strategy, the last of the three strategic business foundations listed earlier (delivery on the South African transformational agenda), has great significance for HR in emerging markets. For Sasol it meant consciously moving from a 'value-of-customer' to a 'value-of-stakeholder' focus. This entailed a far broader focus than had previously been the case, since it explicitly recognises the imperatives of emerging markets. First there was the imperative to recognise the need to deliver on a transformational agenda in the particular emerging market in which the business operates. This implies that a 'licence to operate' in that market must be earned through, inter alia, employing local nationals and acknowledging other local socio-economic imperatives. Second there was the need to recognise that in growing new markets and working in joint ventures globally, a key competency is the ability to influence and manage sensitive partnerships. This competency was highlighted in the Sasol leadership development programme.

In the South African context, in pursuit of the transformational agenda the three imperatives of employment equity, skills development, and boosting the profiles of senior executives and management were both acknowledged and planned for.

Establish a clear organisation people philosophy

In clarifying the role of the HR function in achieving the business strategy, the need to develop a people philosophy became an important base from which to establish coherent and supportive people practices and approaches. Keywords emerging from these conversations were 'talented', 'diverse', 'competent', 'highly technical' and 'inspired'.

This gave rise to the following people philosophy:

Build a profitable, sustainable, and adaptive organisation of talented, diverse, competent and inspired people, who face the future with confidence.

Link the strategic purpose of the HR function to the business strategy and people philosophy of the organisation

From the three group business imperatives, the two relevant foundational elements and the organisation's people philosophy, the purpose of the HR function emerged and was formulated as follows:

> We create business value through the effective and consistent delivery of HR solutions that meet Sasol's strategic and business needs and enable the Sasol people philosophy and employee value proposition, in partnership with all stakeholders.

Set HR strategic objectives

The Sasol strategic agenda identified three foundational elements, of which two were directly relevant to the role and contribution of HR. This was underpinned by a Sasol people philosophy that provided the context within which the purpose of the HR function could be clarified.

Stemming from the above, and informed by a benchmarking exercise, three HR strategic objectives were formulated:

- The right talent in the right place at the right time to enable Sasol's transformation and growth strategy;

- Refine and deliver Sasol's employee value proposition (EVP) to enable employee engagement and a high-performance culture;

- Implement a technology-enabling platform and build HR capability to drive effective and integrated service delivery.

Ensure alignment around and commitment to the HR strategic agenda

Sasol embarked on a rigorous leader-led process of alignment and commitment to the HR strategy, addressing, inter alia,

- seventeen business units, each with their own style and methods of HR practice. Due to a lack of internal consistency, there were effectively 17 different ways of doing things! This highlighted the real need to bring about alignment and build commitment;

- how to obtain alignment and commitment to the HR strategic agenda at a watershed global HR conference attended by 500 delegates. The agenda included an introduction and endorsement of the HR role in the business strategy, as well as presentations from business unit leaders on expectations of

HR as well as challenges facing HR, the results from the group benchmarking exercise and discussions on HR's strategic agenda. (The successful conference produced alignment, garnered commitment, generated excitement and, in particular, brought about company-wide recognition of the leadership-endorsed new role of HR.)

Ensure focused execution

Hard on the heels of the euphoria of the conference, came the need for execution. Some examples of disciplined execution, the essence of strategy, were

- an HR operational plan, developed for implementation within the strategic business units of the group;

- the conscious 'up-skilling' of those HR staff required to deliver the HR strategy. This entailed defining both the generic and the unique HR competencies required to implement the operational plan;

- the establishment of a virtual HR academy;

- continued reinforcement of standard methods of practice, and the removal of bad habits through incentives, via performance agreements emanating from group goals;

- the implementation of a shared services project in the group, so that functional excellence could be realised in key functional areas, including HR. This project involved, amongst others, the restructuring and standardisation of processes and the process mapping of HR systems and procedures, with the view to attaining functional excellence.

Reflection: What were the learning points from the journey?

A journey of this nature inevitably has setbacks, is never totally linear with a clear beginning and end, is often messy, and, above all, enjoys the wisdom of hindsight. These are some conclusions and tips:

- It is critical that the Chief Executive Officer understand the strategic value of people, evidence of this being whether this issue features clearly on the strategic agenda, and whether there is a dedicated HR position at board level;

- A major challenge is remaining consistent and focused: HR divisions have a tendency to seize and drive new concepts and fads when the organisation has not yet digested, let alone implemented, the current approach;

- Continuous communication within the HR team is vital;

- It is imperative not to 'change the model' or even the basic look! HR practitioners tend to do this;

- Ensure that HR practitioners have the capability to deliver the HR strategy;

- Remain flexible and adaptable, always be open to balancing HR and business priorities. However, this must be done within the context of choosing between short-term expedience and long-term sustainability;

- Be aware of the need to manage the challenges of emerging market paradigms, such as

  - the burning issue of cost of labour versus cost of capital and the attendant choices required;

  - gaps in levels of competence in emerging markets and how to address these;

  - the complication of global process standardisation and automation in emerging markets.

- Obtain a full understanding of what the leadership want and need from HR and help leadership to understand the processes and structures required in order to offer a compelling EVP;

- Work towards gaining credibility as a business partner who delivers as soon as possible. It is imperative that quick wins be delivered quickly, especially in the context of a long-term plan;

- Be clear that the HR function does not exist for its own sake, but exists to enable the business and support the business strategy. HR cannot tell the business what to do;

- Identify a critical mass of early adopters of new ideas among line management and enlist their assistance in supporting the HR function. HR is a good development opportunity for high-potential senior line managers;

- And, lastly ... Be patient!!

Endnote

1   Sasol continually reviews its structure and effectiveness, and this chapter reflects the situation as discussed in 2013 – Ed.

PART V: Conclusion

CHAPTER 22: In Conclusion – a Conceptual Model

Tjaart Minnaar

Introduction

It is commonly agreed in preceding chapters that the Human Resource (HR) function needs to be one that adds value to the business through the effective finding, retaining, developing and productive deploying of its people. The business agenda forms the HR agenda.

Gone are the days when HR tries to 'sell' the latest trends to the business. HR needs to be a value-creating business partner, and this is dependent on a few aspects:

1   The Chief Human Resource Officer (CHRO) is an astute businessperson, a visionary and strategist, a savvy negotiator, a people developer, a well-versed HR practitioner preferably with previous line management experience. In short, one of the most respected and influential members of the top management team.

2   The HR team at an execution level understands business, has the ability to translate HR-speak into practices that line managers find functional and easy to use.

3   The HR strategy enables the business strategy to be executed through its people. It is done *for* the business, not *to* the business.

In this chapter I want to focus on a conceptual model that can guide the development of the HR strategy to an outcome congruent with point three above. I contributed to its development over a period of more than 20 years, mostly based on practical experience in numerous industries and various countries.

A conceptual model to guide the execution of business strategy through people

To effectively execute business strategy through people, one needs to concentrate on six key elements. These six elements are driven by the intent to create sustainable value for all stakeholders – for the purposes of this chapter we will call this 'building a prosperity partnership'.

Building a prosperity partnership

Building equates to development and growth and *Prosperity* is both financial and non-financial. *Partnership* equates to mutual trust, long-term mutual benefit and fair distribution of the wealth created. The intent is to add value to the broader society and not only to shareholders. To put it simply: a business with a social conscience, which is compelling to work for, do business with and to invest in.

To achieve this intent HR focus is required in six key areas:

- Ensure clarity of direction and purpose;
- Create performance alignment;
- Develop a pipeline of effective leaders;
- Engage employees;
- Enable innovation and continuous improvement;
- Foster a culture of measurement, positive accountability, recognition and reward.

It can also be depicted in the following model:

Figure 22.1: Building a prosperity partnership

Ensure clarity of direction and purpose

This means an effective strategy definition/formulation process regularly takes place in the business. The aim is to create clarity in terms of vision, strategies and the desired culture, the latter being articulated in the core values.

The HR leader as business person, strategist and facilitator plays an important role to ensure sufficient understanding and appreciation among peers for the role that people play in the successful execution of the organisation's strategy. Key HR themes at this level are leadership, critical skills development and creating the desired culture.

This direction needs to be communicated in such a way that every individual in the organisation understands how the work that he/she does, contributes to the execution of business strategy. There needs to be a line of sight between daily activities and strategy execution. The strategic themes or 'golden threads' must be amplified through effective communication.

A common tool used for this communication is a Strategy Alignment Map or a Strategy Map, which is a visual depiction of 'where we are going, what is important in the business and what do we stand for'. The HR themes here are strategic and change communication.

Key HR role: Strategist, facilitator, strategic communicator and change agent.

Create performance alignment

Once a clear strategy has been established, it needs to be translated in a way that ensures effective operational execution. This is the area of business architecture which is often left to operational and IT experts as it covers information systems as an integral part of the business design, especially in financial services.

The aspects that should be integrated to create alignment are:

- High-level business processes (the high-level *what*);

- Structure, roles and responsibilities (the *who*);

- Business processes, systems, policies, procedures and standard operating practices (the *how*);

- Performance goals, targets and measures also known as performance scorecards (detailed *what*);

- Competencies (knowledge, skills and attributes required to execute goals);

- Rewards and incentives (what's in it for me?).

This design lays the foundation for effective performance management.

Poor design and specifically poor alignment of the above impact negatively on people morale and performance and thus on cost, quality and service levels.

HR needs to play a leading role in this multi-disciplinary design which has a high impact on people deployment, skills and morale. To qualify as a contributor in this context, the HR skillset must include business and business process understanding, organisational and job design, scorecard facilitation as well as competency and reward design.

Key HR role: Business architect, designer and facilitator.

Develop a pipeline of effective leaders

Leaders are, in the first instance, the creators of business culture. Their behavioural example and practices set the tone for 'how we do things around here'.

Culture is about consistency. The logic is that if you create a leadership standard that reflects the desired organisational culture in terms of practices and behaviours and you can establish real, daily consistency of these behaviours and practices, you would have the core of the desired culture.

The aspects important under this element are:

- Define what is expected of leaders (leadership standards of practices and behaviours, defined in everyday measurable terms);

- Assess leaders against these practices and behaviours. This can be done in various ways, from psychometric assessments to peer and team member feedback;

- Develop these leaders through individual development plans and talent pools for young talent. Turn your current leaders into mentors. Pay special attention to first-line leaders who, historically, are not well developed and have a very challenging leadership role;

- Take regular stock of the quality and depth of the pipeline. Determine what future talent is required based on business growth, ageing workforce and societal demands such as employment equity and transformation. Ensure strategies are in place for finding the right talent, their effective deployment and retention.

Key HR role: Leadership developer and mentor.

Engage employees

Engagement cultivates commitment. Engagement can take place in the form of individual engagement through 'traditional' communication channels such as newsletters, social media, campaigns and corporate videos.

In my experience meaningful engagement at a team level is more effective. Ideally, however, you want to enhance and support the use of team conversations with individual engagement through traditional communication channels.

The core of team engagement is conversations about behaviour and performance.

Self-reflection and discussions about individual and team behaviour take place, as measured against the organisational values. To make these discussions more tangible, it is important to unpack values into day-to-day behaviour, relevant to the work people do. Only then do values become measurable and, by implication, easier to manage and improve. For example, the retailer Woolworths has integrity as a value. In the context of the work that people do, integrity in a food store is interpreted amongst others as 'removing a product from the shelf by its sell-by date'. In this way the value instantly becomes measurable and a meaningful conversation can be had.

Team performance discussions, centred on goals, targets and accountability, are core to improving business performance. Through a structured format where 20 per cent of the time is spent on review and 80 per cent on goals, anticipating challenges and action planning, substantial results have been achieved. Team performance conversations are further strengthened through techniques that ensure continuous learning and development.

A vital component of effective and sustainable employee engagement is the meaningful facilitation of conversations by skilful leaders of teams. Coaching of leaders in this respect is critical.

Key HR role: Connector of people and coach.

Enable innovation and continuous improvement

The first four of the six elements create focus, willingness and commitment. These are the elements that inspire and empower people to offer ideas that will bring about incremental or even quantum improvements.

Figure 22:2: : The employee value proposition – the outcome of the prosperity partnership

The result of these improvements can be seen in improved cost, quality and service. It is essential that these ideas are recognised, celebrated and rewarded.

It is worthwhile noting that this is also the right time in the process to focus on (functional) skills development. Skills development in the absence of the right level of focus, willingness and commitment will result in poor transfer of skills and a wasted investment.

Given the high level of understanding and buy-in established in the first four elements, the organisation should also be ready for operational improvement initiatives at this stage.

Key HR role: People developer.

Develop a culture of measurement, positive accountability, recognition and reward

Regular measurement creates understanding about the coordinates and exact position in the journey.

How are we tracking? Are we moving in the right direction? Where are the gaps? Measurement takes place at three levels:

* Organisation
* Team
* Individual.

The purpose of the measurement is not only to determine current position, but also to establish a point from which further planning and implementation can be done. Traditionally there is a bias towards 'hard' business measures versus 'soft' people and organisational measures.

My view is that we are not very effective at measuring organisational and people effectiveness and therefore these measurements are not taken seriously.

This brings me to a dilemma, which I have seen in so many businesses.

Figure 22:3: Organisational versus operational focus

Leaders in the bottom-left quadrant (low organisational focus and low operational focus) are usually quickly identified and leave the organisation. To some extent the same is true of leaders in the top-left quadrant (high organisational focus and low operational focus). These are often recent graduates who are still entangled in theory and (hopefully) in the process of becoming 'streetwise' in applying concepts and principles. Be that as it may, we usually have more patience with these leaders.

Leaders in the top-right quadrant (high organisational and operational focus) are obviously stars. They have the ability to place focus where it is needed – on the organisational and the operational.

The real challenge is those leaders who are in the bottom right-hand quadrant. They have a low focus on organisational aspects – they are not building the organisation for the future, have no time for developmental action and are very focused on operational delivery (providing the profits for this month and this financial year). The question is: Are they adding any value to the organisation? The answer is yes, but only in the short term. You will probably only see the negative impact of their short-term focus once they move on. There will be a lack of capacity because not much organisational improvement effort took place. The challenge here is that in most cases the business will entertain them, even celebrate them, because of their contribution to short-term profits. Part of the dilemma is that organisational capacity-building efforts have a longer time frame, while today's business measurements are from one financial year to the next, driving short-term profits. In addition, and probably for HR the more important challenge, is that we are not good at measuring organisational improvement efforts. These measurements do not have a high weighting on management scorecards. The old saying is relevant – what gets measured gets done!

What, then, must be measured? Besides the financial and efficiency measurements of business, certain organisational measurements are crucial. Culture, climate, engagement effectiveness and leadership effectiveness are all aspects that can be incorporated in measuring the success of progress.

An important aspect of measurement is what we do with those results. Regular feedback at an organisational, team and individual level should take place. Positive accountability must be applied, requiring recognition and reward for positive results and constructive learning from mistakes (no blame!).

Key HR role: Performance managers and mentors.

Implementation and sustainability

Implementation and sustainability can be made easier by using the following steps:

- Define your ideal business;
- Assess the current status;

- Identify the gap between the ideal and actual business results;
- Develop a realistic plan;
- Resource the plan sufficiently;
- Execute.

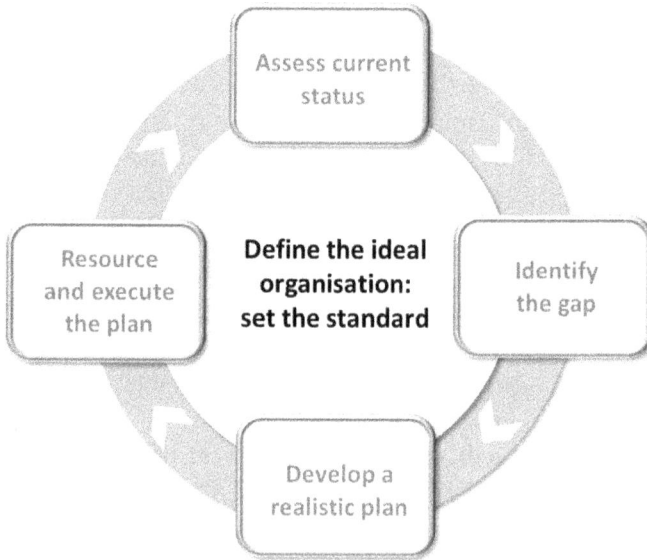

Figure 22:4: Customise and build internal capacity

Conclusion

In many businesses HR has low credibility because it tends to do things on an ad-hoc basis. Therefore business struggles to see the real value-add, beyond payroll and industrial relations.

These six elements provide a blueprint for the development of practical and value-adding HR business initiatives. It is a sustainable model, but to perfect the various focus areas takes time. It is important to stick to the model and continuously improve the same six elements, instead of carrying out partial implementation and then moving on to the next fad – this is a sure way for HR to lose credibility.

The process described above can be likened to Formula One motor racing. Drivers go around the same track time and time again, becoming increasingly better at positioning their cars, braking and accelerating and this results in faster lap times. Similarly, the model provides ongoing focus and improvement in six key business areas. Over time line managers and HR business partners increasingly improve in areas such as communicating direction, facilitating scorecards and engaging employees. Over time, line managers also become more skilled and confident at organisational improvement and move into the top right-hand quadrant (high organisational and operational focus)

By using this approach HR is bound to be seen as a credible business partner which is valued for its contribution to direct bottom line success.

In addition, HR will be experienced as a

- Strategist, strategic communicator and change agent;
- Business architect, designer and facilitator;
- Leadership developer and mentor;
- Connector of people;
- People developer;
- Performance manager and mentor.

Endnote

Prosperity partnership is a registered trademark of OIM Group (Pty) Ltd.

CHAPTER 23: In Conclusion: A Checklist for Action

Dave van Eeden

How does one usefully summarise a book of this breadth and diversity, and avoid merely repeating the content in different words? The most useful way would seem to be to present the key messages of the book in the form of a checklist of questions, structured, for ease of reference, in the same format as the structure of the book. The first person has also been used to make the checklist questions more incisive and direct.

Part I: Context

1. Have I conducted political, economic, social and technical environmental analyses to identify the factors that are likely to impact on people strategy in my organisation?

2. Have I identified factors arising from the changing world of work which need to be addressed in the people strategy of my organisation?

3. Have I considered the role and importance of social capital in the culture of the organisation, and is it being addressed in leadership and transformation initiatives?

4. Do I have absolute clarity on what my CEO expects of me as a leader, as the CHRO and a representative of the HR function?

5. Does the people strategy of the organisation address these expectations?

6. Is my HR function structured and resourced to address these contextual factors?

Part II: Leadership and the role of HR

7. Have I identified the leadership challenges facing the leaders in my organisation? Do I have in place a clear leadership development strategy which is based on a visible competency framework and is supportive of a desired culture?

8. Have I considered the leadership demands which the changing socio-cultural environment places on the leaders in my organisation? Have I incorporated these in my leadership development strategy?

9. Have I identified and clearly defined the cutting-edge HR roles and competencies which my HR colleagues and I need to have, in order to add significant value to my organisation?

10. Have my HR colleagues and I developed clear and visible personal visions of our individual and collective future, underpinned by clear values and a robust code of conduct?

Part III: Dealing with the challenges

11. Do I follow an integrated approach to talent management as part of my people strategy?

12. Do I have an integrated reward and recognition programme which reinforces a clear employee value proposition as part of my people strategy?

13. Am I harnessing the power and reach of social media as a component of my people strategy?

14. Do I have in place a carefully considered employee relations philosophy and strategy which acknowledges socio-economic realities and the need for collaboration, trust, and efficient, strategic conflict resolution?

15. Do I have in place a comprehensive organisational health and wellness strategy and programme, appropriate to the needs of my people?

Part IV: Learning from practice

16. Do I have a well-considered, written personal vision which I regularly review and which guides my life and decisions?

17. Am I aware of the need to have a planned transition to new positions? Do I assist the leaders in my organisation with this process?

18. Are my organisation's core purpose and desired culture clearly stated and reflected in the people strategy?

19. Do I lead the HR function with a clear picture of what HR competencies and values I need to authentically reflect and demonstrate, so that the function, and I, earn personal credibility?

20. Is the value offering which the HR function and I deliver, clear and directly supportive of the organisation's strategy and objectives?

21. Is the design of our strategic HR architecture aligned with the strategic intent of our organisation?

Part V: Conclusion

22. In formulating our people strategy, have I taken account of the following imperatives?

- The role of the HR function;
- Clarity on the key HR components of the business strategy;
- Clear definition of these key strategic HR components;
- Internal stakeholder engagement;
- Clarity of accountability;
- The current status of the HR function;
- A development plan to fill HR competency gaps;
- A clear time horizon;
- A clear organisation people philosophy;
- Clear strategic HR objectives;
- Broad alignment around and commitment to the HR strategic agenda;
- A focused and planned execution plan.

23. Do I have an integrated model that encompasses all the components of the people strategy, and which integrates and links them to organisational performance and improvement?

The following quote is an appropriate way to conclude this book, as it emphasises the critical contribution the CHRO can make:

> The capitalist system is under siege. In recent years business increasingly has been viewed as a major cause of social, environmental and economic problems. Companies are widely perceived to be prospering at the expense of the broader community…
>
> A big part of the problem lies with companies themselves, which remain trapped in an out-dated approach to value creation that has emerged over the past few decades. They continue to view value creation narrowly, optimizing short-term financial performance in a bubble while missing the most important customer needs and ignoring the broader influences that determine their longer-term success…
>
> Companies must take the lead in bringing business and society back together….
>
> The solution lies in the principle of shared value, which involves creating economic value in a way that *also* creates value for society by addressing its needs and challenges. Businesses must reconnect company success with social progress. Shared value is not social responsibility,

philanthropy, or even sustainability, but a new way to achieve economic success. It is not on the margin of what companies do but at the centre. We believe that it can give rise to the next major transformation of business thinking.[1]

Quo Vadis, the role of the CHRO?

Endnote

1   Retrieved September 4, 2014 from http://hbr.org/2011/01/the-big-idea-creating-shared-value/ar/1

INDEX

A

ability, 2, 14, 15, 45, 46, 51–52, 54, 55, 57, 58, 69–73, 76, 77, 91, 92, 161, 167, 184, 245, 246, 307, 308, 371–372
   leader's, 69, 71–73, 77, 162
absence, 70, 131, 139, 144, 247, 258–267, 345, 404
absence frequency rate. *See* AFR
absence management system, 266
absence rates, 258, 261–262
absence severity rate. *See* ASR
absenteeism, 3, 39, 234, 235, 248, 249, 251, 258–260, 263, 265–267, 269
abuse, 259, 260, 262–263, 266, 286
Accenture, 121, 145, 149–150
accessed, 15–16, 171–173, 196, 211, 225, 355, 389
accountability, 57, 61, 65, 67, 68, 71, 73, 128, 167, 241, 277, 280, 306, 358, 359, 403, 411
   positive, 400, 404, 405
action learning projects. *See* ALPs
addition, 50, 52, 53, 89–91, 94, 95, 115, 152, 158, 165, 167, 189, 190, 201, 203, 207, 405, 407
AFR (absence frequency rate), 261–263
African countries, 19, 79, 121, 309
agenda, strategic, 8, 11, 112, 368, 395–396, 411
agility, 23, 26–28, 32, 83, 91, 96, 170, 299
aligning, 8, 51, 60, 104, 209, 293, 295, 297, 299, 301, 303, 305, 307, 309, 311
aligning marketing principles, 343, 345, 347, 349, 351, 353, 355
alignment, 27, 56, 59, 89, 118, 156, 203, 272, 273, 283, 324, 329, 392, 393, 395, 401, 411
   strategic organisational design, 314, 337
allowances, 195, 197, 262, 266
ALPs (action learning projects), 60, 62, 64, 81
amendments, 210, 231, 388
application of strategic HR, 345, 347, 349, 351, 353, 355
architecting, 313, 314, 322
argument, 151, 229, 344
ASEAN (Association of Southeast Asian Nations), 107
ASR (absence severity rate), 261, 263, 264
assets, 31, 33, 191, 369
assignments, 116, 122, 124, 126, 129, 131, 137, 138, 140, 193, 194, 197, 219
Association of Southeast Asian Nations. *See* ASEAN
autonomy, 24, 27, 331–333, 358, 359, 371

B

balance, work–life, 24, 25, 87, 181
BCG (Boston Consulting Group), 5, 13, 15
behaviours, 9–10, 56, 63, 65–67, 69, 159, 257, 275–277, 296–298, 302, 304–305, 308–310, 352, 354, 402, 403
   human, 344
benefits, 156–158, 175, 176, 178, 179, 181, 183, 186, 189–191, 205, 209–211, 219–222, 246, 248, 249, 347–349, 351, 352, 382
   expected, 316, 317, 341
   noncash, 186
better working world, 295, 296, 302
bosses, 99, 220, 228, 275, 285, 287, 291
Boston Consulting Group (BCG), 5, 13, 15
brain drain, 23, 24, 113, 124, 298
brand, 18, 22, 81, 91, 116, 170, 189, 206, 216, 295, 297–298, 349–350, 357
   employer's, 184, 189
Brazil, 1, 4, 7, 8, 18, 21, 23, 26, 83, 87, 107, 115, 116, 130, 131, 147, 152, 155
BRIC countries, 15-16, 21, 26, 29, 87, 155, 156, 160
building blocks, 67, 69, 314, 315, 337, 366
building leadership capability, 60
business, 1–3, 42–44, 51–52, 57, 62–64, 67–69, 88–97, 109–111, 116–119, 181–182, 309–310, 343–345, 379–383, 385–389, 399–401
   aligning, 72, 73
   international, 116, 139
   new, 60, 64, 135, 224, 284
business acumen, 52, 94, 345
business architect, 402, 407
business challenges, 11, 14
business context, 11, 92
business culture, 402
   local, 140
business disablers, 302
business environment, 12, 14, 75, 123, 291
business focus, strategic, 90
business functions, 52, 170
business growth, 80, 402
business imperatives, 61, 393
business issues, 43, 92, 345
business leaders, 2, 51, 82, 111, 115, 118, 257
business leadership cluster, 69
business leadership cluster differentiator, 71
business model, 66, 119, 384
   game-changing, 6, 117
business objectives, 257, 346
business partners, 43, 51, 88, 397

[Created with **TExtract** / www.Texyz.com]

www.ingramcontent.com/pod-product-compliance
Lightning Source LLC
Chambersburg PA
CBHW082124210326
41599CB00031B/5866